D1568176

Early Reading Instruction

Early Reading Instruction

What Science Really Tells Us about How to Teach Reading

Diane McGuinness

A Bradford Book

The MIT Press   Cambridge, Massachusetts   London, England

This book was set in Janson and Rotis Semi-sans on 3B2 by Asco Typesetters, Hong Kong.
Printed and bound in the United States of America.

Library of Congress Cataloging-in-Publication Data
McGuinness, Diane.
  Early reading instruction : what science really tells us about how to teach reading / Diane McGuinness.
     p.   cm.
  "A Bradford book."
  Includes bibliographical references and index.
  ISBN 0-262-13438-1 (alk. paper)
  1. Reading (Early childhood) I. Title.
LB1139.5.R43M34   2004
372.4—dc22   2003066585

10 9 8 7 6 5 4 3 2 1

Contents

Preface   vii

Introduction   xiii

1   Why English-Speaking Children Can't Read   1

2   On the Nature of Writing Systems   11

3   The Structure of the English Alphabet Code   37

4   How to Teach Reading: Lessons from the Past   73

5   How to Teach Reading: Modern Research   107

6   Phoneme-Awareness Training   153

7   Reading Fluency   189

8   Vocabulary and Comprehension Instruction   211

9   How Does Anyone Learn to Spell?   247

10   The Many-Word Problem: More to Spelling Than Meets the I   279

11   New Directions for the Twenty-First Century   317

Appendix 1: How Nations Cheat on International Literacy Studies   349

Appendix 2: Misuse of Statistics   355

Appendix 3: Analysis of Word Lists from Treiman et al. 1995   359

Glossary   363

References   371

Author Index   395

Subject Index   401

Preface

Five thousand years ago, Egyptian and Sumerian scholars designed the first full-fledged writing systems. Though these systems were radically different in form, the Egyptians marking consonants and whole-word category clues, and the Sumerians marking syllables, both were complete and self-contained. Any name, any word, or any word yet to come, could be immediately assigned the appropriate symbols representing that word's phonology.

Schools were established for the sons of the elite—the rulers, priests, administrators, and wealthy farmers, plus the obviously gifted—and not much changed in this regard until the nineteenth century, when the universal-education movement began gathering momentum. Up to this point, no one kept track of which children were more or less successful in mastering this extraordinary invention. But with children sorted by age, and every child in attendance, individual differences in learning rate and skill were hard to ignore. In most European countries, individual differences were minor, and when problems did occur, they impacted reading fluency and reading comprehension. In English-speaking countries, individual differences were enormous. Some children were learning to read quickly but others were not learning to read at all, despite years of teaching. This applied across the board—to decoding, spelling, fluency, and comprehension. Was this failure due to the teaching method, the nature of the written code itself, or something inherent in the child?

Answering this question took most of the twentieth century, and now that the answers are in, there are some huge surprises. Reading and spelling are easy to teach if you know how to do it. Influential theories driving much of the research over the past 30 years are not supported by the data. Meanwhile, the volume of research has snowballed to such an extent that the quantity of studies has become unmanageable. The huge and formidable databases on almost every topic related to reading are an impediment to progress. To get a sense of the actual size of these databases, and the quality of the studies in them, the National Reading Panel (NRP) decided to keep score. They reported that of the 1,072 studies carried out over the past 30 years on methods of reading instruction, only 75 survived a preliminary screening consisting of these criteria: publication in a referred journal, comparison of at least two methods, random selection of subjects into comparison groups, and statistical analysis sufficient to compute effect sizes (National Reading Panel, 2000). On further scrutiny, only 38 studies were found to be methodologically sound. It was the same story for each area of reading instruction. The NRP uncovered a whopping 19,000 papers on the theme that "reading a lot" helps children learn to read. (It does not, but only 14 studies survived the final screening to prove it.) The training studies on phoneme awareness, reading fluency, vocabulary instruction, and methods of teaching reading comprehension all suffered a similar fate.

I faced the identical problems when I set out to write a book that was intended to review the research on reading in the twentieth century. Trying to squeeze all this material into one volume, while adjudicating between reliable and unreliable studies, proved impossible. The result was two complementary, but independent, books. *Early Reading Instruction* deals with the historical and scientific research on reading instruction, including a detailed analysis of the NRP report. The second book (*Language Development and Learning to Read*) focuses on reading predictors—whether or not individual differences in certain perceptual, linguistic, or cognitive skills impact children's ability to learn to read. The proof (or lack thereof) for many of the popular theories in this area of research lies outside the field, in the mainstream research on language development carried out by developmental psychologists, psycholinguists, and researchers in the speech and hearing sciences, and this adds another level of complexity to the mix. The table of contents for the second book is set out following this preface. These books are self-contained and do not have to be read in any order. However, they reference one another whenever a greater exposition (or proof) of a statement or argument is provided in the other volume.

A pronunciation key is provided in the accompanying table. It should be noted that this key does not conform to the International Phonetic Alphabet (IPA). Instead, it represents the most common spelling in English for each phoneme. The IPA is a particularly poor fit to the English spelling system compared to other European alphabets, which are more directly tied to the Latin sound-symbol code. As such, the IPA is confusing to people unfamiliar with it. For example, the IPA marks the sound *ah* with the letter *a*. In English, this letter typically stand for the sounds /a/ (*cat*) or /ae/ (*table*), while *ah* is marked with the letter *o* (*hot*), which is the symbol for the sound /oe/ in the IPA. This muddle exists for most vowel spellings.

A glossary of terms is provided at the end of the book.

English Phonemes and Their Basic Code Spellings

Sounds are indicated by slash marks.

Consonants

Sound	As in	Basic code spelling
/b/	*big*	b
/d/	*dog*	d
/f/	*fun*	f
/g/	*got*	g
/h/	*hot*	h
/j/	*job*	j
/k/	*kid*	k
/l/	*log*	l
/m/	*man*	m
/n/	*not*	n
/p/	*pig*	p
/r/	*red*	r
/s/	*sat*	s
/t/	*top*	t
/v/	*van*	v
/w/	*win*	w
/z/	*zip*	z

The following are combinations of two consonants with special spellings:

/ch/	*chin*	ch
/ng/	*sing*	ng

/sh/	*shop*	<u>sh</u>
/th/	*thin*	<u>th</u>
/*th*/	*then*	<u>th</u>
/zh/	*azure*	—
/ks/	*tax*	<u>x</u>
/kw/	*quit*	<u>qu</u>

Vowels

Sound	As in	Basic code spelling
/a/	*had*	<u>a</u>
/e/	*bed*	<u>e</u>
/i/	*hit*	<u>i</u>
/o/	*dog*	<u>o</u>
/aw/	*law*	<u>aw</u>
/u/	*but*	<u>u</u>
/ae/	*made*	<u>a-e</u>
/ee/	*see*	<u>ee</u>
/ie/	*time*	<u>i-e</u>
/oe/	*home*	<u>o-e</u>
/ue/	*cute*	<u>u-e</u>
/o͝o/	*look*	<u>oo</u>
/o͞o/	*soon*	<u>oo</u>
ou	*out*	<u>ou</u>
oi	*oil*	<u>oi</u>

Vowel + *r*

/er/	*her*	<u>er</u>
/ah/–/er/	*far*	<u>ar</u>
/oe/–/er/	*for*	<u>or</u>
/e/–/er/	*hair*	<u>air</u>

There are nine vowel + *r* phonemes. All but one (/er/) are *diphthongs*—two sounds elided that count as one vowel. Those listed above have special spellings and need to be specifically taught. The remainder use more conventional spellings and can be taught as "two sounds": /eer/ /ire/ /ure/ /oor/ /our/ as in *deer, fire, cure, poor, our.*

Language Development and Learning to Read
Contents

Preface

I   **Does Phonological Awareness Develop?**

1   The Origin of the Theory of Phonological Development

2   Development of Receptive Language in the First Year of Life

3   Speech Perception After One

4   Links: Auditory Analysis, Speech Production, and Phonological Awareness

5   Young Children's Explicit Awareness of Language

6   What is Phoneme Awareness and Does It Matter?

II   **Expressive Language, Reading, and Academic Skill**

7   The Development of Expressive Language

8   The Impact of General Language Skills on Reading and Academic Success

III   **Direct Tests of the Language-Reading Relationship**

9   An Introduction to Reading Research: Some Pitfalls

10   Auditory and Speech Perception and Reading

11   General Language and Reading: Methodological Issues

12   Vocabulary and Reading

13   Verbal Memory and Reading

14   Syntax and Reading

15   Naming Speed and Reading

16   Slow Readers: How Slow Is Slow?

17   Summary: What Do We Know for Sure?

Introduction

It may come as a surprise to many readers that we know how to teach reading so that every child can succeed. Not only this, but there are highly successful programs in all categories of reading instruction, including decoding, spelling, fluency, vocabulary, and comprehension. The knowledge that these programs exist is largely due to the National Reading Panel. They performed an invaluable service for everyone in the field by carrying out exhaustive searches of the enormous databases on reading, and carefully pruning the deadwood. I was able to take advantage of their screening process, and expand on this in this book to look at the successful methods in much more depth than they were able to do.

Early Reading Instruction is about much more than current research on teaching methods. It assesses the most recent discoveries on how writing systems were designed and the implications for how they should be taught. It provides an analysis of the efforts to categorize the English spelling code, and of how our new insight into the structure of this code affects the process of teaching children to read and spell. The book also reviews the historical evidence on important breakthroughs in teaching methods that got lost at the beginning of the twentieth century.

Distilling the lessons from the historical and scientific evidence, I established a *prototype*, or template, for what an effective reading program should and should not contain. The advantage of a prototype is that it is neutral with respect to specific programs, highlighting the elements that really matter, as well as those that have no effect or are even detrimental. When I compared this prototype to the modern research on reading methods, it precisely mirrored the most successful programs, those that boost reading scores one or two years above grade level after a year or less of instruction.

———

This book also addresses a new problem in reading research—what I call the *many-word problem*. This is the fact that, even if a logical or reasonable instructional method for spelling was introduced into the classroom, it will never be possible to teach children how to spell every word in the English language. Because our spelling system is so unpredictable, what cues or kinds of exposure determine how people learn to spell? The answers to this question are new and surprising.

Early Reading Instruction is largely an inductive analysis of the historical evidence and the empirical research on reading instruction. Because reading methods are complex and the field is controversial, I will be addressing methodology in more depth than is usually necessary. In part this is because there is no mechanism in the field for screening out invalid research. Examples of good and bad research alike can be found in every journal (even in the top-rated flagship journals) and are very hard to tell apart. This is just as true of the high-profile studies cited by everyone in the field, as for research on major breakthroughs that nobody knows about. This is particularly an issue for chapters 5 through 8, which review the research screened by the National Reading Panel. To make this material as accessible as possible, I have provided summaries at the end of each chapter.

A Few Facts about How to Teach Writing Systems

This book focuses on the research that bears directly on how to teach the alphabet code, the writing system we inherited from the Greeks and the one we are stuck with. I will not spend more time than necessary considering forms of reading instruction that violate the alphabet principle, for reasons set out below.

As we will see in chapter 2, all writing systems, living or dead, are based on phonological units of sound below the level of the word. Writing systems cannot be based on the whole word, because languages have too many words. The historical evidence shows conclusively that the ability to memorize sound-symbol pairs closes off at around 2,000 pairs. This is an *ultimate limit* requiring years of study. This means no one can learn to read by memorizing whole words by sight.

There have been four (and only four) phonological units adopted for the writing systems of the world (McGuinness 1997c, 1998b). Syllables are used for languages with very few syllable types, like Chinese.

Consonant-vowel units (CV diphones) are used for languages where words are mainly based on those units (CVCVCV), like the languages of India and Japan. An English word with this structure is *potato*. Consonants only (CCCC) are used for languages where consonant sequences carry the meaning load and vowels indicate changes in grammar, like Semitic languages. Phonemes (individual consonants and vowels) are used for all languages with a highly complex syllable structure and no common phonological patterns, like European languages. History shows these phonological units are never mixed in any writing system.

European languages are written in an alphabet, because they cannot be written any other way. This is a fact, and there is nothing we can do about it. The evidence reviewed in this book shows that when you follow the principles by which writing systems are constructed and teach the English writing system appropriately, 4-year-olds can easily learn to read in about 10 to 12 weeks. It makes no sense to continue teaching reading the way we do.

Reading Skills Vary from One Country to Another

The scientific study of reading is about the mastery of a human invention, not the study of natural laws like those in chemistry, physics, and biology. This complicates things. To begin, there is no universal thing called reading independent of a particular language and a particular solution for how that language was written down. A reading problem in one country is not necessarily a reading problem in another. Children in English-speaking countries have far more difficulty learning to read than children in many European countries, a fact that is reflected in how reading is measured. In English-speaking countries, the main test of reading success is *decoding accuracy*, the ability to read isolated words one at a time. Yet in a large number of European countries, decoding accuracy is of little concern, because *every child reads accurately*. There are no standardized tests of decoding skill in these countries. Instead, reading is measured by tests of fluency (reading speed) and comprehension.

These differences are due to the way individual speech sounds called *phonemes* are mapped to symbols in the various alphabetic writing systems. In a highly "transparent" alphabet, like Italian, Spanish, German, and most Scandinavian writing systems, there is mainly one way to write (spell) each phoneme in the language, and one way to decode each letter or letter pair called *digraphs* (<u>sh</u> in *ship*). Transparent alphabet codes are "transparent" in the sense that it is obvious how they work, making them easy to teach and learn.

Highly opaque alphabet codes, like English, have multiple spellings for the same phoneme (*b<u>e</u>, s<u>ee</u>, s<u>ea</u>, sc<u>e</u>n<u>e</u>, f<u>ie</u>ld, d<u>e</u>c<u>ei</u>t, rad<u>i</u>o, mar<u>i</u>ne, luck<u>y</u>, k<u>ey</u>*), and multiple decodings for the same letter or digraph (*s<u>ou</u>p, s<u>ou</u>l, sh<u>ou</u>t, sh<u>ou</u>ld, r<u>ou</u>gh, c<u>ou</u>gh, j<u>ou</u>rney*). Opaque writing systems can be very hard to teach unless teachers use a structured method that mitigates these difficulties. Poor teaching of a difficult code creates enormous confusion and can lead to reading problems and failure.

If success in learning to read is intimately bound to the form of the script, no universal laws can be applied to it. In other words, reading is not a natural aptitude—"a property of the child"—and children who fail to learn to read do so mainly because of environmental causes, not biological causes.

An Opportunity Lost

In the early nineteenth century, Isaac Pitman, a self-taught linguist and author of the famous shorthand method, hit on a solution for how to teach our complex alphabet code. Spelling reformers had been clamoring for changes to our spelling system since the sixteenth century, with no success. John Hart (*An Orthographie*, 1569) and Richard Mulcaster (*The First Part of the Elementarie*, 1582) advocated sweeping reforms almost to the point of scrapping everything and starting over. Mulcaster called for a new phonetic spelling system—a transparent alphabet. Although nothing like this ever happened, Mulcaster did manage to eliminate some oddities, such as the unnecessary letter doublings and <u>e</u>'s at the ends of words (*great<u>e</u>, shopp<u>e</u>*). He was responsible for standardizing the letter <u>e</u> as a *diacritic*, a symbol that signals a pronunciation, as in the words *cam<u>e</u>, tim<u>e</u>, fum<u>e</u>, hom<u>e</u>*.

No true spelling reform of the type that Hart and Mulcaster advocated ever succeeded, despite numerous efforts by highly influential people over the centuries. And while Samuel Johnson was able to standardize spelling in his famous dictionary in 1755, he standardized the spellings for words, but not the spellings for phonemes.

Pitman's solution was to adapt his shorthand method for use in beginning reading instruction by setting up what I call an *artificial transpar-*

ent alphabet, consisting of one letter or special symbol assigned to each of the 40 English phonemes. He developed this into a classroom program called *Phonotypy* with A. J. Ellis in 1847. An artificial transparent alphabet levels the playing field for English children vis-à-vis their continental cousins, and provides the novice reader with critical information about how alphabet codes work:

- They are based on the unchanging sounds (phonemes) in our speech.
- The number of these speech sounds is finite, providing an endpoint for managing the code.
- Letters are not the units of the code but arbitrary symbols for those units.
- All codes are reversible. Reading and spelling (decoding/encoding) are mirror images of one another and should be taught together.

By far the most effective classroom program to stem from Pitman's insights was designed by Nellie Dale (1898, 1902), a classroom teacher at the Wimbledon High School for girls in England. Instead of adopting Pitman's partially artificial script, Dale set up a *basic code* using the most common spelling for each phoneme. This has two advantages: no artificial symbols have to be unlearned, and spelling alternatives can be pegged onto the system with no change in logic. Teachers can say: "We learned the main way to spell this sound. Now I'll show you another way to spell it. Let's look at the words that use this spelling." Dale's program incorporated the insights of a great teacher with those of a great linguist, and soon became popular on both sides of the Atlantic.

The rise of the universal-education movement brought these advances to a halt. By the 1920s, whole-word (sight-word) methods were beginning to dominate, and by the 1930s they had eclipsed any type of phonics teaching. Though the breakthroughs of Pitman, Ellis, and Dale have recently been rediscovered, they could be lost again. It is up to us to see this does not happen. The sad tale of reading instruction in the twentieth century, in contrast to the brilliant programs waiting in the wings, is the main message of this book.

We are in a jam. Reading instruction, if anything, has deteriorated over the course of the past century. We are stuck with disastrous whole-word (sight-word) methods that will not go away. To complicate things, reading researchers are constrained by a seriously flawed theory of children's language development and cannot think past it. According to this theory, children gradually develop an awareness of speech sounds in the order: words, syllables, phonemes—a process alleged to take 7 to 8 years. This has led to the proliferation of phonological-awareness training programs, that are, at best, a waste of time (see chapters 5 and 6). The theory that phonological awareness develops from larger to smaller units of sound, or even that it develops at all, is contradicted by the evidence from the mainstream research on early language development (see *Language Development and Learning to Read*).

We have the knowledge to teach every child to read, write, and spell at an amazingly high level of skill. So far, this knowledge has not been made available to educators, legislators, parents—or to many researchers. The vast quantity of invalid and unreliable research clogging the databases makes it almost impossible for anyone interested in the field to ferret out what is accurate and important and what is not. The National Reading Panel has made an important start on this problem, and the primary goal of *Early Reading Instruction* is to try to finish the task.[1]

---

1. Readers interested in the early history of spelling reform and reading instruction should consult Scragg 1974; Morris 1984; Balmuth 1992; McGuinness 1997c, 1998b.

WHY ENGLISH-SPEAKING CHILDREN CAN'T READ

As the universal-education movement began gathering momentum, educators broke ranks with nineteenth-century traditions. Reading instruction got so far off track that the twentieth century will go down in history as the century of the demise of the English alphabet code. The final reckoning of an unceasing attempt on its life came in the 1990s. For the first time, properly conducted national testing, international reading surveys, cross-cultural studies, and classroom research pointed to the inescapable conclusion that reading instruction in English-speaking countries is a disaster. The functional illiteracy rate for American 9-year-olds is 43 percent (Mullis, Campbell, and Farstrup 1993; Campbell et al. 1996).

International reading surveys carried out by Statistics Canada brought dismal news (Organization for Economic Cooperation and Development, 1995, 1997). In six English-speaking nations, the proportion of functionally illiterate/very poor readers among 16- to 65-year-olds ranged from a low of 42 percent in Canada to a high of 52 percent in the United Kingdom. These figures were in stark contrast to those of many European nations. The comparable figure for Sweden was 28 percent. Sweden's functional illiteracy rate for 16- to 25-year-olds (level 1 of 5 levels) is 3.8 percent. This rate is nearly three times higher in Canada (10.7 percent), and six times higher in the United States (23.5 percent).

In 1993, an astonishing report came in from Austria. Heinz Wimmer set out to study poor readers and initiated a citywide search. He asked 60 second- to fourth-grade teachers in Salzburg to refer their worst readers for special testing. They identified 120 children, about 7–8 percent of the school population. Imagine Wimmer's surprise when the worst readers in the city scored close to 100 percent correct on a test of reading accuracy and did nearly as well in spelling. Clearly, none of these children had any difficulty with the German alphabet code. It turned out their problem was reading *too slowly*. But *slow* is a relative term. How slow is slow?

To find out, Wimmer collaborated with an English researcher (Wimmer and Goswami 1994) to compare *normal* 7- and 9-year-olds from Salzburg and London. The results were startling. The Austrian 7-year-olds read comparable material as rapidly and fluently as the English 9-year-olds, while making half as many errors. Yet the Austrian 7-year-olds had had 1 year of reading instruction, while the English 9-year-olds had been learning to read for 4 or 5 years. Equal speed and half the errors in one-quarter of the learning time is an *eightfold increase in efficiency*!

Wimmer and his colleagues (Landerl, Wimmer, and Frith 1997) got the same extraordinary results when they compared their worst readers (*incredibly slow*) with English children identified as "dyslexic" (*incredibly inaccurate*). The children were asked to read text consisting of nonsense words. The so-called Austrian slow readers were not only more accurate than the English "dyslexics," but they read twice as fast. The average Austrian "slow reader" would be able to read a 500-word passage in about 10 minutes, misreading only 7 percent of the words. The average English "dyslexic" would read only 260 words in this time, and misread 40 percent of the words. It seems the expression "worst reader" is relative as well.

An even more dramatic study was reported from Italy. Cossu, Rossini, and Marshall (1993) tested Down's syndrome children with IQs in the 40s (100 is average) on three difficult reading tests. They scored around 90 percent correct, breezing through Italian words like *sbaliare* and *funebre*. However, they could not comprehend what they read, and they failed miserably on tests of phoneme awareness, the skill that is supposed to be essential to decoding.

What is going on?
The answer is simple. European countries with high literacy rates have a twofold advantage. First, they have a transparent alphabet code, a nearly perfect one-to-one correspondence between each individual sound (phoneme) in the language and a visual symbol—a letter or letter pair (digraph). For languages with more sounds than letters in the alphabet (English has 40+ sounds), this problem was handled sensibly. When a letter or digraph is reused to represent more than one sound, it is marked by a special symbol (a diacritic) to signal a different pronunciation. In

German, an *umlaut* distinguishes the vowel sound in *Bäume* (boimeh) from that of *Baum* (boum). And while a sound can occasionally be spelled more than one way, there is never more than one way to read a letter or digraph. The English spelling system suffers from both afflictions: multiple spellings for the same phoneme, and multiple ways to decode letters and letter sequences. This is the definition of an "opaque" writing system.

Reading instruction is the second part of the equation. To a great extent, reading instruction is a function of the complexity of the spelling code. Teaching a transparent writing system is far easier than teaching an opaque one, because it is obvious (transparent) how it works. Teaching can be streamlined and proceeds at a rapid pace. In Austria, children are taught the sounds of the German language and which letter(s) represents each sound. Reading and spelling are integrated at every step, which reinforces the code nature of a writing system—that is, the fact that the operations are reversible, involving both encoding and decoding. No clutter or noise clogs the process, such as teaching letter names or lots of sight words. Because basic reading instruction is fast and pretty well guaranteed, it can begin late—at age 6 in most countries (age 7 in Scandinavian countries)—and end early (after 1 year or less). Parents sleep soundly in their beds, safe in the knowledge that their child will be reading and spelling by the end of the first year of school. (This is not to say that inappropriate teaching methods cannot nullify the advantages of a transparent alphabet.)

The cross-cultural comparisons reveal that the source of English-speaking children's difficulties in learning to read and spell is *the English spelling system and the way it is taught*. These comparisons provide irrefutable evidence that a biological theory of "dyslexia," a deficit presumed to be a property of the child, is untenable, ruling out the popular "phonological-deficit theory" of dyslexia. For a biological theory to be accurate, dyslexia would have to occur at the same rate in all populations. Otherwise, some type of genetic abnormality would be specific to people who learn an *English* alphabet code and be absent in people who live in countries with a transparent alphabet, where poor readers are rare. A disorder entirely tied to a particular alphabetic writing system is patently absurd and has no scientific basis. English-speaking children have trouble learning to read and spell because of our complex spelling code and because of current teaching methods, not because of aberrant genes.

A Century of Whole-Word Methods

The historical evidence shows that teaching methods most similar to Dale's (and the methods used in other European countries) resemble the programs found to be most effective in recent studies (see chapter 5). These phonics-type methods were replaced early in the twentieth century as a consequence of universal education. Self-appointed education gurus and newly fledged professors of education with little or no knowledge of how to teach reading decreed that old-fashioned phonics had to go. Instead, children should be taught whole words by sight, just as Chinese people were thought to do, using a method known as "look-say." The "whole-word" century was launched, and the alphabet code soon vanished without a trace.

Look-say was replaced early on by a meaning-based sight-word method. Children were introduced to a few words in each lesson, spent most of the lesson learning the meanings of these words (words they already knew), and then read dreary stories where these words were repeated endlessly:

"Come, come, John. See me. I can swing. Come and see."

Phonics lessons came in late or not at all, and made no sense. This approach was the platform for "basal readers" (U.S.) or "reading schemes" (U.K.), products of the educational publishing houses. Basal readers dominated from the 1930s until the late 1970s. In the mid-1960s, a survey showed that basal readers were used in 95 percent of classrooms in the United States. Many people still remember *Dick and Jane* or *Janet and John*.

The extreme dullness and repetitiveness of the basal-reader method, plus other precipitating factors, eventually led to a backlash. Basal readers were swept away by a third whole-word method that came to be known as "whole language" (U.S.) or "real books" (U.K.). The theory behind whole language is that with minimal guidance, children can teach themselves to read naturally. They do this by following along as the teacher reads stories written in natural language, and by reading on their own while using all their "cuing systems." These include everything from guessing words based on context and the illustrations, to sight-word memorization, to attempts to decode by letter names. Children are encouraged to "invent" their own spelling system during creative writing.

The basal-reader approach may have been boring, slow, and wrong, but at least it was *honest*. What you saw was what you got (figuratively and literally). Whole language is based on faith, promising everything and delivering nothing. Children are passed from grade to grade in the belief that they will eventually teach themselves to read. And if they do not, it is their fault. Something is wrong with them. Needless to say, whole language was not a success. It led to skyrocketing illiteracy rates, quite beyond anything produced by basal readers. In California, where whole language was mandated in 1987, the functional illiteracy rate soared to 60 percent, plunging California to last in the nation. The disastrous test scores dampened the enthusiasm of parents and legislators for whole language, but had little or no effect on professors of education, education publishing houses, curriculum specialists, and many classroom teachers. Because they control what goes on in the classroom, whole language is still with us, battered but unbowed, despite lip service to the contrary.

Nouvelle Eclecticism

In the 1990s, reading researchers and directors of research agencies, supported by state and national politicians, launched a campaign to rescue children from whole language, claiming they wanted a return to phonics. But after nearly a century, no one was quite sure what phonics was. Instead, what they proposed was not phonics, but a new kind of eclecticism. In the past, eclecticism referred to a teacher's habit of mixing different approaches and materials in the mistaken belief that children have different learning styles. This form of eclecticism is individualistic and haphazard.

"New eclecticism" is based on the notion of *developmental gradualism*, a consequence of the myth that children become more phonologically aware as they grow older. Children begin by learning whole words by sight, then move on to syllables (clapping out beats), then to word families (words with rhyming endings like *fight*, *might*, *sight*), with the goal of being eased into an awareness of phonemes, a process taking a year or two, if it is completed at all. This not just a passing whim. It is the method promoted by people in charge of research funding in the United States.

Full-blown "nouvelle eclecticism" was recently mandated by the British government, complete with suitcases of lesson plans, charts, and materials sent to every elementary school in the country at a cost to the taxpayer of £56 million.

The Myth of Phonological Development

There is a strange and twisted tale behind this new movement. Inspired by discoveries in speech perception (A. M. Liberman et al. 1967), Isabelle Liberman (Liberman et al. 1974) proposed that phonological awareness "develops" throughout childhood and underpins "reading readiness." Around the same time, paleographers and linguists were launching a new field of study—the comparative analysis of writing systems. Among a spate of books on the topic, by far the most influential was by Ignace Gelb (1963). Gelb proposed that writing systems "evolve." They begin with pictograms (recognizable little pictures standing for whole words), graduate to logograms (abstract signs for whole words), then to syllabaries (syllable signs), and finally to alphabets (phoneme signs). According to Gelb, this is true of every civilization that invented writing. While Gelb was highly regarded for his scholarly work (he was instrumental in cracking the code of the Hittite writing system), his colleagues in paleography were far less enthusiastic about his evolutionary theory. And as more archaeological evidence came to light, it became clear that Gelb's theory was fatally flawed.

For Liberman and her colleagues, Gelb's theory was almost too good to be true. It was assumed that the "evolutionary" order of writing systems mirrored the developmental sequence of speech perception—moving from larger to smaller phonological units (whole words, syllables, phonemes). And because children appeared to differ in when and whether they became "phonologically aware," the theory provided an explanation for dyslexia as well.

There is no scientific support for this theory or anything resembling it (a complete analysis of this issue is provided in *Language Development and Learning to Read*). Instead, the evidence shows that children become less rather than more phonologically aware as time goes by. Tiny babies can discriminate between any consonant-vowel contrasts (*ba* versus *pa*) in every language of the world, an aptitude that disappears by 12 months of age. By 9 months they can tell the difference between legal and illegal phoneme sequences in words (Aslin, Saffran, and Newport 1998; Friederici and Wessels 1993; Mattys et al. 1999). In English, illegal consonant sequences commonly form word boundaries ("wor*d b*oundaries"). Infants use these patterns to wrench words out of the speech stream in order to build a receptive vocabulary. If they could not hear phonemes, it would be impossible to split phonemes from one another. Chaney (1992) found that virtually all 3-year-olds can identify a single phoneme error in a spoken sentence and fix the error. Furthermore, they can blend isolated phonemes into a word and pick that word from a row of pictures with 88 percent accuracy (96 percent scored significantly above chance).

This does not mean that young children know that speech consists of phoneme sequences or that an alphabetic writing system represents these phonemes. They will not make this connection unless it is taught. Even fluent readers are not consciously aware of phonemes until someone points them out, and there is no reason they should be. The brain carries out this analysis so rapidly that it operates below the level of conscious awareness. No one needs to be aware of phonemes unless they have to learn an alphabetic writing system. Anyone, at any age, who has to learn an alphabetic writing system must be taught to unravel phonemes in words to understand how an alphabetic writing system works.

The proposed link between the discoveries in speech perception (its biological foundations) and Gelb's theory of the origin of writing systems (its supposed "evolutionary" foundations) had a powerful impact on reading research in English-speaking countries that has not abated over time. Yet Gelb's theory was wrong, and the analogy to speech perception without merit. Writing systems do not evolve.

The comparative analysis of writing systems was in its infancy when Gelb proposed his theory in 1963. This discipline came of age with the publication of Florian Coulmas's *Writing Systems of the World* (1989), a synthesis of extraordinary breadth and depth. This was followed in 1996 by Daniels and Bright's remarkable compendium. Perhaps it is fortuitous that Coulmas's book appeared at the precise moment in history when we finally learned the ghastly truth about the functional illiteracy rates in English-speaking countries. This is a problem of monumental proportions. It is not merely a question of how to teach our formidable spelling code, but how to shed 100 years of unsubstantiated beliefs about how to teach reading and false theories about why children fail.

Before any real transformation can occur, people need a deeper understanding of the issues. They need to know what a writing system is and how it works. They need to know how a *particular* writing system can and cannot be taught and which skills are important to success. Coulmas gave us the first road map to find our way out of this quagmire. There is no better place to start than with the lessons learned during the 5,000-year history of the origins of writing systems. A writing system has a central logic, and this logic is based on how the human mind works. If this logic is not adhered to, a writing system cannot be taught effectively, if at all.

Before I move on to discuss these new discoveries, I want to present the commonly held assumptions about writing systems that either directly or indirectly affect what goes on in the classroom. It may come as a surprise that *not one of these assumptions is true.*

1. Writing systems evolve from whole-word systems (logographs), to syllable systems (syllabaries), to phoneme systems (alphabets). Logographs are "low" on the evolutionary scale (poor), and alphabets are "high" (best).
2. Ontogeny recapitulates phylogeny. Children go through the same stages during development of speech perception, mirroring the evolution of writing systems: from whole words, to syllables, to phonemes.
3. The evolutionary process (in both cases) is inevitable and goes in one direction.
4. There is such a thing as a logographic writing system.
5. The Chinese have a logographic (archaic) writing system.
6. The alphabet principle was discovered only once and spread by diffusion.
7. Alphabets are superior to other writing systems. Nearly all writing systems today are alphabetic.
8. An alphabetic writing system can be used as a proxy for a logographic writing system. That is, children can learn to read an alphabetic writing system by memorizing whole words (random letter strings) by sight.
9. Different sound-based units can (and should) be mixed together in teaching the alphabet code, including (but not limited to): whole words

(sight words), syllables (*ta-ble*, *droop-ing*), rhyming endings or word families (*and, band, hand, sand*), consonant blends (*br, tw, sl, sts, nt*), and individual phonemes. Children will not be confused by this practice and will clearly understand how the alphabet code works.

10. Over time, every word is read as a sight word. Ultimately, people read holistically, and only rare words or unknown words need to be decoded phonetically.

ON THE NATURE OF WRITING SYSTEMS

The comparative analysis of writing systems sheds considerable light on what the human mind can or cannot remember, and on how human memory and language determine the way writing systems are designed. This knowledge helps us understand how a particular writing system can and cannot be taught.

Comparative analysis came of age when there was a sufficient body of evidence to provide a complete succession of forms from protowriting to full-blown writing systems.

At the beginning of the nineteenth century, these archaic writing systems still awaited decipherment: Egyptian, Sumerian, Babylonian, Akkadian, Hittite, Aramaic, Persian, Mayan, the Cretan scripts of Linear A and Linear B, and many others. The first breakthrough came in 1823 and the last (so far) in 1953. Eleven archaic writing systems still defy a solution. The analysis of an extinct writing system unfolds in a series of steps and can take well over a hundred years. I will take up these steps briefly, because each is relevant to understanding how a writing system works.

The Code Breakers

*A writing system is **a code** in which specific elements of a language are mapped systematically to graphic signs or symbols.* Scholars who decipher ancient writing systems are "code breakers" in exactly the same sense as the cryptographers who crack the enemy's coded messages. Codes have an internal logic and an external system or structure; otherwise they could not be broken.

Code breakers have a formidable task, and breaking the code is almost never solved by one person alone. This is why we should never expect a young child to "break the code" of a writing system unaided. In fact, code breakers need superb analytic skill in combination with expertise in the language in question or a related language. Unless the language is known, or can be linked to some other known language, the code cannot be cracked.

The code nature of writing systems is not well understood, in part because writing systems are imperfect graphic representations of both semantic (meaning-based) and phonological (sound-based) aspects of a spoken language. No writing system is purely one or the other (Coulmas 1989). The fact that codes for spoken language are so complex is important to bear in mind when thinking about reading instruction. The novice reader is, in a very real sense, like a code breaker facing an alien script, and this task can be impossible if instruction is misleading, incomplete, or absent altogether.

All codes are reversible mapping systems (McGuinness 1997c, 1998b). What is put into a code (encoded) can be decoded by reversing the process. A code is more or less transparent to the degree that it has a one-to-one correspondence between the original units, whatever they might be, and their coded form. A completely transparent code is *perfectly reversible*: one symbol is associated with only one unit of something, and that unit has only one symbol. No writing system is completely transparent, but some alphabets—like those listed earlier—come close.

There are many well-known codes with perfect one-to-one correspondences. There are number codes for quantities, codes for musical notation that mark pitch, duration, and rhythmic meter and stress, and computer codes devised to translate binary logic (the zeros and ones of computer hardware) into octal, then into computer "languages" (and back again).

A fundamental aspect of codes is that the *elements being encoded* are logically (not just perceptually) distinct from the symbols of the code (McGuinness 1997c, 1998b). To understand what a code is, to master the system and use it efficiently, a learner should know the direction in which the code was written. This means being made aware, indirectly or explicitly, of what is being encoded and what constitutes the code. Number symbols code *quantity* and are not merely transcriptions of number words. Musical notation codes the *music*, not a particular instrument or the fingerings on a keyboard or strings.

Similarly, letter symbols in alphabetic writing systems represent phonemes. Phonemes are the *basis* for the code, and the letters *are* the code. Letters do not "have" or "make" sounds. People have sounds. Unless this logic is made clear to teachers and used to guide beginning reading instruction, the code will lose one of its essential elements: its reversibility. This is especially critical for learning an opaque writing system. Children are magical thinkers and can easily believe that letters "make sounds," leading them to use one logic to read (decode) and a different logic to spell (encode). For this reason all *phonemes* will be enclosed in slash marks, and all *spellings* (as opposed to readings) will be underlined. It is important to be able to distinguish between what is being decoded and what constitutes the code.

The Translators

Translators take over once the code has been cracked and come from a variety of disciplines. Linguists and grammarians must unravel the phonological, grammatical, and structural properties of the language before a complete translation is possible. When translators work with the vocabulary of a dead language, such as ancient Egyptian, Sumerian, or Babylonian, they must see the same word in different contexts, in a variety of texts, to gain any real insight into what the word implies. Once vocabulary and grammar are tentatively worked out, the translator needs a historian's talent for framing a synthesis that accurately represents the customs, the political system, the economy, and the feelings of the people about all manner of things, including their sense of themselves.

The historical reconstruction of an ancient civilization is critical for an understanding of how writing systems develop. Without knowing anything about the Sumerian economy (that it was agricultural on a large scale, with a temple distribution system and individual ownership of land), or the Sumerian religious practices (that priests and city administrators played a joint and important role in economic matters), or the Sumerian legal system (that it was an effective system of justice), it would have been difficult to discern how and why the writing system developed the way it did.

How Writing Systems Work

One of the major contributions of comparative analysis has been to document and classify the critical elements that determine what, in fact, qualifies as a writing system.

Function

A writing system codes spoken language into a permanent form so that it can transcend time and space. But the most important aspect of a writing system is its *purpose*. For one thing, it should make life better. A writing system that has no effect (being too difficult for most people to learn) or that makes life worse (generating thousands of bureaucratic forms) is hardly worth the bother.

Writing systems make it possible to permanently record important things that are hard to remember, such as rules and laws, and case decisions about breaches of those laws. They can record events of critical importance to everyone, such as migrations, battles, and other historical events, as well as disasters like floods, drought, and crop failure. They can record intentions of good faith, as in a business transaction or in marriage vows. And should disagreements arise, family members, magistrates, or judges do not have to rely on a person's word, or on the testimony of witnesses who may or may not remember or be telling the truth. Recorded accounts of how land and inheritance disputes were settled in the Middle Ages, when most parties and witnesses were illiterate, make fascinating reading (Clanchy 1993). A writing system, plain and simple, makes civilization work, and without a writing system, it cannot work.

Structure

The texts and documents unearthed from civilizations with the earliest writing systems in the world, Sumer and Egypt, show that writing systems originated in the same way for the same reasons. They began as systems for accounting, inventory control, bills of lading, and invoices. This is why protowriting (which is not a system at all) has so many symbols that are stylized pictures or icons. Much more is needed to qualify as a writing system. A true writing system must represent the entire language, and to do so it has to meet certain fundamental requirements. Coulmas (1989) specified three: *economy*, *simplicity*, and *unequivocality*. I would add *comprehensiveness* to the list.

Economy means that the number of symbols used for the system must not only be complete but must be as small as possible. Economy is essential to keep the memory load for symbols manageable. Alphabets, for example, have the fewest symbols and are therefore the most economical.

Simplicity means that the mapping relationships between what is being encoded (elements of speech) are straightforward, in the sense that there is only one way to write a particular word, not half a dozen. Mayan and Egyptian hieroglyphic writing fail the standard of simplicity miserably.

Unequivocality dictates that the meaning of a written expression be determined by its form. This is a complex way of saying that what you read must mean one thing, not many things. Writing systems should not cause confusion by creating ambiguity. Ambiguity poses more of a problem in writing than in speech, because context, facial expressions, tone of voice, and knowledge of the personal history of the writer are absent in written texts. Coulmas used an example of how the written form disambiguates speech patterns by means of variant spellings, contrasting the French phrase *cette heures* (meaning "this time") with *sept heures* (meaning "seven o'clock"). Although Egyptian and Mayan writing systems fail the simplicity test, they meet this criterion with flying colors. There is almost no way to mistake meaning, when the same meaning is cued in several different ways.

Comprehensiveness means that all words, names, and any possible new words in the future can be represented by the writing system with relative ease. That is, you would not need to convene a meeting of the National Writing Board each time a new word appeared in the language, like *computer, hardware, software, Internet, website, hacker, nerd.*

These examples highlight Coulmas's central point, that there is always a trade-off between the elements of the system. Furthermore, one cannot assume that all will be well by opting for economy alone, which would lead to the conclusion that every writing system should be an alphabet. Instead, the syllable structure of a language will dictate which form of the code is "simple," and this turns out to be just as important as economy. As Coulmas notes, the Morse code is extremely economical. Only two values of duration (long, short) plus silence constitute the entire code, but this is not a sufficient reason for it to replace the alphabet.

Comparative analysis has revealed that a perfect, isomorphic mapping between speech and symbol has never been achieved by any culture so far, and probably would never work. Unfortunately, there is not, and can never be, a perfect writing system sufficient to satisfy a linguist's dream writing system, because the needs of the user are remote from the ideal imagined by the linguist. The simple fact that alphabets use different spellings for homophones (*bear/bare*; *knight/night*; *pair/pear/pare*) shows that orthographies work better when they are designed to help the user rather than to satisfy the purist.

In summary, a writing system must meet several constraints in order to work at all. It must be sufficiently easy to learn so that it does not take a lifetime to learn it. A reasonable goal would be that it could be mastered by a child in a short period of time. It must be unambiguous. The printed script should be the most faithful translation of the true meaning of the spoken language that it can possibly be. Finally, it should be comprehensive. There should be a way to record every word and every name in the language, not just some.

Meeting these goals was a formidable challenge. All early writing systems began with the wrong solution and had to change course, often to the point of scrapping everything and starting over. There were stopgap solutions in which special symbols were added to reduce ambiguity. But the more extra symbols that were pegged onto the system, the harder it became to learn. The writing systems with the most props, the greatest amount of redundancy and instability in the size of units for the code, were the Egyptian and Mayan hieroglyphic writing systems, systems so difficult to learn that only the scholar-priests could learn them. We will be looking in more detail at the writing systems that succeeded in all the functions listed above. Do these successful writing systems have anything in common, and if so, what? Are there patterns that can be determined about how and why writing systems differ? Is one form of writing system better than another?

Writing Systems Do Not Evolve
Comparative analysts have more or less agreed on the types or forms of writing and the order in which they appear. Coulmas provides a list that represents the majority view on this issue. However, as he notes, the list is "abstract" in the sense that it is more or less correct, but not specifically correct. Here is a simplified and slightly revised interpretation of the list. There are two levels. The first level is *whole-word writing*. At this level are

the various forms of whole-word symbols: *pictograms* of either a specific person or object (that man, that bird, that ship), or a prototypical form (a bird, a ship), and *logograms*, which are completely abstract signs for whole words.

A writing system in which each word is represented by a unique visual pattern is unworkable for several reasons. First, it would always be in the process of becoming and could never arrive. It would forever fail the standard of comprehensiveness. Second, it fails the criterion of economy as well. Adult speakers know about 100,000 words, and use over 50,000 words in ordinary conversations. If every word was coded by a unique symbol, you would need 50,000 symbols just to begin. (The *Oxford Companion to the English Language* estimates that the English language has about one million words; see McArthur 1992.) Third, because every sign must be individually taught, this does not qualify as a code. If the word is not in your vocabulary, there would be no way to read (decode) the sign. In short, whole-word writing is not a *system*. It has no structure. Learning a logographic writing system would be exactly like memorizing the telephone directory.

For these reasons, the second level—*sound-based writing*—is inevitable due to the unworkability of the first. Here, abstract symbols stand for units of sound in speech. There are far fewer sounds than words in every language by several orders of magnitude, no matter which sound unit is chosen, so this fulfills the requirement of economy. The central logic of a sound-based system is that *the sound unit drives the system and meaning does not*. This is true even though sound and meaning can overlap, as they do in one-syllable words in a syllabary writing system. Another critical factor is that sound units in a language are *fixed in number*, whereas words are never fixed.

Coulmas lists the sound-unit options as syllables or phonemes, but does not specify a sequence. Gelb proposed that writing systems evolved in a fixed order: alphabets must follow syllabaries, and syllabaries must follow logograms. For Gelb, evolution means the inevitability of moving to higher forms. Pictograms are primitive. Alphabets are sophisticated and "best."

Finally, Coulmas includes a kind of mopping-up period in which redundancy is eliminated, and the written form is standardized by the creation of an "orthography" or "standard form."

As we review the development of individual writing systems, it will become obvious that Gelb's position is untenable. Further, I want to take a slightly different orientation to Coulmas and present a more psychological and pragmatic analysis of the similarities and differences between the various systems. This way, we can include what we know from research on human memory and perception, and make this relevant to the classroom. Coulmas is correct that a writing system must be economical due to the limits of human memory, and should be designed to suit the user. But these limits need not be vague. There are precise answers, not only from the psychological research, but from evidence on the analysis of the structure of writing systems. This means we can discover *exactly* what a human learner can and cannot remember, and *exactly* what a human perceiver can and cannot perceive about elements in the speech stream, something that Coulmas does not discuss. In other words, there are even more constraints on the design of writing systems than Coulmas identifies.

The Limits of Human Memory

When early cultures began the transition to a full-fledged writing system, two things happened. Pictograms disappeared relatively quickly. Logograms expanded in number and soon reached asymptote. A logograph ceiling was observed in Sumer, China, and Egypt alike. From the historical evidence, it is obvious that ancient scholars quickly discovered that a logographic (whole-word, meaning-based) system would not work. If it had worked, it would not have been abandoned so early. It was not the comprehensiveness issue that dampened everyone's enthusiasm for logographs, but the *economy* issue. Memorizing thousands of abstract visual patterns is something human brains simply cannot do. But this is only half the problem.

In a logographic writing system, each abstract, meaningless visual pattern is paired with a particular word. Psychologists call this *paired-associate learning*. In a typical paired-associate task, people are asked to memorize a list of random word pairs (*tree-mouth*), and are cued by one of the words later in time: *tree*—? People are particularly bad at this task when the word pairs are unrelated in meaning, as in this example, and are hard pressed to memorize more than about 20 such pairs. And these memories do not survive (Meyer, Schvaneveldt, and Ruddy 1971; Postman 1975; Fisher and Craik 1977).

Paired-associate learning is even more difficult if words are paired with abstract visual symbols. Even with extensive study over a long period, memorizing thousands of abstract visual symbols *and* remembering which symbol goes with which word may be fine for a computer, but it is a very bad idea for a human brain. And the difficulty level would go through the ceiling if the visual symbols consisted of thousands of random sequences of the same 26 letters. This is what sight-word methods require of a child learning an alphabetic writing system, and is the reason no one is a sight-word reader. Nor do people become sight-word readers as adults, as some researchers claim. Only the profoundly deaf read purely by sight, and they reach a ceiling at around a fourth-grade reading/spelling level (Aaron et al. 1998; also see chapter 10, this volume).

The evidence from the study of writing systems shows us not only *that* sight-word reading is impossible, but exactly *when* the memory overload occurs. In the case of Egyptian hieroglyphics, even the priests, the keepers of the sacred script who boasted of their prowess in mastering it, gave up on logographs as the main unit of the system so early that the date cannot be traced. Already in 3000 B.C., the date of the earliest Egyptian writing so far discovered, the writing system had three different components. There were pictographs/logographs standing for whole words indeed, but every one of them had a cluster of clues around it. One clue was a "category determiner," a symbol that stood for a common semantic category (man, water, mountain, grain, and so on).

Other clues consisted of a set of phonetic symbols standing for single-, double-, and triple-consonant sequences. Consonants frame the meaning of a word (its root) in Hamito-Semitic languages like Egyptian. Vowels signal changes in grammar and swap in and out, while the root stays intact. Today, these "consonantal alphabets" are the main writing system for modern Hebrew and Arabic. Sometime before 3000 B.C., the Egyptians had figured this out. Logographs were there all right, but they did not need to be.

Sumer is the only ancient civilization with an unbroken record of the writing system dating back to the remote reaches of time. Symbol tokens carved on clay and inserted into clay balls were used in commerce and have been dated to as early as 10,000 B.C. (Schmandt-Besserat 1978). There were symbols for a number system along with pictograms for the products being conveyed.

A true writing system did not appear until around 3200–3000 B.C. The most primitive form of this system used pictograms, abstract symbols standing for words (logographs), and category determiners for nouns. This changed rapidly due to the nature of the language. Sumerian was an "agglutinative" language consisting mainly of one-syllable words with these syllable types: CV, VC, CVC. In this type of language, one-syllable words are combined ("glued") into longer words and phrases. For example, the plural was indicated by duplication: "I see man-man." Because the Sumerians used the same symbol for the *sound* of the word no matter what role it played in the sentence, the writing system essentially functioned like a syllabary—a sound-based system.

The shift from meaning to sound is not obvious and has misled scholars down through the years. Proportional counts of pictograms and logographs made from the vast number of clay tablets recovered from archaeological digs show that the logograph count has declined over time. In part, this is because scholars initially believed all early writing systems were logographic, leading them to see more logograph symbols than were actually there. In part, it was because the Sumerians shed logographs as time went by. For example, Falkenstein (1964) reported that among the total signs dating back to 3000 B.C. (pictograms, logographs, classifiers), 2,000 were logographs. In subsequent estimates, the logograph tally was much smaller, and it shrank dramatically over the centuries: 1,200 in 3000 B.C., 800 in the period 2700–2350 B.C., and 500 in 2000 B.C. (Coulmas 1989). Yet Michalowski (1996), a leading Sumerian scholar, believes that the Sumerians may have had few, if any, logographs almost from the beginning. He calculated that the entire corpus of symbols (all types) was around 800 by 3200 B.C., stating that the system was virtually complete at this time. A writing system with 800 signs is consistent with a syllabary.

In 2500 B.C., the Semitic Akkadians adopted Sumerian for their administrative language, along with the writing system (much as Europeans borrowed Latin). Over time, it was adapted to the Akkadian language and became a syllabary of about 300 signs (Cooper 1996). By the reign of King Sargon I, in 2350 B.C., any use of logographs had virtually ceased (Civil 1973).

We can trace a similar development in China. Early Chinese writing was discovered late in the nineteenth century on a set of oracle bones dating to the Shang dynasty in roughly 1200 B.C. The characters, which numbered around 2,500, were so complex and numerous that Chinese scholars assume the writing system must have developed much earlier. So far, no further evidence has been found (Chang 1963; Ho 1976).

The Shang characters are identical in *type* to modern Chinese characters, though dissimilar in form. Characters are compound symbols. The main symbol represents a unit of sound (the syllable). A secondary symbol, which is fused with it, represents a semantic classifier, called a "radical." This is a clue to the category of the word: *man, water, food, mountain, earth*, and so forth. These compound symbols constitute the main writing system. Karlgren (1923) estimated that 90 percent of all modern Chinese characters are "semantic-phonetic compounds." Mair (1996) revised this figure to 81 percent.

Chinese, like Sumerian, has a small number of syllable types: CV and CVC. Phonemes combine in these syllable patterns to create 1,277 legal Chinese syllables. Because there are so few syllables in the Chinese language, Chinese (like Sumerian) is riddled with homophones, words that sound alike but have different meanings. This is less of a problem in natural speech, because Chinese is a tonal language. Changes in vocal inflection (pitch) signal a change in meaning. But tones are not marked in Chinese writing, and the category symbols (radicals) are essential clues to meaning. They serve the function of unequivocality.

The number of symbols or characters in the modern Chinese writing system provides a good estimate of the limits of human memory. Children memorize about 1,260 syllable symbols, plus 214 category classifiers, for a total of 1,474 basic signs. They must also learn which word (which of the nine meanings of *tang*) is represented by which particular syllable-plus-classifier combination, because this is not always obvious. Mair (1996) estimated that 90 percent of words in common texts can be written with 1,000 compound characters, and 99 percent with 2,400. He concluded that "there is a natural upper limit to the number of unique forms that can be tolerated in a functioning script. For most individuals, this amount seems to lie in the range of approximately 2,000–2,500" (p. 200).

The Japanese writing system is the only writing system that still retains a large number of logographs (*kanji*). These symbols were originally borrowed from China and used for Chinese loanwords. Today, the Japanese Ministry of Education has set the school requirement for kanji at about 1,860. Children learn half the kanji symbols in elementary school and half in high school, a process taking about 12 years. Mastery of an additional 2,000–3,000 kanji is considered the mark of a highly educated person, and memorizing them can take up to a decade or more of adult life.

Needless to say, 1,860 word signs that take 12 years to learn is scarcely sufficient to represent the 50,000 or so words required by the average Japanese man or woman to read a newspaper or magazine. This is why the lion's share of the Japanese writing system consists of two (redundant) phonetic scripts (*katakana* and *hiragana*) with around 50 symbols each. These represent the consonant-vowel (CV) diphone units so typical of the Japanese language (*ka-ta-ka-na*). The Japanese writing system contains $1,860 + 50 + 50$ symbols, for a total of just under 2,000, plus the addition of Roman letters to represent foreign words. Here is a writing system that fails two out of three of Coulmas's criteria: economy and simplicity. By this measure, it does not qualify as a "successful writing system," yet it works nonetheless.

The numbers from these tallies tell a story. There is a limit on human long-term memory for memorizing abstract visual patterns paired with individual words. This is an *ultimate limit*, present after years of intense memorization. Based on an earlier analysis of known writing systems, I put this limit at approximately 2,000, remarkably close to Mair's estimate based on Chinese (McGuinness 1997c).

Logographs do not a writing system make, that much is clear. But logographs do not even fare well as components of a writing system. It is obvious that no civilization ever thought they did, or developed anything remotely approximating a whole-word system. We have a 5,000-year history to show that writing systems are essentially sound-based systems and that no whole-word (sight-word) reading method can work. The notion that children can learn to read whole words purely by sight, or that adults ultimately become full-fledged sight-word readers, is patently false.

Without exception, in every writing system ever translated, the memory-overload problem was solved by avoiding the word as the unit of the system, and switching to phonological units instead. At this point we reach level 2 of Coulmas's list, and confront a serious dilemma.

The Sound-Based Level: Syllables, Syllable Parts, Phonemes
At this level, a major problem was created by a premature classification system. Put simply, linguists allow words, syllables, and phonemes, but creators of writing systems did not see it that way. They did not stick to syllables or phonemes in choosing a sound-based unit. In a sense, linguists have put a straightjacket on comparative analysis, leaving no wiggle room.

The lack of terminology for writing systems that are neither syllabaries nor alphabets creates unnecessary disputes among analysts. The Egyptian consonant script is a case in point. Gelb claimed it had to be a syllabary, because the consonant symbols automatically imply vowels, and also because no writing system can skip a step in Gelb's evolutionary sequence. Other paleographers argued that because the symbols do not mark which vowel to use, or whether it would precede or follow the consonant (VC or CV), it cannot be a syllabary but must be some kind of alphabet (Jensen 1969). In fact it is neither. It is neither because the reader does the work filling in vowel sounds that are implied but not marked. This is because a goodly chunk of the "writing system" is inferred. It has to be carried in one's head. Furthermore, a writing system like this can only work for languages with a particular structure, where consonants carry the meaning load and stay in a fixed sequence while vowels swap in and out to signify changes in grammar. These are characteristics of Hamito-Semitic languages and no other languages. The mere existence of a consonant-only writing system refutes the notion that there is a universal model that would apply to the development of all writing systems.

The facts, if you look at them impartially, tell us that the choice of a sound-based unit has nothing to do with an evolutionary progression. Nor is the choice an accident, or just "relatively" based on syllable structure, or borrowed haphazardly via diffusion. The choice is governed by the structure of the language in terms of both syllable number and *phonotactics*, the legal phonetic sequences in a given language. For example, the adjacent consonant sequence /str/ is legal at the beginning of English words (*street*), but not at the end. This is not an academic issue, but a living, breathing, language issue. Nine-month-old infants are already hard at work analyzing the phonotactic structure of their language (Aslin, Saffran, and Newport 1998; Friederici and Wessels 1993; Jusczyk 1998; Mattys et al. 1999; also see *Language Development and Learning to Read*).

The idea that the phonotactic structure of a language plays a role in the choice of a phonetic unit for a writing system has been suggested by a number of authors (Mattingly 1985; Coulmas 1989; Katz and Frost 1992; McGuinness 1997c), but it has not been explored in much depth. I have proposed (McGuinness 1997c) that there are four types of sound-based writing systems, not two. These four basic types derive from the syllable structure and phonotactics of individual languages. The choice of a sound unit is based on the principle of least effort—a trade-off between two factors: economy (the ease with which the sound units can be learned), and perception (the ease of discrimination, or "naturalness," of the units to be adopted). This is assuming the other constraints apply as well.

This represents a departure from conventional wisdom on this issue. Nevertheless, it is worth exploring because it provides answers to some quite fundamental puzzles, the first being: If Gelb was so certain that a syllabary is an inevitable step en route to alphabets, where are the syllabaries he refers to? So far, we have met only three (Sumerian, Akkadian, and Chinese). There are the Babylonian and Assyrian syllabaries (languages that were dialects of Akkadian), the Hittite syllabary, plus the classical script for Annamese (Vietnamese) borrowed from China. Seven or so syllabaries in 5,000 years is not an impressive number. Only one, Annamese, was shed for an alphabet, and this was not made official until 1912. A more compelling argument against Gelb's linear evolutionary model is that it cannot explain the many examples where an alphabet was rejected in favor of something more syllable-like. If Gelb was correct about writing systems evolving into higher forms, then evolution could go both forward and backward in time and so would not count as "evolution."

To understand the implications of this new classification scheme, we need to look at the structure of the four types of writing systems and how they were designed. In particular, we are going to look at the critical role that awareness of the phonetic/phonemic level of language played in how the writing system was set up. This illustrates the fact that no scholars could have designed a writing system unless they knew the phoneme corpus of their language, and raises the following question: If they knew this, why didn't they always opt for an alphabetic writing system?

Syllabary Writing Systems   The syllable is the largest phonological unit below the level of the word, in the sense of containing the most phonetic information. The English words *straight* and *I* are both one-syllable words. Syllabary writing systems only work for languages that have an extremely limited number of syllable types. Two major civilizations, Sumer and China, fit this description, and both have a syllabary writing system.

But did the adoption of a syllabary writing system mean that early scholars opted for this solution because they were unaware of phonemes, and could never have discovered that an alphabet was the best solution? No notes remain from the hundreds of hours it must have taken scholars to create a syllabary writing system. One can speculate. There are two solutions. The first would be to work it out orally in a piecemeal fashion. As each syllable comes to mind—*tan, chang, ho, tang, wan, min*—a symbol would be designed for it. This is rather chaotic and dangerous, because people would forget which symbol went with which syllable as the days went by.

Another solution is to work out the individual sounds within syllables (the phonemes) and design symbols for them. There are far fewer phonemes than syllables in any language (Chinese has about 35, and Sumerian 21). If you did this, you could set up a matrix and work it through systematically. This way, you would be far less likely to leave something out, and it would be much easier to keep track of what you were doing.

Here is a partial phoneme solution for creating a syllabary in a language with the vowels /a/ and /o/ and the consonants /b/ and /t/. The problem we are addressing is how many syllable symbols we need to represent every legal syllable (CV, CVC) in a language similar to Chinese. Beginning with symbols for the 4 phonemes, we would end up with 12 possible legal syllables, as the accompanying table shows. The next step is to cross off the syllables that are illegal in the language and design a special symbol for each syllable that remains. These can be recorded on a separate chart.

C	V		C	V		C
	a	*o*		*a*	*o*	
b	ba	bo	*b*	bab	bob	*b*
t	ta	to	*b*	bat	bot	*t*
			t	tat	tot	*t*
			t	tab	tob	*b*

This example is intended to make the point that when your logographic solution crashes into the ceiling of human memory, you have to find a better way, and it must be complete. A partial writing system is no use. The question is, would it be more efficient to begin by assigning symbols to 35 phonemes as a memory device, then set up a matrix and work it through, or to do it randomly, designing each syllable symbol as you went along? We have no clues from Chinese documents as to what was done, but we do have clues from Sumer in the thousands of clay tablets found in temples, palaces, and schools dating back to the fourth millenium B.C. (Kramer 1963, [1956] 1981; Michalowski 1996).

Michalowski (1996) reported that digs in ancient Uruk revealed an abrupt transition, which has been dated to between 3200 and 3000 B.C. The early phase of protowriting had no particular order or structure. At the point where writing proper begins, suddenly order appears. Having observed this material, he wrote: "The structure and logic of the system indicate that it was invented as a whole and did not develop gradually" (p. 35). Michalowski emphasized the fact that from the beginning there was a concern for the structured transmission of the system.

Kramer reached a similar conclusion in his analysis of Sumerian tablets written for and by schoolchildren (about 2000 B.C.). The children were introduced to the syllable signs in a systematic way: all the CV syllables, all the VC syllables, then the CVC syllables, each memorized independently. Next, they learned lists of words in semantic categories. Written symbols were not learned in a random order incidentally as part of reading meaningful text, and it is highly unlikely they were designed that way.

These examples show that it is just as likely the Chinese and the Sumerians were aware of the phonemic structure of their language, as it is they were not. And if they were aware of it, they could have easily observed that an alphabet was extremely economical. Nevertheless, *they chose not to use it.*

CV Diphone Systems When a language has more than three or four syllable types, a syllabary will not work for the simple reason that it would breach the limits of human memory. According to the received wisdom on this issue, the only other option is an alphabet. But this is not remotely what happened. The most common sound-based unit adopted for all writing systems, past or present, is the consonant-vowel unit. CV writing systems work for the hundreds of languages *mainly* built on a repetitive phonological structure like this: CVCVCV. These phonological units appear universally in the utterances of infants: *ba-ba-ba, goo-goo, ba-goo-da.* An English word with this pattern is *potato*. There are no languages where VC units commonly form words: VC-VC-VC (*edit* and *idiot* are about as close as it gets).

These writing systems were identified by McGuinness (1997c) and named *diphone systems* (two sounds). Up to this time, diphone writing systems had been classified as alphabets or syllabaries. Coulmas (1989, 225) referred to one of these systems as "a Devanagari-type syllabic-alphabet," a good illustration of the missing-terminology problem.

The most important word in the first paragraph of this section, is the word *mainly*. All languages written in a diphone writing system have more syllable types than CV alone. If they did not, they would be one-syllable languages, and the writing systems would indeed be syllabaries. But these languages have words that end in a consonant (VC, CVC) and words with consonant sequences (CCV, CCVC, CVCC). This is especially true of Indic languages, all of which are written with a diphone system. One of the features of Indic languages (and all other Indo-European languages) is the variety of consonant clusters or blends.

This means that diphone writing systems are inherently ambiguous. There is a problem of how to mute an extra vowel sound when the word ends in a consonant. *Balam* is a Mayan word, but in their diphone script it would read *balama*. The consonant clusters in *krishna*, an Indic word, would read *karishana*. The solution was to add marks or diacritics indicating when to drop a vowel, and these can become part of the script itself. Indic writing systems use "ligatures" (loops that act as connectors) to signal the reader to drop a vowel between two consonants. This is why a diphone system is different from a syllabary. The fact that a diphone system does *not* mark all the syllable patterns in the language sets it apart.

It would not be practical to list every writing system that used or uses the CV diphone as a sound-based unit for the code, but even a partial list is impressive. The Mayans appear to be unique in designing a compound system, with pictograms and logograms plus a CV diphone script and symbols for vowels. The remaining diphone systems are sound-based only. The earliest so far is Linear B (about 1450 B.C.), found on Crete and later used in commerce by the Greeks. Next come the writing systems based on the Indic Brahmi script, developed sometime after the fifth century B.C. This script led to an amazing number of offspring.[1]

It is assumed that the Indic Pali script, or one like it, led to the creation of the two Japanese diphone systems, hiragana and katakana, via Buddhist missionaries. Other diphone systems include Ethiopian (a Semitic language), circa fourth century A.D., and the Han'gul system developed during the Korean writing reform in the fifteenth century. There is also the writing system of the Cherokee Indians, and a most interesting diphone hybrid from Persia, discussed in more detail below.

The important message is that alphabets may dominate in Western cultures, but they do so for linguistic (phonotactic) reasons, not because they are inherently superior to all other forms.

Evidence on how these diphone systems were set up and designed provides another surprise. At the time the Brahmi script was created, Indian scholars had already designed symbols to represent each phoneme in their language. These "alphabet symbols" were set up in a fixed order and grouped by place of articulation, showing their sophisticated knowledge of phonetics. The same "alphabetical order" was used for dictionaries. There is speculation that this "alphabet chart" was used for novices to learn to chant mantras with precise pronunciation. But it is highly likely the alphabet chart was used to design the Brahmi diphone script, as shown by how it was constructed. Each consonant plus the vowel /ah/ (the primary vowel in Indic languages) was assigned a different symbol. Next, these symbols were systematically modified for each vowel change, as shown in figure 2.1.

---

1. The Brahmi offspring include the writing systems for Kusan, Gupta, the Devanagari script used for Sanskrit, Hindi, and Nepali, plus the scripts for Siamese, Burmese, Kavi or Sinhalese, Bengali, Assamese, Tibetan, Mongolian, Kashmiri, Balinese, Madurese, Tamil, Central Indian, Punjabi, and Malayalam, as well as the important Pali scripts designed for the Prakrit languages associated with Buddhism. These scripts traveled east as Buddhism spread, giving rise to the diphone systems of Sri Lanka, Burma, Thailand, Cambodia, and Indonesia.

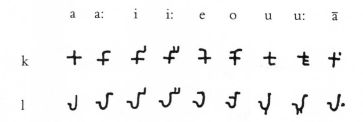

| Figure 2.1 |

Brahmi script 5th century B.C. Examples of diphone symbols for 2 consonants and 9 vowels

Judging from the evidence on how these systems were set up, and the large number of people who adopted and designed them (about 200 of these scripts have been attested in India alone), it would have been obvious to ancient scholars that an alphabet could work as a writing system. *Yet an alphabet was never adopted for this purpose.*

The Han'gul writing system from Korea is an even clearer example, because its design is more transparent. First, each vowel and consonant was assigned a symbol and these were set up in a matrix, 10 vowels across the top and 14 consonants down the side. At each junction of consonant and vowel, they needed a symbol for all the CV pairs in the Korean language. Instead of designing 140 new symbols like everyone had done before them, they had a better idea. Rather than wasting the alphabet symbols, these symbols were fused into pairs, as shown in figure 2.2.

There is one more example from Old Persia, during the reign of Darius I (522–486 B.C.), the most curious so far. It is written in cuneiform symbols, no doubt borrowed from the Babylonian script. This is a hybrid system of 36 symbols. There are 13 consonant-only signs that are used with 3 vowel signs (an alphabet). In addition, there are 20 different consonant signs that include an inherent vowel and vary according to which vowel is indicated (CV diphones). Another surprise is that the "alphabetical" order of these signs is identical to the one used in India, with consonants grouped by place of articulation. Our alphabetical order derives from the West Semitic (Phoenician) system and is quite different. Whether this alphabetical order is original to Persia or to India is unknown, because both writing systems appeared around the same time.

		Vowels									
		ㅏ	ㅑ	ㅓ	ㅕ	ㅗ	ㅛ	ㅜ	ㅠ	ㅡ	ㅣ
Consonants		a	ya	ŏ	yeo	o	yo	u	yu	eu	i
ㄱ	g(k)	가	갸	거	겨	고	교	구	규	그	기
ㄴ	n	나	냐	너	녀	노	뇨	누	뉴	느	니
ㄷ	d	다	댜	더	뎌	도	됴	두	듀	드	디
ㄹ	r(l)	라	랴	러	려	로	료	루	류	르	리
ㅁ	m	마	먀	머	며	모	묘	무	뮤	므	미
ㅂ	b	바	뱌	버	벼	보	뵤	부	뷰	브	비
ㅅ	s	사	샤	서	셔	소	쇼	수	슈	스	시
ㅇ	※	아	야	어	여	오	요	우	유	으	이
ㅈ	j	자	쟈	저	져	조	죠	주	쥬	즈	지
ㅊ	ch	차	챠	처	쳐	초	쵸	추	츄	츠	치
ㅋ	k	카	캬	커	켜	코	쿄	쿠	큐	크	키
ㅌ	t	타	탸	터	텨	토	툐	투	튜	트	티
ㅍ	p	파	퍄	퍼	펴	포	표	푸	퓨	프	피
ㅎ	h	하	햐	허	혀	호	효	후	휴	흐	히

| **Figure 2.2** |
Diphone symbols for combinations of vowels and consonants in Han'gul

Old Persian was an Indo-European language. However, the administrative language of the Persian empire was Semitic Aramaic. The Aramaic writing system originated around the ninth century B.C. and marked only consonants, using simple letter-like characters similar to the Phoenician script, the ancestor of our alphabet. It seems the Persian script was influenced by two factors: the form of the script (cuneiform) plus the CV diphone system by the Babylonians, and the concept of consonant-only symbols featured in the Aramaic writing system. Whatever turns out to be correct, it is clear that the Persians designed at least a partial alphabet but *failed to use it* for a writing system. We now have three clear examples of "evolution" going backward.

Consonant Cuing Systems Writing systems based on consonant sequences (no vowels) are unique to Semitic languages. There are scores of consonant cuing systems in the Near East and Middle East, both past and present, the prototype being Egyptian hieroglyphics (3000 B.C.). In one sense these systems cannot be classified, because they are so dependent on the reader knowing all possible words and conventions of the spoken language before the text can be decoded. One could think of them as shorthand versions of a diphone system, except this would be inaccurate, because the script provides no indication of which vowels must be added to the reading. If the reader saw p t t (CCC), and a diphone rule was operating, the reader would think: CVCVCV, "this might be *potato*." But the script does not indicate where the vowels go. The sequence could be read any number of ways: VCVCVC (*oputot*) or CVVCVCV (*piatuti*).

This is not really a writing *system*. It is more like a sketch or a sequence of clues. For example, it would be impossible to read a word that was not in your vocabulary. Consonant cuing systems are about as economical as it gets, so much so that they fail both the unequivocality and the comprehensiveness tests. Modern consonant systems, like Hebrew and Arabic, use diacritics to indicate vowels when texts are difficult. This applies to books for beginning readers, to sacred or classical texts, and to highly technical books. With the addition of specific vowel markers, these systems turn into alphabets.

Alphabets When a language has too many syllable types (English has 16, not counting plurals), when it lacks a basic diphone structure CVCVCV or any other simple structure, or when it does not have the "consonant-root" nature of Semitic languages, it must be written some other way. At this point we are nearly out of sound-unit options, and the only other way is *down*—down one more level below the CV unit, to the individual consonants and vowels (phonemes).

All writing systems based on the phoneme are called *alpha-bets* after the first two letter names (*alpu*, *beth*) in the Old Phoenician consonantal script. The Greeks borrowed these symbols in the eighth century B.C. to set up the first alphabetic writing system. They used the 22 Phoenician consonant symbols to represent similar sounds in Greek. Any leftover letters were assigned to vowels, and new letters were created for the remaining sounds. When they were finished, there was one letter symbol for each phoneme in the Greek language, a perfect or transparent alphabetic writing system. This was certainly not the first alphabet ever designed, but it was the first one *used as a writing system*. Everyone who speaks a European language today uses an alphabet derived from the early Greek alphabet through the process of diffusion.

A transparent alphabet, like the Greek alphabet, is very efficient and has no ambiguity. Alphabets have a small set of easily remembered symbols. No props, rules, or clues, like determiners or classifiers, are required (syllabaries), no vowel sounds have to be dropped (CV diphone systems), and no vowels have to be supplied by the reader (consonant cuing systems), a major advantage. Why then aren't there more alphabets in the world? Why are CV diphone systems the most common type of writing system?

Now we are at the heart of the matter. The history of the development of writing systems shows that ancient scholars must have been aware of alphabets. It is extremely unlikely that any writing system could be designed without one. Examples of alphabet charts, of patterns in the symbols of the scripts, show that scholars were well aware of phonemes. Yet they avoided using an alphabet even when one was staring them in the face. It is hard to escape the conclusion that the phoneme was an unpopular unit for a writing system.

Diphone systems, on the other hand, have a number of useful features. They are well within the memory limit. (A diphone system for English could scrape by with around 315 symbols, although it would never work.) They are designed for a highly salient unit of sound, easy to hear in the speech stream. They fit natural-language patterns in ways that individual phonemes absolutely do not. There is more phonetic information per symbol than in an alphabet, so like syllabaries, they are faster to read and write (nearly twice as fast).

By contrast, phonemes overlap each other in the speech stream and slip by so quickly that people are not aware of them. If children are not made aware of phonemes when they learn to read, they will misunderstand how an alphabet works. Because people find it unnatural to analyze and isolate phoneme sequences in words, this is undoubtedly the reason alphabetic writing systems are not found everywhere. It seems that when an alphabet could be avoided, it was.

Implications for Teaching and Research

The major types of writing systems have been described in some detail to emphasize the fact that writing systems are inventions. They require time to design and develop. They have a complex structure. They must be designed by scholars with sufficient access to power and influence to convince everyone to learn the system. The efforts that went into the design of early writing systems were monumental. That it was possible to represent the fleeting sounds of human speech in symbols that mark every word in a language is nothing short of miraculous. These facts have important implications for research and for reading instruction.

The assumptions about writing systems held by many educators and researchers were listed at the end of the last chapter. Here is a recap on why these assumptions are false.

First, there is no support whatsoever for a fixed evolutionary sequence in the development of writing systems, nor any evidence that ancient peoples "gradually evolved" into being able to hear phonemes. What appears evolutionary (the transition from whole-word to sound-based systems) is due to historical/logistical factors in trying to use graphic symbols designed for economic purposes in a full-fledged writing system for broad cultural ends. During this transition, logographs quickly hit a ceiling, then decreased as the sound-based system took precedence. At least this was the pattern in civilizations where writing systems were created from scratch.

The logograph holdout, in the case of Japan, can also be explained in terms of historical factors. Early on in the development of their writing system, the Japanese borrowed Chinese characters and used them as logographs (kanji) for Chinese loanwords. These logographs were subsequently used for Japanese words with the same or related meanings. A kanji symbol today has many "readings," another reason it takes so long to learn them.

Second, a writing system is an *invention* and not part of our biological heritage like spoken language. People must be trained to use inventions. A reading method must ensure that the nature and logic of the writing system are transparent to the learner, and that the elements of the system are mastered. Methods that ask the child to "guess" how the writing system works (whole-language) are utterly irresponsible.

Third, no writing system was ever based on the whole word, nor were whole-word symbols (logographs) ever more than a minute fraction of any writing system. Languages have too many words. Human memory for abstract symbols overloads at about 2,000 symbols, and even achieving this takes many years. A reading method either totally or partially based on whole-word memorization of sight words will cause the majority of children to fail. These facts also refute the notion proposed by some cognitive psychologists, that people ultimately read all words by sight. It cannot be done. (For a description of these theories and what they imply, see chapter 11.)

Fourth, all writing systems are based on one of four specific meaningless phonological units, specific because *phonological units are not mixed*. Teaching methods that train children to be aware of the particular sound unit for the writing system, *and only that unit*, and that show them how these sounds are represented by the symbols, will be effective. Teaching a potpourri of other sound units (words, syllables, syllable segments, word families) that have nothing to do with the writing system will lead to confusion and failure for many children.

Fifth, writing systems are designed to fit the phonological structure (phonotactics) of the languages for which they were written. The choice of the sound-unit basis of the writing system is not arbitrary. Civilizations adopted an alphabet solution out of necessity and not from choice, because no other solution would work. The Greeks, for example, already had a diphone writing system (Linear B), which they used for commerce. But it was useless for representing the Greek language, with its complex syllable structure. All Linear B texts used by the Greeks consist of bills of lading, inventory lists, and invoices. And it is quite obvious, viewing these texts, that the CV diphone units of Linear B map extremely badly to the Greek language (see Robinson 1995).

Finally, history shows that alphabets tend to be avoided if possible. Scholars from different cultures, separated widely in time and place, designed alphabets for other reasons, but failed to use them for a writing system. The record shows that a larger, clearly audible, phonological unit was the preferred solution, especially if the number of these units was well below the magic 2,000 limit. People are not normally aware of phonemes, and it is unnatural to isolate phonemes from each other. This has important implications for instruction. Children who learn an alphabetic writing system need to be taught to listen at the phoneme level of speech, and need to learn how to link phonemes to letter symbols. They have to be trained to listen at the *right* phonetic level and to look at the *right* symbolic units (letter(s) in a letter string). Any reading method that teaches the wrong unit of sound or multiple units of sound (words, syllables, syllable fragments) risks misleading children, causing them to fail.

THE STRUCTURE OF THE ENGLISH
ALPHABET CODE

A writing system is an *encoding* device for representing units of sounds in the language by a set of symbols. What we call "spelling" (encoding) is the fundamental or basic operation, the process of turning sounds into symbols. What we call "reading" involves decoding those symbols back into sounds to recover the words. Reading and spelling are reversible processes, and should be taught in tandem so that this reversibility is obvious. Unfortunately, in English-speaking countries it is common practice to teach reading and spelling as if they had nothing to do with each other, using different words, different forms of instruction, taught on different days. This practice totally obscures the code nature of our writing system, and makes learning to read and spell far more laborious and confusing than it needs to be.

Structural reversibility, however, does not mean psychological reversibility. Reading and spelling are structurally reversible, but they draw on different memory skills. Decoding, or reading, involves *recognition memory*, memory with a prompt. The letters remain visible while they are being decoded. Encoding, or spelling, involves *recall memory*, memory without prompts or clues, which is considerably more difficult. To spell a word, you must first identify each phoneme in sequence in your mind, remember how each phoneme in that particular word is spelled, and then write it down. What you can spell, you can easily read (recognize). But what you can read is not necessarily easy to spell (recall). The fact that spelling is the primary process and has 100 percent spin-off for reading has been known for centuries, one reason Noah Webster wrote a "speller" in 1793 and not a "reader." Maria Montessori strongly advised teachers to teach children to write (spell) first, and then allow them to discover that they can read what they have written.

The Sumerians understood this 5,000 years ago. The thousands of clay tablets containing stories and exercises discovered in the ruins of ancient Sumer are a testament to a number of important facts about writing systems and how to teach them. Based on the historical record, there is a high probability that the people who designed the Sumerian writing system played a significant role in setting up the schools to teach it. No other culture in history has provided such a clear picture of how the designers of the writing system thought the system should be taught.

It is evident from this material that children were taught each syllable in their language and the symbol that represented it. They learned this through a series of exercises beginning with the basic syllable forms (CV, VC, CVC), moving systematically to more complex multiple-syllable words (CV-CVC-VC-CV). Encoding (spelling) and decoding (reading) were connected and learned as a *reversible process* at every step. The students copied syllables, words, and sentences, or wrote them from dictation. They then read aloud what they had written to their teacher.

Five thousand years ago, the Sumerians bequeathed to us the basic guidelines for how to teach reading and spelling for any writing system:

1. Make sure the complete structure of the writing system has been worked out (or thoroughly understood) before a method of instruction is developed.
2. Teach the specific sound units that are the basis for the code. (Do not teach other sound units that have nothing to do with the code.)
3. Teach the arbitrary, abstract symbols that represent these sounds. These symbols constitute the code.
4. Teach the elements of the system in order from simple to complex.
5. Ensure that the student learns that a writing system is a code and that codes are reversible.
6. Make sure that encoding (spelling) and decoding (reading) are connected at every level of instruction via looking (visual memory), listening (auditory memory), and writing (kinesthetic memory).

It is hard to imagine a better list of guidelines. Unfortunately, education practice has strayed so far from its roots that hardly any educators or classroom teachers adhere to even *one* of these principles, let alone all six.

We cannot begin to implement reform unless educators (and researchers) understand how writing systems work in general, and how our writing system works in particular.

Children must be made aware that specific sound units (phonemes) in the language are the basis for a written code, and that symbols representing these sounds constitute the code. It should be made clear that sounds are "real," and letters are "unreal," arbitrary symbols for those sounds. Letter do not "have sounds," or "say" anything, as children hear so often in phonics lessons in the English-speaking world. And they certainly do not "say" letter names.

The important message is this: a writing system is a code with a systematic relationship between units of sound and visual symbols. All codes are reversible. That is the nature of codes. If a code cannot reverse (through encoding/decoding), it will not function as a code.

There are good codes and bad codes, codes that are obviously reversible (like those in Germany, Italy, Finland, Sweden, and Norway) and codes that cannot reverse unless they are taught correctly. Purpose-built codes, like the Greek and the original Anglo-Saxon writing systems, were designed by scholars familiar with the nature of codes and how writing systems work. These purpose-built systems were designed in a short period of time and tend to be "good codes." A good code is efficient (entailing a reasonable memory load), comprehensive, and transparent— only one symbol is used for each sound in the language (whichever unit of sound is chosen). Transparent codes are transparently reversible. The student can easily see that the code works in both directions: encoding and decoding. The sound /d/ is always written *d*, and the letter *d* is always read as /d/. For this reason, transparent codes are much easier than opaque codes to teach and learn.[1]

Venezky (1973) discovered just how easy it is to learn a transparent alphabet in a study on 240 Finnish children in grades 1 through 3. Children begin reading instruction in Finland at age 7 (grade 1). A nonsense-word reading test was designed that included words spelled with every

---

1. As a reminder, phonemes are enclosed in slash marks and spellings are underlined.

possible deviation from a one-to-one correspondence in Finnish orthography. At the end of first grade, the children scored 80 percent correct on this test, a value that remained unchanged through third grade. College students scored 90 percent correct, failing the words with the most obscure Finnish spellings. In other words, it takes a year or less for Finnish children to be able to read and spell nearly as well as the average college student.

As noted in chapter 1, Wimmer (1993) found that the worst readers in the city of Salzburg, Austria, scored close to 100 percent on a difficult test of reading accuracy and did nearly as well in spelling. Wimmer and Landerl (1997) compared Austrian and English children on a spelling test of English and German words balanced for complexity of spelling patterns. The English children made twice the spelling errors (of all types) as the Austrian children. More importantly, 90 percent of the errors made by the Austrian children were legal (phonologically accurate), compared to only 32 percent for the English children.

Geva and Siegel (2000) reported on 245 Canadian children who were learning to read and write English and Hebrew at the same time. English was the first language in most cases. Hebrew is written with a consonant cuing system where symbols represent consonants, and diacritic marks are used for vowels when texts are difficult, as for beginning readers. The consonant symbols and diacritics are nearly 100 percent consistent, making Hebrew a highly transparent writing system. By the end of first grade, the children scored 79 percent correct on a Hebrew reading test, but only 44 percent correct on the English version of the test. Children did not reach the 80 percent competency level in English until fifth grade, and by this time they scored 90 percent correct in Hebrew.

Writing systems that evolve over long periods of time tend to be opaque, lacking consistency between sounds and symbols. This happens for two reasons. The first has to do with the arbitrary nature of the process; the designers are pioneers and there is no prior model of a code or a writing system. The process proceeds by trial and error, and as insight is gradually gained, no writing reform occurs to correct early mistakes.

The second reason is historical accident. A country (England) with a transparent writing system (Anglo-Saxon or Old English) is conquered by a people who speak a different language and have a different way of writing (spelling) the same or similar sounds (Norman French). The language and the spelling system are superimposed on the existing system. Or a country (England) with a transparent writing system (Anglo-Saxon) adopts Latin for religious, legal, and academic purposes. The Latin spelling system uses different symbols for the same or similar sounds. Over time these words become part of the vernacular, and Latin words along with their spellings are pegged onto the existing system. And no writing reform ever takes place to correct these problems. In addition, spoken language slowly changes over time. Vowels shift in pronunciation. Consonant sequences may become illegal (drop out of the language). In the Anglo-Saxon word for "know" (spelled cnāwan), the /k/, /n/, and /w/ were pronounced "k-na-wan."

By "reform," I do not mean spelling reform, tinkering with the problem by standardizing spelling, but real reform in which the one-to-one correspondence between sound and symbol is restored.

Because the English language and the English writing system were assaulted by several foreign-language invasions, it is not an exaggeration to say that the English writing system is one of the most opaque writing systems in existence. It represents five languages and their spelling systems superimposed on one another: Anglo-Saxon, Danish, Norman French (a patois of Danish, Romanz or Old French, and Latin), Classical Latin, and Greek. The bonus has been one of the most expressive languages in the world, but the downside is one of the highest functional illiteracy rates among literate nations. There is no question that the high functional illiteracy rate in English-speaking countries is largely a product of our formidable spelling code and the way it is (or is not) taught.

The central argument in this chapter is that a complex, opaque spelling system like the English spelling system needs to be taught with great care. It cannot function as a code (cannot reverse) if it is taught with the wrong logic and in the wrong direction: from letter to sound only. Here's why. There are 40+ phonemes in the English language, and about 176 common ways to spell them (see below). This number would explode if every rare spelling was included (Venezky 1970, 1999). If the code is taught in the direction in which it was written, 40 sounds to multiple spelling alternatives and back again, the code nature of the writing system remains intact. *The 40 sounds are the only constant in the system.*

If the code is taught the wrong way around, from 176 spellings to 200+ "sounds," there is no way to get to the 40 English phonemes. This destroys the logic of the writing system. Confusion can start to creep in quite early and unravel students long before they get anywhere close to 176 alternative spellings (these spellings would never be taught anyway, because teachers do not know what they are).

Here is a typical example of a common error. Mrs. Jones is keen to include phonics principles in her teaching. She works entirely from visual logic: letter to sound. She teaches the letters k, c, and the digraph ck, but not at the same time. She says something like: "The letter see says /k/." (Mrs. Jones is careful not to say "kuh," which is good.) She writes the words *cat*, *cup*, *car*, and *cow* on the board. A week or so later, she says: "This letter is kay, and it says /k/." She writes the words *keg*, *keep*, and *kill* on the board. Several weeks later, she says: "The two letters see-kay say /k/." She writes the words *back*, *duck*, and *sick* on the board.

If children remember the first lesson (which many will not), they may think they probably got something mixed up. What they heard a week ago was not really /k/, but something else they cannot remember. Other children will assume that the sound /k/ that the letter c says is a different /k/ from the one the letter k says, and a different /k/ from the one the letters *ck* say. Young children make this kind of mistake a lot. They believe, or actually *hear*, the same phoneme as sounding differently depending on where it comes in a word. To some children the /b/ in *bat* sounds different from the /b/ in *cab*. Acoustically, they *are* different. The /b/ in *bat* is considerably more bombastic than the /b/ in *cab*. These subtle distinctions are known as *allophones* (variants on the same sound). But our writing system is based on phonemes, not allophones. If children are taught the 40 phonemes in the first place, this kind of confusion could never occur.

Here is what Mrs. Jones should have said: "Today we're going to learn the sound /k/. There's more than one way to spell this sound. I am going to teach you some patterns to help you remember when to use each spelling."

Now the message is clear. The children will not think that they are losing their minds, or that they are too stupid to learn.

Given the fact that the English spelling code is highly complex, one would imagine that considerable effort has been expended to work out its structure by linguists, curriculum designers, and researchers studying how children learn to read and spell. This has not happened. The nature and structure of the English spelling code are virtually unknown. As a consequence, research on how children master a writing system is carried out without any knowledge of its structure, or even of the fact that it is a code. This is like studying what children do when they are put in a room for several hours a day over a period of years, with a piano, some musical scores, a few CDs, and no lessons on how to read music. For the most part, reading research has largely demonstrated two things: the enormous ingenuity and versatility of the young mind in the absence of suitable instruction, plus the miraculous fact that some children actually learn to read and spell.

A Tower of Babble

Confusion in the field begins with basic terminology like *orthography*, *spelling rules*, and *regular spelling*. The word *orthography* appears in almost every research report on spelling and in much of the literature on reading as well. *Orthography* means "standardized spelling," *ortho* meaning uniform or standard, and *graphy*, written signs or symbols. We have a standardized spelling system thanks to Samuel Johnson, but knowing correct spelling tells us nothing about the structure of the spelling code. Yet researchers frequently confuse the word *orthography* with this structure and with "spelling rules." Many believe that "orthographic rules" govern why and how words are spelled in particular ways, despite the fact that no one is quite certain what these rules are. Yet it is precisely these "rules" that children are supposed to grasp intuitively and internalize as they work their way through pages of print and spelling tests over the years. Here is a summary of the terminology problem. When the basic terminology of a discipline is misused, or never properly defined, the researchers do not understand what they are studying.

Rules

Clymer (1983) wrote an insightful and entertaining paper on spelling rules, or as he put it, on "spelling generalizations." In his words, "We were careful not to call the generalizations 'rules,' for all our statements had a number of exceptions. As the class finally formulated a generalization regarding the relationships of letters, letter position, and sounds, such defensive phrasing as 'most of the time,' 'usually,' and 'often' appeared as protective measures" (p. 113).

Clymer stumbled onto the truth about "generalizations" while teaching an elementary school class. He was advised in a course on reading instruction to let children discover spelling rules through exercises in categorizing spelling patterns. While Clymer and his students were busily engaged in this activity, one student ("Kenneth") spent his time pouring through the dictionary, locating exceptions to the generalizations as fast as the class could create them. When Clymer explained that the dictionary was filled with unusual words, Kenneth turned his attention to the basal-reader word lists instead, with the same results. His interest piqued, Clymer decided to track down phonics spelling rules in various manuals and programs. Using a corpus of 2,600 words, he worked out how many words did or did not fit 45 common rules. The only rules that held up 100 percent of the time specified which letters formed digraphs (*sh* in *ship*). Every other rule failed in some way or other. This includes the stalwart: "c = /s/ before *e*, *i*, *y*" (*crusta__ce__an*, *suspi__ci__on* break the rule), and the infamous "when two vowels go walking the first one does the talking," a rule that fails 55 percent of the time.

A broken rule is not a rule. If "washing hands before meals" is a family rule, washing hands "some of the time" breaks this rule. Nor does it help to fudge matters by calling rules "generalizations": "*Most of the time* we wash our hands before meals in this house." This begs the question what "most of the time" means. In any case, even assuming that rules or generalizations were reliable, they would never work. Children cannot remember rules, much less apply them, something Noah Webster observed and commented on in his speller over 200 years ago. Many of the rules Clymer lists do not even make sense: "In two- and three-syllable words, the final *e* lengthens the vowel in the last syllable" (a rule that is broken 54 percent of the time).

There are no spelling rules. Forget about rules. Forget about generalizations.

Regular Spelling

The expression "regular spelling" is used all the time in publications on reading, as well as in descriptions of reading and spelling tests. The casual use of this expression, and the fact that it is never defined, implies that everyone is supposed to know what "regular spelling" means. Some authors refer to "regular grapheme-phoneme spellings," others to "grapheme-phoneme correspondence rules" or "GPCs," apparently in the belief that there are rules governing which decodings are "regular" and "irregular." But there are no such rules.

Nevertheless, some spellings are obviously more common than others, and in the absence of any definition for "regular spelling," I will provide one here. "Regular spelling" is the only spelling for a particular phoneme (including letter doubling), or the most probable or least ambiguous spelling. For example, the sound /b/ is always spelled b̲ or b̲b̲. The spellings e̲e̲ and e̲a̲ are the most probable (common) spellings for the sound /ee/, and represent this sound equally often. However, e̲a̲ is ambiguous (*bead, head*) and e̲e̲ is not.

Note that "regular spelling" means regular *spelling*, not to be confused with regular *decoding*, which is often how this term is used. For instance, the digraph o̲a̲ is supposed to be "regular" because it is usually *decoded* as /oe/ (*broad* and *oasis* are exceptions). But o̲a̲ is not the most common (regular) *spelling* for the sound /oe/, one of the many problems that arise when the code is analyzed the wrong way around. (The most common spelling of /oe/ is o̲-e̲, as in *home*.)

Orthography

Wagner and Barker (1994) unearthed 11 definitions of *orthography* in publications by leading reading researchers. Each definition was different. Three were circular, using the word *orthographic* or *orthography* to define *orthography*. According to Szeszulski and Manis (1990, 182), for example, "Orthographic coding allows direct access to a mental lexicon for familiar words based on their unique orthography." Other authors stressed the function and structure of the spelling code, the "general attributes of the writing system," which included things like "structural redundancies" (Vellutino, Scanlon, and Tanzman 1994) or similar structural features (Leslie and Thimke 1986; Jordan 1986). Some incorporated phonological processing into the definition (Foorman and Liberman 1989; Ehri 1980; Goswami 1990; Olson et al. 1994), while others took pains to exclude it, stressing that orthography was different from "phonological mediation" (Stanovich and West 1989). Perfetti (1984, 47) came closest to the real meaning, defining *orthographic ability* as "the knowledge a reader has about permissible letter patterns."

I will reserve *orthography* for its true meaning (standardized spelling) to avoid further confusion. The goal of this chapter is to establish a set of criteria that define the structure of the spelling code. One of these criteria, as Vellutino and colleagues correctly pointed out, is "structural redundancy" or *probability*. But a "probability structure" is not an orthography. Probability refers to the fact that some alternative spellings for a particular sound are more or less likely than others. This is a statistical likelihood, most definitely not a rule or a generalization. Statistical likelihood can be estimated reliably, whereas rules and generalizations are unreliable, as we have seen.

In an opaque writing system, the only factors that make it a code and not chaos are reversibility and statistical likelihood, the incidence of predictable structural patterns.

The complexity of our spelling code has led most people to believe that the English spelling system goes on to infinity with no end in sight. This is why classroom teachers, curriculum designers, and researchers find such solace in "word families" (*damp, lamp, clamp, stamp*), those little islands in an endless sea of chaos, the few discernible patterns in the system. The view that English spelling is untamable, and thus unteachable, has been reinforced by three well-known attempts to fathom the constraints or limits of the system. All were unsuccessful, though for quite different reasons. Before outlining why these attempts failed, let's look at the peculiar complexities of our spelling code. Here is a laundry list of the woes of the English spelling system:

1. There are not enough letters in the alphabet for the 40 phonemes in the English language. To solve this problem, the Anglo-Saxons followed the Romans' lead by reusing letters in combination (digraphs) to stand for a single phoneme (<u>sh</u> in *ship*).
2. There are only 6 vowel letters for approximately 23 English vowel sounds (15 vowels, and 8 vowel + *r* vowels). The multiplicity of vowel digraphs and phonograms (<u>igh</u> in *high*) make vowels particularly difficult to read and spell.
3. There are multiple ways to spell the same sound: *spelling alternatives*.
4. There are multiple ways to "read" the same letter(s): *code overlaps*.
5. The connection between spelling alternatives and code overlaps is not straightforward. This creates the false appearance of two independent

systems, one specific to encoding (spelling) and one specific to decoding (reading).

As an example of points 3–5 above, the sound /ee/ can be encoded (spelled) ten ways: ee (as in *green*), ea (*mean*), e (*be*), ie (*siege*), ei (*deceive*), e-e (*serene*), ey (*key*), y (*folly*), i (*radio*), and i-e (*marine*). The spelling ee is always decoded /ee/, but the remaining spellings can be decoded in a multiplicity of other ways. The spelling ea can be decoded as /e/ (*head*) or /ae/ (*break*), the spelling e as /e/ (*bed*) or /ə/ (*the*), and the spelling ie as /ie/ (*die*), /ue/ (*view*), /e/ (*friend*), or /i/ (*sieve*), and so forth.

Given this complexity and the disorganized manner in which reading and spelling are taught, it is easy to see that, for a child (as for teachers and reading researchers), the spelling code appears to lack any discernible structure. But brains are pattern analyzers and cannot code or retrieve randomness. They actively resonate with recurring regularities in the input, and automatically keep score of the probabilities of recurring patterns. By 9 months of age, infants can learn the statistical redundancies of four alien syllable sequences in spoken words in about 2 minutes of listening time (Aslin, Saffran, and Newport 1998). True randomness, unpredictable relationships between sound and symbol, is unlearnable, in the same way that the telephone directory is unlearnable. The fact that the majority of people learn to spell tells us the spelling code cannot be random. It must have a probability structure in which recurring patterns are more or less predictable. And if there are patterns, these can be classified so that they can be taught.

Attempts to Classify the Spelling Code

Webster

The first attempt to classify the English spelling code, as well as to set out a sequenced method for reading and spelling instruction, was carried out by Noah Webster and published in 1783. The book became known as the *American Speller* or the *Blue-Backed Speller*. Webster was well aware that the spelling code works from sound to print and back again from print to sound, and that the spelling system is the code: "Spelling is the foundation of reading." But, perhaps because "sounds" are hard to represent in print, he set up the speller from print to sound only. Here are his opening remarks on how to use the speller: "Let a child be taught first the Roman letters, both small and great … then the Italics … then the sounds of the vowels; not pronouncing the double letters a and u separately, but only the sound that those letters united express … then the double letters. All this a child should know before he leaves the Alphabet and begins to spell" (Webster 1783, 28). The speller consists mainly of word lists organized by syllable length (up to seven syllables) and by types of suffixes. The only phonological structure imposed on these lists was the use of word families (rhyming endings). There was no attempt to provide the common patterns of sound-to-symbol relationships in our spelling code. No change to this basic format occurred in the six editions of the speller over 100 years. (For a thorough discussion of Webster's analysis of the problem, see McGuinness 1997c, 1998b.)

Venezky

Since that time, surprisingly few attempts to assess the structural elements and limits of the code have been made. Venezky (1970, 1995, 1999), also using a letter-to-sound approach, analyzed the incidence and variety of *code overlaps* (point 4 on the list above). As he put it, "Orthography concerns letters and spellings, the representation of speech in writing. That's not exactly what this book is about, however. Here only one direction in the speech-writing relationship—that from writing to speech—is stressed" (Venezky 1999, 3).

Venezky set himself the task of discovering all possible ways a particular letter or letter combination can be decoded, using a corpus of 20,000 words. For example, he identified 17 different ways to decode the letter o. There are 48 ways to decode the five (single) vowel letters. However, Venezky tends to give equal weight to all options, which only serves to highlight the number of exceptions. He did not write, for example: "Most of the time, the letter o is decoded three ways—/o/, /oe/, and /u/, as in *hot, told, among.*" Instead, common and weird spellings alike are set forth (*sapphire, catarrh*), and while these curiosities are interesting, they lead the reader to believe that the English spelling system is beyond redemption.

Venezy did not work out the probability structure of these code overlaps, but he did offer two classification systems. In the first system, letters were categorized functionally as relational units, markers, or silent. *Relational units* signal a particular decoding (a phoneme); *markers* refer to letters used as diacritics; *silent* letters serve no function. However, letters are not confined to just one category (i.e., are not mutually exclusive), so it is not clear what function this classification scheme serves. For example, the letter e is a relational unit for three decodings (*be, bet, the*), it is a marker or diacritic for both vowel and consonant pronunciations (*can/cane; bulge*, not *bulg*), and it is silent in *axe*.

In the second classification scheme, Venezky labeled spelling patterns as *invariant, variant but predictable*, or *unpredictable*, meaning that the decoding is either fixed (b is always read /b/), or limited to a set of alternatives, or unknown without instruction. But Venezky did not specify which letter patterns fit which of his classification schemes, and did not clarify the connection between them. Can a letter or digraph be a "variant but predictable" "relational unit"? Because few examples were provided to illustrate these categories, no overall structure can be developed from them. One gets a sense of hopelessness about our spelling code, and it seems Venezky (1995, 29) did as well: "If orthographic patterns were symmetrical, pronouncing words from their spellings and spelling words from their pronunciations would be relatively similar tasks.... Such symmetry would allow a collapsing of the teaching of reading and spelling, as well as simplifying the description of orthographic patterns. But alas, English orthography is painfully asymmetrical."

This is a surprising statement on two levels. First, it is a confession that there is no symmetry if the code is analyzed backward, solely from print to sound (the way he did it). Second, it is tantamount to a claim that our spelling system is not reversible. But if it is not reversible, it cannot be a code. And if it is not a code, no one can learn it. Venezky's statement was followed by three pages of illustrations and descriptions of the startling complexity created by multiple spelling alternatives for the sounds /k/ and /z/, and of how these, in turn, can be decoded in a multitude of unrelated ways. These examples have the effect of shocking the reader into recognizing the utter futility of trying to fathom the limits of our spelling system.

The American Way of Spelling (Venezky 1999) is the most systematic of Venezky's writings and is devoted to an analysis of our spelling system. The title belies the contents, because the purpose of the book is to set out the "decodings" of the various spelling patterns, not how the 40 phonemes in our language can be spelled. The book begins with an in-depth account of the many spelling patterns in our system and ends with a chapter on phonics instruction, setting out a more simplified list of which spelling patterns should be taught and in what order. Despite including a chapter on the phonetic distinctions in English, the book provides virtually no analysis of how the spelling patterns are related to these distinctions, or an explanation of the relevance of this phonetic structure to the nature of the code or the teaching of reading and spelling.

Venezky's primary goal in this book is to provide some type of order, a set of categories or "rules" for how our spelling system works, although he recognizes that no one can learn to read by trying to memorize or apply these rules. His search for rules is actually a search for logic, as if our spelling system was idiosyncratic *by design*. Thus, he makes many observations like "Visual identity of meaningful word parts takes precedence over letter-sound simplicity"—this to explain why the plural s signifies two pronunciations (as in *cats* and *dogz*). He searches for patterns in homophone spellings, such as the use of "silent letters" (*plum, plumb*; *rain, reign*; *him, hymn*), as if their use was intentional. Some of his observations are correct and quite general (useful), such as the consistent way simple vowels govern the spelling of final consonants: final /k/ is spelled ck after simple vowels (*sick, sock, sack*), but not after digraphs (*weack, seeck*) or consonants (*milck, sharck*). Final consonants usually double after simple vowels (*well, stuff*) but not after digraphs or consonants (*real, leaf, girl, self*).

Venezky attempts to look at "regularity" in two ways. One has to do with pseudowords or pronounceable nonwords. As he points out, "No full set of rules for generating legal spellings for pseudowords has ever been published." He tries to set up some rules here, such as "all one or two letter words are irregular by strict criterion," listing *ebb, odd*, and *egg* as examples of why the final letter is doubled. (But there are many regular spellings that do not follow this rule, such as *in, is, it, at, am, an, as*.)

The second way is to identify every consonant and vowel spelling, and establish a frequency count of how often each spelling is used in the overall corpus of words and in the initial, medial, and final positions in these words. A table is provided for consonants, but not for vowels. One problem with this endeavor is that the 20,000-word corpus contains foreign words and proper names, which make the tallies misleading. Examples include *Ghent, khaki, khan, Slav, Yugoslav, Chekhov, leitmotiv, Himalayas, Maya, Sawyer, Agassiz*, and *Suez*. The consonant spelling rrh for /r/ appears in six Greek words for diseases (*cirrhosis, diarrhea*).

From this exercise we learn that the most common initial consonant letter is c, the most common medial letter is r, and the most common final letter is m. But this does not tell us which *sounds (phonemes)* are common in these positions or how these sounds should be spelled. Nor does it tell us how these letters are decoded. For example, knowing that c is most common in initial position does not tell us how often it represents /k/ or /s/ (*cut, cent*).

The chapter on consonants traces the history of 38 consonant spellings, such as where the letter(s) itself came from, the regular and irregular types of spellings or words it can appear in, and the sound or sounds into which it can be decoded. The letter b is usually decoded /b/, can double in certain words (bb), and is subject to being "silent" in *debt, doubt,* and *subtle*, is subject to "pre or postjunctural deletion" (silent) in *bdellium, bomb*, and so on, and is subject to "medial cluster leveling" (silent) in *subpoena*. The 38 consonant spellings are listed in alphabetical order and include many alternative spellings, including: ck, dg, gh, gn, kh, ph, pph, rh, rrh, sch, tch, u (u stands for /w/ in a words like *quiz, anguish, persuade*). As a reminder, there are only 23 consonant phonemes in English, including /zh/ (vision) plus /kw/ (qu) and /ks/ (x).

The chapter on vowel spellings lacks a table of spelling patterns and frequencies (i.e., no probability analysis for vowel spellings). Instead, the vowels are set out in a categorical scheme. This goes as follows:

Major primary patterns: a, e, i, o, u, y. These letters signify vowels that are "checked," as in *cat, bet, sit, hot, cut, gym,* or "free," as in *cake, mete, kite, home, cute, why.*

Primary subpatterns. Final *e* pattern: corresponds to spellings as above: a-e, e-e, i-e, o-e, u-e.

Geminate consonant pattern. Special decoding for vowels in conjunction with double consonants: *mamma, albatross, coffee, gross, doll, pudding.*

Consonant influences: Vowel + *r* Venezky sets out 15 vowel + *r* patterns, plus 12 exception patterns. There are too many overlaps in both spellings and pronunciation for this to be valid. Linguists usually recognize about 5 to 6 vowel + *r* phonemes. I could only find 9, as listed in the preface.

Before final l or ll. This refers to so-called "l-controlled" vowel pronunciation in words like *ball, doll, almond, calm.*

w-controlled a: As in: *wand, swan,* where the w signals the vowel /o/.

<u>i</u> before <u>nd</u>, <u>ld</u>, <u>gn</u>.: As in: *kind, mild, sign*.

Suffix Patterns: Syllable stress and schwa vowel.

Exceptions to decoding words with final <u>e</u> spellings: *hav<u>e</u>, moral<u>e</u>*.

Major Secondary Patterns: <u>ai</u>, <u>ay</u>, <u>au</u>, <u>aw</u>, <u>ea</u>, <u>ee</u>, <u>ei</u>, <u>ey</u>, <u>eu</u>, <u>ew</u>, <u>ie</u>, <u>oa</u>, <u>oi</u>, <u>oy</u>, <u>ou</u>, <u>ow</u>, <u>ui</u>, and <u>uy</u>.

Minor secondary patterns are low-frequency spellings: <u>aa</u>, <u>ae</u>, <u>eau</u>, <u>eo</u>, <u>ieu</u>, <u>iew</u>, <u>oe</u>, <u>ue</u>, <u>ye</u>

In the final chapter, Venezky states that 100 "common graphemes" should be taught initially in beginning phonics instruction, a process he estimates will take two to three years to complete, and this does not include the additional time for learning prefix and suffix spelling patterns. These graphemes consist of 58 consonant spellings and 38 vowel spellings, plus 4 spelling rules (for a total of 100). However, the chapter lists only 34 vowel spellings and 23 consonant spellings, plus one rule, and there is no explanation for why the remaining spelling patterns are omitted. The list excludes 32 common spelling alternatives in my system (see page 55) but includes many spellings that children will not need at this level, such as: <u>t</u> for /sh/ in *nation*, <u>c</u> for /sh/ in *ocean*, <u>s</u> for /zh/ in *measure* (the phoneme /zh/ is not mentioned anywhere in the book), <u>ch</u> for /k/ in *chord*, <u>h</u> is silent in *honor*, and <u>b</u> is silent in *bomb*. (The phoneme representations are mine.)

Also provided is a list of 37 "exception words" (sight words), plus 32 prefixes and suffixes. Sixteen of these words have perfectly regular spellings and are in no way exceptional. There are no guidelines for how these spelling patterns, rules, exception words, and affixes should be taught. Only a few words are provided for each spelling, and rare spellings are just as likely as common ones. In short, it is difficult to see how teachers are supposed to use this material, and difficult to understand how reading can be taught without reference to the 40 phonemes in our language.

Venezky suggests that spelling should be taught along with reading, but he provides no information on how this should be done. He often uses a logic that is contradictory to the way the code works, one which blocks teaching spelling in any meaningful way. For example, he urges teachers to reinforce multiple ways to decode the same spelling: "Students should be asked repeatedly 'what other sounds could that letter (digraph) *have*?'

and 'do you know a word in which it *has* a different sound?'" (p. 232, italics mine).

Letters do not have sounds. People do.

Hanna, Hanna, Hodges, and Rudorf

In the third well-known attempt to come to grips with the spelling code, the code was analyzed properly from print to sound, the way it was designed. This project was much more ambitious than Venezky's. Using a corpus of 17,310 English words, Hanna et al. (1966) worked out all the spelling alternatives for sounds in the English language, apparently the first attempt to do so. Their goal was to classify the various spelling alternatives according to the "frequency" with which particular spellings appeared within this 17,310-word corpus.

I want to distinguish here between frequency in terms of probability within a corpus of words (how often a particular spelling appears in all words), and frequency in print (how often words with particular spellings appear in text), which is not what Hanna et al. were interested in. For example, <u>ee</u> and <u>ea</u> are the most probable spellings for the sound /ee/. But <u>e</u> is the most frequent spelling because words with this spelling appear frequently in print (*be, he, she, me, we*), and this spelling also appears in common prefixes (*de-, e-, be-, re-, pre-*). I will use the word *probability* for the former and *frequency* for the latter. Both are important in working out the structure of the code and in setting up a curriculum for how to teach it.

Hanna et al.'s work is a monumental effort in every sense of the word, and it is unfortunate that a series of major blunders and other problems led to a largely unusable outcome. The classification was based on 52 English phonemes, about 10 too many. These include 15 primary vowels: /a/, /e/, /i/, /o/, /u/, /ae/, /ee/, /ie/, /oe/, /ue/, /o͝o/, /o͞o/, /ou/, and /oi/, plus schwa (ə), an unaccented /uh/ sound. The vowel sound /aw/ was omitted. Also included were five of the eight vowel + *r* vowels: /ar/, /er/, /or/, /air/, and /eer/. Omitted were /ire/, /ure/, and /our/.[2]

---

2. Vowel + *r* vowels are known as "rhotacized" vowels ("*r*-colored"). Because /r/ by itself is a vowel (/er/ in *her*), a vowel + *r* is effectively a digraph that represents a diphthong. This is like other vowel-vowel combinations that

Some vowel sounds were counted twice: /er/ (*her*) and /ur/ (*fur*); /o/ (*soft*) and /o/ (*odd*). There were numerous errors in classifying vowel spelling alternatives. The most serious stemmed from misunderstanding the role of *e* as a diacritic marker for consonants in words like *juice*, *dense*, *live*, *siege*, *judge*, and *soothe*. The *e* was erroneously coded with the vowel, producing several nonexistent spelling alternatives like oo-e (*choose*) and ui-e (*juice*), plus hundreds of misclassified words where the *e* works with the consonant but was coded as working with the preceding vowel: e-e (*license*), o-e (*dodge*), and i-e (*massive*).

There are 23 consonants in English (25 if one includes the letter symbols for consonant clusters: x /ks/ and qu /kw/). Hanna et al. listed 31. These included /ks/ and /kw/, plus silent h (*honest*) and several phonemes that do not exist, marked with a glottal stop /'l/, /'m/, and /'n/, as in *table*, *chasm*, and *pardon*. These are two-syllable words. Every syllable, by definition, must have a vowel, not a glottal stop. These words are pronounced *ta-bəl*, *kazzəm*, and *pardən*, with a schwa vowel in the second syllable.

Hanna et al. uncovered a total of 174 spellings for 52 phonemes (93 for consonants and 81 for vowels), including the spellings for the Latin and Greek layers of the language. The spelling alternatives were classified in turn according to whether they appeared in a stressed or unstressed syllable. However, English spelling is largely unrelated to syllable stress. The schwa vowel always appears in an unstressed syllable, but knowing this does not tell you which of its six spellings to use. Next, Hanna and colleagues classified multisyllable words according to whether a spelling appeared in the initial, medial, or final syllable, another exercise in futility. Spelling patterns are affected by phoneme position *within* a syllable, not between syllables in multisyllable words. All this greatly increased the level of complexity of their results.

There were errors in data entry. People were trained to classify words by phoneme and by spelling alternative. Initially, there was a high success rate with a trial corpus of 565 words. This level of accuracy was not

---

count as one vowel: /ou/ = *ah-oo* (*out*); /oi/ = *oh-ee* (*oil*). Vowel + *r* vowels are most affected by dialect, and in some dialects the /r/ portion is not sounded. There is considerable disagreement among linguists as to how many vowel + *r* vowels there are.

maintained, however, and Hanna et al.'s study is replete with hundreds of data-entry errors. The most glaring mistake was putting the words with the vowel sound /ue/ (*cue*) into the lists of words with the vowel sound /oo/ (*coo*), an error that does not appear in the vowel tables at the front of the book.

But there was a far more serious problem, essentially dooming the whole endeavor. They did not separate the Latin (or Greek) layers of the language from common English words (Anglo-Saxon and Norman French). This needs to be done, because there are major structural differences in the spelling code for Latin words, and there are special spelling patterns for words of Greek derivation.

The inaccurate set of spelling alternatives, the complex and unnecessary syllable-classification scheme, plus the inclusion of an abundance of affixed forms of the same root word (*idea, ideal, idealism, idealistic, idealize, ideally*), led to an unwieldy tome of 1,716 pages, taking up the space of four large books on the library shelf. The awesome complexity of this document along with its bulk only confirmed in another way that our spelling system is too wild to tame.

These efforts had the effect of convincing researchers that spelling could not be taught. The fact that children learned to spell at all was taken as evidence that children go through "developmental stages" (see chapter 9). The extreme form of this notion is tantamount to a belief that *English* brains evolved to learn to spell the English writing system. This specificity is a requirement of the model, because the spelling errors English children make as they progress through these so-called spelling stages do not appear for children learning transparent orthographies who receive appropriate instruction (Venezky 1973; Wimmer and Landerl 1997; Geva and Siegel 2000).

McGuinness
The most recent attempt to classify the spelling code is my own (McGuinness 1992, 1997a, 1997c, 1998a, 1998b). This classification is based on a strict sound-to-print orientation like that of Hanna et al. But the goals and the procedure were different, in that the purpose of my classification was similar to Webster's—to systematize and illuminate the spelling code so that *it could be taught*. The process began with the phonotactic structure of the English language (legal phoneme sequences

in words). All phonotactically legal syllables were determined. If a syllable constituted a real word, or was part of a real word, its spelling was recorded. Based on this analysis, it was estimated that there are over 55,000 legal English syllables. Contrast this to the 1,277 legal syllables in Chinese, and you have the reason our writing system is an alphabet and not a syllabary.

Basic Code   The first step in any classification process is to establish limits or endpoints. Endpoints create a frame or boundary. This is essential for codes, because they must have a pivot point, around which the code can reverse. This endpoint or pivot is the finite number of phonemes in the language. Once the student knows 40 phonemes, there are no more to learn.

The next step is to set up a basic code (an artificial, transparent alphabet) using the most probable spelling for each phoneme, as defined in the section "Regular Spelling" above. A basic code can easily be taught to 4- or 5-year-olds in a relatively short period of time (Johnston and Watson 1997, forthcoming; also see chapter 5, this volume), though this should not be mistaken for the complete code. A basic code makes it possible to read and write a large number of common one- and two-syllable words. It is transparently reversible, so children can see and experience the logic of a writing system. The idea of a basic code is not new (Ellis 1870; Dale 1898), and it is common to several phonics programs today, particularly in the United Kingdom. But nearly all programs stop here, or at best, teach only a fraction of the remainder of the code.

The Advanced Spelling Code   The major hurdle in our writing system is mastering the multiple spellings for each phoneme. This is the reason English-speaking children have so much difficulty learning to read and spell. It is the "advanced code" that causes the major problems for poor readers, and teaching this turns out to be far more important during remediation than training phoneme-awareness skills (C. McGuinness, D. McGuinness, and G. McGuinness 1996).

Because of its complexity, the advanced code itself needs a classification scheme with limits and boundaries. All classification systems are somewhat arbitrary, and whether this one is best for the purpose remains an empirical question. The first hurdle is to find out which spelling alternatives are common and which are rare, and the number of words sufficient to establish a bona fide spelling alternative. The number of spelling alternatives needs to be kept within reasonable bounds, while at the same time avoiding hundreds of special exceptions. If an improbable (uncommon) spelling of a phoneme occurs in a few words or less, what should be done with these words? The solution was to create *four more categories* at the advanced-code level.

The first category comprises the *major spelling alternatives* beyond the basic-code level. Spellings that did not qualify as major were classified in one of three ways: as a *special group* (few words, improbable spelling, high frequency in print), as *sight words* (singular spelling, high frequency in print), or *omitted* (singular spelling, low frequency in print).

In making these distinctions, probability (how many times a spelling alternative is used in a large corpus of words) was a key determiner of a major spelling alternative, whereas frequency in print was more important for inclusion as a "special group" or a "sight word." Special groups like *could*, *would*, *should*, and *door*, *floor*, *poor*, and *break*, *great*, *steak* are important high-frequency words with improbable spellings.

Another decision was to avoid "silent letters" by merging them into digraphs or multiletter phonograms whenever possible. Thus <u>igh</u> is one of four main spelling alternatives for the sound /ie/ (*high*). This helps teachers avoid making nonsensical statements like this one: "In the word *high*, the *I* says its name, and the gee aitch is silent." This solution works well except in rare cases. For words like *honor*, *hour*, and *honest*, there is no choice but to tell the children: "The first letter isn't sounded in these words."

Every effort was made to avoid classifying a word as a sight word. Most reading programs produced by the major publishing houses include a large list of sight words, many using "regular" spellings. It is a bad idea to teach sight words to children learning *any* writing system, as we saw in chapter 1. But there is more at stake. Teaching whole words by sight promotes a faulty decoding strategy. This happens because memorizing whole words seems logical and is relatively easy initially, leading to a false sense of security. But a whole-word strategy will inevitably collapse, depending on the child's vocabulary and visual-memory skills. Meanwhile, this strategy can harden into a habit that can be difficult to break (McGuinness 1997b).

For these reasons, the sight-word category was reserved for common words where one or more phonemes have a unique spelling that is hard to decode without direct instruction. There are almost no words where *every* phoneme has an unpredictable spelling. By this criterion, there are remarkably few true sight words. The following sight words and special-group words did not fit a major spelling category in a large corpus of words of English/French origin. There are approximately 100 sight words:

/a/	*aunt, laugh, plaid*
/e/	*friend, leopard*
/i/	*been, busy, sieve, pretty, women*
/o/	*abroad, broad, cough, father, gone, trough, yacht*
/u/	*a, because, does, blood, flood, of, once, one, the, was, what*
/ae/	*straight, they* Group: <u>ea</u> *break, great, steak*
/ee/	*people, ski*
/ie/	*aisle, choir, I, height, sleight*
/oe/	*sew*
/ue/	*beauty, feud, queue*
/o͞o/	*move, prove, shoe, deuce, through* Group: <u>o</u> *do, to, who, whom, whose*
/o͝o/	Group: <u>oul</u> *could, would, should*
/ar/	*are, heart, hearth* Group: <u>orr</u> *borrow, tomorrow, sorrow, sorry*
/er/	*acre, glamour, journey, syrup, were* Group: <u>ure</u> *leisure, measure, pleasure, treasure*
/or/	*drawer, laurel* Group: <u>oor</u> *door, floor, poor*
/air/	*bury, heron, scarce, their, there, they're, very, where*

Final /k/—<u>c</u> or <u>ch</u> *arc, tic, ache, stomach*   Group: /k/—<u>lk</u> *baulk, caulk, chalk, stalk, talk, walk*

/t/—<u>bt</u>   Group: *debt, doubt, subtle*

Final /th/—<u>th</u> *smooth* (final voiced /th/ is usually spelled <u>the</u>, as in *breathe, clothe*)

Final /v/—<u>f</u> *of*

Initial <u>h</u> is not sounded: *honest, honor, hour*

Initial /h/—<u>wh</u> *who, whom, whose, whole*

The "omitted" category eliminates nuisance sight words—those rare, low-frequency words with rogue spellings that only clog up the system, like *sapphire* and *catarrh*. These words are usually easy to decode and only hard to spell. They need to be seen a lot or looked up in a dictionary until they are memorized.

So far, this analysis covers words derived from Anglo-Saxon and Norman French. There are 132 major spelling alternatives for these words, 55 for consonant spellings and 77 for vowels (including 4 vowel + *r* spellings). Once this structure was worked out, it was set up in an easily accessible form as a "spelling dictionary" organized by phonemes. All words containing a phoneme with a particular spelling were listed under the appropriate heading and alphabetized in two dimensions down the page. Spelling alternatives were listed in a row across the top of the page from most to least probable, with words spelled in basic code on the left. Thus, a corpus of over 3,000 common English words could be presented in only 75 pages, providing a clear visual display of the probability structure of the spelling code (McGuinness 1997a). This structure is obvious, even to a child. A page from the dictionary is shown in table 3.1.

Very little active memorization is necessary when learning is based on exposure to predictable patterns (structural redundancies). Our brains do the work for us. The only active memorization required is to learn the 40 phonemes in the language and their basic-code spellings. Spelling alternatives for each phoneme can be mastered through controlled exposure and varied repetition, via dictionary activities, fail-safe worksheets, specially designed stories, copying, and creative writing.

Once the structure of the spelling code is set up visually, numerous features and patterns come to light. Use of these patterns can dramatically speed up learning while reducing the memory load, and is essential for setting up a sequence of instruction. Here are some of the most important patterns.

Structural Features of the Code
1. Some phonemes have no, or rare, spelling alternatives. Apart from consonant doubling, there is no way to misread or misspell them:

/b/, /d/, /l/, /p/, /th/, /a/, /ar/

Table 3.1
Sound: /ae/ Key word: *came*

	Spelling alternatives				
	a-e	ai	a	ay/ey	ei/eigh
h		hail			
	hale		halo		
	haste				
	hasty				
	hate		hatred	hay	
	haze			hey	
i	inflate				
j	jade	jail		jay	
l			label		
			labor		
	lace		ladle		
			lady		
		laid			
		lain			
	lake				
	lame				
	lane				
	late				
	lathe		lazy	lay	
m	mace				
	made	maid			
		mail			
		maim			
		main			
		maize	major		
	make				
	male				
	mane		manger		
			maple		
	mate			may	
	maze				
n		nail			
	name				
	nape		nasal		
			native		
			nature		
			naval		
			navel		
			navy		neighbor
o				obey	

Source: McGuinness 1997a.

2. Because some phonemes have one or two spelling alternatives used in a very small number of words, it is possible to teach by exclusion: "This sound is spelled in basic code except in these words."

/g/, /h/, /m/, /n/, /ng/, /t/, /i/

3. Some consonant spellings are determined by whether the consonant is in the initial or final position in a syllable.

/j/   *jinx barge bridge*
/th/   *this bathe*
/v/   *vain groove*

4. Some consonant spellings in final position are determined by whether they are preceded by one of the five "checked" vowels: /a/, /e/, /i/, /o/, and /u/. (There are exceptions.)

/ch/   *lunch beach catch*
/j/   *siege barge hedge*
/k/   *beak milk sick*
/l/   *girl fool dull*

5. There are 76 legal consonant blends (adjacent consonants) in the English language, and only 3 appear in both initial and final position in a syllable. These are *sk*, *sp*, and *st* (*skip/ask*; *spoon/gasp*; *stop/fast*). Nearly all consonant blends are always spelled in basic code, something very useful to know. If children can segment them, they will always be able to read and spell them correctly.

6. Patterns within patterns (statistical regularities) make learning multiple spelling alternatives more manageable. Once these are known, they can be taught directly. Exposure (practice) is the key, not rules or memorization. For example, /ee/ has the most spelling alternatives of any phoneme. These can be broken down in several ways. Multisyllable words ending in /ee/ are spelled y or ey most of the time (exceptions: *cookie, collie, coffee, toffee*), and these spellings rarely represent /ee/ in other slots. Children should learn this by exposure—by reading, writing, and spelling a range of multisyllable words ending in the sound /ee/. Teaching these patterns

chips away at the complexity, by accounting for when and where specific spelling alternatives are used. By a process of exclusion, the complexity is reduced from 10 spellings for /ee/ to 8, and can be reduced to 7 by memorizing the few words and prefixes where /ee/ is spelled e (*be, he, me, she, we, be-, de-, pre-, re-, tre-*), and so forth.

7. The classification reveals danger zones, such as spelling alternatives with no obvious or memorable patterns, or those with conflicting code overlaps, signaling the need for more exposure. This can be illustrated with another example from the /ee/ spelling complex. The two main ways to spell /ee/ (ee and ea) are equally probable in common English words: *bean, clean, green, mean, queen, seen, screen, teen, wean / beat, beet, bleat, feat, feet, fleet, greet, heat, meet, neat, peat, seat, sleet, street, sweet, treat, wheat.* I have set these up in the *een* and *eet* families to make the point that "word families" do not help you spell. Because there are no clues for which of these spellings to use, the only solution is to see and write these words often.

THE LATIN LAYER OF THE CODE A different type of classification is required for the Latin layer of the spelling code, one that relates to the morpheme level of language (McGuinness 1998a). A morpheme is the smallest unit of sound that signifies meaning. English, Norman French, Latin, and Greek are *compounding languages,* in which root words can combine with other root words or affixes to alter parts of speech, change verb tense, or create entirely new words like *deadline, firefly, household, hotdog,* and *railroad.* Teaching spelling alternatives in Latin words in the context of this compounding structure greatly simplifies the nature and type of spelling alternatives that need to be taught. It considerably enhances multisyllable decoding and spelling, while building vocabulary at the same time.

The compounding structure of English, French, Latin, and Greek words, along with special issues like adjacent vowels, homophones, and the schwa, can be fully addressed with an additional corpus of 3,000 words.

We will skip over the details of English compounding and the transformations that occur when English prefixes and suffixes are added to root words. These are reasonably well known and sufficiently orderly (see McGuinness 1998a). For example, if a root word ends in e, this must be dropped prior to adding a suffix that begins with a vowel, such as -ing or -<u>ed</u>. When adding a suffix to CVC-type words with "simple" vowels, if the suffix starts with a vowel (-<u>ing</u>, -<u>ed</u>, -<u>er</u>, -<u>y</u>), the final consonant is doubled to preserve the vowel sound. Examples involving *bat* include *batting, batted, batter,* and *batty* (not *bating, bated, bater,* and *baty*). This is a fairly stable convention, coming about as close as it gets to a rule in our spelling code. Adding prefixes poses no problem, because no transformations are necessary.

The Latin layer marches to a different drummer. In the first place, it is rare that a Latin root word is an English word (*fact, duct,* and *port* are exceptions that come to mind). This means that the core of Latin/English words is bereft of meaning, a definite disadvantage. English/Latin words are compounded by prefixes, suffixes, or both. As an example, the root word *struct* ("to build") is not an English word, but is "English" in a number of common affixed forms: *instruct, construct, instructor, instruction, instructed, construction, constructed, destruction, indestructible, structure, obstruction,* and so forth. (The prefix *in-* means "in," *con-* means "with," *de-* means "undo" or "opposite to," and *ob-* means "in the way of" or "against." The suffix *-or* means "a person," and "shun" (-<u>tion</u>) means the word is a noun.)

Fortunately, Latin roots and prefixes are usually spelled in basic code, which is a bonus. But Latin suffixes are not and pose particular problems if they are taught as a sequence of individual phonemes. This would produce a dazzling array of spelling alternatives and code overlaps. The phoneme /sh/ can be spelled <u>ti</u> (*nation*), <u>si</u> (*tension*), <u>ci</u> (*magician*), <u>ce</u> (*ocean*), <u>shi</u> (*cushion*), <u>sci</u> (*conscious*), or <u>xi</u> (*anxious*). It is tidier to keep Latin suffixes intact as multiphoneme units. This is a radical departure from the approach used for the English layer of the language.

A good example is the suffix "shun," the most common Latin suffix. It has three main spelling alternatives and four rare ones. Far and away the most common is -<u>tion</u>, which appears in tens of thousands of English words. The next most common is -<u>sion</u>, followed by -<u>cian</u>. The rare spellings are -<u>tian</u> (*dietitian, gentian, Martian, titian*), -<u>cion</u> (*coercion, suspicion*), -<u>cean</u> (*crustacean, ocean*), and -<u>shion</u> (*cushion, fashion*). There are lots of useful clues for these "shun" spellings:

• When in doubt, spell -<u>tion</u>.
• If an occupation or person, spell -<u>cian</u>.

• The suffix -<u>sion</u> usually attaches to word stems ending in /s/: *access, compress, concuss, confess, convulse, depress, digress, discuss,* and so on, though other word stems take this spelling as well: *admit/admission, ascend/ ascension.*
• Memorize the words that use the -<u>tian</u>, -<u>cion</u>, -<u>cean</u>, and -<u>shion</u> spellings.

What is more, -<u>tion</u> and -<u>sion</u> get around. They move as a unit, another reason to teach them as a unit. They pop up as spellings for "zhun" (*equation, vision*), and for "chun" (*digestion, question, suggestion*). In all, there are 38 Latin and 2 Old French suffix spellings that need to be taught. This brings the total of spelling alternatives to 172, plus 4 extra "Greek" consonant spellings at this level, a total of 176. This is surprisingly close to the tally of 174 reached by Hanna et al., but for quite different reasons.

Teaching these Latin suffixes requires a different instructional approach, and keeping the suffixes intact has a number of spin-offs. One is that it makes long, scary words like *advantageous* and *unconscious* easy to read and spell. Knowing that the formidable -<u>geous</u> or -<u>scious</u> spellings are merely "jus" or "shus" in disguise makes them far less daunting. Once these suffixes are demystified, they can be identified first, making the rest of the word easy to decode and spell: ad-van-ta-/<u>geous</u>, un-con/<u>scious</u>. The front ends of Latin-derived words are remarkably well behaved and usually spelled in basic code, or with a highly probable spelling alternative.

A second spin-off is that suffixes attach to root words in predictable ways. When -<u>tion</u> attaches to a root word, the most common form involves adding the letter <u>a</u> to the root: *inform-information, limit-limitation.* When word stems ends in <u>e</u>, the <u>e</u> is dropped: *agitate-agitation, create-creation.* A large family of -<u>ate</u> words follow this pattern, another reason to group words when teaching these suffixes.

Greek words came into the language via philosophy, medicine, and science, originally in Greek, and later as transliterations with special "Greek" spellings. If one steers clear of specialist or technical words, the Greek invasion is remarkably less intrusive than people believe. Very few common words use these spellings, and only eight of these spellings appear in familiar words. These words can be listed on a single page. The spellings include <u>ch</u> for /k/ (*chorus*), <u>y</u> for medial /i/ (*myth*) or /ie/ (*cycle*), p̲h̲ for /f/ (*dolphin*), and rarer spellings like p̲n̲ for /n/ (*pneumatic*), r̲h̲ for /r/ (*rhapsody*), p̲s̲ for /s/ (*psalm*), and x̲ for /z/ (*xylophone*).

This is not to say that everything is solved by classification alone. Other elements of our spelling system present different challenges, and some make heavy demands on visual memory. Words with adjacent vowels are a problem because they tend to look like common digraphs and sometimes overlap with them. This group includes words like *poet, briar, ruin, create, fluent, denial, radio, annual, oasis, alien,* and *idiot.* Children need lessons on how to break these words into syllables.

The biggest spelling headaches, those that never go away, are when to double consonants, and how to spell a schwa. These are the spelling errors most responsible for the wavy red lines produced by your computer spell-check feature. The schwa, an unaccented "uh" sound, appears in tens of thousands of multisyllable words. Though initial and final spellings were standardized to a̲ (*among, agenda*), there is no rhyme or reason for how to spell the schwa anywhere else in the word: *hesi̲tate, benefi̲t, relia̲nt, gratify, impo̲lite, culti̲vate, econo̲my, importa̲nt, adjace̲nt,* and the list goes on. Letter doubling in Latin-based words is supposed to be resolved by word-derivation rules. But because nobody knows Latin any more, this is no help at all. Which of the following spellings is correct: *recomendation, reccomendation, recommendation, reccommendation?*

Research Based on Spelling-Classification Systems

The ultimate question is, does classifying the spelling code so that it can be taught make it easier for children to learn to read and spell? There is almost no research on spelling (or reading for that matter) based on an informed understanding of the spelling code, so little, in fact, that while the National Reading Panel's report (2000) has sections on phoneme awareness, reading, fluency, vocabulary, and comprehension, it has no section on spelling. I know of no applied research that relies on Hanna et al.'s efforts to systematize the code or on their subsequent recommendations (Hodges 1981, 1982). A few studies use the spelling levels proposed by Venezky (1995), and at least one study uses my classification system. These studies shed considerable light on the difference in outcome between teaching the code from letter to sound (visual strategy) versus from sound to letter (phoneme strategy).

Berninger et al. (1998) created a set of 48 words derived from eight levels or sequences proposed by Venezky. These levels are letter driven, so it is important to point out that they are *decoding levels*, not spelling levels (the code taught backward). The levels are as follows:

0. CVC words: *bat nut men mad hit wet*
1. mixed words: *flag back last ask drop club*
2. words with <u>a-e</u>, <u>i-e</u>, <u>o-e</u> spellings
3. words with consonant and vowel digraph spellings: <u>sh</u> <u>ch</u> <u>ng</u> <u>oy</u> <u>ou</u> <u>aw</u>
4. words with vowel digraph spellings: <u>ai</u> <u>ay</u> <u>ee</u> <u>ea</u> <u>oa</u> <u>ow</u>
5. words spelled with single or double <u>l</u>
6. words with vowel + *r*: <u>ar</u> <u>er</u> <u>ir</u> <u>ur</u> <u>or</u>
7. words spelled with <u>wr</u> <u>kn</u> <u>igh</u> <u>mb</u> <u>tch</u> <u>dge</u>

Altogether, there are 33 phonemes here represented by 47 spellings. Missing from the list are seven phonemes (/ue/, /o͝o/, /o͞o/, /th/, /*th*/, /v/, and /z/), 5 vowel + *r* vowels, and the spellings <u>qu</u> and <u>x</u>. This arbitrary, visual approach is typical of many phonics programs, and I want to unpack it to illustrate the problems created by a letter-to-sound approach like this. Bear with me, because if this confuses you, think how it will confuse a child.

The first two levels introduce words with letters that stand for these phonemes:

Level 0: /b/, /d/, /t/, /m/, /n/, /h/, /w/, /a/, /e/, and /i/
Level 1: /f/, /l/, /g/, /k/, /s/, /t/, /p/, /o/, and /u/

Level 1 words (see above) include three spellings for the sound /k/: <u>c</u>, <u>k</u>, and <u>ck</u>, as seen in the words *club*, *ask*, and *back*. Do the children learn these as three spellings for the *same* sound, or as three *different* sounds? At level 2, children learn to decode words with the vowel spellings <u>a-e</u> (*lane*), <u>i-e</u> (*fine*), and <u>o-e</u> (*tone*). At level 4 they learn alternative spellings for two of these vowels (/ae/ and /oe/): <u>ai</u> (*hail*) and <u>ay</u> (*day*); <u>oa</u> (*soap*) and <u>ow</u> (*snow*). The <u>ow</u> spelling is also a code overlap for the phoneme /ou/ (*cow*), so it is not clear which sound is meant. The question is, do children learn the level 4 vowels as new sounds, or do they learn that <u>ai</u>, <u>ay</u>, <u>oa</u>, and

<u>ow</u> are alternative spellings for two sounds they learned at level 2? And if this is the case, where are the spelling alternatives for the sound /ie/ that was also introduced at level 2? These alternatives are <u>i</u> (*find*), <u>y</u> (*cry*), and <u>igh</u> (*high*).

Level 5 is devoted to teaching words spelled with single and double l's. Why this is important is unclear. There is no "level" for the equally tricky single and double *f* spellings (*elf*, *staff*) or any other spelling where final consonant doubling is an issue: *bag, egg; gas, dress; quiz, buzz.*

At level 6, children learn <u>ar</u> and <u>or</u>, as well as three spelling alternatives for the sound /er/: <u>er</u>, <u>ir</u>, and <u>ur</u>. Again, do children learn <u>er</u>, <u>ir</u>, and <u>ur</u> as different sounds, or as three spellings for the same sound? If the latter, why aren't the main spellings for /or/—<u>ore</u> (*bore*), <u>oar</u> (*soar*), and <u>our</u> (*your*)—listed here as well? (/ar/ has no common spelling alternatives).

At level 7, children see a mix of common and rare digraphs and phonograms. There is no logical or structural reason why these are here. Five are spelling alternatives for phonemes previously taught, but it is highly unlikely the children will ever know this. One assumes that <u>igh</u> is taught as a "new" sound, bearing no relationship to the /ie/ sound taught five levels earlier.

Level 7 plays havoc with the structure of the code by divorcing spelling alternatives from the basic code. The basic-code spelling for /ch/ is <u>ch</u> (taught at level 3). Do children learn that <u>tch</u> (level 7) stands for the same sound? Are they told which is used only in word-final position, and when? The spelling <u>dge</u> for the sound /j/ (also a word-final spelling) is introduced here as well. But the basic-code spelling *j* was never taught. How then should children spell words like *just, June,* and *jelly*? Are they to be written <u>dgeust</u>, <u>dgeune</u>, and <u>dgeelly</u>?

This approach and its haphazard organization are notable for the total disregard of the sounds in the language. This makes it impossible for children to understand that our writing system maps 40 speech sounds to a set of spellings, because these sounds are never taught.

Using Venezky's system, Berninger et al. trained a large number of third and fourth graders identified as "poor spellers." The children were divided into several groups that received different kinds of training, plus a control group. They were taught to spell 48 words over a period of

4 months (24 sessions of 10 minutes each, totaling about 4 hours). The control group was trained in phonological awareness and letter-name knowledge and did not see these words.

After training, the children took a spelling-dictation test on "transfer words," which differed in some minor way from the training words. Most (75 percent) involved a simple change of the initial consonant. The investigators found that children in the training groups spelled the 48 transfer words more accurately than the control group (40.5 correct versus 30). There was no difference as a result of different types of training. It did not matter whether children memorized the words as sight words, or via phoneme segmenting, "onset-rime" analysis, or any combination thereof. In effect, these results show that if you study the same 48 words on 24 occasions, you will be more likely to spell nearly identical words correctly than if you have never seem them before.[3]

The critical test is whether the spelling instruction transferred to standardized measures of spelling. It did not. The authors reported that they "failed to find any reliable differences between the treatments as a group or singly and the control groups, or among the different treatments on the standardized normed measures that contained different words than the words that were taught" (p. 596).

In short, teaching words based on Venezky's sequence of spelling levels had no greater effect on spelling skill measured by a standardized spelling test *than teaching nothing*, and this was true no matter what training emphasis (whole-word, phonemes, onset-rime) was employed.

Henry (1989) added a multisyllable component for the Latin and Greek layers of the language to a phonics program developed by her and Calfee (Calfee and Henry 1985). The phonics program, *Project Read*, had been ongoing in 14 classrooms prior to this study. This is a letter-driven

---

3. The authors reported "no significant differences" between the different instructional approaches, but this was not the message in the abstract or the closing section. *Abstract*: "Combining whole word and onset-rime training is most effective in achieving transfer of the alphabet principle across word context." *Final summary*: "Explicit training in whole word and onset-rime connections led to greater transfer of the alphabet principle to untrained monosyllabic words" (p. 603).

program very similar to Venezky's. Eight classrooms of third and fifth graders used Henry's new addition (READ PLUS) along with the Project Read lessons. A control group was taught with a basal-reader method. READ PLUS consisted of 5 lessons 30–45 minutes long, spread out over 5 weeks (2.5 to 4 hours). The lessons included Latin root words, prefixes, and suffixes, grouped by common spellings, with several examples of each. Unfortunately, the results of this study are unclear. The reading and spelling tests were not standardized tests, and reliabilities were only "fair." Also, because the reading and spelling test scores were combined in the data analysis, the separate impact of the training on reading and spelling cannot be determined.

The gain scores (raw scores) for "reading/spelling" over the school year were 6.2 points (controls), 6.7 (Project Read), and 9.0 (READ PLUS). READ PLUS children had significantly higher gains ($p < .05$). However, when scores on the reading/spelling test were converted to percent improvement over the year, gains were not impressive and groups did not differ. Furthermore, the Project Read children scored identically to the children in the basal-reader group, suggesting this phonics program is not particularly effective.

A study using a spelling program based on my analysis (McGuinness 1997a, 1998a) was carried out in New Zealand (Smith 1999) on teenagers 13–14 years old. All had extreme reading and spelling delays as measured by standardized tests. They were between 2:6 and 5 years below chronological age on word recognition, and 5 to 8 years below on spelling dictation. Everyone was below the 25th percentile on reading comprehension. The students received 12 hours of one-on-one instruction in spelling up through the Latin layer of the spelling code using a corpus of over 6,000 words.[4]

Students with such extreme profiles are hard to shift, especially in only 12 hours, and results were very encouraging. Average standard-score gains on the Woodcock Reading Mastery subtests and the Test of Written

---

4. The instruction involves lessons designed around an English and a Latin spelling dictionary, fail-safe worksheets, stories featuring a phoneme and its multiple spellings, and spelling dictation.

Spelling–3 (TWS-3; Larson and Hammill 1976) were as follows: word recognition improved by 10.6 standard-score points to a final score of 88, word attack by 18.6 points to 100, word comprehension by 14.8 to 104, passage comprehension by 10.4 to 96, reading comprehension by 12.8 to 100, and spelling by 9 to 90 for regular words and by 7 to 78 for irregular words. Gains of this magnitude for this age range are equivalent to an average increase (all tests combined) of 27 percentile points, bringing the students up to the mid-average range (50th percentile) overall.

One of the most important results of this study is that a program designed specifically to teach the advanced spelling code had an even greater effect on decoding and reading comprehension than on spelling. This is proof (though tentative due to the small sample size) that teaching the complete spelling code the right way around, from sound to print, allows the code to reverse. What people can spell, they can automatically read. The program does not directly teach multiple decodings (code overlaps) of the same spelling (_soup_, _out_, _soul_), yet children learned them anyway. This means that Venezky's concern over the lack of symmetry between decoding and encoding is unfounded. The code is asymmetric only if you teach it the wrong way around. These results support and extend the findings of Ehri and Wilce (1987) and Uhry and Shepherd (1993) that children score higher on reading tests when they are taught to spell than when they are taught to read!

Spelling scores did not improve at the same rate as reading and comprehension scores. As noted earlier, spelling relies on recall memory (no clues or prompts available), while reading requires only recognition memory. It will take longer than 12 hours for spelling patterns to leave a stable trace in long-term memory. However, spelling scores are rarely impacted even in long-term interventions of this type (National Reading Panel, 2000; see chapter 5, this volume), so a gain of 9 standard-score points is remarkable.

There are a number of problems with these studies. Much more research is required to assess the value of spelling/reading instruction based on an analysis of the spelling code. Smith's study used a small sample and there was no control group. Gains in standard scores were compared to pretest scores and to norms on the test, but there is always the chance that these norms may not be truly representative of the children in the study.

Berninger et al. used a large sample, well-matched groups, plus a control group. While transfer of training did occur for words nearly identical to those that had been taught, it did not generalize beyond these words to standardized tests. Furthermore, children taught a whole-word (sight-word) strategy did just as well as everyone else, suggesting the results were due to exposure (visual memory) and not to any particular method. Henry's results for READ PLUS were encouraging, but reliable (and separate) reading and spelling tests are essential to allow comparisons to other research.

We return to this topic in chapter 9, which reviews the evidence on how children learn to spell using the traditional spelling methods that have nothing to do with the structure of the spelling code. In these methods, children are given lists of spelling words chosen at random, or that feature structural patterns like word families that are irrelevant. Given the fact that our spelling system is highly complex, how children learn to spell under these circumstances is somewhat of a mystery. Recent studies have provided some surprising information about how the brain is able to code the probability structure of our spelling system nonetheless.

At this point we move on to reading instruction.

HOW TO TEACH READING:
LESSONS FROM THE PAST

In 2000, several committees of scholars, convened as the National Reading Panel (NRP), released a report reflecting an extensive review and analysis of the research on reading instruction. The topics were reading programs, phonological-awareness training programs, and instructional methods designed to improve reading fluency, vocabulary, and comprehension. This formidable undertaking provides an enormous service to educators and to the research community by screening a database of thousands of papers for scientific merit, and by assessing the major outcomes of the better studies.

My goal in the next two chapters is to compare the lessons from the past with the research findings over the last 40 years. To begin, I want to summarize what we have learned from the comparative analysis of writing systems and the structural analysis of the English alphabet code, and work forward in time. This will allow us to establish the basic parameters for an effective reading program—a *prototype*—and to match these parameters to the most successful programs identified in the NRP survey.

Lessons from the Past
We begin with what we have learned from the attempts to design a functional writing system.

Lesson 1   The ancient scholars who designed the first writing systems began by using the same logic people had used to set up accounting systems: one symbol for each word. This attempt failed quickly, irrevocably, and universally. Scholars were forced to abandon the word for a sound unit below the level of the word due to the extreme limitations of human memory for mastering sound-symbol pairs. The average person has an upper memory limit of about 2,000 of these pairs, no matter which sound unit is chosen. This is an ultimate limit, a memory ceiling, which does not improve with further training. Thus, this type of paired-associate learning obeys the law of diminishing returns.

We have abundant evidence, dating back over 5,000 years, that a whole-word, meaning-based writing system does not work, never did work, and never will work.

The evidence from the NRP report provides incontrovertible support for this conclusion. Whole-word teaching methods lead to consistently lower reading test scores than methods that emphasize phoneme-grapheme correspondences.

There is another problem with whole-word methods: they are highly misleading. Children and adults alike are strongly biased in favor of linguistic meaning. A whole-word (sight-word) reading method is very appealing to children, especially because memorizing letter sequences and "word shapes" is quite easy early on. This gives children the false impression that they are learning to read. But it is just a matter of time before this strategy begins to implode. Whole-word memorization starts to fail toward the end of first or second grade, depending on the children's vocabulary and visual-memory skills, and unless they figure out a better strategy, their reading will not improve (McGuinness 1997b).

Lesson 2   Only four types of sound units have been adopted for the writing systems of the world: the syllable, the CV diphone, consonants only, and the phoneme. Which unit is chosen depends on the phonotactic or phonetic structure of the language. *These sound units are never mixed.* If more than one unit was adopted, this would make the writing system highly ambiguous and extremely difficult to learn.[1]

A reading method must teach the sound for which the writing system was designed, and no other unit. This rules out "eclectic" or "balanced" reading methods that teach whole words, syllables, syllable fragments like rhyming endings, and phonemes. This is tantamount to teaching four

1. Japan is an exception since they added the Roman alphabet to their two CV diphone scripts.

writing systems simultaneously. The NRP report confirms this also. Methods that introduce a variety of phonological units, or the wrong phonological units, are much less successful than methods that stick to phonemes.

Lesson 3   Ancient scholars avoided adopting the phoneme as the basis for a writing system. Yet there is abundant evidence they were well aware of the phonemic structure of their language and used this to set up the writing system and to design dictionaries. The fact that phonemes are harder to isolate or segment than larger phonological units appears to be the primary reason, perhaps the *only* reason, why every civilization today does not have an alphabetic writing system. For this reason, it makes sense to teach children to segment (and blend) phonemes if they have an alphabetic writing system. A method that includes this type of instruction ought to be more effective than one that does not. This too is confirmed by the NRP report. Reading methods that include phoneme-analysis tasks are far more successful than methods that do not.

Here is the message so far: *If you have an alphabetic writing system, you must teach an alphabetic writing system. There is no use pretending you have something else.*

Lesson 4   The English alphabet code is highly opaque. There are two ways to mitigate this problem and help children manage this complexity. The first is to ensure that children understand the direction in which the code is written, *from* each sound in speech *to* its spelling. For an opaque writing system to function as a code, it must be anchored in the finite number of sounds of the language and not in the letters or letter combinations of the spelling patterns. Unless this is done, the code nature of the writing system is obscured, and the code cannot reverse. A code that cannot reverse will not function as a code.

By contrast, transparent codes are relatively easy to learn and to teach. The second way to help children master an opaque alphabet code is to set up a temporary "artificial transparent alphabet" or basic code. This reveals the nature or logic of an alphabetic writing system, making it "transparent" or accessible to a child. It also provides a platform, a foundation, from which the code can expand, and spelling alternatives can be pegged onto the system without changing the logic. Reading programs based on these two principles ought to work better than programs that are not. So far, no analysis, including the NRP review, has focused on these possibilities: a sound-to-print orientation, and teaching via an artificial transparent alphabet.

We begin this analysis here, and it continues in the following chapter. It is of considerable interest to follow the history of these new ideas, and track the programs that meet these guidelines from the nineteenth century to the present time. This way we can evaluate how a prototype reading program based on these principles fares in well-conducted research.

The Origin of the Artificial Transparent Alphabet

Scragg (1974) and Morris (1984) provide an interesting history of reading instruction in Great Britain and of the attempts over the centuries to improve the spelling code. As noted in the introduction, the major breakthrough in how to teach our opaque system derived from Isaac Pitman's shorthand, which he designed in 1834 using common letters plus invented letters for the leftover phonemes. He collaborated with a colleague, A. J. Ellis, to develop a classroom reading program based on this new alphabet. This was subsequently redesigned by Ellis in a program called *Glossic* in 1870. The final transformation occurred when Nellie Dale, a classroom teacher at Wimbledon School for Girls, wrote a more practical and user-friendly version, using the most common spelling for each of the phonemes in English and no special characters—in other words, what I call a "basic code." This is the first true classroom program based on a basic code and taught from sound to print.

Dale's program was set out in a teachers' manual titled *On the Teaching of English Reading* in 1898, and was expanded in 1902 (*Further Notes on the Teaching of English Reading*). She described 83 innovative lessons that could be taught to the whole class, and that "worked well for classes of up to 70 children." Sounds of the language were the first emphasis. Children were taught to listen for a target phoneme in the initial, middle, and final position in words, learned how phonemes were produced, and found out what articulatory features they had in common. For example, consonants with the same place of articulation (/b/, /p/) were identified as "brothers." Children checked which one was voiced (vocal cords vibrating) by touching their windpipe.

Once several phonemes had been taught, and children practiced combining them, they were shown large, cutout wooden letters. As each sound-letter correspondence was taught, a letter was hung on a frame at the front of the room according to its articulatory features. A space was reserved at the bottom of the frame for word building. Children copied each letter on a blackboard inside the lids of their desks, saying the sound as they wrote the letter. In other exercises, children moved about the classroom "becoming" a phoneme or a letter. Children made words by standing in a row (left to right) according to the order of their sounds (/k/ /u/ /p/), or their letters (*c-u-p*), while the class blended the phonemes into a word.

There were no standardized reading tests and no statistics in the early twentieth century, so the success of Dale's program can never be known. Based on what we know today, her program would have been highly successful. Teachers certainly thought so at the time, and it sold well on both sides of the Atlantic.

These innovations were soon to be eclipsed by the expansion of universal education in the early twentieth century. Reading instruction was hijacked by newly minted education gurus in collaboration with the fledgling educational publishing houses. Dale's program, and other phonics-type programs, began disappearing from classrooms during the 1920s, to be replaced by whole-word (sight-word) methods of the "look-say" or basal-reader variety.

While a few phonics-type programs survived, lingering on in some parochial and private schools, the basic code did not. It resurfaced 40 years later in three different reading programs. One owed its origin to family ties. Pitman's grandson, Sir James Pitman, designed the *initial teaching alphabet* or i.t.a. (Pitman and St. John 1969). Pitman believed that digraphs (sh in *ship*) were confusing for beginning readers. For this reason, i.t.a. used an artificial (temporary) script with special symbols for digraphs. The two other programs were American, though one had obvious ties to Dale, linking phonemes to an analysis of their speech patterns and mouth movements. This method, *Auditory Discrimination in Depth*, was designed as a remedial program by Pat and Charles Lindamood in the late 1960s (Lindamood and Lindamood 1969). The third method had some name changes in its history. It began life as *Hay-Wingo*, named after its authors Julie Hay and Charles Wingo. This was the program used by Rudolf

Flesch in *Why Johnny Can't Read* (Flesch [1955] 1985). It was later revised and expanded to include stories and exercises by McCracken and Walcutt (1963), and since then it has become known as the *Lippincott* program, after the publisher. We will look at the success of these programs in the following section.

At this point, I need to say a few words about phonics. By the 1960s, the term *phonics* could mean any method that had to do with teaching letters, letter names, and/or letter-sound correspondences. It could refer to such disparate forms of reading instruction as teaching the 26 names and sounds of the letters of the alphabet, or a linguistic-phonics program as sophisticated as Dale's. *Phonics* came to have quite different connotations in different countries. In the United Kingdom, for example, phonics is more likely to mean something similar to Dale's program. In the United States, phonics commonly refers to letter-driven methods, like the one set up by Webster (see McGuinness 1997c, 1998b). For this reason, the so-called methods wars, which began in earnest in the 1960s, cannot really be characterized as a debate between phonics versus whole-word methods. Framing the problem in these simplistic terms is not helpful.

Early in the twentieth century, decisions about what should go into a reading method and how it should be structured came to be based on partiality to the alphabet principle or partiality to the logograph principle, and subsequently sparked the reading "wars." Prior to the 1960s, there was no way to determine whether one type of reading method worked better than another. Logic alone could not resolve this issue. There was little understanding of how writing systems work. There were no reliable tests to measure the success or failure of a teaching method, and no scientific or statistical tools. Despite the rhetoric and the rancor, there was not a scrap of evidence that a particular phonics method or whole-word method worked better in the classroom or anywhere else.

We needed solid research on the content of reading programs and on which components were most effective for young children. We had to wait a very long time. The first major efforts began in the mid-1960s, and we turn next to the monumental studies from that decade.

Doing Research on Reading Methods Is Not as Easy as You Think
Prior to the 1960s, educators assumed that a reading method was autonomous, so much so it would override everything else: the school, the

children, the classroom, the teacher, the parents, and so forth. Thus, it seemed reasonable to compare classrooms using method X to classrooms using method Y. If, on the whole, children taught with method X had better reading test scores, then everyone could rejoice and switch to X. Several problems came to light as these studies accumulated.

The first problem was that results from one study to the next were contradictory. Method X would work well in one school but not in another. It would work well in one classroom but not in another *in the same school.* As people searched for reasons, they became aware that the children, the teacher, the principal, the parents, and the reading tests mattered more than they thought. People realized that baseline measures had to be taken before methods X and Y were compared, because children enter school with widely varying skills.

The measures themselves had to be valid and reliable. The tests had to accurately reflect the types of performance you wanted to measure, and provide information on a broad range of aptitudes. For example, reading tests should include measures of decoding, spelling, comprehension, and fluency. The tests should be normed and standardized. They should be reliable, so that when they are given at different times (on alternative forms), students get similar scores. These elements, if uncontrolled, can add up to a multitude of "confounding variables," which is a fancy way of saying that the results are not a consequence of the method but of an unknown factor or factors.

A persistent question dogged many thoughtful people. If method X is "better," then how much better is "better"? From a practical standpoint, is an average reading score of 26 compared to an average score of 19 on a reading test sufficient for the entire school district to scrap everything, train teachers, and purchase new materials? Is an improvement of two months above age or grade-level norms worth the bother and expense? Until the 1960s, data were reported in simple means or average scores, because statistical tools were not well known. The first statistics textbook for the behavioral sciences, *Psychological Statistics* by Quinn McNemar, was published in 1949. McNemar commented in the preface that he wrote the book for his students, because there was nothing else available. Of course, statistics is only part of the answer to the question "how much better is better?"

There is another problem. Reading programs are not "pure." They are sequenced differently, take various lengths of time, and contain a variety of activities. If method X was found to be better than method Y (even highly significant on powerful statistical tests), what exactly was it about method X that made the difference? Was it the emphasis on memorizing sight words, the encouragement to engage in shared reading, the time spent chanting letter names, a focus on the sounds of English, the stress placed on the code nature of a writing system, or the emphasis on guessing words in context? This is still the key issue in reading research, though we have some important answers (see the next chapter).

For all these reasons, research on reading made little headway until the 1960s. In recounting this history, Graves and Dykstra (1997) thought the major catalyst for a more rigorous approach to research was the publication of *Why Johnny Can't Read*. It certainly stirred the pot. But Flesch's book appeared in 1955, and the pot had long since stopped boiling before anything happened. Some rumblings were heard at a meeting of invited participants at the National Conference on Research in English in 1959. And from one person's animated concern, a famous study emerged.

Jeanne Chall's Road Map

In 1961, Jeanne Chall began an intensive quest to provide a thorough analysis of reading programs and teachers' performance in the classroom, and to do a survey of research on reading. The project took three years and resulted in the publication of the book *Learning to Read: The Great Debate* in 1967. The investigation involved interviews with 25 authors and editors of reading programs, an analysis of 22 reading programs, over 300 hours of classroom observations in the United States, England, and Scotland, and a review of the research literature.

Chall was trying to connect the opinions of authors and curriculum developers with the actual program content in the manuals and materials, with what teachers did in the classroom, and hopefully with children's reading achievement. At this time, about 95 percent of U.S. classrooms were using basal-reading programs. Basal-reader authors tended to imitate one another, even holding the same contradictory set of assumptions. On the one hand, they agreed that children should learn to read with words in their vocabulary, memorizing these words by sight. On the other hand, the bulk of the lesson was devoted to exploring the meaning of the new words in the lesson, words the children already understood. These authors believed that reading should precede writing and viewed reading and writing as entirely separate processes. This meant that for most beginning readers, from the 1920s to the time of this study, the encoding aspects of the writing system were never mentioned. Letters and words were neither traced nor copied, spelling was not taught, and there was no creative writing to be seen. Most programs did not introduce writing or spelling until the second or third grade.

When basal-reader authors were asked why they thought some children failed to learn to read, they provided a laundry list of amorphous causes unsubstantiated by any facts: dysfunctional families, an unsupportive culture, substandard schooling, poor teachers, lack of funding, overcrowded classrooms, the children's emotional and psychological well-being, physical disabilities, and so forth. Of course, the authors whose methods were out of favor said "methods" were the primary problem. Spelling reformers focused on the spelling code, claiming that children would continue to fail until the spelling code was revised.

A Program Analysis

Chall did an analysis of program content and sequence, plus an in-depth account of three programs. The basal-reader programs as a group featured very few words in their stories and "readers." Neither spelling regularity nor word length was considered important. Letter-sound correspondences were introduced late, and children learned slowly, gradually being exposed to the word from whole to part, a method known as *analytic* or *intrinsic phonics*. These lessons do not begin until around second grade and continue for several years. Details on two basal-reader programs are presented in the following section.

The programs described as *synthetic phonics* were much more variable. Chall described these methods as having reading vocabularies based on spelling regularity and word length. Early words were simple and short, gradually increasing in complexity. The emphasis was on mastering letter-sound correspondences, and new words were introduced rapidly. To this end, children were taught to blend and segment sounds in words and to connect sounds to letters.

A third group, the *linguistic* programs, had several features in common. First, they were written by linguists. There was little emphasis on meaning for obvious reasons, and the focus was on the alphabet, especially letter names. The reading vocabulary consisted of predictable, short words set out in lists that abounded with word families: *cat, rat, sat, mat*. Children were expected to spontaneously detect the sound-symbol regularities from these spelling patterns and read words as wholes, not to "sound them out." Oddly, the linguistic aspect of the code was the most ignored and most distorted. Sounds of the language were not taught. No segmenting or blending was allowed. If children encountered a new word, they were to spell it aloud with letter names, then read it as a whole. Illustrations were minimal or absent. Visually, these programs look remarkably like no-nonsense spellers, and if Noah Webster's speller had been among them, it would have fit in perfectly. It is difficult to understand what is "linguistic" about these programs.

Two programs in the synthetic group fit the prototype—a sound-to-print orientation and a basic code. These were the Initial Teaching Alphabet i.t.a. and the Lippincott program. As noted above, the i.t.a. uses a special script to represent 44 phonemes of English, and children are obliged to transition to conventional letters and spelling. The i.t.a. program has a strong emphasis on writing. Writing begins as soon as possible, and creative writing is especially encouraged. The Lippincott program will be discussed below.

Chall studied three programs in depth from the prereader phase (kindergarten) through third grade. Two were basal-reader programs: Scott-Foresman and Ginn, the most popular programs in the United States. The Scott-Foresman program will be familiar to anyone who remembers Dick and Jane. The third program was the Lippincott program.

The basal-reader programs were very much alike. The stories gradually increased in length through repetition. New words were introduced slowly at a constant rate of 1 to 2 words per 100 running words in a story across all grades. By the end of third grade, children had seen about 1,500 words. Teachers were instructed to focus on meaning as well as on the visual elements of the word—its length and its shape, or pattern of ascenders (*b, d, f, h, l,* and *t*) and descenders (*g, j, p, q,* and *y*). The Ginn program actually had lines around new words to emphasize their shape. Illustrations were numerous and colorful, especially in the early books, with 6.5 pictures per 100 words.

The word count of what the teacher was supposed to say in the partially scripted lessons, versus what the children were allowed to contribute, was always overwhelmingly in favor of the teacher. Despite this verbal barrage, Chall could not find a single statement about the fact that the alphabet is a code in pages and pages of teacher instructions in either program. Comments on sound-symbol relationships, or segmenting and blending, were absent entirely until the end of first grade/beginning of second grade.

In excerpts from the so-called phonics lessons in the basal-reader manuals, it was obvious that the authors had no idea how the alphabet code works. Elements were introduced at random, and the statements in the lesson make no sense. In a grade 2 example, children were supposed to tell the teacher "which *i* and which *a*" (letter names) they heard in the words *sit, night, bird, hand, rain, car,* and *ball.* This assumes that children "get it" that letter names stand for the letters, and that letters, in turn, represent sounds.

The Lippincott program was an extreme contrast. Each lesson introduced a phoneme and its most common spelling, plus a story with the target sound appearing in all positions in the word (no word families). Lessons began with the five "simple" (short) vowels and moved on to consonants. Consonant blends came next, followed by vowel and consonant digraphs. Toward the end of first grade, vowel-spelling alternatives were taught, including phonograms (*ough* in *bought*). Alternative spellings and code overlaps (*out, soup*) were sometimes introduced together to illustrate certain problems with the code.

There was a strong emphasis on teaching the relationship between sounds and letters, and connecting this immediately to words. Twenty-two percent of the lesson time was devoted to writing, compared to zero in the basal programs. Children copied words and were given spelling dictation. Reading aloud was emphasized.

This approach led to a rapidly increasing reading vocabulary. By the end of first grade the children had been introduced to over 2,000 words, ten times as many words as the basal-reader children had seen at this stage, and 500 more words than they will see by the end of third grade. Because the Lippincott children were taught to decode, whereas basal-reader children were not, their skills transferred easily to decoding unfamiliar words.

Classroom Observations

The third phase of Chall's investigation included visits to over 300 classrooms in kindergarten through third grade. The observations consisted of subjective impressions of elusive qualities like "mood of the classroom," "restlessness," and "interest" on the part of the children, as well as "momentum," "support," and "expectations" on the part of the teacher. Chall opted for variety (300 classrooms in several months) over stability (fewer classrooms studied repeatedly), to study the impact of lots of different reading methods on the children's enthusiasm for learning them, *and* on their success in learning to read. However, the second goal turned out to be a fruitless quest. In some cases, school records and test scores were not made available. In other cases, records were incomplete, or the tests used by different schools measured different things, or children were tested at different ages. In short, testing was haphazard and differed to such a degree that test scores could not be compared.

What remained was Chall's impressions and insights. She observed that a good teacher can make children enthusiastic about a lesson that an adult would think was dull, and a poor teacher can make children listless or fidgety during a lesson that should have been interesting. Many of Chall's comments were essentially descriptions of good teaching. Good teachers have control of the class, get the children excited about the lesson, push them to the limits of their confidence and no further, move the lesson along at a good pace, confront and solve problems quickly and fairly, and involve as many children as possible in the lesson. No surprise here. But one wonders, are these qualities sufficient to make a poor reading program succeed, and their absence sufficient to make a good reading program fail? Without objective data on the children's reading performance, these questions cannot be answered.

One of Chall's most important discoveries was that teachers tend to be eclectic. If teachers are asked, or decide, to change to a new program, they do not abandon old activities and lessons from programs they enjoyed teaching or felt were important. Nor do they abandon their philosophies. This can create a situation where elements from different programs with contradictory logics cancel each other out, such as an emphasis on decoding *and* an emphasis on memorizing the shapes of words. This has profound implications for classroom research, because it means that there will always be an overlap of different methods, depending on the teachers' training and on how many different methods they have been asked to teach. It seems highly unlikely a particular method will ever be taught "pure," unless a teacher really commits to it, or the program is so effective it succeeds in spite of the odds.

A Research Summary

The last component of Chall's review was an analysis of classroom research on reading methods. All the comparison studies between look-say and phonics were published between 1912 and 1940, and will not be discussed further. The findings from the studies were summarized in a series of tables. The method that produced the best outcome on tests of word recognition, comprehension, spelling, and so on was indicated by its initials. Thus, if look-say did "better" on a particular test, an LS was reported. (Synthetic phonics = SP; intrinsic or "basal" phonics = IP.) Words and phrases like *better*, *higher*, and "had an advantage" were used to describe these outcomes. *Better* was not defined and no numerical data were provided.

What kind of data did Chall rely on? The majority of the studies reported outcomes in average scores. It appears that no statistical analysis of the data occurred before the 1960s, as shown by the fact that "no difference" was indicated by E (for equal) in all studies prior to the 1960s, but as NS (not significant) from the 1960s on. The tables are peppered with SP's, showing a huge "advantage" for synthetic phonics. In the comparisons listed from first through sixth grade, SP was "better" 68 times, IP only 11, and there were 34 draws (29 E's and 5 NS's), giving the impression that synthetic phonics was the overwhelming winner. This is very misleading.

The absence of numerical data, the reliance on average scores to determine *better*, and the failure to define what *better* means, make it impossible to draw any conclusions from this review. Chall leaves us with a basic contradiction. If synthetic phonics is vastly superior, as her tables seemed to show, then the quality of teaching is far less important than the method. In fact, teaching skill pales into insignificance compared to the overwhelming superiority of synthetic phonics according to the tables. Yet Chall's classroom observations indicated that the teacher's ability can override the method, at least in making the lesson exciting and stimulating. On the one hand, the message from the classroom is that the teacher matters as much as or more than the method. On the other hand, Chall's presentation of the research seemed to show that the method matters far more than the teacher. Which conclusion is true?

Chall mapped out the important issues and asked the fundamental questions, many of which have still not been answered and need to be. But the form her research took and her conclusions from it failed to persuade people that we had been doing something terribly wrong and needed to change our ways. As Chall began her study, another project was underway that had precisely these goals.

The Cooperative Research Program

In 1963 a dedicated group of scholars, including Chall, Bond, Clymer, and Durrell, convinced the U.S. Department of Education to fund an ambitious project that would settle the basal-reader/phonics debate once and for all. This project was called the *Cooperative Research Program in First-Grade Reading Instruction*, and the project directors were Guy Bond and Robert Dykstra from the University of Minnesota. The project was funded in 1964. The first published report appeared three years later (Bond and Dykstra 1967) and was reprinted in *Reading Research Quarterly* (Bond and Dykstra 1997). There is no better place to begin an in-depth analysis of quantitative research on reading than with this pioneering study and all that it implies.

Project proposals were requested by the funding agency on the topic of reading methods and their efficacy, and had to conform to one requirement: since basal readers were used in 95 percent of classrooms, every project had to compare a basal-reader program to something else. The rationale went like this: if "Johnny can't read," is this the fault of those ubiquitous basal-reading programs? There was actually no hard evidence that "Johnny" could or could not read, and neither Flesch nor Bond and Dykstra had a word to say about student test scores. The issue was more subjective. It had to do with the war between the whole-word enthusiasts and the phonics enthusiasts.

A large number of proposals were received, and 27 projects were funded. Probably nothing on this scale will ever be seen again. The key to the success or failure of the entire enterprise was the degree to which it could be ensured that all project directors used the same measures to the same standards. The study proceeded as follows. First the world was divided up by types of reading programs. Everything that anyone could

Table 4.1

Comparison of five methods: Number of Projects, subjects, Classrooms, and means

Methods	Projects	Group testing			Individual testing
		N	No. of classes	No. of means	N
Basal		1,038	49	98	149
vs.	5				
i.t.a.		1,055	48	96	163
Basal		722	33	66	161
vs.	4				
Basal + Phonics		1,002	42	84	204
Basal		1,523	61	122	138
vs.	3				
Language Experience		1,431	60	120	134
Basal		597	25	50	120
vs.	3				
Linguistic		760	31	62	146
Basal		525	24	48	97
vs.	3				
Lippincott		488	23	46	94
Total N		9,141			

think of that might affect learning to read was measured as precisely as possible. The clock was started and time ran on without interference for 140 classroom days (7 months) of first-grade instruction. Several reading tests were given. Table 4.1 sets out the overall structure of this study.

This study is highly complex. Classrooms are nested within Projects, Projects within Methods, and Methods within the Study as a whole. (I capitalize the terms "Study," "Method," "Project," and "Classroom," which represent the variables in the research design, to distinguish them from their generic form.) Here is a glossary to help keep these components straight.

Study. Refers to the Study as a whole, including all Methods and Projects.

Method. The particular Method being compared to basal-reader instruction. Five different Methods were investigated.

Projects. Each Method comparison included several Projects run by different people in different geographic locations.

Classrooms. Each Project included a large number of Classrooms.

Data Collection

Baseline Measures   Demographic data were collected on the children, the teachers, the community, and the school. For the children, these were age, sex, months of preschool experience, and days absent. Teacher variables included sex, age, degrees, certification, years of experience, marital status, number of children, attitude toward teaching reading, days absent, and supervisor-rated teacher effectiveness. Community-/school-based information included median education of adults, median income, population, type of community (urban, rural, and so on), classroom size, length of school day/year, per-pupil costs, and so forth.

These data can be dismissed rather quickly. None of the community and school variables were more than modestly correlated with the children's reading test scores. "Teacher experience" was the only marginally relevant teacher variable ($r = .30$). Sex was found to be a strong predictor, and for this reason, it was included as a variable in all further statistical analyses.

The children took a battery of tests thought to be predictive of subsequent reading skills. These included auditory- and visual-discrimination tasks, tests of letter-name knowledge, reading readiness, and IQ. When this testing was completed at each school, the 140-day clock started running.

Outcome Measures   At the end of the 140 days, children were tested once more on various reading tests. They were given the five subtests of the Stanford Reading Test, which had just been renormed. This is a group-administered test. The subtests are *word reading* (word recognition), *paragraph meaning* (comprehension), *vocabulary* (receptive vocabulary), *spelling* (spelling dictation), and *word-study skills* (tests of auditory perception as well as decoding skill).

In addition to the Stanford Reading Test, four individually administered tests were given to a subsample of children, randomly selected from every classroom. The total number of children in this sample was 1,330. The tests were the Gilmore Tests of Accuracy and Rate, the Fry Word

List (decodable, regularly spelled words), and the Gates Word List (based on word frequency, including many irregularly spelled words).

Correlational Analyses

The first question was whether scores on the baseline tests correlated with (predicted) scores on the Stanford Reading Test seven months later. There were complete data on 8,500 children. Correlations were computed separately for each Method, and also for Basal-reader Classrooms combined across all Projects and Methods.

Group-Administered Tests   The best predictors of performance on the Stanford tests were the Murphy-Durrell Letter-Name and Phoneme Discrimination tests, and the Pitner-Cunningham IQ. In the phoneme test, the child makes same/different judgments between two spoken phonemes (/b/ versus /b/ or /v/ versus /t/). Correlations for the six Methods ranged from .48–.55 for letter-name knowledge to .37–.48 for phoneme discrimination and .32–.50 for IQ. However, these measures were correlated with each other: letter-name knowledge correlated with the phoneme-discrimination test at .50. IQ was correlated with letter-name knowledge at .43, and with the phoneme test at .46. Had IQ had been statistically subtracted, it is unlikely the letter-name and phoneme tests would have had much predictive power. The remaining baseline tests (Metropolitan Reading Readiness, Thurstone visual discrimination tests) were not strong predictors of reading skill. The correlations were positive but low (.20–.35).

The subtests of the Stanford Reading Test were found to be strongly correlated *with each other* in every case. Apart from vocabulary, these ranged from .63 to .76 ($\overline{X} = .67$). This shows that, for first graders, all aspects of reading skill—decoding, spelling, comprehension, and phonics skills—are strongly related, and doing well on one predicts doing well on the others. Vocabulary was correlated with the reading measures at around .50.

Individually Administered Tests   No correlations were carried out between the baseline tests and scores on the individual tests (Gilmore, Fry, and Gates). However, the individual and group reading tests were correlated with each other. Apart from the Gilmore Rate of Reading test (correlations from .45 to .62), all other correlations were very high indeed, ranging from .61 to .86. Clearly, the group tests and the individual tests were measuring the same skills. This shows that both the individual data and the group data were valid and reliable measures of reading skill.

A particularly important result was the almost-perfect correlation (.86) between the Fry Word test (a test of decoding regularly spelled words) and the Gates Word test (a test of visual recognition of mainly irregularly spelled words or sight words). This was surprising, because people assumed, as many still do, that decoding and sight-word memorization require different skills. Children trained to memorize sight words (basal-reader groups) were expected to be good on the Gates and worse on the Fry. Conversely, children taught to decode regularly spelled words (phonics only/few sight words) were expected to do the opposite. These patterns would produce low to moderate correlations. Instead, performance on one test almost perfectly predicted performance on the other. There is only one interpretation: children who are good decoders are good decoders, no matter how words are spelled. Children who rely mainly on visual memory (nondecoders) are not only poor decoders but fare just as badly on sight words.

Comparison of Reading Methods

The major focus of the study was on the comparison of the different types of reading programs to the basal programs. The Projects were reduced to 15 from the original 27, so that at least three Projects were using the same method. The Methods were the *Initial Teaching Alphabet* (i.t.a.; five Projects), *Basal + phonics* (four Projects), *Language experience* (four Projects), *Linguistic* (three Projects), and *Lippincott* (three Projects).

The basal-reader programs were described earlier. The most frequently used basal in this study was the Scott-Foresman series (Dick and Jane). Details on the other Methods are provided in the following paragraphs.

The *i.t.a.* uses standard and special letters to provide separate symbols for 44 phonemes in English. There is a one-to-one correspondence between each phoneme and its symbol in all materials, which included readers. Children are encouraged to do lots of writing and reading. Later, children transition to conventional spelling. It was noted that many children had not made this transition by the end of the first year.

The *Basal + phonics* condition added a separate phonics component to the Basal-reader curriculum in half of the classrooms. The add-on phonics programs were either *Speech to Print, Phonic Word Power,* or *Phonic Exercises,* all of which are code-emphasis programs. Descriptions of these programs were not provided.

The *Language experience* program involves highly individualized one-on-one interactions between teacher and child. The idea is to develop reading and spelling ability directly from each child's vocabulary. The process begins by the child telling a story, which is copied by the teacher. The child reads what the teacher has written, copies the words, and gradually develops enough skill to write on her own, using whatever spellings she can. Teachers listen to children read their own work, correct spelling, and so forth. Later, children move on to books of their choosing.

The *Linguistic* programs were described earlier as being the least "linguistic" of any phonics program. These were the McGraw-Hill program, and programs authored by Fries and by Bloomfield and Barnhart. Both Fries and Bloomfield were linguists.

The *Lippincott* program was used in three Projects in this group. A detailed analysis of the Lippincott program was presented in the previous section.

Results from the Stanford Reading Test (Group Administered)   At this point, in this otherwise impeccably controlled research, several statistical blunders took place that essentially voided most of the results. The authors decided to use mean scores from each classroom instead of individual scores, one for boys and one for girls. This reduces the data from 20–30 children in a classroom to a prototypic boy and girl. Next, the data were analyzed with analysis-of-variance (ANOVA) statistics for the five Methods separately. Reducing data to means invalidates the use of ANOVA statistics, because the mathematics is based on *variances* derived from normal distributions of individual scores, not on group means—hence its name.[2]

---

2. There is currently a theory that the unit of instruction must also be the unit of analysis. If the "treatment" is the whole class, then the measure must be the

By substituting means for the children's individual test scores, two things happened. First, the focus of the study changed. Now all the variance (variability in each outcome measure) was due to the variability *between classrooms*, instead of variability between children *within classrooms*. This turns a study comparing children learning different Methods into a study comparing Classrooms (teaching skill perhaps?). Second, this represents a huge loss of statistical power. Table 4.1 illustrates the contrast between the actual number of children in the study and the number of scores used for the data analysis, a tenfold reduction (100 to 10).[3]

I will examine the Basal-reader-versus-i.t.a. comparison to illustrate the kinds of problems this created. There were large main effects of sex (girls' better $p < .001$), effects of Method (i.t.a. better on the Word subtest, Basal readers better on Spelling), and effects of projects (some did better than others). However, there were also highly significant Project × Method (treatment) interactions on every test except Vocabulary. Sometimes Basal Classrooms did better and sometimes i.t.a. Classrooms did better, depending on which Project they were in. This is the ultimate muddle in methods research, the experimenter's worst nightmare: "Now you see it here, now you see it there, now you don't see it anywhere."

The investigators tried to reduce or eliminate these interactions by covariance analyses (ANCOVA) on the assumption that the erratic results occurred because children started out with different levels of skill. ANCOVA helps to level the playing field by equalizing scores on the

---

whole class as well (mean scores). This is a doubtful practice, and, as far as I am aware, unknown to Bond and Dykstra at that time. A full analysis of this problem is presented in appendix 1.

3. The authors provide no explanation for why they reduced the data to classroom means and analyzed the methods comparisons one at a time. When this project was carried out, computers were physically big and computationally small. The data and the program-code information went onto punch cards. To compare 15 projects in one analysis requires a four-factor design with 300 cells! It is unlikely anything this complex could have been handled by computers at that time. Mean scores may have been used for the same reason. ANOVAs are simple to compute by hand (by calculator) if the data set is small (a few hundred), but nearly impossible when numbers run into the thousands.

baseline tests (letter-name knowledge, phoneme awareness, IQ, and so on) and making corresponding adjustments to the Stanford Reading tests. If a child did too well on the baseline tests, reading scores are adjusted down, and vice versa.

However, covariance analysis must meet stringent requirements. McNemar (1949) cautioned that covariance should be used only when groups being compared cannot be randomly assigned, or if they have something that will cause differences in performance between the two groups. For example, differences in IQ will impact the ability to learn new skills.

The Bond and Dykstra study in no way met these criteria:

1. The only skill that would directly "cause" subsequent reading performance is initial reading performance, and this was not measured.
2. Correlates of reading scores cannot be used to infer causality, and in any case the baseline measures are correlated with each other, so it is impossible to know what is causing what.
3. One valid covariate in this study was IQ, but IQ was not used as a *separate* covariate in the ANCOVA analyses.

The authors do not report what kind of data were used for the covariance analyses, but the tables reveal that mean scores were used again, which voids the use of ANCOVA statistics. (You cannot do covariance analyses with mean scores.) The tables also reveal that grossly inflated degrees of freedom were used on all analyses. (These problems are discussed more fully in appendix 1.)

Despite these statistical manipulations, the Project × Methods interactions did not go away. Something else was causing this effect. The researchers decided to reanalyze the data for each Project separately (see their table 23). Two Projects had strong across-the-board results favoring i.t.a. over the Basal-reader groups. Three Projects essentially found no differences between the two methods, except for spelling. Basal-reader classes had significantly higher spelling scores. On closer inspection, the explanation was obvious. Many of the children in i.t.a. classes were still using nonstandard script, and scoring did not allow for this. However, it was not at all clear why two Projects produced a strong i.t.a. advantage on the remaining tests, and three Projects did not. The authors could not explain this result. Using means instead of individual data in the analysis could have produced this effect, or alternatively, it could be a real effect. There is no way to tell.

Data from the other Methods comparisons (Basal + phonics, Linguistic, Language experience, Lippincott) were analyzed in the same way, producing the same erratic mix for the same reasons. Because of the problems of data analysis raised above, I will not review these statistics further. Instead, I have reassessed the data and will present the results later.

Individually Administered Tests   Analyses of the individually administered tests (Gilmore, Fry, and Gates) did use individual data instead of means. This was good news, especially because there were more individual scores than mean scores (see table 4.1, right column).[4]

Here are the results for the most discriminating of the individual tests, the Fry and the Gates. The children using the Lippincott program were superior on both the Fry and the Gates to the Basal-reader controls in all three Projects (6 out of 6 comparisons: 100 percent at $p < .01$). i.t.a. classess also did well. They were superior in 7 out of 10 comparisons (70 percent). Basal + phonics were superior in 5 out of 8 comparisons (62 percent), Language experience in 2 out of 6 (33 percent), Linguistic in none. Basal-reader groups were not superior on any of the 36 comparisons, despite the fact that the Gates is a sight-word test and contains many of the same words these children were taught to memorize.

A New Look at Old Data   There are 92 tables in this report but no table summarizing the entire project. In view of the inappropriate use of the data in the statistical analyses, a summary of combined data from these more than 9,000 children is in order. It will be far more informative and more valid than its predecessor. I calculated the grand means across all Classrooms within a particular Method. These results are shown in tables 4.2 and 4.3. The tables illustrate the number of children who contributed

---

4. The degrees of freedom were incorrect here as well. However, when I compared their probability values to statistical tables *using the correct degrees of freedom*, the probability values were accurate.

Table 4.2
Mean scores and grade-level equivalents on the Stanford Reading subtests

Group	Word Reading	Grade-level equivalent	Paragraph Meaning	Grade-level equivalent	Vocabulary	Grade-level equivalent	Spelling	Grade-level equivalent	Word Study	Grade-level equivalent
Basal (1,028)	20.1	1.7	19.6	1.7	22.0	1.9	11.4	1.9	35.9	1.9
i.t.a. (1,055)	23.3	1.9	20.9	1.8	21.9	1.9	10.8	1.9	38.6	2.0
Basal (722)	19.0	1.7	16.7	1.7	20.2	1.7	8.7	1.7	32.8	1.7
Basal + phonics (1,002)	20.9	1.8	20.5	1.8	21.1	1.8	10.8	1.9	35.3	1.8
Basal (1,523)	20.0	1.7	20.7	1.8	21.2	1.8	12.1	2.0	36.6	1.9
Language experience (1,431)	21.5	1.8	21.1	1.8	22.1	1.9	12.3	2.0	37.3	1.9
Basal (597)	19.1	1.7	19.2	1.7	21.5	1.9	10.8	1.9	36.3	1.9
Linguistic (760)	19.0	1.7	15.8	1.6	19.6	1.7	9.3	1.7	33.8	1.8
Basal (525)	19.6	1.7	19.6	1.7	22.2	1.9	10.8	1.9	36.1	1.9
Lippincott (488)	26.6	2.2	24.4	1.9	23.7	2.2	14.1	2.2	41.4	2.2
Basal total (4,405)	19.6	1.7	19.2	1.7	21.4	1.8	10.8	1.9	35.6	1.9

Table 4.3

Mean scores on individual tests

Group	N	Gilmore Accuracy	Gilmore Rate	Fry Word	Gates Word
Basal	149	23.3	59.0	7.4	13.3
i.t.a.	163	26.0	60.0	17.2	19.3
Basal	161	21.6	59.2	6.2	12.1
Basal + phonics	204	23.5	59.9	9.9	14.5
Basal	138	18.9	52.2	5.9	12.1
Language experience	134	21.8	53.0	9.1	13.8
Basal	120	23.3	59.1	6.5	12.1
Linguistic	146	17.9	43.8	7.8	10.5
Basal	97	24.4	56.2	6.0	12.3
Lippincott	94	29.5	62.4	18.4	20.5
Basal grand means		22.3	57.2	6.4	12.4

to these means. With numbers this large, *statistical tests are not necessary*. One can confidently assume a normal distribution, and the mean is the most accurate measure of this distribution if standard deviations are low. Fortunately, table 75 in the Bond and Dykstra paper provided the standard deviations for each subtest on the Stanford Reading Test for every Method, and for all Basal-reader groups combined. These standard deviations were computed correctly on the children's individual test scores. All were low and extremely consistent, indicating the excellent psychometric properties of the Stanford tests as well as outstanding testing and data collection. Thus we know we are dealing with normal distributions, and combining means across Classrooms is a valid indication of what happened in this study. The table values represent only the nontransformed (noncovaried) data.

Table 4.2 provides the grand means for the Stanford subtests, plus grade-level conversions (in decimals, not months). The expected grade level for these children at the end of the Project was 1.7 (first grade, eighth month). The Basal-reader groups consistently scored at or near this level across all measures. Because the Stanford tests had recently been normed on American children, 95 percent of whom received Basal-reader instruction, the match in table 4.2 between grade-level norms and Basal-reader children's test scores is no surprise. But it gives one a good deal of confidence that the data are real. Table 4.3 contains the grand means on the individually administered tests. Unfortunately, no conversion table was provided for these raw scores, so it is not possible to translate them to grade level or age.

The tables illustrate that, overall, the phonics-type programs worked somewhat better than Basal-reader instruction, but not much better. The main result is the clear and unassailable evidence that one method (Lippincott) is consistently superior to the rest, something not reported in the article. This method produced the highest scores across the board, in both group and individual test results. The value 2.2 translates to *six months above grade level*. This is in striking contrast to the small or nonexistent effects of the other programs. There is something about the Lippincott program that worked in the classroom in a way that the Linguistic programs and other phonics programs did not.

The obvious next step would have been to look in detail at the Lippincott program. What was it about this program, and what was going on in Lippincott classrooms, that worked better compared to other programs like the Linguistic programs, which were surprisingly unsuccessful. Could this lack of success have been due to the emphasis on letter names in the Linguistic programs to the exclusion of phoneme analysis and phoneme-to-letter correspondences? Could it be due to the fact that they were designed by linguists with no experience in the classroom? Did the teachers or the children find any elements in these programs that were especially good or especially confusing? Surprisingly, issues like these were not addressed as a consequence of this report, and the Lippincott program never received the attention it deserved.

What Really Happened in This Study?

Bond and Dykstra's summary of the Methods comparisons tended to be biased toward the statistical results that favored phonics or linguistic methods. Comparing the Basal-reader and i.t.a. methods, they wrote: "The i.t.a. treatment produced superior word recognition abilities as measured by the Word Reading subtest of the Stanford and the Fry and Gates word lists" (1997, 414). This is true, but they did not report that this was the only Stanford test on which i.t.a. children excelled, nor did they mention that this effect did not occur in three out of the five Projects.

Rather than pursue these issues further, especially in view of the many problems with data handling and statistical analysis, the following is a summary of what this study demonstrated.

The Study Design and Measurement   The investigators made an excellent choice of baseline and outcome measures. The study also employed a thoughtful (useful) set of demographic variables, which helped to rule out a wide range of factors as contributing to reading performance. Finally, there was superb control over this study from the top down to every Project director and every test site. This led to extremely reliable testing and highly robust data for such a vast undertaking. (The authors commented on the excellent spirit of cooperation among the Project directors.)

The Results   Sex differences favoring girls were very large and consistent and appeared on every test in every comparison.

Correlations between the baseline measures (IQ, phoneme discrimination, letter-name knowledge) and the Stanford Reading tests were modest, with the best predictors accounting for about 25 percent of the variance. However, there was a high degree of overlap (shared variance) between these baseline measures that was not controlled.

The fact that phoneme discrimination predicted 20–25 percent of the variance in subsequent reading scores was a new finding, and needed to be followed up.

The correlations between group and individual reading tests were very high, indicating good test administration and good validity.

There was unequivocal evidence that good decoders can decode both regularly and irregularly spelled words with the same facility, and that sight-word memorization does not work (see the scores of the Basal-reader children on the Fry decoding test in table 4.3).

Classroom means were used in the ANOVAs for the Stanford tests, and incorrect degrees of freedom were used on about 75 percent of the analyses. As a consequence, grand means have greater validity. These showed that children who were taught with the Lippincott method scored six months above grade on nearly all the Stanford tests, and were *superior to all other method groups on all tests*, and there were large effect sizes on all measures except vocabulary. These conclusions were strengthened by low and consistent standard deviations on the test scores.

Bond and Dykstra provided 15 numbered paragraphs in their final conclusions on the Methods' comparison data. Many comments are ad hoc and unwarranted by the findings, even if the statistics had been reliable. However, paragraph 15 stands out as the most prescient statement in their summary:

It is likely that improvement would result from adopting certain elements from each of the approaches used in this study.... For example, the i.t.a. and the Phonic/Linguistic [Lippincott] programs, both of which were relatively effective, have in common a vocabulary controlled on sound-symbol regularity, introduction of a relatively large reading vocabulary, and emphasis on writing symbols as a means of learning them. It would be interesting to know which of these elements, if any, are primarily responsible for the effectiveness of the program. (1997, 416)

In paragraph 13, Bond and Dykstra wrote that these two programs "encourage pupils to write symbols as they learn to recognize them and to associate them with sounds" (1997, 416).

This is the first time in the report that the reader has some idea of the specific characteristics of the Lippincott program, and it is the first time that Bond and Dykstra give any indication that they are aware of what happened in this study. From what we know today, had these suggestions been followed up with appropriate research, we might be one or two decades ahead of where we are now, and we might have prevented the unnecessary suffering of hundreds of thousands of children who have struggled to learn to read. But these suggestions were not followed up. One cannot help wondering why.

Missing Variables　The problem with doing pioneering research is that you miss things. Hardly any of the demographic, school, or teacher variables the authors thought to measure ahead of time were found to correlate with reading performance. Of course, this information is just as valuable as finding out what *does* correlate. In this project, and in follow-up publications (Dykstra 1967, 1968b), the authors pondered what they might have missed. In the conclusion to their study, they wrote: "Evidently, reading achievement is influenced by factors peculiar to school systems over and above differences in measured prereading capabilities of pupils" (Bond and Dykstra 1997, 415). They did not speculate on what these factors might be. They suggested that teachers needed better training, though they did not explain why they thought this, or what it implied.

Throughout their 1967 paper, Bond and Dykstra commented that the results were unstable because of large Project effects, and possibly because of a novelty effect, arguing that new programs "undoubtedly influence" and were "likely" to have contributed to the better performance of children in the classrooms using novel programs. Chall also held this view, and added the insight that the teacher's personality may contribute to these results. Yet "novelty" cannot explain the dismal showing of the Linguistic programs both in this study and in Chall's observations, or the absence of any strong effects for the Basal + phonics approach or for the Language experience program.

The Importance of the Teacher   In a commentary on the reprint of Bond and Dykstra's 1967 article, David Pearson (1997) related a story told to him by Dykstra when the original project was ongoing. One day, Dykstra popped into a project teacher's classroom unannounced. This teacher, assigned to the Language experience method (individualized teaching), was happily doing a phonics lessons with the whole class. When asked about this, she explained that children needed phonics to be able to learn to read. She obviously thought, or had ascertained, that her students were not learning to read, at least to her standard, with the other approach.

This experience prompted Dykstra to raise the issue of "treatment fidelity" in his article on the second-grade extension of this study (Dykstra 1968b). Were the teachers teaching the methods they were assigned to teach to the same standard in the same way? Were they mixing methods or leaving out elements? Dykstra wrote: "One of the most important implications of this study is that future research should center on teaching and learning situation characteristics, rather than method and materials" (p. 66). This echoes Chall's observations on the success or otherwise of different teachers using the same program, and underscores the fact that teachers tend to be eclectic. However, research approaches emphasizing teachers and methods are not mutually exclusive. Both could be studied at the same time.

The story about the wayward teacher is supported by Chall and Feldman's (1966) classroom observations that teachers' reports of their activities did not tally with their observational notes. Teachers do not always do what you think they are doing, nor do they always tell you what they are doing, so asking them to fill out forms or keep a record is no use either. Also, teachers may not always know or remember what they did. There are interruptions; a lesson that is going well will be extended; something the teacher intended to do does not get done. There is, regrettably, only one solution: sit in the classroom and record what the teacher does and for how long.

The teacher's behavior in Pearson's story also highlights a real ethical dilemma. If a teacher sincerely believes that what she has been asked to do in a research project is not working, she is entirely within her rights to stop doing it. She is responsible for human lives. Nonreaders and poor readers do not do well in our society. Anyone who has ever tutored poor readers can attest to the amount of suffering they and their families have endured. The teacher's dilemma is similar to what occurs in medical/clinical trials when some patients are allocated to the miracle-drug group, and others to the placebo group.

The Impact of the Study

This study appeared to have a strong negative impact on future research. Pearson (1997) wrote that the value of a scientific project is determined by how much research it generates. He observed: "By that standard, the First-grade Studies were a dismal failure ... they, in conjunction with Chall's book, marked the end of the methodological comparisons in research on beginning reading (at least until the 1990s)" (p. 431).

Of course, a study like this almost shouts out: "Now top this!" Perhaps because this study was so complex, with its 92 statistical tables, which only seemed to highlight the unpredictable outcomes, other researchers were intimidated by it. This was also the last decade where research funding flowed like water from a tap, and the 1970s saw a severe cutback in support for research of all kinds. No study like this one ever appeared again.

Nevertheless, there are so many tantalizing leads here that it is surprising that no one was inspired to follow them up. Here are some of them:

• Phoneme discrimination may be important in learning to read.
• Being taught how to decode is more beneficial than being trained to memorize sight words. Basal-reader children had serious decoding problems.
• A reading method with the following characteristics produced far larger gains than all other methods in this study: sound-symbol regularity, a controlled but large reading vocabulary introduced systematically, copying letters, words, and phrases, saying the sound the symbol stands for, and reading stories that target a particular phoneme.
• What teachers do in classrooms can be unpredictable, matters a lot, and needs to be investigated quantitatively in tandem with classroom research on methods.

What We Have Learned about Research
It is easy to look back to 1967 and say: "Well, we don't do things like that any more." We have powerful computers to handle complex data sets like these, and all is well. This perception may be comforting, except it is not accurate. In some ways the problem is worse because we have become complacent. We assume that in every scientific report, the correct statistics were used on the appropriate data for the right reasons, and that the interpretation of the findings in the study is an accurate reflection of what really happened. We assume that all the flaws will be picked up by the reviewers, that we can rely on the reviewing process totally, and that we can accept the findings and the author's conclusions at face value. Unfortunately, these are dangerous assumptions, as witnessed by the fact that the Bond and Dykstra article was reprinted in 1997 without any comment about the problems with data handling and statistics in the original study. The editors were either not aware of this or chose not to comment. The NRP report (see the next four chapters) is witness to the serious methodological problems that plague this field.

A Postscript: Follow-On Studies

In 1968, Dykstra (1968a, 1968b) published two brief reports on follow-on data for 960 children who had completed second grade. They came from ten Projects: two each for Basal reader, i.t.a., Language experience, Linguistic, and Lippincott. No Basal + phonics groups were included. In addition, 250 students were followed up on the individually administered tests.

Correlational data revealed much the same results as those found in first grade. The same three baseline tests—letter-name knowledge, phoneme-discrimination, and IQ—correlated with the Stanford Reading subtests: Vocabulary and Comprehension (the only two tests reported). Each of the baseline measures accounted for approximately 16–25 percent of the variance on the Stanford scores.

Reading achievement measured at the end of second grade correlated with reading at the end of first grade at values ranging from .60 or higher, showing that reading achievement is the best predictor of reading achievement. This led Dykstra (1968b, 60) to conclude:

The best predictor of success in learning a task is prior success in learning a similar task.... There is little indication that any of the readiness subtest skills uniquely related to success in the various types of programs.... Results indicate that it is not feasible to place pupils differentially in instructional programs on the basis of a profile of readiness tests administered early in the first grade.

In the Method comparisons, i.t.a. and Lippincott were superior to the other Methods on most comparisons, and Basal readers superior on none. However, no tables or numerical data were provided to support these statements. Sex differences favoring girls were still in evidence. Dykstra concluded: "On the average boys cannot be expected to achieve at the same level as girls under the current methods." There was no indication from these reports that the statistics problems had been solved, or that individual scores had been used in these analyses. All Method comparisons are still subject to the same criticisms raised earlier.

There was one other large-scale project from this period. This was Project Follow Through, involving research on how to prevent children in Head Start programs from losing gains after preschool. Altogether, 22 instructional approaches were examined. These fell roughly into three groups: those that focused mainly on academic skills, those that emphasized cognitive development, and those that emphasized affective or emotional development. A survey of the outcomes of the various methods conducted by Abt Associates and Stanford Research Institute (Stebbins et al. 1977) proved difficult. Data had not been collected on the same measures, and testing was not synchronized in time nor reported in a similar fashion.

This research lacked the advance planning and uniform controls imposed by Bond and Dykstra in their study, and only the vaguest conclusions could be drawn. There was a tendency for the academic approach to be most successful, and within this group the direct-instruction method known as DISTAR was most effective. DISTAR was designed at the University of Oregon by Engelmann and Bruner (1969) and was intended for disadvantaged children in small-group instructional settings. It requires minimal teacher training, because lessons are scripted and teachers are strongly encouraged not to deviate from the script.

DISTAR includes a variety of components, including math and language. The reading program is phonics oriented and features a modified script. Letters vary in size depending on their perceived importance in decoding, or are marked to indicate pronunciation. Children do not learn to segment but to read the "slow way" by stretching the sounds. The long-term effects of the complete DISTAR program were reviewed by Becker and Gersten in 1982. They provided an analysis of the follow-on data for fifth and sixth graders collected in 1975. These children had been in a three-year DISTAR program for reading, language, and mathematics, beginning in first grade in 1969–70. When DISTAR training ended at third grade, children had gained over 20 standard-score points on the Wide Range Achievement Test (WRAT) for reading, 9 points in spelling, and 7.5 points in arithmetic. Percentile scores were 67, 40, and 45 (50 is the national average). These are good results.

There was a further follow-on at fifth and sixth grade after the DISTAR children had been transferred to schools with normal instruction. Compared to a matched control group, they were significantly ahead in WRAT reading in 23 out of 31 comparisons. At fifth grade, DISTAR children were superior in one-third of the comparisons on the Metropolitan Achievement Test (MAT) battery, and equal to the controls on the remaining two-thirds. By sixth grade this advantage had dwindled to around 10–20 percent of comparisons.

However, when compared to national norms, these children did not do well. When Becker and Gersten plotted the average percentiles and standard scores for the children across six grades, the DISTAR children showed a strong peak (near norms or well above norms) at both second and third grade (during the period of DISTAR instruction), followed by a sharp decline by fifth and sixth grade. WRAT reading tumbled into the 30th percentile and MAT reading into the teens, along with math scores. Despite these declines, the DISTAR children were still ahead of the matched control groups, and kept this advantage at a ninth-grade follow-on (.8 of a grade equivalent).

The failure of these children to maintain their hard-won gains is both puzzling and troubling. Becker and Gersten believed that they suffered from a lack of challenging work, and that once the DISTAR program ended, "without effective instruction which continues to build on these skills in the intermediate grades, the children are likely to lose ground against their middle-income peers" (p. 89). The results also suggest that teachers did not assess these children's skills appropriately when they transferred to normal classes at age 9. This study was important for showing what can be accomplished with disadvantaged youngsters, and for illustrating the critical importance of longitudinal data.

As these monumental studies faded from memory, the insights they provided were lost. A proper reading of this work could have saved much time and impelled us toward studies that did not appear for another 30 years.

HOW TO TEACH READING: MODERN RESEARCH

It is the ultimate irony that Chall's book and Bond and Dykstra's study had the opposite effect from the one they intended. Bond and Dykstra's analysis of the data failed to reveal what really happened (that is, the superiority of the Lippincott program on all measures), and seemed to show that the success of a reading method was completely unpredictable. This message undermined Chall's assessment of the research (that synthetic phonics was the clear and unassailable winner) and gave more weight to her observations on the impact of the teacher. Taken together, the projects pointed to the same conclusion: *teachers matter more than the method.* Dykstra (1968b) even suggested this in a follow-up report, expressing concern that teachers needed to be monitored in future research.[1]

The net effect of Bond and Dykstra's project was to virtually shut down applied research on classroom reading methods. If the teacher matters more than the method, the method is largely irrelevant. If basal-reader programs are no worse than anything else, there is no reason to change. And unless some way can be found to neutralize or stabilize the teacher's input into the process, any future research on methods is a waste of time. There was no point in funding this kind of research when a study of over 9,000 children failed to show anything definitive. The fact that only 38 research reports on reading methods passed the final screening in the recent National Reading Panel survey says it all. And of these 38 reports, half are tutoring programs for older readers. Twenty valid studies

---

1. Much later, Chall offered a more chilling explanation at a conference I attended, stating that research on reading methods in the classroom is impossible.

on classroom reading programs in 30 years is two studies every three years, one reason we have made so little progress in establishing solid scientific evidence on how to teach children to read.

The 1960s projects had even more ripple effects, opening the door for the whole-language movement. Chall's book (in company with Flesch's book in 1955) unmasked the basal programs. The facts were there for all to see, complete with virtual pages from those boring readers. By the end of third grade, children had been exposed to a reading vocabulary of a mere 1,500 words. They did not learn to spell. They did no writing of any kind until second grade.

This was the antithesis of what should happen, according to the founders of the whole-language movement, who believed that learning to read was as "natural" as learning to talk. Children should learn to read *by reading* and use stories written in natural language, not in the stilted and repetitive style of the Dick and Jane readers. This way, children could apply all their linguistic skills (vocabulary, syntax, sensitivity to context) to understand what they read. According to Goodman (1967), reading is a "psycholinguistic guessing game," where the main goal is to follow the gist of the story. Accuracy is largely irrelevant.

Of the face of it, the "natural-language" approach sounded like a better solution, and had the added bonus of being fun—fun for the teacher whose main task was to read interesting stories from real children's literature out of Big Books, and fun for children who got to listen and "read along" in little books. It was fun for teachers to encourage creative writing and watch in admiration as children invented their own spelling system, and fun for children to "write stories" regardless of whether anything they wrote could be deciphered. It was motivating for children to believe they were learning to read, write, and spell, despite the fact they were not. The whole-language movement was the third (and final) whole-word method of the twentieth century, and it took the English-speaking world by storm—with catastrophic consequences (see chapter 1).

The founders of whole language were not alone in believing that natural-language development had something to do with learning to read. This has been a major theme in reading research as well. Most of the research on spelling derives from the belief that children go through developmental spelling stages (see chapter 9). As noted in chapter 1, the dominant theory in reading research for the past 30 years has been that "phonological awareness develops," a theory unsupported by any data. This gave rise to a proliferation of phonological-awareness training programs, the topic of the following chapter.

Since the early 1970s, the phonological/language-reading connection dominated the landscape in scientific studies on reading. At a rough estimate, approximately 90 percent of the scientific research over the past 30 years has been descriptive or correlational, addressing the following question: What phonological or linguistic skills do good readers possess that poor readers lack? (See *Language Development and Learning to Read*.) The remaining 10 percent of published studies is applied and deals with more fundamental issues, like pinning down what matters most for teaching children to read.

Only a few studies in this 30-year period have addressed the critical problem that Chall and Dykstra identified. What is the relative contribution of the teacher and the method to children's reading skill? This is the most important question of all, because unless we can answer it, methods research is largely a waste of time.

Methods and Teachers Matter

In their observational study, Chall and Feldman (1966) discovered that what classroom teachers said they did bore only a vague resemblance to what was recorded on their observational checklists. Perhaps this is not surprising. It is difficult to monitor your own behavior when you are part of the action. Classrooms are highly dynamic, and what happens minute by minute is unpredictable. Lessons get interrupted. A lesson that is going well may be extended. A lesson that was planned never gets done.

This means that asking teachers to keep diaries or fill out checklists on what they did in the classroom that day or that week is not the most productive way to find out what is really going in the classroom. It is certainly not the way to find out which of the activities students engage in really matter for learning to read. The only way to do this is to sit in the classroom and record what the children are doing minute by minute. Few researchers have had the fortitude to do this, and the first rigorous study did not appear for 20 years.

Canadian psychologists Evans and Carr (1985) carried out observations on first-, second-, and third-grade classrooms. Ten classrooms followed the language experience (LE) format described in the preceding chapter. Lessons are developed around the child's vocabulary. The child tells a story to the teacher. She writes it down and copies the words onto cards. These become the child's "word bank," which he is supposed to memorize by sight. This phase ends when the bank reaches around 150 words. After this, the child works with published materials, following the tenets of whole language. In another ten classrooms, the children were using a program based on "traditional phonics." Children memorized sight words, learned to link letters and sounds (decoding), filled in phonics workbooks, practiced writing letters, words, and sentences, and read phonics-type readers.

Each of the 400 children in the study was observed on 50 different occasions for 10-second periods. Observations covered the entire school day. Behaviors were coded into categories, and the total "time on task" for each category was recorded.

The two types of classroom were noticeably (and significantly) different in how time was allocated. Children in the LE classes worked independently about two-thirds of the time, while children in the phonics-oriented classes spent over half the time (57 percent) in whole-class, teacher-led activities. They spent far more time on word analysis and decoding—three times longer in groups, and six times longer when working alone. They also spent more time writing letters and words, more time reading silently, and less time reading out loud.

On direct comparisons of several standard tests of reading comprehension at the end of the year (the only reading skill measured), children in the phonics classes were significantly ahead. There were no differences between the two groups on any tests of cognitive and language skills.

The critical aspect of this work was the relationship between the time spent on the various activities (time on task) and reading test scores, *irrespective of the reading method* (all classes combined). There were several key findings. Time spent memorizing sight words was negatively correlated with every reading test. This was true in both group and independent settings (median scores: −.32 group, and −.63 independent). The negative correlation means that the more time the children spent memorizing sight words, the lower their reading scores. Time spent reading aloud (to teacher or class) was uncorrelated with reading skill. Interestingly, lessons on comprehension and on how to use context to understand the story were unrelated to reading comprehension (correlations at zero). All classes benefited from *group* silent reading (correlations strongly positive) but not from independent silent reading (no correlation). Apparently, it is easier to focus on reading when everyone in the class is silent than when only you are silent.

Other findings were more specific to the types of instruction. Children in the phonics classes spent far more time copying words and in various writing activities. These activities were positively correlated with reading comprehension scores (range $r = .37$ to $.75$). There was a modest relationship between reading and time spent on phonics-type activities whether done by the whole class or independently (range $r = .04$ to $.41$). The children in the LE classrooms engaged in far more oral-language activities led by the teacher (lessons on vocabulary and grammar, listening to a story). Time spent in these activities was strongly negatively correlated with reading skill at surprisingly high values (range $r = -.70$ to $-.80$).

The authors commented on the negative outcome for several of the independent-learning tasks, and suggested that children "may be at risk for degenerating into almost random learning which may detract from or interfere with more systematic practice of reading skills" (Evans and Carr 1985, 344). The one exception was writing practice, which was highly predictive of reading skill and rarely took place in a group setting. Talking about the meaning of words and listening to the teacher read stories takes time away from more productive activities. Time spent on these activities had negative consequences for reading comprehension.

Sumbler (1999) in Toronto used a similar approach. Ten kindergarten classrooms were using a linguistic phonics program called Jolly Phonics (JP), a program close to the prototype. The alphabet principle is taught from sound to print using a basic code. Children get extensive practice in blending and segmenting sounds and letters in real words, both orally and in writing. We will look more closely at this program later in the chapter. The other ten classes were using a "balanced" approach, which included a wide range of activities chosen at the discretion of the teacher.

The children were attending half-day sessions in senior kindergarten. The average age was six years at midyear when the training and the observations began. Observations followed the format developed by Evans and Carr. Every child in every classroom was monitored for a brief time period on numerous occasions, and the observations continued for several months.

Overall activity patterns were similar in the two types of classrooms. Children went out to play for the same amount of time, spent the same amount of time transitioning between activities, and were interrupted equally often. However, children in the "balanced" classes spent a significantly larger proportion of the time in non-literacy-related activities (35 percent versus 28 percent). Of the ten literacy activities coded, there were significant differences on four, with JP children participating significantly more often in each one. JP children spent 10 percent of the language period on phonics-related activities (explained below), compared to 2 percent for the other children. They spent more time on auditory phoneme-awareness tasks (7 percent versus 3.7 percent), and more time memorizing sight words and learning about grammar, though the last two activities were infrequent in all classrooms. There were no differences between the two types of classroom in the time spent on the remaining categories: learning concepts of print, like the order of words on the page and order of pages, reading aloud or silently, "pretend writing" sentences, copying letters/words/sentences and writing them from memory, learning letter names, and vocabulary lessons. Vocabulary work took up by far the most time in both types of classrooms (18 percent and 20 percent).

The children took five standardized reading and spelling tests at the end of the school year. Children in the JP classrooms were significantly ahead on every test. When scores on these tests were correlated with time on task for the various activities, only two activities were significantly (and positively) related to reading and spelling scores. These were phonics activities (range $r = .48$ to $.62$), and copying/writing letters and words (range $r = .50$ to $.55$). The correlations between time spent on auditory phoneme analysis (no letters) were essentially zero for all five reading measures. Although no other values were significant, the following activities were consistently *negatively* correlated with all five reading and spelling tests, with values for r ranging from $-.20$ to $-.31$: learning letter names, vocabulary lessons, and "nonliteracy" activities (15 negative correlations out of 15 would not occur by chance).[2]

The phonics category consisted of five subcategories: oral spelling: spelling out loud with letter names, visual spelling: saying letter names of words, learning sound-letter correspondences, word analysis: sounding out and blending sounds in words using letters, and Jolly Phonics "actions." These actions only occurred in the JP classes. Because they always overlapped with learning sound-to-letter correspondences (nonindependent categories), they will not be discussed further.

Children spent little time doing either oral or visual spelling, and comparisons were not significant. JP children spent 8 minutes a day learning sound-to-letter correspondences and 8 additional minutes on word analysis (segmenting, blending). The children in the "balanced" programs averaged less than a minute per day on either activity. Time spent on these two activities was significantly correlated with reading and spelling (correlations ranged from $r = .35$ to $.55$ across the reading and spelling tests).

The negative impact of story time on children's reading skill was also shown by Meyer et al. (1994). Two large cohorts of children in three different school districts were followed from kindergarten to the end of first grade. At kindergarten, the more time the teacher spent reading to the class, the lower the children's scores on a variety of reading tests, especially tests of decoding ($r = -.44$ to $-.71$). Reading to children in either kindergarten or first grade had zero impact on first-grade reading scores. However, time spent teaching decoding skills was strongly correlated with reading skill on five tests ($r = .44$ to $.62$).

These findings are remarkably consistent. Time devoted to learning sound-to-letter correspondences, segmenting and blending sounds in words, and writing letters and words predicts subsequent reading and spelling skill in both beginning readers and more advanced readers. Most other "literacy activities" have no effect, while memorizing sight words, doing vocabulary lessons, and listening to stories have a consistently negative effect.

---

2. It should be noted that the "subjects" in this study were "classrooms," which sharply reduced N and statistical power.

The importance of writing for locking sound-symbol correspondences into memory has been investigated by Hulme and his colleagues (Hulme 1981; Hulme and Bradley 1984; Hulme, Monk, and Ives 1987). They compared learning speed for mastering phoneme-grapheme correspondences for copying, using alphabet cards, or using letter tiles. Children learned much faster when they wrote the letters. Hulme and colleagues (1987) concluded that *motor activity* promotes memory, and this assists children in learning to read. But this is only part of the answer. Copying letters forces you to look carefully and hold this image in mind while you are writing. This, plus the act of forming the strokes, makes it clear how letters differ. (See McGuinness 1997c for an analysis of how copying assists memory.)

Cunningham and Stanovich (1990b) reported the same effect for spelling accuracy. First graders memorized spelling lists using three different methods: copying by hand, utilizing letter tiles, and typing the lists on a computer keyboard. Children spelled twice as many words correctly when they learned by copying the letters than with letter tiles or typing. They also found that saying letter names while writing letters had no impact on spelling performance.

The most surprising result to emerge from the observational studies was the large number of activities that were either nonproductive (zero relationship to reading) or actually detrimental (negative correlations). Negative correlations can mean either of two things: time wasted (a trade-off between learning one thing at the expense of another), or a negative outcome, like the creation of a maladaptive strategy. Correlational research can never prove causality, but it is hard to imagine that vocabulary activities and listening to stories are "bad" for children. Here, the time trade-off argument makes sense, especially because vocabulary work and listening to stories took up more time than any other literacy activity in most classrooms. (The big question is whether time spent on vocabulary work actually improves *vocabulary*. We will come back to this question in chapter 8.)

On the other hand, we know that time spent memorizing sight words can cause a negative outcome by promoting a strategy of "whole-word guessing." This is where children decode the first letter phonemically and guess the rest of the word based on its length and shape. This strategy is highly predictive of subsequent reading failure (McGuinness 1997b). It is well known that program emphasis (sight word, context-based guessing, part-word analysis, phonemic decoding) strongly affects the child's decoding strategy, and that this strategy quickly becomes entrenched (Barr 1972, 1974/1975; Vellutino and Scanlon 1987; McGuinness 1997b, 1997c).

Boronat and Logan (1997) showed convincingly that what you pay attention to is automatically encoded by the brain and automatically cued in memory. As they put it, "What one pays attention to acts as a retrieval cue that draws associations out of memory" (p. 45). What you ignore, even though it is physically adjacent to what you are looking at, is not encoded at all. The more a child focuses on the wrong patterns and combinations of letter sequences in words, the more automatic (habitual) this becomes.

In the observational studies, time spent memorizing sight words was negatively and weakly correlated with reading scores for the kindergarteners, but negative and strongly correlated for the older children (6 to 8 years). A sight-word strategy begins to overload between 7 and 8 years. I found that children who adopted a whole-word strategy by the end of first grade had not improved their performance when they were followed up in third grade (McGuinness 1997b). These children often made the same decoding errors on the same words they had made two years earlier, and they were uniformly the worst readers in the class.

The observational studies are incredibly powerful, because they do something that research on classroom methods cannot do. They cut through the noise of curriculum details and teacher variability and get to the heart of the matter. They make it possible to link success in learning to read and spell to what is actually being taught. Training in listening for the sound units of the writing system, learning the correspondences between these units and their symbols, and grasping how the units link together to make words are the essential ingredients of a successful reading method. The more these skills are practiced by eye, by ear, and by hand, the better.

After 5,000 years, the Sumerians have been vindicated by science.

Spelling Helps Reading, But Seeing Misspelled Words Is Bad for Spelling
There were other important discoveries during this 30-year period. Two sets of studies, in particular, bear directly on the importance of writing and spelling practice. One group of studies looked at the impact of spelling

practice on reading skill. The second group of studies stemmed from concern about teaching methods that advocate misspelling words as a strategy for learning to spell, or that tolerate the writing of misspelled words by children.

In chapter 3, I pointed out that learning to spell (correctly) impacts reading, because spelling requires *recall memory*, a substantially more comprehensive (deeper) form of memory than what reading entails. Reading relies on *recognition memory* (memory with a prompt), a more superficial type of memory. This is why learning to read is less likely to impact spelling than the reverse. Smith (1999) found that very poor readers scored normally on tests of word recognition and reading comprehension after 12 hours of structured lessons on the advanced spelling code. Other scholars have investigated this more directly.

Learning to Read by Learning to Spell

Ehri and Wilce (1987) taught one group of 5-year-olds to spell nonsense words with letter tiles, and another group to read the same words, using a slightly modified alphabet of 10 letters. After training, the spelling group had higher *reading* scores than the reading group on a transfer task (same letters/different words). In a more thorough investigation, Uhry and Shepherd (1993) trained two groups of first graders matched for reading skill for 40 minutes a week for 28 weeks. One group received segmenting and spelling training, while the other group received a mirror-image version consisting of blending and decoding (reading) training. At 32 weeks, the children took a battery of tests. The segmenting/spelling group was significantly ahead on all tests of *reading*, spelling, and phoneme awareness (including blending). These children used letter tiles or typed on a computer keyboard to spell words. Based on the evidence that writing letters speeds up learning, one would expect this to make an even greater difference.

Invented Spelling

There is little research on the consequences of invented spelling, because spelling is assumed to follow natural developmental stages. When children are encouraged to "just write" and "invent" their own spelling system, the most common pattern that emerges (other than complete randomness) is letter-name spelling (so, for example, the word *far* would be spelled *fr*), as noted in chapter 1. This is not a "stage of development," as researchers claim. Letter names are all the children have been taught. (If they had been taught the sounds the letters stand for, correctly spelled words would appear a lot earlier in spelling development.)

We know that chanting letter names as you spell has no effect from Uhri and Shepherd's research, and we know that saying the sounds does from the Lippincott results. It turns out that *using* letter names to spell is actually detrimental. Treiman and Tincoff (1997) discovered that learning letter names focuses children's attention on the syllable instead of the phoneme (*es, em, ef, kay, pee, are*), blocking their conceptual understanding of how an alphabet works, to say nothing of the fact that they will not learn how to spell.

The argument for teaching letter names to young children has always been that the names contain the sound the letter stands for. But this is another myth. Try this little game with a friend. Write out the following letter-name sequences on a piece of paper and ask a friend what they spell: *sea-oh-double-you, aitch-ee-ay-tee,* and *ef-are-oh-gee.*

It is obvious that invented spelling, by definition, will impede, halt, or otherwise delay correct spelling. Does correct spelling eventually emerge from this mess, as educators believe? So far, there are no studies on children that shed light on this issue, but there are studies on adults.

The Negative Impact of Seeing Misspelled Words

Any teacher or college professor knows that after hours of marking student papers, one's sense of the spelling code begins to falter. What was once easy (spotting spelling errors effortlessly) now becomes tentative. Is it possible that a sense of the "wrongness" or "rightness" of particular spellings (learned over decades) could start to evaporate in such a brief period?

This phenomenon was first documented by Pintner, Rinsland, and Zubin (1929) and by Nisbet (1939). They discovered that if students took a spelling test, then saw some of the same words misspelled, when they took the spelling test again the spelling errors increased by about 15 percent. More recent studies have supported these results. Brown (1988) gave college students a spelling-dictation test of intermediate difficulty. Half the students saw half the words again and had to generate two possible phonetic spellings (misspelled) for each word. The other students did an unrelated task. The original spelling test was given again. The spelling errors increased by 17 percent for the experimental group versus 7 percent for the controls, a highly significant result.

In a second experiment, Brown looked at the effect of *seeing* misspelled words rather than creating them. The experiment was run on a computer. The format was similar: a spelling-dictation test, then a spelling-recognition test (or not), followed by either a dictation or recognition test. The spelling-recognition test consisted of several spellings of the same word (*tramendous, tremendus, tremendous, tremmendus*), and the task was to choose the correct spelling. Students also had to rate each misspelled word according to how closely it resembled the correct spelling. The control group did a jigsaw puzzle. On the final dictation test, spelling errors were twice as high for the experimental group.

One of the most intriguing and complex studies on this topic was carried out by Jacoby and Hollingshead (1990). They were interested in whether merely seeing misspelled words was sufficient to depress spelling skill, as compared to active processing, which requires decisions or writing out the words. College students saw hard-to-spell words one at a time on a computer: 20 spelled correctly, 20 incorrectly. Students were assigned to one of three conditions: *read* the words out loud, *type* the words exactly as spelled, or *print* the words exactly as spelled. All students were told that some of the words were misspelled. After this, they took a spelling-dictation test on the same 40 words plus 20 new words of equal difficulty.

Spelling accuracy (the dictation test) was strongly affected by previous exposure to the correct and incorrect spellings alike. The results were the same whether the students had previously read, typed, or printed the words. Scores were as follows: old correctly spelled words (93 percent), new correctly spelled words (87 percent), incorrectly spelled words (83 percent). Seeing misspelled words significantly depressed spelling scores, and the probability of using the same misspelling was high (.76). This shows a "priming" effect in that recent exposure to correctly spelled words improves spelling (93 percent) for those words, as compared to correctly spelled words not seen recently (87 percent).

While spelling accuracy did not vary with the three types of exposure, typing speed did. The groups that had typed or printed in the exposure phase, typed faster in the dictation test than the group that just read. This suggests that motor involvement has more of an impact on efficiency than on accuracy. In a recognition-memory test ("Was this word on the list?"), performance was also superior for the groups that typed or printed.

In a second experiment, students saw the same word lists. This time, one group copied each word while it remained in view. A second group studied the word for 3 seconds, then did a distracting task for 10 seconds. Both groups took the same spelling-dictation and spelling-recognition tests. The two groups did not differ in accuracy on the spelling tests, and scores mirrored the first experiment: correctly spelled words (92 percent), new words (86 percent), incorrectly spelled words (80 percent). This shows that an interfering task does not erase the negative impact of seeing misspelled words or the priming effect of seeing correctly spelled words. Not only this, but recognition memory was higher for the distraction group (85 percent correct versus 65 percent).

Jacoby and Hollingshead explored several possible theoretical explanations for these results and dismissed most of them. For example, no "template" theory, in which every spelling has a special memory trace, or a system prompted by "recollection" or "spelling rules," can explain these findings. Unconscious (automatic) processing is at work here. We will come back to what these results mean shortly.

A similar study was carried out with undergraduates in the United Kingdom (Dixon and Kaminska 1997). Good and poor spellers were selected on the basis of their performance on words from *The Awful Speller's Dictionary* (Krevisky and Linfield 1990), which contains difficult-to-spell words. They first took a spelling-dictation test consisting of 60 words from the above dictionary, then did one of three intervening tasks: read misspelled words from the same test, read correctly spelled words from the same test, or read correctly spelled words not on the test. A final spelling test was given immediately and again one week later. The delay had no effect. Exposure to misspelled words depressed the spelling scores, and they did not rebound at all over the week. Seeing correctly spelled words twice had no more beneficial effect than seeing them once. Good and poor spellers were not differentially affected by any of these manipulations. That is, good and poor spellers alike were equally prone to the impact of misspelled words immediately and after a delay.

The authors of all three studies strongly cautioned educators and researchers to not use spelling-recognition tests, either for school testing or for spelling research. This type of test appears in well-known test batteries like the California Achievement Test, Comprehensive Test for Basic Skills, Metropolitan Achievement Test, and the McGraw-Hill Basic Study Skills. There are two reasons for concern. First, a spelling-recognition test is an invalid method of testing spelling ability. It is a test of recognition memory ("choose the spelling that looks 'familiar'"), not a test of recall memory. Second, merely taking the test can create spelling amnesia for the misspelled words. Jacoby and Hollingshead reported on the experience of the second author who ran the experiment many times, exposing her to the misspelled words again and again. This seriously eroded her confidence or sense of what correct spellings looked like, not only for these words, but for other words as well.

These studies provide considerable insight into the process by which the brain codes and remembers spellings. The fact that a single exposure can erase or degrade a particular spelling shows that memory traces, especially for complex spellings seen infrequently, are extremely unstable and can easily be overwritten by brief exposure to something "almost correct." The brain is a statistical pattern analyzer par excellence. Incoming patterns are instantly matched to prior representations of the same or similar patterns. If a small deviation (a spelling change) in a relatively unfamiliar word exists, statistical probability will shift in the direction of the new form. That we have stable memories of spellings at all, given the idiosyncrasies of the English spelling code, seems miraculous. The instructional implications are enormous. First, a regime of "invented spelling" makes it impossible to form stable memories of correctly spelled words. Second, the spelling techniques and tricks widely used by classroom teachers where children are told to write out all the ways a word can be spelled to see what looks right, are fatally flawed.

truble, trubble, trubbel, troble, trobble, trobbel, trouble, troubble, troubbel

The argument is that children should do this, because adults commonly try out different spellings when they forget how to spell a word, or when a spelling "looks funny." But adults try out likely spellings, not a list of highly improbable, intentionally misspelled words. And adults know how to spell; otherwise a misspelled word would not "look funny" in the first place, prompting the need to try another spelling. Children do not know how to spell, and so writing out lists of all possible spellings, carefully scrutinizing each one, then crossing it off, is a sure-fire "antispelling method." Children will see far more incorrect spellings than correct spellings, making it impossible for the brain to do its job. Consistent patterns lead to accessible memories. The brain cannot code randomness. As Boronat and Logan's research showed, what you are forced to pay attention to is what you remember. Rightness or wrongness makes no difference to this automatic process.

The Prototype: An Update

Before moving on to an analysis of reading programs in light of this new information, here is what a successful reading/spelling program should or should not contain based on our discussion so far:

- No sight words (except high-frequency words with rare spellings).
- No letter names.
- Sound-to-print orientation. Phonemes, not letters, are the basis for the code.
- Teach phonemes only—no other sound units.
- Begin with basic code (a one-to-one correspondence between 40 phonemes and their most common spelling).
- Teach children to identify and sequence sounds in real words by segmenting and blending, *using letters*.
- Teach children how to write each letter. Integrate writing into every lesson.
- Link writing (spelling) and reading to ensure children learn that the alphabet is a code and that codes are reversible: encoding/decoding.
- Spelling should be accurate or, at a minimum, phonetically accurate (all things within reason).
- Lessons should move on to include the advanced spelling code (the 136 remaining, common spellings).

Reading Instruction: The National Reading Panel Results

This section reviews the evidence from the National Reading Panel's (NRP) survey on instructional methods for reading. My goal is to look more closely at the programs in the NRP database that have the greatest and most consistent success. How well do these programs align with the prototype program I have been assembling in the last two chapters?

In the introduction to the project, the NRP reported that a general screening of the databases unearthed approximately 100,000 research studies on reading published since 1966. To handle the volume of this material, the NRP divided "reading" into five topic areas. I will discuss one of these areas—reading instruction—in this chapter. The remaining areas (phoneme-awareness training, methods for improving fluency, instruction in vocabulary, and instruction in comprehension) will be taken up in the following chapters. Spelling instruction was not included in the NRP survey, no doubt because so little research is available on this topic.

The panel held hearings for parents, teachers, researchers, and other interested parties who were the intended audience for this report. Here is one of the seven themes they identified from this input: "The need for clear, objective, and scientifically based information on the effectiveness of different types of reading instruction and the need to have such research inform policy and practice" (National Reading Panel, 2000, 1-2).

From these themes they developed more specific questions to guide their search. The general statement above was narrowed considerably, producing questions like; "Does phonics instruction improve reading achievement? If so, how is this instruction best provided?" (p. 1-3).

At no point do they explain why they limited the focus to phonics, specifically to "systematic phonics," as you will see below. Part of the reason appears to reflect the panel's preference, though the main reason may lie in the fact that whole-language advocates rarely conduct research on their approach. The same can be said of publishers of basal-reader programs.

This is a very curious state of affairs. The dominant reading method is accepted universally without a shred of evidence attesting to its efficacy, while phonics advocates continually have to prove that phonics programs work. One would imagine that there would be voluminous research on whole language, a method used in 90 percent of classrooms for 30 years, and that research on other programs, like phonics, would be hard to find. Yet the opposite is true, not only in terms of volume, but in terms of quality. This says a lot about why our schools are in trouble.

Of the original 1,072 studies on reading instruction screened by the NRP, only 75 passed the first screening based on these guidelines:

- An experimental or quasi-experimental design with a control group.
- Published in a refereed journal after 1970.
- Must provide data testing the hypothesis that systematic phonics instruction improves reading performance more than alternative phonics instruction or no phonics instruction (i.e., other programs).
- Reading must have been measured as an outcome.
- Adequate reporting of statistics sufficient to compute effect sizes.

Other problems came to light as the NRP reviewed the 75 studies in more depth, such as missing control groups, too limited a focus or time span, incorrect or inadequate statistical analysis, inappropriate outcome measures, and duplicate studies (or data) found in another publication. As a result, only 38 research reports (a total of 66 individual comparisons) passed the final screening—a sad state of affairs.

Yet even this dismal showing is better than the research database on whole language. In 1989, Stahl and Miller attempted to review the whole-language/language experience research and provide a quantitative synthesis of the research findings. The search was exhaustive and dated back to 1960. It included all the obvious databases, dissertation abstracts, and bibliographies. Personal letters were sent to the major figures in the field, asking for information and help. Apart from Bond and Dykstra's research on the language experience method, only 46 studies were found, and only 17 had sufficient statistical data to compute effect sizes. These 46 studies constituted the total pool of research on the whole-language and language experience methods. Contrast this with the 1,027 studies found by the NRP. These studies compared whole language/language experience to various basal-reader programs.

Because Stahl and Miller located so few studies, none could be excluded, regardless of the numerous methodological problems they detected and the fact that most of these studies had never passed peer review. They were obliged to report the outcomes in a table similar to the one used by Chall. The table showed that 58 comparisons were not significant, 26 favored whole language/language experience, and 16 favored basal readers. On closer inspection, the advantage to whole language was entirely on nonreading tests, like "concepts of print," and only in the kindergarten classes. Of the 17 programs with sufficient statistical information to compute effect sizes, only 4 were published papers. Of these 4, whole language had marginally higher effect sizes on "print concepts" and "readiness." Otherwise the results were either nonsignificant or in favor of the basal programs.

In contrast, all studies in the final NRP data pool were published. All had data sufficient to compute effect sizes and to provide a meta-analysis of the results. Before reviewing this evidence, I need to discuss what a meta-analysis is, and what it can and cannot do. Readers who are knowledgeable about meta-analysis may want to skip to the next section.

Meta-Analysis Made Simple

The NRP converted each statistical comparison between reading methods to an *effect size* (ES). These ES values are used in a meta-analysis, which is essentially a grand average of all effect sizes for a large number of studies. To make sense of the NRP findings, one has to understand what this means.

An effect size provides a common metric for comparing two reading methods on any test, by transforming means and standard deviations into *standard deviation units*. An effect size is computed by taking the difference between the two means of the methods being compared on a given measure, and dividing this value by the average of their standard deviations $(m1 - m2/s.d.1 + s.d.2 \times .5)$. This provides an estimate of the magnitude (effect *size*) of the difference. An ES of 1.0 represents a one-standard-deviation difference between the two groups, very large indeed. This would reflect 15 standard-score points on a standardized reading test, the difference between scoring at the 50th percentile (score of 100) or the 15th percentile (score of 85).

A meta-analysis pools the effect sizes from a large number of studies and adjusts values according to the number of participants in each study. After this, studies can be sorted into baskets and compared in different ways. This provides very useful information. For example, training phoneme awareness in tandem with letters has a much greater impact on reading test scores than when the training is purely auditory.

Despite its usefulness, meta-analysis is not a magic bullet. There are a number of constraints and difficulties with this technique. A meta-analysis requires a large number of studies to make reliable generalizations. *Studies need to be as alike as possible.* Children should be the same age and grade. The general content or teaching time within categories of reading methods (phonics, whole language) should be similar. Because of the enormous variety of reading programs, and the variability with which they are taught, this constraint is impossible to meet. For this reason, I will be looking at the studies in much more depth than the NRP was able to do.

Another difficulty with meta-analysis is that an effect size is entirely dependent on the control group or contrasting group. Applied research on methods typically contrasts two different programs with the goal of finding out which is best. If one program is truly better than another, the ES value will be large. But not all research designs are alike. There are several studies in the NRP database where "at-risk" children were compared to "normal" children who got no special training. The purpose of the training was to get the at-risk children caught up. If this effort has been successful, the two groups will not differ, and the ES values will be close to zero. This means an effect size cannot tell you anything absolute. It can only tell you something relative to something else. When a large number of studies with different research designs or other methodological variations are combined in a meta-analysis, they will partially cancel each other out, giving a false impression of what is true. A meta-analysis is rather like taking a census by counting houses instead of counting the people in the houses.

I also need to add that I computed effect sizes using the formula provided by the NRP. For the most part my values were identical or comparable to those reported by the panel. However, in some cases differences were very large, and I will comment on this as we go. The most likely explanation for these gross discrepancies are mathematical errors in the NRP report.

A Quick Overview

With these reservations in mind, we will explore what the NRP's meta-analysis showed about the global effectiveness of the different types of reading programs. For the most part, the studies in the database compared a phonics-type program with something else. It was rare to find two phonics programs being compared. Taking all cases (66 ES values), the mean ES after training was .41 for combined reading scores. At follow up (62 cases), it was .44 (see table 5.1). The positive value shows an advantage of phonics methods over contrasting methods. These effect sizes are a composite value that represents every reading measure, on every age

Table 5.1

National Reading Panel: Reading-instruction effect sizes for phonics versus other

	N cases	Read-ing	N cases	Spell-ing	N cases	Compre-hension
All studies						
Immediate testing	65	.41				
End-of-year testing	62	.44				
K and 1st grade only	30	.55	29	.67	20	.29
2nd to 6th grade	32	.27	13	.09	11	.12

group, on normal and special populations alike, and for all types of research designs. It is interesting to see what happens when a subset of studies is subtracted from the mix. A general summary of ES values for the studies as a whole is shown in table 5.1.

I separated the studies on beginning readers (kindergartners and first graders) from the studies on older readers (children receiving remedial tutoring). For beginning readers, the ES value increases for phonics methods (30 cases, ES = .55). For older, poor readers, it is reduced substantially (32 cases, ES = .27). The first value is moderately large and significant, and the second is neither. Does this mean that phonics-type programs do not work for older, poor readers? Well, no, it does not. But it does mean that a large proportion of the remedial programs in this *particular* database were unsuccessful. For instance, programs based on the Orton-Gillingham model were particularly ineffective (10 cases produced an ES value of only .23).

Because my analysis will focus on beginning reading instruction, we can unravel this further by examining what the ES value of .55 represents. The 30 individual comparisons that contributed to this value tell us, by and large, that a phonics-type program produces a 0.5-standard-deviation advantage over a non-phonics-type program. Not all phonics programs were equally successful. Particularly weak were programs described as *rime analogy*. These programs teach larger sound units, like word families, and encourage children to make analogies to other words by swapping word parts (*cr-own*, *fr-own*, *d-own*). The average effect size was .28 for this group of studies, not significantly different from the comparison programs.

Studies on Reading Mastery, or Direct Instruction (DISTAR), produced highly inconsistent results. It is informative to compare the NRP's pool of these studies to a recent meta-analysis on DISTAR carried out by Adams and Engelmann (1996). They located 350 studies, reduced by careful screening to 37. To meet criteria, the study had to include a comparison group, pretest scores, means and standard deviations, and substantial training (no short-term studies were allowed). Moreover, DISTAR could not be confounded with some other method. Studies did not have to be published, however, which *was* a requirement in the NRP's protocol.

Of the 37 studies, only 13 were specific to reading or spelling. After excluding studies on adults and one on DISTAR's advanced spelling program (seventh grade), this left 6 studies on special-education populations and 4 on classroom reading instruction (normal children). The effect size for children in special education was solid (ES = .74), but DISTAR was less impressive in the normal classroom (ES = .40).

Because only one study appeared in both databases, I will assess the studies in the NRP database separately. I eliminated three. Gersten, Darch, and Gleason (1988) had an unusual study design, comparing children who received two years of DISTAR, but who either did or did not participate in the DISTAR kindergarten program. Effect sizes were close to zero. In another study, first-grade "at-risk" children were individually tutored, but children in the control group were not, producing an overly large effect size. The third study involved seven different teaching approaches (tutoring, computers, small groups, and so on), some of which combined DISTAR with other methods. The cumulative effect size was zero.

After eliminating these studies, the total effect sizes for the remainder were higher than those reported by Adams and Engelmann: ES = 1.1 for reading and .45 for spelling. Nevertheless, the variability between the studies was still large for no obvious reason. Because of this, DISTAR will not be included in any further analysis. I also excluded the one-of-a-kind studies using an unknown and unpublished reading program. It is impossible to generalize from a single study, especially when authors fail to describe the program adequately.

There are several reading programs in the NRP database that closely resemble the prototype. I will take them up in turn to see how they compare with the total effect sizes reported in table 5.1. Before I do this, however, I need to provide a glossary of common terms.

A Glossary

Basal readers or *traditional basal* is jargon for a complete reading curriculum of any type published for the schools by an educational publisher. The word *basal* means "basic" and "comprehensive." In the United Kingdom, basal readers are called *reading schemes*, a more descriptive term. These programs contain all the necessary components for the classroom teacher: teacher manuals, lesson plans, suggestions for activities, workbooks, over-heads, graded readers, and recommended-reading lists.

Basal programs tend to be alike (publishers copy one another). Most hedge their bets and include all possible ways to teach reading: sight-word memorization, part-word decoding (word families), and specialized readers, along with a sprinkling of phonics lessons and worksheets. It is typical for the content and logic of the phonics lessons to mismatch the readers, and for everything to mismatch the spelling lessons. There are differences in emphasis; some programs are more oriented to whole language and others more oriented to phonics. By and large, *phonics* in this context does not conform to most people's notion of phonics.

Phonics is a problematic word. In most research reports, the description of what passes for phonics is exceedingly vague. The phrase "letter sounds were taught" could refer to the 26 sounds of the letters of the alphabet, or to the 40+ sounds of the English language and their common spellings, or neither. In the United Kingdom, the term *letter sound* is nearly synonymous with *phoneme*, a practice that is causing a great deal of confusion. On rare occasions, the reader might be able to decipher what is meant from other clues. Griffith, Klesius, and Kromrey (1992, 86) wrote this about a traditional basal-phonics unit: "Instructional focus is primarily upon the acquisition of letter-sound correspondence information and less upon the mapping of spoken language onto written language. In fact, during first grade children are exposed to approximately 90 different individual sounds. It is felt that through direct instruction on individual letter-sound correspondences children will learn to both decode and spell words."

Griffith and colleagues have no problem with the statement that children learn 90 different sounds, despite the fact that there are only 40 sounds in English! Nevertheless, this statement tips off the reader that the phonics component of this program is entirely letter driven and far removed from the prototype.

Some basal-phonics lessons resemble a guessing game or a cognitive puzzle rather than anything to do with instruction. It is the student's job to decipher what the teacher is talking about, discover the purpose of the game, and then solve the problem. A teacher may ask a question like "Is the short sound of 'a' in these words?" and point to a set of pictures. Note that she uses a letter name, not the sound /a/, and assumes the child can make the connection between letter names and sounds without any knowledge of how to do this. The child has been asked to ponder something that does not exist—the "short sound" of a vowel letter name.

We need much better descriptors for the different types of phonics. The NRP reading group has made one attempt, but they do not operationalize their classification in terms of exactly what is taught and how it is taught. In the introduction to the NRP report on phonics instruction, *phonics* is defined as a means of teaching the alphabetic system by explicit and systematic instruction in letter-sound correspondences and spelling patterns. The report goes on to specify variations among phonics programs that fit this general category, as follows:

Synthetic phonics programs teach children to convert letters into sounds or phonemes and then blend the sounds to form recognizable words. *Analytic phonics* avoids having children pronounce sounds in isolation to figure out words. Rather children are taught to analyze letter-sound relations once the word is identified. *Phonics-through-spelling* programs teach children to transform sounds into letters to write words. *Phonics-in-context* approaches teach children to use sound-letter correspondences along with context cues to identify unfamiliar words they encounter in text. *Analogy phonics* programs teach children to use parts of written words they already know to identify new words. (National Reading Panel, 2000, 2-89)

This classification is unsatisfactory because it does not identify the critical difference in logic between programs that teach the code backward from print to sound, and those that teach it forward from sound to print (linguistic phonics). They describe "phonics-through-spelling" as a sound-to-print method, but this appears to refer to a strategy for teaching spelling, not a method for teaching both decoding and spelling. There is also the problem that the United Kingdom, in particular, and some other English-speaking countries, use *phonics* (specifically *synthetic phonics*) to refer to reading instruction based on a "basic code." This kind of phonics is anchored in the 40 phonemes and their major spellings. This is not what Americans mean by *phonics* or by *synthetic*, as can be seen above.

To avoid this kind of confusion, I have set out a new classification system:

JUNK PHONICS   The practice of teaching aspects or elements of the alphabet code in a chaotic, nonsensical, and unstructured fashion. Most basal phonics comes under this heading.

VISUAL PHONICS   The short version (a) teaches the 26 "sounds" of the 26 letters of the alphabet. The long version (b) teaches 40 to 256+ "sounds" of the letters, digraphs, and phonograms.

WHOLE-TO-PART PHONICS   (also known as *embedded, analytic, intrinsic*). The practice of easing children into phonemes by starting with whole words, then word parts (word families, blends), then individual phonemes, either overtly or covertly (embedded). This is tantamount to teaching three different writing systems one after the other, each canceling out the one before.

(Whole-to-part phonics is not the same as an eclectic reading program, which contains elements from any of the above, plus sight-word memorizing, plus whole language.)

MULTISOUND PHONICS   Same as above, but the different-size sound units are mixed up and taught in a random fashion.

LINGUISTIC PHONICS   (Not to be confused with "linguistic programs" circa 1960s.)
a. *Incomplete*. (Called *synthetic* in the United Kingdom.) Teaches from the sound to the letter. Teaches the 40+ phonemes of English and their main spellings (basic code), plus some spelling alternatives.
b. *Complete*. Includes (a) above plus 136 spelling alternatives.

THE PROTOTYPE   Fits (b) above, plus the other components of the prototype listed earlier. There are no programs that fit all the elements of the prototype in the NRP database, though some come close.

Programs Predicted to Shine
The programs outlined in this section are those most representative of the prototype.

Lippincott and i.t.a. The Bond and Dykstra 1967 study included two reading programs close to the prototype: the initial teaching alphabet (i.t.a.) and the Lippincott program. (See chapter 4 for descriptions of these programs.) Bond and Dykstra's study was not included in the NRP database because of their 1970 cut-off date. I am adding it here, because the effect sizes represent over 3,000 children, providing the most accurate estimate of the power of these programs. I computed the effect sizes for i.t.a. and Lippincott on the Stanford Reading Test subtests. ("Word study" is a measure of phonics knowledge.) The comparison groups were the basal-reader classrooms (see chapter 4).

Table 5.2 contrasts the effectiveness of these two programs. The Lippincott program has much higher effect sizes than the i.t.a. program and is superior to the basal programs in all respects (ES = 1.12 for reading, .61 for spelling, .62 for phonics knowledge, and .57 for reading comprehension). Perhaps having to learn, then unlearn, a special script (i.t.a.) wastes time and/or causes confusion. More recent studies on Lippincott that are in the NRP data pool are shown in table 5.2. Effect sizes are smaller but generally confirm the Bond and Dykstra results, which are far and away the most accurate reflection of the strength of this program.

Lindamood: Auditory Discrimination in Depth Another program that partially fits the prototype (basic code, sound-to-print orientation) is the Lindamood program. This program was originally designed to remediate poor readers. Like Dale's program, it focuses on how speech sounds are produced and includes a number of exercises for classifying and analyzing phonemes. Lessons were designed around various materials, such as pictures of mouth postures, letters and digraphs printed on cards, felts, and tiles, plus colored blocks and special charts. There is no writing component in this program. A movable alphabet is used instead. The program adheres largely to a one-to-one correspondence between phonemes and their basic-code spellings. A major departure is that word work tends to be confined to nonsense words. Some alternative spellings are taught (about

Table 5.2
Initial teaching alphabet, Lippincott program, effect sizes

	Word recognition	Phonics knowledge	Decoding	Spelling	Comprehension
Bond and Dykstra 1967 (all comparisons to basal readers)					
i.t.a. $N = 2,100$					
Grade 1	.49	.31		.11	.03
Lippincott $N = 1,000$					
Grade 1	1.12	.62		.61	.57
Lippincott (comparisons to whole language or basal)					
Brown and Felton 1990 $N = 48$					
Grade 1	.02		.94	.51	
Grade 2	.52		.68	.38	
Fulwiler and Groff 1980 $N = 147$					
Grade 1	.81	1.65			.76
Silberberg, Iversen, and Goins 1973 $N = 69$					
Grade 3	.70				.36

Tests: Stanford Achievement Test, Woodcock Reading Mastery, Canadian TBS, TWS Spelling, DST Decoding.

16) but no common sight words are included. Spelling activities are indirect in the sense that children build and alter nonsense words using letter tiles. The program takes, on average, 80 hours for poor readers to reach normal reading levels.

Because of the population for which it was written, the Lindamood program requires some modification and flexibility to teach beginning readers. The exercises on phoneme analysis need pruning, and lessons on the 40+ phonemes and their basic-code spelling need to be speeded up. With these modifications, the program can be highly effective in the classroom when taught in small groups. This was shown in the work of Howard (1982, 1986) and in an unpublished study by Lindamood (1991)—studies that did not appear in the NRP study pool.

Two studies using Lindamood were in the NRP database. These are McGuinness, McGuinness, and Donohue 1995, a study on normal first graders, and Torgesen et al. 1999, a study on at-risk kindergartners. In the study I and my colleagues carried out, two classrooms were taught the Lindamood program in small groups of five to eight children. The control classroom was also taught in small groups for the same amount of time, but received a combination of whole-language instruction, invented spelling, and a sprinkling of phonics. The training took 40 minutes a day for one school year, about 100 hours per group, roughly 15 to 20 hours per child.

In the Torgesen et al. study, children were tutored individually for 80 minutes a week starting in the middle of kindergarten and continuing to the end of second grade (if necessary), for an average of 88 hours. There were three control groups, two of which were also tutored. One was taught an embedded-phonics program designed by a local teacher, which included sight-word memorization, letter-sound training, and reading text. The second group was tutored on whatever was being taught in the classroom, and the third control group had no tutoring. The results of the two studies are shown in table 5.3. Results from the McGuinness, McGuinness, and Donohue 1995 study include both my own analysis and that of the NRP. I computed the effect sizes for the standardized tests only from the Torgesen et al. study. I omitted the kindergarten data due to large floor effects (too many zero scores). Because the Lindamood training relies on nonsense words almost exclusively, test scores on "word attack" (nonword decoding) always exceed "word-recognition" scores.

The two sets of results are difficult to compare, given the different formats. In one school year, the normal children taught in groups by a single classroom teacher made at least the same gains as the at-risk children with 2.5 years of individual tutoring plus their regular classroom program. One would expect individually tutored children to do much better, and in a shorter space of time. There are several possible reasons why they did not:

Table 5.3
Lindamood effect sizes

	Word ID	Word attack	Spelling	Comprehension
McGuinness, McGuinness, and Donohue 1995 $N = 42$				
Grade 1	.30	1.66		
Torgesen et al. 1999 $N = 180$				
K to grade 1	.32	.71		.25
Grade 2	.48	.89	.43	.53
$N = 138$				

Tests: Woodcock Reading Mastery (reading, comprehension), WRAT (spelling).

1. There was a clash of methods in the tutoring study, with children getting one method during tutoring and a different method (unknown) in the classroom.

2. The Lindamood program is not easy to teach. In our study, I and my colleagues used highly experienced classroom teachers who were trained for one full week prior to the study, plus refresher workshops. In the Torgesen study, 9 lead tutors received 18 hours of training initially, plus extra bimonthly sessions. However, the "instructor aides" who appear to have done the bulk of the tutoring received only 2.5 hours at the outset, followed by 2.5 hours per month after this. The Lindamood clinic recommends 2 weeks of training before teaching this program.

Training is important with this method, because the speed through the program is based on the child's input moment by moment. Unless the tutor/teacher knows how to present an activity properly, help children correct errors quickly and effectively, and judge when an activity has become counterproductive, they can get stuck reteaching the same exercise over and over again. A typical example is phoneme-manipulation training using colored blocks. The child is asked to alter a row of colored blocks to match a sequence or chain of nonsense words: "If that is *ip*, show me *pip*." (If /i/ is "blue" and /p/ is "red," the child must add another red block on the left.) This task has a high cognitive load, and is significantly correlated with age, vocabulary, auditory and visual short-term memory, and oral comprehension, with all values exceeding $r = .40$ (McGuinness, McGuinness, and Donohue 1995).

3. The third explanation is related to the second. If children are young, developmentally delayed, or have low verbal IQs (all of which was true in the tutoring study), the program will be harder to teach, and tutors need to be even more skilled. In our small-group study, the children were older, came from upper-middle-class families, had high verbal ability, and had the guidance of well-trained and highly experienced teachers. These children had few problems with any of the lessons.

Nevertheless, we know from Lindamood's own study in the Santa Maria school district that with proper teaching, even sons and daughters of migrant farmworkers can be taught effectively. In this study, first graders were taught by the classroom teacher trained in the method plus an experienced tutor from the Lindamood clinic who was in the classroom each day. At the end of first grade, average reading scores were three years above age norms. No child did worse than one year above national norms. These children have been tracked for several years by the local school district and continue to score well above norms. Because this study was never published, we have no knowledge of how or whether the lessons were modified to suit these children. The format in the study by McGuinness and associates was similar to the one in Santa Maria, minus the expert aide. Our results were far more modest, and the obvious conclusion is that teaching expertise is critical to the effectiveness of this program.

Open Court There is only one study in the NRP database on the Open Court program. This is unfortunate, because this program has received a good deal of national attention, and because it is a good fit to the prototype, at least according to the description provided by Foorman et al. (1997, 67):

Components of the first grade program include: 1) Phonemic awareness activities during the first 30 lessons (10–15 minutes daily); 2) Forty-two sound/spellings are introduced in the first 100 lessons, one per day in lessons 11–30, and at a slower pace thereafter; phonics principles are reinforced through sound/spelling cards, alliterative stories, and practice stories whose vocabulary is tightly controlled for the sound/spelling just taught; 3) Blending is regarded as the key strategy for applying the alphabetic principle, and, therefore, 8–10 new words are blended daily; 4) Dictation activities move from letter cards to writing words sound by sound, to whole words (by lesson 17), to whole sentences (by lesson 27); 5) Shared reading of Big Books; 6) Text anthologies (with uncontrolled vocabulary), plus workbooks are introduced in the middle of first grade, when all sound/spellings have been introduced; and 7) Writing workshop activities are available in individual and small group formats.

There are some peculiarities in this program, such as the extensive use of color-coded text (both background and print) to mark consonants and three types of vowel spellings. There is little empirical support for the use of color-coded text, and there is a risk that children will come to rely on the colors to the exclusion of noticing the specific print features. Transferring to normal text may cause difficulties. The program includes some aspects of whole language, which can muddy the waters.

The second-grade program starts with a review of the sound-to-letter correspondences, includes more blending exercises, and adds two new anthologies. There is no mention of how spelling is taught after the basic code has been mastered.

The study by Foorman et al. (1997, 1998) was ambitious, involving 375 children (1997), reduced to 285 (1998), who received tutoring through Title 1 in addition to a classroom program. There were three control programs: whole language with no special teacher training, whole language with teacher training, and an embedded-phonics program with teacher training. Open Court teachers (and tutors) were taught by Open Court trainers. The embedded-phonics program was developed locally, and was a visually driven method based on letter patterns and featuring an "onset-rime-analogy" type of instruction.

These children were scattered among 70 classrooms in all (70 teachers). The three methods were taught to the whole class, but *only the tutored children participated in the study*, about 3 to 8 children per classroom. Classroom time for literacy activities was 90 minutes daily, and tutoring was provided for 30 minutes per day. Whether these periods overlapped is unknown. This was a complex study design in which the tutorial method sometimes matched the classroom program and sometimes did not. To complicate matters further, the tutors had been trained the previous year

Table 5.4

Open court

	Reading	Spelling	Compre-hension
Foorman et al. 1998 $N = 285$			
Grades 1 and 2 combined scores			
OC vs. embedded phonics	.58	.36	.37
OC vs. whole language (trained teachers)	.48	.38	.31

Test: Wide Range Achievement.

Note: The NRP had access to data not in the published report and broke out ES values by grade. However, their values—first-grade reading ES = 1.63 and spelling ES = .56, as well as second-grade reading ES = .32 and spelling ES = −.19 —do not tally with the published data. The NRP values are too large.

in Reading Recovery (a whole-language-type intervention program for children who fall behind), and had to be retrained in one of the two new methods. Half of the tutors had to deliver two different tutorial methods.

The results from the complete study, which lasted from early grade 1 to the end of grade 2, are in Foorman et al. 1998. I have computed the ES values from the results presented in that article, which combines first- and second-grade test scores. I also provide the ES values from the NRP report (see table 5.4). The NRP appears to have had access to data not available to the public, and broke out the first- and second-grade scores. However, these values do not tally with the published data (the ES values are too large).

This study did not provide a fair assessment of the Open Court program, and better research is called for. So far, there is no published study on Open Court *in the classroom*. The research design was overly complex and there were other methodological problems. The authors stated that the matched versus mismatched tutorials had "no effect," and for that reason "tutoring was ignored in subsequent analysis." It is hard to understand why extra one-on-one help for 2.5 hours per week for one school year had no effect, especially when the lessons matched what was ongoing in the classroom.

Jolly Phonics   Jolly Phonics was developed by Sue Lloyd (1992), a classroom teacher in England who devoted many years to perfecting this program. It takes its name from the publisher, Chris Jolly. Jolly Phonics meets nearly all the requirements of the prototype, and goes beyond it in some respects. Jolly Phonics is the product of what can happen when popular myths of how to teach reading are challenged.

First to go was the myth that reading is hard to teach. Second to go was the notion that a linguistic-phonics program cannot be taught to the whole class at the same time. Third to go was the age barrier. Jolly Phonics is taught to 4-year-olds. Fourth to go was the belief that young children cannot pay attention for more than about 10–15 minutes at a time. Fifth to go was the related belief that if young children are kept at a task for longer than about 15 minutes, they become bored and frustrated and are unable to learn. Sixth to go was the idea that teachers need extensive training to teach the alphabet code properly.

Lloyd's initial goal was to reduce the lessons to the essential elements and present them at an optimum rate, as quickly and as in depth as possible. Undoubtedly, her greatest insight was in figuring out what these elements are. Certainly nothing in teacher training provides any useful information on this issue. The next questions were how these elements should be taught and how early and quickly they could be taught, given the appropriate sequence and format. She discovered that young children forget what they have learned when lessons are spaced too far apart. This necessitates constant reteaching and review, wasting an extraordinary amount of time.

Lloyd discovered that a comprehensive reading program can be taught to young children in a whole-class format if three conditions are met. First, the lessons should be fun and stimulating and engage all the children. Second, sufficient backup materials for individual work have to be available to support what is taught in the lessons. Third, parents need to be involved enough to understand the program and know how to support their child at home. When lessons are enjoyable and when children see that they and their classmates are actually learning to read, they have no trouble paying attention for up to an hour.

Lloyd found clever and ingenious ways to engage the whole class and keep them interested. She invented simple action patterns to accompany learning each phoneme. Children say each phoneme aloud accompanied by the appropriate action. An undulating hand movement accompanies the sound /s/, a finger to the lips represents the sound /sh/, and so forth. Apart from being fun for the children, the action patterns fulfill a number of functions. They help anchor the speech sounds in memory. Because the actions are visible to everyone, including the teacher, they ensure that all the children are engaged (no daydreamers allowed). In this sense, they function as gentle peer support for everyone to get on board and learn quickly. A similar group activity is used when writing training begins. However, it is possible that these actions are not essential, and research is needed to sort this out.

Jolly Phonics proceeds rapidly. Children learn one phoneme per day, along with the accompanying action and letter symbol. They get handwriting training almost from the beginning, and are soon able to write the basic-code spellings for the phonemes taught so far. The basic code is taught in 9 to 10 weeks, taking about 50–60 hours of direct instruction. After this, children move on to simple phonics books, are given spelling dictation for words and sentences, and begin to learn spelling alternatives (22 spelling alternatives are taught). Little teacher training is necessary. There is a simple handbook with brief, clear instructions, and an excellent video.

One study using the JP program (Stuart 1999) was included in the NRP database, but there are several other studies in the literature from the United Kingdom and Canada. Some were ongoing when the NRP completed its search. I have calculated the effect sizes for these studies (unless provided by the authors). Table 5.5 sets out the average scores on standardized tests to illustrate the extraordinary gains. Table 5.6 provides the effect sizes for each study.

None of these studies were exactly alike. The study truest to Lloyd's intentions was the study by Johnston and Watson (1997), which was carried out at Lloyd's school. The children were matched on a wide range of skills (IQ, phoneme awareness, and so on) with a control group in Scotland that was learning the traditional Scottish method, known as *analytic phonics* (similar to whole-to-part phonics). Children also learn to identify phonemes in initial, final, then middle position, but these are taught in isolation over an extended period of time.

Johnston and Watson's second study (2003) used a variant of the JP program designed by Watson, called: *Fast Phonics First* (FPF). The study

Table 5.5
Jolly Phonics standardized tests in age-equivalent or standard scores

	N	Initial age	Training	Read-ing	Spelling	Compre-hension
Johnston and Watson 1997			10 weeks 50 hours			
JP	25	4:8	age at test	5:9		
AP	29	4:9	5:1	5:0		
JP			age at test	6:7		
AP			5:4	5:3		
JP			age at test			8:3
AP			7:6			7:5
Johnston and Watson 2003			16 weeks 26 hours			
JP/FPF	117	5:0	age at test	6:0	6:0	
AP only	109	5:0	5:4	5:4	5:2	
AP + Phon	78	5:0		5:4	5:3	
JP/FPF			age at test	7:7	7:8	7:3
AP + Phon + FPF			6:7	7:5	7:5	7:0
Stuart 1999			12 weeks 60 hours			
JP	55	5:0	age at test	7:1	6:8	
WL	57	5:0	6:6	6:3	5:8	
Sumbler 1999			20 weeks 33 hours	Word ID	Word attack	Spelling
JP	145	6:0	age at test	107	100	104
Eclectic	120	6:0	6:5	101	86	98

JP = Jolly Phonics, FPF = Fast Phonics First, AP = Analytic Phonics, Phon = phoneme awareness, WL = whole language.

included all beginning readers (337) from Clackmannanshire, the smallest county in Scotland (nicknamed "Wee County"). Children from the towns with the most free lunches and clothing allowances were in the FPF classrooms. The more affluent children constituted the control groups. There were several modifications to Lloyd's format. The action patterns were dropped. Phonemes were introduced in the same order as in JP, but at a slightly slower rate (just under one per day). The lesson periods were shortened and spaced out over 16 weeks, totaling about 26 hours overall. Magnetic letters were used to teach blending and spelling simple words from the beginning. Otherwise, the content and sequence were the same, with the exception that no consonant blends or spelling alternatives were taught.

There were two control groups. Both received the standard analytic-phonics fare, but were taught the same phonemes in the same sequence as the FPF children. The children spent the same amount of time on the lessons, but only 16 sound-letter correspondences could be taught in this time frame. One of the control groups split the time with a phonological-training component (no letters). This involved onset rime and phoneme segmenting and blending. As can be seen in table 5.6, the phonological training added something above analytic phonics alone. The effect sizes for FPF versus AP + Phon are smaller than for FPF versus AP only. Effect sizes were large across the board in favor of the FPF program, close to 1.0 for reading and over 1.0 for spelling.

Stuart's famous "docklands' study" (Stuart 1999) was carried out in London's east end, in the impoverished docklands area. Children had little spoken English, and 53 percent knew no English words whatsoever. The JP program followed Lloyd's format closely, and children had about 60 hours of instruction. Despite the fact that these children had such impoverished English-language skills, the results are remarkably like those of Johnston and Watson's in almost every respect. Furthermore, they held up well over time.

In Sumbler's observational study discussed earlier, half the children were taught with JP. The duration of the lessons was considerably shortened, and they were extended over the entire school year. The results provide scientific support for Lloyd's assertion that learning should be fast and intense for maximum effect. The problem was not in the study design, but in the reluctance of the kindergarten teachers to teach at this pace.

Table 5.6
Jolly Phonics effect sizes

	Phoneme segmentation	BAS reading	Young reading	Nonword decoding	Spelling	Comprehension
Johnston and Watson 1997 $N = 53$						
JP vs. analytic phonics						
Immediate (5:1)	1.46	1.52	.90			
1st posttest (5:4)	.73	3.27	1.0			
JP group 2 (7:6)						1.1
Johnston and Watson 2003 $N = 304$						
FPF vs. analytic phonics (5:4)		.91			1.45	
FPF vs. AP+PA (5:4)		.85			1.17	
Stuart 1999 $N = 112$						
JP vs. WL						
1st posttest (5:6)	1.80	1.18	.63	1.49	1.39	
2nd posttest (6:6)	1.13	.71	.62	.74	.86	.37

Sumbler 1999 N = 265	Phoneme segmenting	Word ID / All reading	Word attack / Nonword decoding	Spelling	Comprehension
JP vs. eclectic (6:5)		.52	.68	.44	
GRAND MEANS	1.65	.84	.89	1.22	.73

UK tests: Yopp-Singer segmenting; British Ability Scales: reading, spelling; Young Reading; Primary Reading Test; Neale Comprehension; Schonell Spelling; Willows Spelling.
Canadian tests: Woodcock Reading Mastery.

They did not believe that young children could learn a phoneme and letter per day, or endure hour-long sessions. There was a compromise. Lessons were reduced to 20 minutes or less, and total recommended hours were nearly cut in half. As noted in the discussion of the observational study, the JP program was taught along with a mix of other language activities, reducing time still further. We can see the impact of the slower delivery of the program, plus the lack of focus, in the lower effect sizes (table 5.6). Sumbler commented that after working with the program, some teachers realized that children could learn this material much more quickly and had begun speeding up the training.

There were three follow-on studies among this group. Johnston and Watson (1997) followed the children for an additional year, to 7.5 years old. JP children maintained their gains and were about one year ahead of the control group and national norms. Furthermore, one-third of the control children scored more than one standard deviation below the mean, but only 9 percent of the JP children scored this low. Stuart's one-year follow-up produced much the same results.

Johnston and Watson (2003) followed up the "Wee County" children for an additional year. However, because of the initial success of the program, school officials insisted that the entire county be switched to FPF, and group differences were eliminated by the end of the next year. Now all the children in the Wee County scored one year above national norms. Further follow-on studies (see Johnston and Watson 2003) showed that the advantage for all the children increased over time to two years above national norms by age 9.5 on reading (decoding), and one year ahead in spelling. Reading comprehension was only marginally above norms (see table 5.7).

None of the prototype programs include anything other than the most rudimentary attempt to teach the advanced spelling code. Yet spelling scores were surprisingly high, certainly much higher than the national norms. Because norms are based on the current status quo, this tells us what a parlous state spelling instruction is in. Merely teaching the basic code the right way around, getting the logic straight, and adding a dozen or so of the 136 remaining spelling alternatives makes an enormous difference.

Several of the studies in this group measured phoneme awareness in addition to the reading and spelling tests. Table 5.6 shows the enormous

Table 5.7

Fast Phonics First: Clackmannanshire follow-on results. Johnston and Watson (2003)

Age		Age-equivalent scores in years:months	Years:months Above national norms
7:9	Reading	9:4	1:7
	Spelling	8:6	:9
	Comprehension	8:0	:3
8:9	Reading	10:6	1:9
	Spelling	9:6	:9
	Comprehension	9:2	:5
9:7	Reading	11:9	2:2
	Spelling	10:9	1:2
	Comprehension	10:0	:3

U.K. tests were: British Ability Scales (reading); Schonell Spelling Test, Primary Reading Test (comprehension).
Source: Scottish Executive Education Department. Internet publication: *Insight* www.scotland.gov.uk/sight/

impact of the JP/FPF programs on phoneme-awareness scores. Johnston and Watson used the Yopp-Singer segmenting test, a reliable test that is highly correlated with decoding skills. This raises the question of whether special (additional) phonological-awareness training programs are really necessary—the topic of the next chapter.

What is most remarkable about the Jolly Phonics research is the consistency of the results. This is in striking contrast to most of the studies in the NRP database. The grand means are provided in the final row of table 5.6, and these values act as a benchmark for what can be achieved in whole-class beginning reading instruction.

Potpourri

Before we leave the assessment of reading methods, I want to report on some of the other programs that made it into the NRP database. A brief synopsis of these studies provides a startling glimpse of the confusion and variability that abound in research on reading methods, and in the use of the term *phonics*.

A major source of this confusion is the lack of specificity of program content. As a general rule, reading researchers with a background in experimental psychology ignore what is being taught in the classroom. They craft clever training programs and carefully match all the groups in the study on important variables, like age, IQ, and so forth. The experimental groups then get special training (described in great detail) while the control group participates in the "usual classroom program," whatever this might be. The actual program content is presumed to have so little impact (positive or negative) on the outcome of the study that the program itself is not even identified. But the classroom program could be complementary or contradictory to one or more of the experimental treatments. We saw this problem in Torgesen's study above, where children were individually tutored in a highly structured linguistic-phonics program, while they participated for at least 5 hours a week in some unidentified "classroom program," probably whole language.

Researchers with a background in education take more care to provide information on the classroom programs, but these descriptions are often vague and misleading. As noted earlier, descriptions of "basal phonics" make so little sense that they strain the imagination.

More Phonics   A new phonics program designed by Blachman et al. (1999) was included in the NRP's database for reading instruction. This program was an extension of a kindergarten phoneme-awareness training program designed by Ball and Blachman (1991). The study design (kindergarten through grade 2) does not allow for an independent assessment of the two programs. For this reason, the Blachman program will be considered in the following chapter on phoneme-awareness training.

Two published programs were tested in citywide or countywide studies using large numbers of students. The first was a reading program designed by Beck, called the *New Primary Grades Reading System* (NRS) (Leinhardt and Engel 1981). It was tested over a two-year period on first and second graders. It was described as "an eclectic code-breaking approach as opposed to a whole word approach," with explicit instruction in letter-sound correspondences along with extensive blending practice. After initial learning (levels 1 and 2) children read books and listened to audiotapes. The content of these tapes was not described. The contrast programs were basals, either Scott-Foresman, Harper and Row, or Houghton-Mifflin.

At the end of the school year, the first-grade children were tested on the Stanford Achievement Tests (SAT) reading total, and the second-grade children on the California Test of Basic Skills (CTBS) reading total. The NRS program worked well in first grade but did not hold up in second grade. The ES values for the SAT for three large first-grade studies were .76, .67, and .44. The ES values for the second-grade children were essentially zero, reasons unknown. Unfortunately, there was a major confound in this study. NRS teachers assigned about 100 more minutes of reading instruction per week than the basal-reader teachers, which essentially invalidates this study.

Bond et al. (1995–1996) looked at the impact of a published program called *Sing, Spell, Read, and Write* (SSRW). This was a partial test of the method, because the district agreed to allow only 20 lessons. A feature of the program is singing, as the title suggests. There are several audiotapes of songs about "phonics generalizations" (term unexplained). Otherwise, this is visual phonics, strongly letter driven. Early lessons involve memorizing the "sound" of each letter of the alphabet. "Phonetic Storybooks" are introduced after a few letter sounds are learned. Spelling and writing activities are included in the program. The program was tested on three age groups: kindergarten, first grade, and second grade, using nearly 900 children. Effect sizes for the Woodcock letter-word identification test were low across the three grades (.39, .24, .44), but much higher for "word attack" (first grade .60, second grade .56). Most kindergartners scored zero on this test. There was no special advantage of the SSRW program for oral reading (first grade .02, second grade .33).

Whole Language   There were three studies specifically oriented to whole language. Klesius, Griffith, and Zielonka (1991) compared whole language to a "traditional basal" program that emphasized "explicit phonics." The experimental question was whether first graders in a whole-language environment, who were "submerged in print" and doing a "range of reading and writing activities," could learn the alphabet principle "implicitly" without direct instruction. (This is the general claim of whole-language advocates.) There were 112 children from 6 classrooms in the study.

Teachers received additional training and continuing help from the researchers. The whole-language activities were typical and involved listening to the teacher read children's books, poems, and rhymes, while the children read along. The children did a lot of writing, far more than the children in the basal classroom. However, they had little, if any, formal spelling instruction.

The basal program was not well described, other than that it included "isolated skill instruction," including "letter-sound correspondences," plus directed reading from basal readers. There were weekly spelling tests. The amount of writing varied extensively from one classroom to the next. Children also worked independently on phonics workbooks, doing exercises like circling words or objects that started with the same sound.

The basal-phonics program produced generally higher scores on a battery of reading, spelling, and writing tests. Effect sizes were low for comprehension (.10), marginal for word recognition, spelling, and writing (range .30 to .34), moderate for phoneme awareness (.56), and large for nonword decoding (.71). This, of course, does not mean that this "traditional basal" program is a good program, only that whole language was worse. (The NRP ES values were highly discrepant from the values shown above.)

In a second study on the same two reading methods by the same team (Griffith, Klesius, and Kromrey 1992), children were selected on the basis of extreme scores (high, low) on a phoneme-awareness test. The goal was to find out whether children with high phoneme awareness did better overall, and whether the type of reading program was influenced by phoneme-awareness skills. Unfortunately, when children are sorted into extreme groups, other factors come into play. IQ is a major factor on some phoneme-awareness tests, and this was not controlled. Nor was home environment. The children with high phoneme-awareness skills may have been taught to read at home. In any case, children with high phoneme awareness did better in both types of classrooms. For the most part, the type of reading instruction made no difference (results were not significant). This study had too many uncontrolled variables to be valid. Also, several reading test scores were at ceiling for the high-phoneme-awareness children. (The NRP reported very large effect sizes in favor of the basal-reader group, which is clearly incorrect and misrepresents what happened in this study.)

The final study (Eldredge 1991) was an attempt to improve whole language by adding a phonics component for 15 minutes each day. Three classrooms of "modified whole language" were compared to three classrooms using basal-reader programs. Children were all "low achievers" in first grade. From the description of the phonics supplement, this was partly visual phonics ("20 vowel-team graphemes"), plus a variety of phoneme-analysis activities: identifying sounds in initial, middle, and final positions in a word, lessons in segmenting and blending, and so on. Children learned spelling patterns for certain syllable types. The basal program (Houghton-Mifflin) also appeared to be whole language oriented. Most of the activities were devoted to reading, vocabulary training, and sentence building. Some letter-sound relationships were taught, but no segmenting or blending.

Results showed a consistent superiority of whole language plus phonics over the basal programs. The effect sizes were .44 for phonics knowledge, .55 for word recognition, .73 for reading total, and .83 for comprehension (the last three tests from the Gates-MacGinitie battery). This is the only study to show a substantially higher effect size for comprehension than for basic tests of word recognition and word attack. However, this study was comparing apples and oranges, and the evidence is not convincing that whole language plus phonics causes the advantage, or simply phonics alone.

Conclusions

How valid and reliable is a meta-analysis for research of this complexity where nearly every study uses a different method, involves different types and ages of children, employs different research designs, and utilizes different measures of reading and spelling competence? I should point out that nearly all reading and spelling measures in these studies were properly constructed, normed, standardized tests. This does at least ensure that the effect sizes (when computed accurately) are statistically valid and reliably represent group differences on these measures. This is a bonus, because standardized tests are very much the exception in the phoneme-awareness training studies reviewed in the next chapter. Nevertheless, effect sizes will vary for other reasons, such as study design and extraneous factors.

I have taken special care to analyze each study separately in detail and to compute effect sizes myself (many times). This revealed that the computations in the NRP report were not always accurate. Sometimes this was due to misunderstanding the study design. For example, one study in the database (Martinussen and Kirby 1998) had nothing to do with comparing reading methods. Instead, it focused on whether teaching different *strategies* for learning the *same* reading program made any difference. Results were not significant for reading, and there were huge floor effects on the Woodcock reading tests with standard deviations three times higher than the means. Yet effect sizes were computed anyway.

Besides noting anomalies like this, I was concerned about the fact that my values sometimes deviated significantly from those in the NRP's tables, especially since we were using the identical formula. In part, this was because I was more interested in individual test scores, whereas the NRP was more likely to collate the data from several tests. However, in other cases, there were gross computational errors. For example, Griffith, Klesius, and Kromrey (1992) (see previous section) reported no significant differences between two contrasting reading methods on every reading and spelling test except one. "No significant differences" translates into low or zero effect sizes, which is what I found. The NRP, however, reported large effect sizes in every case (some higher than 1.0) in favor of whole language. Errors like these bias the general meta-analysis results (in this case away from phonics and toward whole language).

In view of the nature of meta-analysis as a statistical tool, and the problems outlined above, the overall summary of the panel was disappointing. They relied exclusively on the summary tables and argued from global effects to conclusions. There were sweeping generalizations like the following: "Phonics instruction failed to exert a significant impact on the reading performance of low-achieving readers in second through sixth grades" (National Reading Panel, 2000, 2-133). This is a dangerous statement. It implies that *no* phonics instruction works for poor readers or that *none* of the programs in the NRP database was effective for this population, neither of which is true. The statement also gives the false impression that all remedial-phonics programs found their way into their data pool, when this was far from the case. In fact, the most successful remedial-reading programs today were missing (see D. McGuinness 1997c; C. McGuinness, D. McGuinness, and G. McGuinness 1996).

As for beginning reading instruction, the panel concluded that the meta-analysis value (MS = .44), the one we started with at the beginning of this section, "provided solid support for systematic phonics" (p. 2-132), when this value is marginal and was the outcome of a composite of every program comparison.

In a question-and-answer section (on pages 2-132 to 2-136), they asked the question "Are some types of phonics instruction more effective than others?" They answered it by loosely grouping the studies (66 cases) into three types. They found no statistical differences between the effectiveness of these types and concluded that the type of phonics program did not matter. Once more, this statement is misleading. As we have seen, the type of phonics program matters enormously. The real issue here is how you classify them.

The term *synthetic phonics* is particularly troublesome. It was defined as "teaching students to convert letters (graphemes) into sounds (phonemes) and then to blend the sounds to form recognizable words." This definition suggests synthetic phonics is synonymous with what I call *visual phonics*. The panel does not seem to recognize the distinction between visual phonics (letter driven) and linguistic phonics (phoneme driven), which is clear from the way the summary tables are coded. Visual-phonics programs and linguistic-phonics programs were both coded as "synthetic phonics."

The problems created by (visual-phonics) logic appear in the question-and-answer section. The panel asked this question: "How many letter-sound relations should be taught and how many different ways of using these relations to read and write words should be practiced?" Later, they posed the same question again and answered it: "It is clear that the major letter-sound correspondences, including short and long vowels and digraphs, need to be taught."

But what is clear? And what is "major"?

In linguistic-phonics logic, neither the question above, nor the answer, makes sense. Children need to be taught the 40 sounds in the English language and their most common (probable) spelling. Everything follows from this. The real question is: When and in what order should the remaining 136 spelling alternatives be taught?

When the NRP addressed guidelines for future research, many questions the panel raised were already answered by studies in their data pool, or by the research literature reviewed in this chapter. These were questions like the following: "How many months or years should a phonics program continue?" (It takes one semester to teach the basic code.) "What are the active ingredients of effective systematic phonics programs?" (The key components include sound-to-letter logic, a basic code marking all 40 phonemes, the integration of reading and spelling, the teaching of segmenting and blending, and lots of writing.) "How does the use of decodable text as early reading material contribute to the effectiveness of phonics programs?" (Certainly, text that is too difficult to decode contributes nothing.)

As for my own conclusions, I think the news is exciting. The linguistic-phonics programs—those most like the prototype—were the clear winners, nearly all producing very large effect sizes, despite the enormous variation in subject populations (including children who had no spoken English). Moreover, these effect sizes are sustained or even increase over several years. We do know how to teach reading efficiently and effectively. What we need is more research on these good programs to pin down the details. This would include an exploration of materials, activities, sequence, and pace, plus an assessment of the value of special program features like the Jolly Phonics "actions," or the analysis of articulatory motor patterns used in the Lindamood program. Do they really help? We need to compare the various linguistic-phonics programs with one another and stop doing research comparing "phonics" to whole language and basals. We know that whole-word methods do not work. We have abundant evidence that whole language is a dismal failure, and that the majority of basal-reader programs are not far behind.

In chapter 11, I provide more information on important research questions for the twenty-first century. Meanwhile, we will look at phoneme-awareness training programs. Are they really necessary?

PHONEME–AWARENESS TRAINING

The importance of phonological- or phoneme-awareness training for mastering an alphabetic writing system has been the dominant theme in reading research for 30 years (*phonological* refers to all sound units, including words, syllables, and phonemes). The NRP located nearly 2,000 studies on phoneme awareness. There is no question that performance on certain phonological tasks correlates strongly with reading and spelling skills. What is in question is the nature of this correlation, the type of phonological skills that are important, and their precise role in reading and spelling.

According to the theory that "phonological awareness develops" over childhood, children gradually become aware of words, syllables, syllable fragments, and phonemes, in that order. Development is long and slow, with "explicit awareness" of phonemes emerging around age 6 or 7 (Liberman et al. 1974; Adams 1990). This theory has had a profound impact on the design of phonological training programs, with important consequences for when phonological awareness is taught, what is included in the lessons, and in what order.

Research on speech perception and language development, as well as the training studies themselves, do not support this theory. Awareness of phoneme contrasts (*ba-da*) is present at birth, and phoneme analysis becomes operational by about 6 months of age, when infants begin to extract words from the speech stream (spoken phrases) and build a receptive vocabulary. At the babbling stage, infants learn how spoken language is produced mechanically, and check on how they are doing through auditory feedback (Vihman 1993; also see *Language Development and Learning to Read*). That children are truly aware of individual sounds is evident from the fact that they begin to self-correct mispronounced phonemes in their speech before age 3 (Chaney 1992). (These studies are reviewed in depth in the companion book cited above.)

Two-year-olds are generally incapable of demonstrating that they know what they know, but 3-year-olds can. Chaney found that 93 percent of 3-year-olds (average age 44 months) could listen to a sequence of isolated phonemes, blend them into a word, and select this word from a set of pictures with accuracy well above chance, scoring 88 percent correct. This was the second-easiest task in a battery of 22 language tasks. The easiest task was saying a "word" ("Can you say a word for me?"), showing that young children are well aware of what a "word" is, despite another myth to the contrary. Another easy task was detecting a mispronounced phoneme in a phrase and fixing the error by saying the words in the phrase correctly.

On the other hand, children had enormous difficulty with tasks that, according to the phonological-development theory, are "developmentally early," like word play, rhyming, and alliteration. Few children could judge whether a word "sounded like" a series of spoken rhyming words, and almost no one could provide a matching rhyming word. They had even more difficulty with alliteration (matching initial sounds). These findings show two things: children's natural sensitivity is to words and phonemes, and children have difficulty making abstract judgements such as whether fragments of words "sound alike."

This is not to say that explicit awareness of phonemes is instantly on tap when children have to learn an alphabetic writing system. As perception and production of speech increase in efficiency, they begin to run on automatic pilot, operating below the level of conscious awareness, *the exact opposite of the developmental theory.* Adults are not aware of individual phonemes as they listen or speak; their attention is focused on meaning. Yet most people can detect a phonemic error and correct the speaker without a moment's hesitation, though they may be uncertain where the error occurred. The brain performs these functions for us, and we do not need to monitor them.

The only reason anyone would need to be aware of phonemes is if they had to learn an alphabetic writing system. But once the necessary skills are mastered, phonemes "go unconscious" once more. Ask a family member or friend how many sounds are in the word *straight*, and you will get a number between 4 and 8. (Try it yourself.) Because phoneme analysis occurs below the level of conscious awareness, children (or illiterate adults) must be taught to *pay attention* to the phonemic level of speech to learn an alphabetic writing system. This does not necessarily require *explicit awareness* ("awareness that"), as Cossu, Rossini, and Marshall's (1993) research on children with Down's syndrome has shown. These children were able to learn the sound-symbol correspondences of the Italian alphabet code by simple matching and repetition, and could read (decode) real and nonsense words at fairly high levels of skill. Yet they could not comprehend what they read and failed dismally on phoneme-awareness tests.

Another powerful component of the myth is that phoneme awareness is difficult to teach. This is said to be because phonemes are coarticulated and hard to tease apart, and because consonants cannot be produced in isolation from a vowel. Thus the best rendering of a segmented word like *cat* is "kuh-aa-tuh." Neither statement is true. Only five of the 40+ English phonemes are hard to produce in isolation. These are the voiced consonants: /b/, /d/, /g/, /j/, and /l/. But even they can be managed by keeping the vowel extremely brief. No other consonants need to be produced with a vowel, and certainly not /k/ and /t/.

Because the evidence shows that children have good phoneme sensitivity, and isolating phonemes in words is not nearly as difficult as researchers seem to believe, do we really need special phoneme-awareness training programs? More to the point, children *do* need to be made aware of phonemes to use an alphabetic writing system and to learn to match each phoneme to its letter symbols. But this is what a linguistic-phonics program teaches. What special benefit, then, does a phoneme-awareness training program confer?

Are Special Phoneme-Awareness Training Programs Really Necessary?
Answering this question will take up most of this chapter. To help with this comparison, let's review how a linguistic-phonics program works in practice.

Lessons begin by drawing the children's attention to a particular phoneme by producing it in isolation (/sss/), and/or having the children discover it by listening to a little story that features the sound over and over. For example, here is the opening section of a story for introducing the sound /p/ in a program I designed (McGuinness, forthcoming).

Pretty Penny is happy.
She has a pig named Poppy.

Poppy is a pet.
The best pet yet.

Most pigs are sloppy.
Not Poppy.

Poppy is perfectly pink and pale.
From the top of her head to the tip of her tail.

Notice that the sound /p/ appears in all positions in a word. After the children learn to hear this sound, and to say the sound in first, middle, and last positions, they see the letter p and are told that this letter represents the sound /p/. They practice tracing, copying, and writing each new letter until its shape is firmly embedded in memory. As they write, they say the sound the letter stands for.

Once a few sounds are introduced, they are combined to make real words (not nonsense words). This way children get to "meaning" as soon as possible and understand the value and purpose of the exercise. Real words can be written down, sound by sound, and retrieved (decoded) from print. Phonemes and their basic-code spellings are introduced as quickly as children can learn them, every lesson building on the one before, until all 40 phonemes and their spellings are mastered. Spelling alternatives follow next.

Children learn to segment and blend phonemes by seeing and writing letters. They learn that phonemes occur one after the other over time, and that letters are sequenced one after the other over space (left to right). Reading and writing (spelling) are integrated in the lessons so that children learn the code nature of our writing system.

These are the basic building blocks of a good linguistic-phonics program.

The central question is whether a phonological-training component adds anything to what I have just described. Will it enhance phoneme analysis, reading, and spelling skills beyond the programs that fit the prototype outlined in the previous chapter? To prove that it does, it would have to produce still larger effect sizes for reading, spelling, and phoneme awareness than the successful phonics programs alone, with ES values well above 1.0.

To answer this question, I will draw on the efforts of the National Reading Panel once again. Their focus was on *phoneme* awareness. To meet the selection criteria, the study had to include training in phoneme awareness. The panel unearthed 1,962 articles referenced by this term, and they were screened by these criteria:

- Had an experimental or quasi-experimental design with a control group.
- Appeared in a refereed journal.
- Tested the hypothesis that phoneme-awareness training improves reading beyond some alternative form of training or no training.
- Phoneme-awareness training was not confounded with other types of training.
- Statistics had to be adequate to compute effect sizes.

Only 78 studies passed this screening, and careful reading eliminated 26 more, leaving 52 studies in the NRP database. These 52 studies included a total of 96 comparisons or "cases." Using the NRP values, I prepared a simplified, summary table of the important findings (see table 6.1). Bear in mind that these studies are just as variable in their own way as the studies on phonics instruction. The table sets out the most informative comparisons. First, we see that teaching phoneme awareness improves performance on phoneme-awareness tests, compared to alternative training or no training, proving, at least, that phoneme awareness is easy to teach.

However, being "phonemically aware" has little functional utility unless there is some causal impact on learning to read and spell. A major tenet of the "phonological-awareness-develops" theory is that children should learn to read *after* they become aware of phonemes, with the added proviso that if phoneme awareness is not "developing" in a timely fashion, children need additional help. Nevertheless, the important question is whether phoneme-awareness training per se has an impact on learning to read.

The simple answer to this question is no. Here is the evidence. For the combined data (72 cases), the meta-analysis showed that phoneme-awareness training has a moderate impact on reading (ES = .53) and

Table 6.1

Phoneme-awareness training effect sizes by category based on NRP analysis

Contrast	N cases	Phoneme aware- ness	N cases	Read- ing	N cases	Spell- ing
Immediate	72	.86	90	.53	39	.59
Follow-up	14	.73	35	.45	17	.37
K only	39	.95	40	.48	15	.97
1st grade only	15	.48	25	.49	16	.52
English	61	.99	72	.63	32	.60
Foreign language	11	.65	18	.36	7	.55
Letters used	39	.89	48	.67	27	.61
No letters	33	.82	42	.38	12	.34
Teacher/trainer	64	.89	82	.55	33	.74
Computer	8	.66	8	.33	6	.09
In-house test			58	.61	24	.75
Standardized test			39	.33	20	.41
Composite* eliminating: 3rd grade or higher Foreign language Computers $N = <20$ Hours $= <3$	14	1.10	45	.74	24	1.01

*Not corrected for letters/no letters or for in-house vs. standardized tests.

spelling (ES = .59). But when the training is purely auditory (subtracting all studies where letters were used), the impact on reading and spelling is substantially reduced (ES values shrink to .38 and .34). Also, if reading is measured by a standardized test instead of an experimenter-designed test, the impact of phoneme-awareness training on reading and spelling shrinks as well (ES = .33 and .41). In-house tests inflate effect sizes, because they measure what was taught.

Another meta-analysis of phonological-awareness training studies was provided by the Dutch team of Bus and Van IJzendoorn (1999), using a smaller database (36 studies). They focused mainly on phoneme awareness, excluding training on rhyme and syllable segmenting. They reported an effect size of 1.04 for the impact of phoneme-awareness training on phoneme tests, and .44 for reading. However, follow-on studies showed the impact of phoneme-awareness training on reading was nil (ES = .16).

Bus and Van IJzendoorn commented on the enormous variability between these studies. In an attempt to reduce the "noise" in the data, they recomputed the meta-analysis using only the studies from the United States where children were randomly assigned to groups or matched. Surprisingly, the effect size for the impact of phoneme training on phoneme awareness declined (ES = .73), while it rose considerably for reading (ES = .70). Bus and IJzendoorn were overly optimistic about this result: "The training studies settle the issue of the causal role of phonological awareness in learning to read: Phonological training reliably enhances phonological and reading skills. About 500 studies with null results in the file drawers of disappointed researchers would be needed to turn the current results into nonsignificance" (p. 411).

We will see shortly that a more careful reading of these U.S. studies will turn *these* results into "nonsignificance."

The NRP's data pool reflected a similarly diverse group of studies with different types of training, different tests measuring different things, and different populations in different countries. Eleven studies were carried out in non-English-speaking countries, including Israel, which does not even have an alphabetic writing system. Some of these countries have transparent alphabets (Finland, Germany, Spain, Sweden, Norway), and some do not (Denmark). In countries with a transparent alphabet, standardized reading tests measure reading speed (fluency), not accuracy, while the reverse is true for countries with opaque alphabets. Subtracting foreign-language studies increases the connection between phoneme awareness and reading for studies in English-speaking countries (English: ES = .63; foreign: ES = .36). Eliminating the computer-training studies, which were singularly unsuccessful, had the same impact: (teachers: ES = .55; computers: ES = .32).

The NRP summary tables illustrate shifts in effect sizes when one variable at a time is subtracted. However, tables were also provided for each study, listing individual effect sizes along with information on important descriptors, like the number of children in the study, the country where it was conducted, the number of hours the training lasted, and so forth. This makes it possible to subtract studies that obscure a true picture of the findings. To this end, I recomputed the average ES value for reading and spelling (see the bottom row of table 6.1) after eliminating studies with these characteristics:

• Foreign-language studies
• Computer-training studies
• Total *N* less than 20 children
• Training lasting less than 3 hours
• Studies on older poor readers (grade 3 or higher)

The new ES values are now much larger: ES = .74 for reading and ES = 1.01 for spelling. These results are more in line with the results from the good phonics programs, and in better agreement with Bus and IJzendoorn's stripped-down meta-analysis of U.S. studies. This seems to show that phoneme-awareness training has a strong impact on reading and spelling. But does it?

Two pieces of information were missing from the NRP's tables on the individual studies. The first is whether *letters* were included in the training, and the second, which reading tests were employed. After careful reading of the remaining studies in the data pool, and recomputing many of the effect sizes, I again found that the NRPs effect sizes were not always accurate, and I will comment on any discrepancies as we go along.

NRP's effect sizes were often based on the combined scores of in-house and standardized tests. Reviewing the individual studies, I found that in-house tests lacked reliability estimates and were highly specific to what was taught. This will grossly inflate effect sizes, giving a false picture of what these training studies accomplished. By contrast, the effect sizes for reading instruction were based on standardized tests (see the previous chapter). If one wants to know the true impact of a phoneme-awareness program on *reading*, the same rigorous measures of reading and spelling must apply. To examine this problem more closely, we have to turn to the studies themselves.

In the remainder of this chapter, I will be reviewing those studies left in the data pool after the studies in the categories listed above were eliminated. I will be looking at studies that compared phoneme-awareness training with or without letters, and examine the outcomes for experimenter-designed tests versus standardized tests. I will also examine the impact of various types of training, such as programs using larger or smaller phonological units, and how, precisely, phoneme awareness is taught. To this end, I have included a few well-designed foreign-language studies that investigated neutral factors such as the impact of teaching phoneme awareness with or without letters.

A Glossary

Before we move on to the analysis of the individual studies, I want to clear up some terminology problems. There are several types of phoneme-awareness skills. Suffice it to say that there are no standardized tests of these skills, and few tests have norms. The descriptive terms for these skills vary as well. Here is a glossary of how I intend to use terms.

Discrimination. Telling phonemes apart. "Are the sounds /v/ and /v/ the same or different?"

Identification. Being able to identify (say the sound) when asked for a phoneme in a particular location in a word (first, middle, final position). "What is the first sound in *cat*?"

Sequencing. Being able to say phonemes in the order in which they appear in a word. There are three teaching methods:

• *Stretching phonemes.* mmmmmaaaaannnn for *man.*
• *Segmenting.* Isolating each phoneme in sequence: /m/ /a/ /n/.
• *Blending.* Being able to join up isolated phonemes to form the word.

Manipulation. Mentally delete, add, or reverse individual sounds in words, close up what remains, and say the word: "Say *stand* without the /t/."

There is considerable confusion about the terms *segmenting* and *blending* and how these relate to reading and spelling. Many people believe that reading involves blending, and spelling involves segmenting. According to this view, when we read, we rapidly translate letters into phonemes and *blend* them into the word. When we spell, we say the word, *segment* the sounds, translate each sound into a letter or letters, and write it down. This is not what happens.

Children see an unfamiliar word: *sting*.

To read the word, they sound out each phoneme (segmenting): /s/ /t/ /i/ /ng/. Then they blend the sounds into the word and check the outcome. It is quite common for beginning readers and poor readers to segment correctly and blend incorrectly: /s/ /t/ /i/ /ng/—*sing*.

To *spell* the word *sting* the children say the word, hear each segment in sequence, and blend the segments into the word as they write. Segmenting and blending are intimately connected in both reading and spelling. Even when reading and spelling are efficient, and it seems like processing is instantaneous, it is not. The same sound-by-sound analysis continues, only at a phenomenal speed. This is what is meant by *automaticity*. Our brains operate in the realm of milliseconds, while conscious reflection operates in the realm of seconds.

We become aware of the interplay of these two processes when we see a word we cannot read or start to write a word we cannot spell. My spelling occasionally falters when I write technical words on the board, an interesting phenomenon caused by the 90 degree rotation from the normal plane and by the wider visual angle. To solve this I have to consciously slow down, segment each sound, then deliberately blend the sounds vocally as I write.

As I review the individual studies in the next section, the litmus test for evaluating the relevance of a phoneme-awareness training program will be the evidence from the Jolly Phonics research that 4-year-old children can learn the 40 sounds of English and their basic-code spellings in about 11 weeks of whole-class teaching. At the end of the school year, these children were one year advanced on standardized reading and spelling tests compared to the control groups, *and* compared to national norms. The average effect sizes for the JP studies were 1.60 for phoneme segmenting, 1.0 for reading, and 1.42 for spelling. Follow-on data showed that an effect size of 1.0 for reading held up for 3 years, the longest time measured. To make the case for a separate phoneme-awareness training regime, it would have to produce results better than this.

An Analysis of the Studies in the Data Pool

Phonological-awareness programs differ in a number of ways, including the size and the type of phonological units taught, how much of the focus is on larger versus smaller units, how many phonemes are taught, and how long it takes to teach them. Many programs in my selected data pool teach larger units of sound as well as phonemes. What works best?

Big and Little Phonological Units

Lundberg, Frost, and Petersen (1988) designed a training program that adhered to the phonological-development theory. This Swedish team tested their program on 400 Danish kindergartners. Kindergarten begins at age 6 in Denmark. Lessons included segmenting sentences and phrases into words, segmenting syllables, and playing rhyming games, which took up 14 weeks of an 18-week program. Matching initial phonemes began in week 15, and phoneme-segmenting and phoneme-blending tasks did not appear until week 17. This program had no impact on reading measured later in time compared to the control group that got no training (play is the main activity in Danish kindergartens). The effect size for reading was ES = .19. Results were much better for spelling (ES = .60).

In an earlier correlational study on Swedish children (Lundberg, Olofsson, and Wall 1980), performance on rhyming and syllable tasks was found to be weakly correlated with tests of reading and spelling, while correlations between phoneme tasks and reading and spelling were moderate to high, with *r* ranging from .41 to .78 for reading, and from .49 to .58 for spelling. These results indicate that phoneme-analysis skills are useful in learning to read, and rhyming and syllable segmenting are not. In view of these results, it is odd that Lundberg's training program focused so extensively on skills that were found to be unrelated to reading and spelling.

A similar result was reported by Williams (1980) in a study on older poor readers (grades 2 and up). She made two attempts to design and implement a remedial-reading program with a phonological-awareness component. In the first study, a good deal of time was devoted to word and syllable exercises, and the results were not encouraging. The program was revised, the word and syllable work was dropped, the phoneme training was increased, and lessons in segmenting and blending CVC words were added. Now there was a strong impact on decoding words and non-words made up of the phonemes that were taught. Though standardized tests were not used, this study does show, at least, that word and syllable training is simply a waste of time.

One of the most famous studies in the literature, and frequently cited as proof that the phonological-development theory is correct, was carried out in the United Kingdom by Bradley and Bryant. A preliminary report appeared in the journal *Nature* (1983) and the full report appeared as a book (1985). The study was based on the premise that children are more sensitive to rhyme (vowel plus final consonant(s)) and alliteration (first sound) early in development, and this leads ultimately to phoneme awareness and to reading skill.

The study was set up in two parts. The first part measured whether early skill in rhyming and alliteration was correlated with subsequent reading test scores. The second part was a training study. The "Sound Categorization" task was designed to measure phonological awareness. In this task, the child must identify the "odd one out" among a set of words and point to one of three or four pictures. The "odd one" can be a phoneme in the initial position (first sound), as in the set *bud, bun, rug, bus*, or in the middle (*red, lid, fed, bed*), or in final position (*pin, win, fin, sit*). The middle and final sound matches are part of the rhyme (*ed* versus *id* and *in* versus *it*). The word sets were heavily biased toward rhyme, and the initial training phase strongly emphasized rhymes. Bradley and Bryant found that children had less difficulty judging middle- and final-sound contrasts (part of the rhyme) than initial sounds. This was interpreted as rhymes being more "salient" or developmentally "early" than alliteration. A simpler explanation is that it is easier to discriminate between vowel-consonant pairs (VC) than between initial consonants (C).

There were two age groups in the study. One group had just turned 5, and the other group was 5.5. The Sound Categorization task was simplified to three words per set for the younger children. In tasks where people choose among a small number of items, a certain proportion will be correct by chance. To correct for guessing, a binomial test must be carried out. This estimates how many answers need to be correct to score better than chance at $p = .05$. This estimate is based on the number of choices and the number of items on the test. After computing this value, I found that the younger children did not score above chance.

However, scoring was well above chance for the 264 older children. With age, IQ, and memory controlled, rhyme scores (middle and final sounds) did not predict performance on standardized reading and spelling tests. Alliteration (first sound) was a significant predictor, accounting for 5 to 8 percent of the variance. But there was a problem. Alliteration predicted *math* test scores even better (10 percent of the variance)! Whatever the alliteration test is measuring, it is not specific to reading. In short, nothing was found in this study. The ability to detect a contrasting phoneme (the "odd one") in initial, middle, and final position in three-sound words does not predict reading and spelling test scores.

Problems with the Sound Categorization test were reported by Schatschneider et al. (1999), who were strongly critical of tests where guessing plays a major role. In their normative study on 945 children in kindergarten through second grade, they investigated the overlap (redundancy) of seven phoneme-awareness tasks, one of which was the Sound Categorization task. Six phoneme tasks were highly correlated with each other. The Sound Categorization was an outlier in this analysis. Nor did it "load" on a general factor of phoneme awareness at high levels like the other tasks. It was also extremely unreliable, producing a wide range of scores (high standard deviations). This led the authors to conclude that "an inspection of the difficulty parameters for the Sound Categorization subtest revealed that item difficult is highly dependent on where the target word is placed in the string of words. This dependence, coupled with the low discrimination parameters associated with these items, indicates that this subtest is a relatively poor indicator of phonological awareness" (Schatschneider et al. 1999, 448). Despite Bradley and Bryant's disappointing results, they did not abandon their hypothesis. Instead, the data were interpreted to fit the hypothesis, both in the conclusions to this study and in the introduction to their training study, which opens with this line: "Children who are backward in reading are strikingly insensitive to rhyme and alliteration" (Bradley and Bryant 1983, 419).

The training study is presented in the next section, because it primarily demonstrates the benefit of using letters during phonological training.

Overall, these studies show that teaching larger phonological units has little impact on reading and spelling skill. There is no evidence, either from correlational studies or from training studies, that children need to be eased into phonemes from larger units of sound. Large-scale correlational studies like those of Lundberg, Olofsson, and Wall (1980) and others (Share et al. 1984; Yopp 1988; McGuinness, McGuinness, and Donohue 1995) show that phoneme-analysis skills are strongly correlated with reading and spelling, while syllable segmenting and rhyming are not. Williams found that children in the control group could segment and manipulate syllables just as easily as the children who had spent weeks practicing this.

Phoneme Analysis with and without Letters

One of the most consistent findings in the literature, and evident in the NRP's meta-analysis, is that when phoneme-awareness training is meshed with teaching letter-sound correspondences, this has a much stronger impact on reading and spelling than training in the auditory mode alone. Overall, ES values for reading were .67 with letters versus .38 without, and for spelling, .61 versus .34.

Studies on phoneme training with and without letters go back over 25 years. Haddock (1976) reported that blending training with letters was far more effective than auditory training alone or training on letter-sound correspondences alone. Bradley and Bryant's training study is in this tradition. Children in the age range 5.5 to 7.5 years were selected on the basis of their poor performance on the Sound Categorization task, and divided into four groups. Each child received 40 individual lessons over a period of 2 years. There was no information on how long the lessons lasted or how often they occurred. Bradley reported later at a conference that the total time per child was less than 10 hours. This would be about 30 minutes per month in a school year.

Bradley and Bryant's use of the terms *categorizing*, *rhyme*, and *alliteration* is misleading in the context of their training study, and obscure what was actually taught. Instead, I will classify the tasks in keeping with the glossary above. Groups I and II got phonological-awareness training using picture sets like those in the Sound Categorization test. The word sets were unsystematic, using 15 consonants and the five simple vowels, plus a sprinkling of vowel digraphs. Children named the pictures and had to discover and say the common sound: "What is the common sound in *mix*, *dip*, *swim*, *sick*?" This is a phoneme-identification task. Next, they learned how to find the odd one out among items in a set (phoneme discrimination and identification). In the final exercises they worked with sets of rhyming words. There were no phoneme-sequencing activities (no blending or segmenting).

Group I worked exclusively in the auditory mode. Group II did the auditory tasks and worked with plastic letters, as described below:

In the second half of the training sessions Group II was taught with the help of plastic alphabet letters as well. Whenever a new sound category was introduced, it was demonstrated first with the help of the picture cards in the normal way. But the child then made each word in the set with plastic letters. (All of the children had by this time attended school for at least two years, and they were quite familiar with the alphabet.) (Bradley and Bryant 1985, 88)

Group III (control) had an equal number of lessons with the same picture cards, but sorted them into semantic categories, like animals, furniture, and so forth. A final control group (Group IV) had no special training.

If these English children had been in school for "at least two years" and "were quite familiar with the alphabet," they would be reading at some level. The groups should have been matched for reading skill, and they were not.

The training was not how it was portrayed. Children did not "categorize" sounds, they did phoneme-identity tasks. Nor were children trained in phonological awareness prior to learning to read. We have no idea what the children were taught in the classroom. This study cannot test the authors' central hypothesis that training in phonological awareness "causes" reading, because reading was well underway, and children's reading skill was not controlled.

Furthermore, plastic letters were not simply added to the mix as support for phoneme identification. They were used primarily for spelling dictation. After the children had identified each phoneme in a word set, they were asked to spell the words with plastic letters, which they selected from a box. The authors commented that many children learned to "withhold certain letters" (not put them back in the box) when the word sets shared phonemes in common: *sand, band, land.*

After 2 years of training (and 4 years of classroom reading instruction), the children were tested on standardized reading and spelling tests. Group II (phoneme identification plus spelling with plastic letters) was the *only group to score in the normal age range* (8 years). They were significantly ahead of the two control groups on reading (a 1-year advantage), ahead of all groups in spelling, and had a 2-year advantage over the untreated control group. Group I (phoneme awareness only) was superior to the untreated control group (6 months ahead in reading, and 1 year ahead in spelling) but *not to the semantic-categorizing group*. The two control groups did not differ from each other.

The NRP used a special formula to compute effect sizes for this study because standard deviations were not provided. These effect sizes were unusually high, especially for Group II (phoneme + letters): ES = 1.17 for reading compared to the semantic-categorizing group, and ES = 1.53 compared to the no-treatment controls. Effect sizes for spelling were even higher: ES = 1.59 and 2.18. It strains credulity that 10 hours of lessons spread over 2 years would generate such large effects.

A number of factors challenge the validity of these results and/or the NRPs calculations. First, there was the failure to control for initial reading skill. Second, there was the small sample size (13 children per group). Third, the effect sizes computed by the NRP were far too large. Even in the comparison between Group I (no letters) and the no-treatment control group, ES values were .86 and 1.0. Recall that Group I was trained with pictures, saw no printed words or letters, identified phonemes in the auditory mode only, did no phoneme sequencing of any type, and *never read or spelled anything*. In the NRPs' meta-analysis (see the previous chapter), the ES values for this type of training were .38 for reading and .34 for spelling compared to no-treatment control groups. Thus the majority of studies are distinctly at odds with this result.

Fourth, interpretation of the results is problematic, even if they were accurate. The main effect appears to be a spelling effect, not a phoneme-awareness-plus-letters effect. If phoneme-identification training was really effective, then the phoneme-only group would have been superior to the semantic-categorizing group, but it was not. Nowhere in the description of these exercises did children ever *read* any words. Even for Group II, the only reading was indirect, a consequence of spelling with plastic letters. If these data are valid, this study has demonstrated the impact of spelling practice on reading skill, supporting findings by Ehri and Wilce (1987) and Uhry and Shepherd (1993).

Unless this study is replicated and these issues addressed, Bradley and Bryant's results cannot be relied on. So far, this has not occurred.

The NRP report provides convincing evidence that learning phonemes in conjunction with letters is better than learning with none. But there are two ways to train phoneme awareness without letters. One is to do this in the auditory mode alone, and the other is to use unmarked tokens or counters to represent each sound. The token method does seem to have some success.

Cunningham (1990) divided kindergartners and first graders into three groups. She provided a program similar to Williams's program, with a range of activities to teach phoneme analysis, segmenting, and blending. Tokens, but no letters, were used. Children were taught in groups for 10–15 minutes twice a week, for 10 weeks (5 hours). One group was taught with a matter-of-fact "skill-and-drill" approach, and a second group with a more cognitive "metalevel" approach," in which explanations and goals were provided. A third group got no special training.

The results were puzzling. In kindergarten, the "meta" and the "skills" groups scored much higher than the controls on three phoneme-awareness tasks (ES values all above 1.0), and did better on the Metropolitan Reading Test as well (ES = .57 and .43). The "meta" and "skills" groups were very much alike. They did not differ in reading, or on the Lindamood Auditory Conceptualization (LAC) test of phoneme discrimination/manipulation, or on the Sound Categorization test, although the "meta" group was superior on the difficult phoneme-deletion test (ES = .81).

The first-grade results were different. Although the "skills" group far outshone the controls on all the phoneme-awareness tasks (ES range = .76 to 1.46), this apparently had no impact on reading (ES = .09). The "meta" group did even better compared to controls on the phoneme tasks (ES range = .83 to 2.08), and this did impact reading (ES = .53).

Something external to the study may be responsible for the strange result, in which a high degree of expertise in phoneme awareness confers no benefit for reading in one group of children but does in another. Perhaps reading test scores were nonnormally distributed for these two groups, or something was going on in the classroom that affected these results. Otherwise, one would have to argue, despite the vast amount of evidence to the contrary, that phoneme awareness taught in first grade has no effect on reading unless you receive a "metalevel" explanation for why you are learning it! This seemed to be Cunningham's argument. She stated that a metalevel explanation was "not an important factor in kindergarten-age children's transfer of phonemic awareness to a measure of reading achievement"—whereas in first grade it was "a more effective method of instruction than a skill and drill approach" (p. 441). It is hard to understand why this should be the case.

Brady et al. (1994) also reported a beneficial effect of a phoneme training program that used blank tokens. One group of kindergarten children got weekly phonological-awareness activities for about 4.5 months (20 hours), and a matched control group participated in the usual whole-language instruction. The first 4 weeks were spent on rhyming activities and syllable segmenting, the next 6 weeks on phoneme-isolation tasks, and the final 7 weeks on segmenting and blending phonemes using tokens. Elements of the Lindamood program were used, including exercises on monitoring mouth postures for each phoneme. At the end of the program, when the children were 6 years old, there was no effect on reading or spelling measured by standardized tests due to floor effects. One year later, they were able to locate 42 of the original 96 children, who were tested on the Woodcock Word ID and Word Attack subtests. The trained group were superior to the controls on Word ID (ES = .68) and Word Attack (ES = .71). These children scored about 5 to 8 months above age norms as well.

These results beg the question that if blank tokens are effective, wouldn't letters be even more effective?

In a direct test of the letters-versus-blank-tokens question, Hohn and Ehri (1983) found that letters were more powerful aids to segmenting than blank disks used in the same exercises. The segmenting-plus-letters group was superior to the blank-disks group and to an untrained control group on tests of phoneme segmentation, phoneme deletion, and on simple decoding tests. In comparison to the control group, ES values were .20 for blank disks versus .68 for letters. The fact that letters (symbols for specific sounds) are more beneficial to phoneme segmenting suggests that letters provide a memory aid for remembering *which* phonemes appear in the sequence. Hohn and Ehri observed that they helped the learner distinguish the correct size of the sound to be segmented.

The same effect was demonstrated in another way by Ball and Blachman (1988, 1991), who looked at learning letter-sound correspondences with and without phoneme-awareness training. The children were 5.5

years old and nonreaders. They were divided into three groups and given 20-minute lessons four times a week for 7 weeks (about 9 hours). The first group did phonological exercises, learned letter names and sounds for nine letters (*a, m, t, i, s, r, f, u,* and *b*), practiced segmenting and blending, and did "word assembly" with tokens and letter tiles. Children in this group never used more than two letter tiles (plus blank tiles) in any one session, and so never saw the words spelled in full. The second group focused on general language activities (vocabulary, categorizing), but also learned the nine letter names and sounds. There was no phonological training for this group. The third group participated in their ordinary classroom lessons.

An in-house reading test was designed with words composed of the letters that were taught. Recall that none of the groups had seen these words, though group 1 had seen portions of them. Group 1 read 10.9 words correctly, group 2, 3.9 words, and the control group, 2.2 words. The effect sizes comparing group 1 and the other groups were substantial (ES = .71 and .98). However, this did not transfer to a standardized reading test. This was reported as a "significant difference," yet there were large floor effects on the reading test, which puts statistical analysis off limits.

The definitive study on this issue was carried out in Germany by Schneider and his colleagues (2000). It is notable for the extensive and informative test batteries that were employed. These provide a clear picture of which phoneme skills are easy or hard to teach (a direct test of the developmental theory). And, by adding an extra experimental group, they were able to pin down the value of teaching phoneme awareness alone, letter-sound knowledge alone, or a combination of the two. This was a complex study, and before I get into the details, I need to alert the reader to certain factors that influence how these findings can be interpreted.

First, in Germany, where kindergarten originated, it was intended to be precisely that: a "children's garden," where children play and interact socially. From a research standpoint, this is useful, because children in the control group are really taught *nothing* about how to read, and parents are discouraged from teaching reading at home. Second, parents and teachers in Germany have strong feelings about the value of this practice. The authors reported that many parents and teachers were opposed to introducing any type of training at the kindergarten level, and obtaining parents' permission was difficult. Third, the German alphabet code is nearly transparent. If the German writing system is taught properly, children learn to read and spell in the first year of school (Wimmer 1993). All that remains is mastering a few quirks of the spelling code. There are no quirks of the reading code (no code overlaps). If you know the code and can segment and blend phonemes, there is no way to misread a word. Fourth, because everyone reads accurately, standardized reading tests measure speed and comprehension, not accuracy. All these factors play a role in how the results are interpreted.

At the start of the study, over 700 kindergartners were tested on a normed "reading-readiness" test, which measured phoneme awareness, phonological memory, verbal-processing speed, and visual attention. Parent permission was obtained for 138 of the kindergartners who had low scores on the test. These at-risk children were divided into three matched groups, with each group receiving different training. The control group consisted of 115 children who scored normally on the test.

The goal of the training regime was to ensure that the at-risk children *caught up* to the normal controls on reading and spelling skills measured later. If phoneme training and/or learning letter-sound correspondences was important, then effects sizes on reading and spelling tests should be *close to zero*, with no difference between the at-risk children and the normal control group.

The three types of training were phoneme awareness only (PA), letter-sound training only (LS), or both (PA+LS). The hypothesis was that the group that got both types of training would be most successful. The lessons were taught to the whole class at the same time for 10–15 minutes each day. This continued for around 5 months, for a total of approximately 20 hours.

A phonological training regime was based on Lundberg's program but dramatically speeded up. For the phonological-awareness group, large phonological units were taught in the first month (words, syllables, rhymes), and phoneme-analysis tasks were introduced in the second month. This group had 20 weeks of training. The letter-sound group learned 12 sounds and 12 letters, which took 10 weeks. A phoneme was introduced in a story and in various games, then children were shown the letter for that sound. Games and activities included alphabet cards, identifying initial phonemes in matching sets of pictures, and so forth. There was no writing in this component. The combination group that had both types of training learned fewer letters and spent less time on the phonological tasks. This group had 20 weeks of training.

Special tests were designed to measure phonological-awareness skills, along with verbal short-term memory, naming speed for colors and pictures of objects, and measures of early literacy such as letter knowledge and word recognition. These tests were given prior to the start of training and after training was completed. Pretraining scores on the phonological tasks were poor for everyone, and when children had to choose among alternatives, performance was no better than chance. Test scores were reliable after training was completed in July.

It is informative to look at the order of difficulty of these tasks. This order was nearly identical for all groups regardless of the type of training. From easy to hard, the order was: (1) Identify (say) an initial phoneme in a word. (2) Blend isolated phonemes into a word. (3) Segment phonemes in a word. (4) Identify the odd one out in a set of rhyming words that varied in the final phoneme (part of the rhyme). (5) Delete phonemes. Say the word that remains after the initial phoneme is deleted. (6) Carry out the "alliteration" portion of the odd-one-out task. Children did not score above chance on this test.

These results support Chaney's findings reported earlier (Chaney 1992). In her study, blending phonemes was the second-easiest phonological task for 3-year-olds, and the alliteration tasks were the most difficult out of 22 tasks. The results also support Schatschneider et al.'s (1999) finding that the Sound Categorization task is one of the most difficult among a variety of phoneme-awareness tests. As seen above, even the phoneme-deletion test, the most difficult of the phoneme tests, was easier than the alliteration task.

Schneider et al. found a large impact of training on phoneme-awareness skill for both the PA group and the PA+LS group. Both groups did significantly better than the normal control group, with the PA group having a decided advantage. However, none of the groups had much success reading simple words.

In the fall of the same year, children entered first grade and were taught to read in the usual way. The authors do not describe the reading

Table 6.2
Effect sizes from Schneider, Roth, and Ennemoser 2000: kindergartners at risk vs. normal controls, three types of training

Kindergarten	Phoneme synthesis	Phoneme analysis	Initial phoneme
Pretest			
PA+LS vs. controls	−.45	−1.0	−1.12
Posttest			
PA+LS vs. controls	.34	.61	.90
PA only vs. controls	.55	.96	1.18

	Reading speed	Spelling	Comprehension
End grade 1			
PA+LS vs. PA only	.17	.27	
PA+LS vs. LS only	.22	.49	
PA+LS vs. controls	−.38	−.17	
End grade 2			
PA+LS vs. PA only	.31	.30	.19
PA+LS vs. LS only	.48	.48	.20
PA+LS vs. controls	−.30	−.32	−.50

Note: Tests used: German standardized tests on reading fluency, spelling, and comprehension. PA = phoneme-awareness training. LS = letter-sound training.

method, but the German writing system is typically taught with a linguistic-phonics approach (Wimmer 1993). Reading and spelling tests were administered at the end of grade 1 and again the following year. Intelligence tests were also administered at the end of grade 1. Because the control groups had significantly higher IQs, IQ was controlled (covaried) in all statistical analysis. These results are described below. The effect sizes (IQ not controlled) are shown in table 6.2.

With IQ controlled, the control group was superior to the PA and the LS groups, but not to the PA+LS group at grade 1 and grade 2 on tests of decoding speed and reading comprehension. Results were similar for spelling, except that the PA+LS group was also statistically superior to the LS group, especially at the second testing. In other words, *the PA+LS combined training had largely eliminated the difference between these at-risk children and the normal children.* Training in phoneme awareness alone, or learning 12 letter sounds alone, did not erase this gap.

I calculated the ES values for the most successful group (PA+LS) versus all other groups. We can see that this group is ahead of the PA group, and especially the LS group, in reading, spelling, and comprehension. Although the ES values are consistently negative in the comparisons to the normal control group, most values are not statistically significant. It would be interesting to see what happens in the future. Differences in IQ may come to matter more over time, especially because the training did not eliminate the difference between the normal children and the at-risk (low-IQ) children on the comprehension test.

This study showed that phoneme-awareness exercises alone, or sound-symbol associations alone, have little impact on learning to read. At least this is the case in countries with a transparent alphabet, where teaching is appropriate. But we are left wondering what would have happened if all the phonemes had been taught (and their letters) and not just 12 of them, and if the letter-sound group had had the same 20 weeks training that the other two groups received.

These at-risk children, apart from having lower IQs, started off at a distinct disadvantage compared to the normal children on several of the readiness measures. They knew half as many letter-sound correspondences as the normal children, and had lower phoneme-identity and phoneme-segmenting scores. These things have to be taught. It may be the case that the "normal" children entering kindergarten had more of a boost at home than their parents let on. (Wimmer reported that, in Austria, some first graders know all the letter-sound correspondences and some know none, even though parents are told to teach nothing.)

Although programs combining phoneme and letter training always produce a greater impact on reading test scores than either alone, if we ask whether any of these combination programs does a better job than a good linguistic-phonics program, the answer is still no. The only exception here is the study above, which measured fluency and comprehension for children learning a transparent alphabet.

Contrasting Types of Phoneme-Awareness Training

Earlier I provided a glossary of the different types or measures of phoneme awareness. Two training studies focused specifically on types of
phoneme training.

*Phoneme Identity and Letter-Sound Training versus Normal Classroom In-
struction* Byrne and Fielding-Barnsley (1989, 1990) began a quest to
determine what preschool children, ages 4 and 5 years, found easy or
difficult to learn. They investigated the children's ability to make sound-
symbol associations. The training focused on phoneme identity for phonemes in initial and final position, and for segmenting initial phonemes.
They discovered that identity training generalized to words made up of
the same phonemes in new combinations and concluded as follows:

Preschool children can be taught to recognize the identity of phonemic segments, both consonants and vowels, across words, whether the phonemes are
singletons or members of a consonant cluster, and the position of the target
phonemes in the word appears to make no difference.... Successful instruction in phoneme identity can, when combined with relevant letter-sound
knowledge, promote acquisition of the alphabetic principle. (Byrne and
Fielding-Barnsley 1990, 810)

In 1991, they reported a study on a preschool program based on this initial research called *Sound Foundations*. Two groups of 4.5-year-olds were
matched on vocabulary scores and received either the training program or
regular kindergarten lessons. The training program focused on learning
nine consonant phonemes and one vowel. Training took 30 minutes once
a week for 12 weeks (6 hours). The trained children had larger gains on a
phoneme-identity test for sounds in both initial and final position. They
also could generalize this knowledge to phoneme sequences in spoken
words that had not been directly taught.

The children were followed up at the end of kindergarten when they
were 6 years old (Byrne and Fielding-Barnsley 1993). They were given
phoneme-identity and phoneme-blending tasks, a test of letter-sound
knowledge, and reading and spelling tests. The children who had the training were superior on the phoneme-identity task for the final sound only.
No significant differences were found for blending or letter-sound knowl-

edge, both groups doing well (24 correct). Likewise, both groups did well on the Woodcock Word ID subtest, and phoneme-identity training played no role (ES = .21), nor did the training affect an in-house spelling test (ES = .09). However, the trained group did outshine the controls in decoding on an in-house nonword test (ES = 1.2). This result suggests that the training had oriented the children toward the alphabet principle.

At this point in the data analysis, the authors chose to re-sort the children into two new groups (regardless of the prior group assignment) based on whether they passed or failed the phoneme-identity test at the end of kindergarten. (The pass/fail cutoff was 66 percent correct.) The new groups were compared statistically on various reading and spelling tests. When groups no longer reflect who did or did not get trained, there is no way to measure the outcome of training! Furthermore, this brings uncontrolled factors into play, raising the following question: Why would some children trained on "phoneme identity" fail a phoneme-identity test, and some of the untrained children pass? IQ and home environment become important, and neither variable was controlled. The new results were highly significant, which was not the case previously.

The reassignment of children to groups based on their ability explains the extremely high effect sizes reported by the NRP for this group of studies. The NRP averaged the results together with those of the original groups, enormously inflating effect sizes for this study as a whole. (ES = 1.61 for reading and 3.14 for phoneme awareness, by far the largest values we have seen.) This grossly exaggerates the impact of this training program, as well as the meta-analysis values as a whole. We know these values are false by a table of first-order correlations from the 1993 publication, which showed that the strongest contributors to reading and spelling test scores were blending skills and letter-sound knowledge, not phoneme-identity skills.

In subsequent follow-on reports on these same children, similar results were found at the end of grades 1 and 2, and at grade 5 (Byrne and Fielding-Barnsley 1995, 2000). In-house tests were used to measure reading and spelling in the early grades. The two groups did not differ on these tests, with the exception of a small but significant effect for nonword decoding. At the fifth-grade level, most tests were standardized tests. The trained group, now 11 years old, outscored the control group on the Woodcock Word Attack test ($p < .04$), though the effect size was small

(ES = .34). No other comparisons using normed, standardized tests were significant. (It should be noted that pass-fail groups were reconstituted in this report also, with the same exaggerated impact on effect sizes in the NRP report.)

It appears that a short (6-hour) training program on phoneme identity, using nine consonants and one vowel, had a small but lasting effect on nonword decoding. Why this is so is not clear, because the same training had no impact on other reading and spelling skills at any time. Finally, it should be noted that the NRP effect sizes for this series of studies are far too large and need to be revised.

Phoneme Identity versus Phoneme Sequencing   A study in Norway (Lie 1991) provided 208 first graders (age 7) with one of two phoneme-awareness training programs. Children learn to read at age 7 in Norway, and Norwegian is written in a transparent alphabet. The training took 15 minutes per day for 9 weeks (11 hours) and was delivered by the classroom teacher as part of normal reading instruction. The two programs had an emphasis on articulation, listening for a phoneme in sound-targeting stories, and learning to recognize individual phonemes in words. Children learned 27 phonemes at a rate of 3 per week. Overall training was the same for both groups with the exception that the phoneme-identity group learned phonemes in isolated positions in the word, and the phoneme-sequencing group learned phonemes in the correct sequence. A third group had lessons in concept categorization. No letters were used in this training, but children were learning letter-sound correspondences in their regular lessons.

At the end of the school year, the sequencing group was consistently superior to the phoneme-identity group and to the controls in reading (ES = .42 and .62) and in spelling (ES = .42 and .68). However, this effect did not persist. At second grade there was no difference between the identity and sequencing groups, though both groups were marginally ahead of controls (ES values ranging from .33 to .53). This shows that phoneme-awareness training can contribute to reading and spelling skills above and beyond a linguistic-phonics program. The sequencing approach is more effective, at least in the short term. It is interesting that this program made a difference even in a country with a transparent alphabet where reading is properly taught.

On the whole, the evidence is not compelling that an independent phoneme-awareness training regime has a special benefit over and above a good linguistic-phonics program. The really effective reading programs reviewed in the previous chapter have far more impact than anything we have seen here. Surprisingly, the strongest support for a positive impact of special phoneme-awareness training comes from the European studies (Schneider and colleagues; Lie) in countries with transparent alphabets, and where traditional classroom instruction is likely to be similar to linguistic phonics. However, neither Schneider and associates nor Lie reveal what *specifically* was being taught in the classroom.

Studies Comparing Phoneme Training with Classroom Programs

Several studies have combined or compared phoneme-awareness training with training in specific classroom reading programs. For various methodological reasons, none provide a direct test of how or whether a phoneme-awareness program is necessary.

Blachman (Blachman et al. 1999) used the findings from her earlier research (Ball and Blachman 1991) to develop a kindergarten phoneme training program and mesh this with a new first-grade phonics program. There were 159 at-risk (inner-city) children in the study. The hypothesis was that early intervention in kindergarten can help at-risk children, especially when followed up by a good phonics program that links these phoneme-analysis skills to reading instruction.

Half the at-risk children had phoneme-awareness training in kindergarten for 11 weeks. This consisted of 15–20 minutes of group lessons 4 days a week, for a total of about 13 hours. Training was limited to 8 letters (*a, m, t, i, s, r, f*, and *b*). The children were taught to segment words orally and move blank disks to represent each phoneme while saying the sound ("say it and move it"). Later, letters were pasted on the disks. Children were taught the letter names and sounds for the 8 letters. There was phoneme-identity training: matching pictures with first sounds in common. The remaining at-risk children (controls) participated in their usual kindergarten program (unspecified).

At the end of kindergarten, the children were tested on phoneme segmenting, letter-sound knowledge, and two reading tests. One was an in-house reading test consisting of words made up of the 8 sounds/letters that had been taught. This, not surprisingly, showed a strong advantage for the special kindergarten program (ES = 1.08). However, this knowledge did not transfer to a standardized reading measure. (The ES value for the Woodcock Word ID test was −.17.) It goes without saying that scores on phoneme-segmenting and letter-sound knowledge were higher for the children who had been taught these things than for children who were not.

The experimental group was followed into first grade and given a phonics program that completely replaced the usual program. The kindergarten activities were continued and letter-sound knowledge was gradually expanded to "all letter sounds." Whether this means the "sounds" of all the letters of the alphabet, or all the sounds in the English language, is not clear. Children were taught some vowel digraphs, but how this was done was not specified. Children did workbook exercises connecting letters and sounds, learned some common sight words, and practiced sequencing using the DISTAR phoneme-stretching technique ("mmmm-aaaaannnn"), instead of segmenting. (Blachman subscribes to the view that segmenting consonants in isolation from a vowel is difficult.) Slingerland's pocket-chart technique was used to sequence letter cards to make words. Children practiced with flash cards to improve decoding speed. They read simple phonics books with "regular" spellings, such as the Primary Phonics series, and wrote words and sentences to dictation. This looks like a sensible phonics program, but there was insufficient detail to make a valid judgment.

Toward the end of training, children were introduced to six syllable types: "closed," "open," "final *e*," "vowel team" (vowel digraphs), "vowel + *r*," and "consonant + *le*." This classification scheme is a feature of Orton-Gillingham remedial programs. English spelling patterns are not specific to syllable types. Furthermore, these types are not mutually exclusive, and therefore do not constitute independent categories.[1] Teaching this only adds unnecessary complexity and will create confusion.

---

1. The same spelling for the same sound can occur in more than one of these syllable types. The spelling *o* for the sound /oe/ occurs in both "open" and "closed" syllables: *go, most*. Ditto *ee* as in *fee* and *feed*; *ie* as in *die* and *died*; *ue* as in *cue* and *fuel*; *oo* as in *too* and *food*. The same word fits more than one syllable type: *goat* ("vowel team" and "closed"), *care* ("final *e*," "vowel + *r*"), *soar*

The control group followed the Scott-Foresman basal series. This is a sight-word, plus basal-reader, plus disconnected-phonics curriculum. Teachers also used parts of the DISTAR program as well. Children read trade books from classroom libraries. This is a typical eclectic mix.

Both groups of children were taught in a whole-class format. And both groups received whole-class spelling instruction using the Scott-Foresman spelling program, which is vaguely phonics oriented ("regular" CVC words first, followed by the "long-vowel" words, blends, and digraphs, gradually increasing in length and complexity).

The teachers in the experimental program received 13 hours of training. No special training was given to the teachers of the control group.

The comparison between the two programs showed that the experimental group had much higher phoneme-segmenting and letter-sound knowledge scores (ES values = 1.0), as would be expected. However, they were only marginally better on standardized reading and spelling tests (ES = .35 for word recognition and .38 for spelling). The children were followed up at the end of second grade, and standardized reading and spelling tests were given again. Effect sizes for reading improved slightly, in favor of the experimental group: ES = .44 for word-recognition tests and .46 for word attack. However, the ES value for spelling was zero. These values are not particularly remarkable for 2 years of special teaching.

This study had a major design flaw if one of the goals was to evaluate the impact of the kindergarten phoneme-awareness training. It is missing a critical control group, and possibly two. This would be a group of children who did not receive the kindergarten phoneme-awareness program but did receive the first-grade phonics program. To be absolutely certain that the kindergarten program was relevant, a fourth control group is also needed. This group would receive the kindergarten program but be switched to Scott-Foresman at first grade. Instead, the control group got neither the kindergarten program nor the new reading program. In view of this, one would expect to find a much more substantial advantage for the experimental group, especially if both the kindergarten program and

---

("vowel team," "vowel + r"). Furthermore, this classification scheme does not fit multisyllable words at all, which make up about 80 percent of the words in English.

the first-grade program were effective. Instead, effects sizes were modest, suggesting that neither program is as effective as it could be, and/or the teachers were not committed to them.

Hatcher, Hulme, and Ellis (1994), in England, compared a phoneme-awareness program to a remedial-reading program known as *Reading Recovery*, based on work by Marie Clay (1985). Hatcher and colleagues trained 125 second-grade children (7.5 years) who had been identified as poor readers. The training consisted of individual tutoring taught by classroom teachers over a period of 25 weeks (two half-hour sessions per week) for a total of 20 hours. After this, the children were retested, and they were followed up 1 year later and tested again. The groups were matched for age, IQ, and initial reading test scores.

The children were divided into three experimental groups and a control group. A phonological training group received a program similar to the one designed by Lundberg and colleagues. It involved identifying and producing words, syllables, rhymes, and a range of phoneme-analysis tasks. These included lessons on segmenting, blending, omission, substitution, and transposition of phonemes in words.

A reading training group received lessons based on Reading Recovery (see Clay 1985). Teaching was visually oriented (reading and rereading the same books), included some strategies for decoding (unspecified), frequent diagnostic tests, plus writing activities (invented spelling) involving letters, words, and stories. Children learned letter names but no letter-sound correspondences.

The phonological-plus-reading group received both types of instruction. There was a trade-off due to time constraints, and only half the phonological tasks were completed. This group also got new activities that linked reading and phonological awareness. These included learning letter-sound correspondences, using plastic letters to spell words, and writing words while attending to sound-to-letter correspondences. These "linking" activities took up 10 minutes of every session.

The ordinary classroom instruction (received by everyone) was described as "phonics" minus phonological-awareness training. There was no description of what "phonics" meant or which program was used. The control group received only this "phonics" instruction, and some children from this group had outside remedial help as well (program and time unspecified).

From this description, it appears that the children in the combined group (phonological awareness + reading + linking activities) got a Mulligan stew of reading methods: a variant of whole language in Reading Recovery lessons, some type of phonics in the classroom, multisound-unit phonological tasks, a variety of phoneme-analysis tasks, plus exercises to "link" phonological knowledge and the alphabet code.

Perhaps this mix was too confusing, because neither the combined group (predicted to be superior to all groups) nor any of the other groups did particularly well. No differences between the groups were found on an in-house word-recognition test or on the British Ability Scales, a standardized test of word recognition. There was a small but consistent advantage for the combined PA + read group on the remaining standardized tests, as shown in table 6.3. The other groups did not differ from one another.

Table 6.3
Effect sizes: Data from Hatcher, Hulme, and Ellis 1994

	Neale Accuracy	Neale Comprehension	Schonell Spelling
Testing age 8:1			
Read + PA vs. read only	.45	.41	.31
Read + PA vs. phonemes only	.40	.52	.14
Read + PA vs. controls	.52	.61	.33
Testing age 8:10			
Read + PA vs. read only	.46	.47	.35
Read + PA vs. phoneme only	.35	.44	.22
Read + PA vs. controls	.38	.57	.30

Read + phonological group only	Testing: age 8:1		Testing: age 8:10	
	Age-equivalent score	Years below age	Age-equivalent score	Years below age
Neale Accuracy	6:1	2:0	6:8	2:2
Neale Comprehension	6:4	1:9	7:0	1:10
Schonell Spelling	6:8	1:5	7:2	1:8

The comparisons between the combined group and the other three groups produced similar effect sizes (see table 6.3), with ES values in a modest .30–.45 range. This is not much to show for 20 hours of one-on-one help. In other words, neither Reading Recovery nor phonological-awareness training *on its own* provided any greater benefit to these poor readers than what was taught in the phonics classroom, which was not much.

More revealing were the combined PA + read group's age-equivalent scores on the standardized tests at beginning and end of training, and at follow-up 9 months later. These scores are shown at the bottom of table 6.3. The children began the study scoring 1.5 years below age norms on all tests. The table lists the years:months these children lag behind age norms for reading and spelling at two testing times (ages 8:1 and 8:8 years). The discrepancies between these scores and national age norms actually increased over time.

For reasons unknown—the mix of methods, the training programs themselves, poor teacher training or monitoring—these programs were not effective in getting the children caught up. Other intervention programs work much better, and in a much shorter space of time (see D. McGuinness 1997c, 1998b; C. McGuinness, D. McGuinness, and G. McGuinness 1996). The rule of thumb for successful remediation is to remain faithful to the prototype, and to avoid teaching skills that have nothing to do with an alphabetic writing system.

Finally, Brennan and Ireson (1997) carried out a study that, despite methodological problems, is the most direct test of whether phonological-awareness training provides any particular advantage over a good phonics program. They adapted a Lundberg-type program for kindergartners (age range 4:10 to 6:1 years) attending an American school in England. The children spent 3 months on phonological units above the level of the phoneme. These included listening to nonverbal sounds, playing rhyming games, clapping out syllable beats, and using markers to represent syllables in multisyllable words. In the middle of the third month, children began learning phonemes in initial position, and subsequently in all positions over the course of the school year. Lessons were mainly in the auditory mode only (no letters). However, there was a major confound in this study. The phonological program took up 15–20 minutes of a 2-hour language-arts period, during which children learned letter names and sounds, copied letters, and wrote "stories" using invented spelling.

The phonological training group was contrasted with two other groups. One group was using a published phonics program (*Success in Kindergarten*) designed to integrate learning sounds and letters. Copying and writing words was a particular emphasis. The third group was taught "Letterland" characters (letters drawn to look like animals) to teach letter sounds. This is a visually driven approach that focuses on letter shapes and "the sounds the letters make." Lessons include hands-on activities to do with memorizing letter forms, such as tracing letters in the sand tray and making letters out of play dough. Children recite rhymes related to the target letter.

Both the phonological training group and the Success in Kindergarten group were considerably advanced on standardized reading and spelling tests compared to the Letterland group at the end of the year. However, the phonological-awareness group was not superior to the Success in Kindergarten group. When I compared the two programs, effect sizes were in favor of Success in Kindergarten: ES = .38 for Schonell reading, .56 for "high-frequency words," and .23 for Schonell spelling. (These values are different from the NRP's effect sizes.)

Brennan and Ireson do not report which phonemes were taught for any group, or how they were taught, and there is the fact that about 90 minutes of other reading activities were ongoing in the classrooms. In contrast to the situation in most other European countries, children in the United Kingdom *are* taught to read in kindergarten. The only clear result was the extremely poor showing of the Letterland program. There is no way to tell whether the differences between the other two programs had anything to do with specific characteristics of these programs.

Conclusions

As a general observation, one of the most consistent findings to emerge from these studies is that phoneme-identification and phoneme-sequencing (segmenting/blending) training are the only phoneme-analysis skills that consistently impact reading test scores. This confirms the evidence from the correlational research. Helfgott (1976) was among the first to discover that segmenting skill for CVC words was the highest correlate to reading 1 year later ($r = .72$) among a variety of phoneme-awareness skills.

The definitive study was that of Yopp (1988), who measured kindergartners' performance on 11 phonological-awareness tests. She investigated the statistical overlap between these tests and correlated each test score with the time to learn to read novel words. Yopp's findings mirror the training studies. The highest correlates of learning rate were "sound isolation" (phoneme identification) ($r = .72$), and phoneme-sequencing tasks (blending and segmenting) (average $r = .67$). Auditory discrimination ($r = .27$) and rhyming skills ($r = .47$) did not predict learning rate. Phoneme-deletion tests were too difficult for this age group.

For those knowledgeable about factor analysis, phoneme-identification and phoneme-sequencing tasks loaded on the same factor (factor I) at values ranging from .76 to .89. Auditory-discrimination and rhyming skill loaded on none, and phoneme-deletion tests loaded on a separate factor (the Rosner test loaded on factor II at .94).

It should be noted that phoneme identification and sequencing are precisely the skills that are trained in a linguistic-phonics program as a matter of course.

Despite the overall agreement between these studies, most studies reviewed in this chapter have a number of design flaws that make it difficult to know exactly how or whether a phonological training program impacts reading and spelling. There is little attempt to discern which of the many phonological tasks are truly necessary. Often there is no description of which phonemes and letters (if used) are taught. And when this information is provided, too few sound-symbol correspondences are included in the program, and far too much time spent teaching them. On the whole, the majority of programs grossly underestimate what 5-year-old children (or even younger children) can learn. One is struck by the fact that the balance is exactly backward between the number of phonemes taught (and their spellings), and the time spent on larger phonological units. The unwritten assumption seems to be that teaching phonemes and letters is hard for young children, but teaching lots of "unnatural" and conflicting phonological tasks is not. This appears to be one of the many legacies of the phonological-development myth.

The evidence is not convincing that special programs for teaching phoneme awareness and letter-sound correspondences instead of using a good linguistic-phonics program at the outset provides any additional benefit.

This was not the conclusion of the NRP, which seemed to take it for granted that phoneme-awareness skills are so hard to learn that separate phoneme-awareness training is a necessity. The panel commented in the introduction to the report that Texas and California have prescribed the inclusion of phoneme-awareness training as part of early reading instruction in the context of praising these two states for their forward-looking policies. (We have already seen what happened the last time California mandated a curriculum.)

If special phoneme-awareness training is essential, precisely which of the many training programs reviewed here should teachers adopt? And what is the evidence that any of these programs confers a benefit beyond what a good linguistic-phonics program confers? So far there is none.

The summary to the NRP report on phoneme awareness ("Implications for Reading Instruction") shows that the authors have not considered the overlap between phoneme-awareness training and a linguistic-phonics program. For example, in a question-and-answer section, the NRP addressed the question of whether phoneme-awareness training helps children learn to read and spell. The panel stated that teaching children to manipulate phonemes "transfers and helps them learn to read and spell. PA training benefits not only word reading but also reading comprehension. PA training contributes to children's ability to read and spell for months, if not years, after the training has ended" (p. 2-40).

As to which phoneme-awareness method has the greatest impact on learning to read, they wrote: "Teaching students to segment and blend benefits reading more than a multiskilled approach. Teaching students to manipulate phonemes with letters yields larger effects than teaching students without letters.... Teaching children to blend the phonemes represented by letters is the equivalent of decoding instruction" (p. 2-41). No, it is *identical* to decoding (reading) instruction.

As for spelling: "Teaching children to segment phonemes in words and represent them with letters is the equivalent of invented spelling instruction" (p. 2-41). No, it is *identical* to proper spelling instruction. Spelling should never be "invented."

The authors of the NRP report appeared to be satisfied with the quality of the studies and the validity of the large effect sizes reported in their analysis—effect sizes that, as we have seen, are grossly inflated due to invalid in-house tests and other methodological anomalies. Nowhere is this more evident than in a statement that misrepresents the fact that effect sizes based on standardized tests are marginal (i.e., ES = .33 for reading, ES = .41 for spelling).

According to the report, "The NRP analyses shows that the evidence rests solidly on well-designed studies. Significant effect sizes were apparent on standardized tests as well as experimenter designed tests" (p. 2-42). As noted in the previous chapter, the effect sizes in the NRP report for *the individual studies themselves* are not always accurate. The problem is compounded when these inaccurate values are averaged together in a meta-analysis. As we have seen from this review, many studies were not "well-designed," and many test instruments and much data manipulation were invalid. I cannot recall more than one study where reliability estimates were computed for an in-house test.

Of course, it is difficult to measure the impact of a phoneme-awareness training program on reading and spelling before children are taught to read and spell, which is the case in most kindergarten studies. Researchers are justified in trying to ascertain whether the training impacted decoding and spelling without having to develop their own reading and spelling tests from scratch, complete with norms and standard scores. However, there are other criteria for a valid test. Test reliability is crucial, as is item analysis. Items may be too difficult or too easy. Some items may not measure the construct (construct validity). Schatschneider et al. (1999), for example, discovered in their analysis of phoneme-awareness tests that items in the same test often varied enormously in difficulty in an idiosyncratic fashion.

As a final comment, let's return to the third criterion used in the initial screening of these studies: "Test the hypothesis that phoneme awareness training improves reading beyond some alternative form of training or no training" (p. 2-15). By "alternative form of training," the panel meant something similar or parallel to phoneme-awareness training. But what if the "alternative form of training" was a linguistic-phonics program like Lippincott or Jolly Phonics? In only one case in this group of studies was this hypothesis even marginally tested, and until this is done, the conclusion must be that separate phoneme-awareness training programs like those reported here do not come close to "improving reading" compared to a good linguistic-phonics program. Phoneme awareness programs do not even produce comparable results on tests of phoneme awareness.

READING FLUENCY

The goal of reading instruction is to ensure that children learn to read accurately and fluently. But while researchers in English-speaking countries carefully measure accuracy in all its forms, fluency is rarely measured. In the eight slots for effect sizes on outcome measures in the NRP report on reading instruction, there was no slot for reading fluency or speed. Very few standardized test batteries include such a measure.

For the most part, researchers and educators believe that fluency is a by-product of accurate decoding. It is certainly the case that inaccurate decoders are halting, dysfluent readers. But the reverse is not true. A slow reader is not necessarily inaccurate. The slow but accurate reader is a common phenomenon in countries with a transparent writing system. As we saw in the last chapter, reading tests in these countries measure reading speed and comprehension, not accuracy. When Wimmer (1993) tested Salzburg's poorest readers, no one had decoding or spelling difficulties but nearly everyone read very slowly.

This means there are two types of slow readers, children who read slowly because they cannot decode (inaccurate), and children who read slowly despite good decoding skills. The first type of reader needs most help with decoding skills (perhaps followed by fluency training), and the second type needs fluency training only. How fluency can best be trained is the topic of this chapter.

Before we look at the training studies, we need to understand why a reader would read accurately but slowly, and address the question of whether it matters if a child is a slow but accurate reader. The standard answer has been that a ponderous decoding speed prevents children from comprehending what they read. However, the evidence to support this theory is largely anecdotal. For the most part, the correlational studies have been carried out on English-speaking children who read slowly *and inaccurately*, so when reading speed and comprehension are correlated, we cannot know why. And other factors like age, sex, and IQ have a major impact on processing speed but are rarely controlled in the correlational studies. Wimmer found that 80 to 85 percent of slow readers at first and second grade were boys, and that verbal IQ scores for these slow readers were significantly below those of normal readers by a wide margin ($p < .001$).

The only way to answer the question raised above is to control both fluency and comprehension at the same time. If slow reading has no effect on comprehension, there is no reason to be concerned. We also need a better conceptual grasp of potential causes. The children may be lagging developmentally, or may not have been taught letters and sounds prior to going to school. They may have been victims of poor instruction, causing them to have an inefficient (slow) decoding rate.

Speaking Rate and Brain Speed

What is the optimum reading rate? One would imagine that reading speed ought to be close to speaking rate. Speaking rate is extremely rapid due to the fact that phonemes are coarticulated (physically overlap). Each phoneme in a word modifies the one preceding it. This is a kind of "backward propagation" in which the last phoneme in a word controls the speech patterns of the one before it, and so on, backward through the entire word. When we begin speaking (forward in time), the brain has already made this calculation before we utter the first phoneme. The /g/ in the word *dog* modifies the vowel /o/, which in turn modifies how the /d/ is physically produced. As a result, the /d/ in *dog* and the /d/ in *dip* have different acoustic profiles, quite easy to distinguish on a paper printout of spectral patterns, even with the naked eye. Coarticulation speeds up speech enormously, making the transfer of information from one brain to another more efficient.

Articulation speed (speaking rate) needs to be optimal for the human brain to extract meaning from speech utterances. Speak too quickly, and it sounds like gibberish; speak too slowly, and the sentence falls apart. Listening to slowed speech is such hard work for the listener that interest wanes with every word. (The same applies to music played too quickly or too slowly.) Speaking rate is surprisingly uniform across different languages, considering the variations in their phonetic structure. This rate is measured by the number of words uttered per unit of time in normal conversations. The natural speaking rate for English is about 250 to 300 words per minute (wpm).

Because this rapid speaking rate makes conversation possible, one would imagine that for readers to process meaning at the brain's preferred rate (to comprehend what they read), they should be able to decode at the same rate as people speak. What might this optimal reading rate be? In his review of eye-movement research, Rayner (1998), described a study with this goal. College students were identified by their excellent performance on a reading-comprehension test. They were asked to read passages at their optimum reading rate. The fastest reader was clocked at 380 wpm and the slowest at 230 wpm. The average for this group of expert readers was 308 wpm. This is about the same as the optimal speaking rate, and even this takes years to accomplish. The normal second-grade reader reads about 90 wpm. This jumps to 150 wpm at fourth grade. By sixth grade, the average reader is closing in on the rate of the slowest college reader (200 wpm).

The variability across age, and the individual differences in reading speed, mean that defining a "slow reader" is not going to be easy. The problem is compounded when English children are compared to children who learn a transparent alphabet. As noted earlier, Wimmer, in collaboration with English colleagues (Wimmer and Goswami 1994; Landerl, Wimmer, and Frith 1997), compared normal children from Salzburg and London. The Austrian 7-year-olds with 1 year of school read as fast as English 9-year-olds with 4 years of school, making half the number of errors, an eightfold increase in efficiency. When the worst readers in Salzburg (very slow) were pitted against the worst readers in London (very inaccurate), the Salzburg children read the same material *twice as fast* while misreading only 7 percent of the words. The English children not only read more slowly, but misread 40 percent of the words. "Slowness," it seems, is a function of the writing system, not a property of the child.

If "slow reading" is relative, tied to a particular writing system and method of instruction rather than to age or innate ability, there are no guidelines for determining an optimum reading rate other than anecdotal reports of the teachers or complaints of individual children. To complicate matters, the content of the reading material also determines reading rate.

Difficult material is read more slowly, with many more regressive fixations, than simple material.

For the time being, I will adopt the average second-grade reading speed of 90 wpm as a base rate, below which comprehension may become difficult. This rate applies to text with simple vocabulary used to describe content that is familiar or conventional. Anything less than 90 wpm will not be adequate to process meaning.

For children whose reading speed falls below this value, what kind of training might help? One clue comes from the eye-movement research. Rayner (1986) found that adults and children utilize different amounts of information in their peripheral visual field as they read. This is known as a *perceptual span*. The span is larger on the right than the left due to the left-right direction of our writing system. It takes about a year of reading practice for this asymmetry to be established.

The average perceptual span for adults is around 14–15 characters to the right of fixation, and adults use all this information. The span is similar for children, but Rayner (1986) found that younger children's *functional* spans are smaller, about 11 characters or less. Children rely more on central (foveal) vision, and do not take advantage of the information to the right of fixation until they are around 12 years old. Perhaps slow readers make less use of this information than normal readers. Their plodding, word-by-word-by-word decoding style suggests they are focusing on one word at a time.

Despite the fact that humans cannot see detail in their peripheral visual field, they can see something. Everyone with normal vision, including slow readers, can make out the first two letters of the following word quite well. Beyond this, the remaining letters provide a blurry, global impression of the word's length and shape, its pattern of ascenders (b, d, f, h, l, and t) and descenders (g, j, p, q, and y). For this information to be accessible it must be coordinated "online" (in real time) with meaning and sentence structure. Readers have to be aware of syntax and anticipate what part of speech is due next: "The little boy _____ [verb goes here]." Readers also have to be aware of *context*—what is going on in the story (the boy just tripped over a log).

These four clues (initial letters, word length and shape, syntax, context) narrow the choice of words that go in the next slot in the sentence. The brain, given half a chance, will automatically toss out a few suitable words that begin with those particular letters, have that shape, fit that slot, and relate to the meaning of the story. Human brains are especially good at associative pattern matching, and superb at anticipating meaning, a phenomenon first reported by William James. Today, this is known as *analysis by synthesis* or *top-down processing*. Listeners continually anticipate words that are coming up next in a speaker's utterance. This is the reason that puns, other forms of word play, and sudden or odd shifts of context are surprising and amusing, because certain words mismatch our expectations.

Of course, people usually do not do this consciously. No one reading this book is aware that they see print they are not looking at. Nor can we monitor the fact that our brain is busily putting this "nonseeing" to good use. How then can we get slow readers to make use of this peripheral information to speed reading along? One way would be to train this faculty directly, by setting up a series of exercises for slow readers to practice making peripheral glances or to fixate straight ahead while trying to identify blurred shapes on the right. However, it turns out that there is a much simpler solution, one that produces the same results without the need to make an unconscious process conscious.

The NRP's Analysis of Fluency-Training Studies

In the introduction to the NRP's analysis of this topic, the authors pointed out that the old notion of "automaticity" as a natural outcome of accurate decoding has to be modified. In particular, they discussed the importance of syntax—"the ability to group words into meaningful grammatical units"—plus comprehension. It is not merely that fluency frees up "cognitive resources" for interpretation, but that fluency is implicated in the process of comprehension because it allows for "preliminary interpretive steps." This anticipatory analysis is similar to the notion of top-down processing discussed above. They link this to "parallel processing," the ability to perform multiple perceptual and cognitive tasks at the same time.

They also bring up another important point, that automaticity is not simply present or absent, but develops gradually with practice over a period of time. Reading speed is on a continuum, and, as we have seen from the developmental norms, there is no definitive measure of reading fluency. The reader is referred to the panel's excellent analysis of the problem of defining *automaticity* and *fluency* (National Reading Panel, 2000, 3-5 to 3-11). The introduction to the section on fluency is one of the highlights of the NRP report.

There are various approaches to training fluency. The NRP found studies on only two of these approaches: the process of "encouraging students to read more" and the technique of "rereading." We can dispense with the first at the outset after discussing some extraordinary facts. There is, perhaps, no more entrenched belief than that "reading a lot" plays a causal role in turning children into accurate and fluent readers who comprehend what they read. "Reading a lot" is supposed to increase vocabulary as well. One would imagine that this long-standing belief has been put to rigorous tests a number of times and been upheld, but this is far from being the case.

Nothing in the field of reading has spawned a more bountiful crop of articles and papers than the belief that "reading a lot" makes a difference with respect to reading skill, attitudes toward reading, and a host of other language and cognitive skills. The NRP search revealed 30 different approaches to how to increase children's reading volume. Using these 30 terms as search terms in one database (PsychINFO), they unearthed over 19,000 papers! Combining these terms with the primary areas of interest—reading speed, reading comprehension, reading skills, and so on—this number reduced to just over 1,000 (900 after foreign-language articles were eliminated). This was repeated with the ERIC database and overlapping articles eliminated.

Limiting the studies to those that appeared after 1991, there was a final set of 603 articles. The NRP investigators looked for studies that met the following criteria: research studies only, English K–12 reading education, and publication in a refereed journal. This eliminated all but 92 studies, of which only 79 could be located. After a close reading of these articles, only 9 could be retained, because most of this research was correlational. They extended the search to the bibliographies of the 79 studies. This produced 10 more likely candidates, of which only half could be retained. They now had 14 bona fide experimental investigations involving the *scientific* study of the impact of "reading a lot." Unfortunately, most of these studies had such a weak research design or other methodological problems that no meta-analysis could be applied to them. This is an appalling state of affairs.

The 14 studies were reviewed briefly. Most of these studies measured the impact of "sustained silent reading" or a similar approach. There was no evidence to support the idea that having children read for a fixed period of time, inside or outside the classroom, made any difference to vocabulary, reading comprehension, reading attitude, word recognition, or performance on general achievement tests and standardized tests. The NRP authors concluded as follows: "None of these studies attempted to measure the effect of increased reading on fluency. Instead, most of these studies considered the impact of encouraging more reading on overall reading achievement as measured by standardized and informal tests. It would be difficult to interpret this collection of studies as representing clear evidence that encouraging students to read more actually improves reading achievement" (p. 3-26).

They went on to stress that the poor quality of this research provides no definitive proof, one way or the other, that a regime of scheduled or controlled silent reading helps reading achievement. Given the fact that the outcome measures included the whole spectrum of reading compe-tence (except fluency), this is a scathing indictment. This pattern has been observed in every topic area so far. It is clear that we urgently need a proper database for scientific research on reading. ERIC has certainly never fulfilled that function, and now, it appears, neither does Psych-INFO. The NRP's discovery that only three of the studies in their review were methodologically sound is also an indictment of the research journals themselves and their editorial boards. Teachers need our help. Teachers should be able to find out how or whether time spent reading makes a difference to reading skills.

Rereading

Teachers have known for a century or more that rereading text will in-crease reading speed. Slow readers read faster after they have read the same story or passage many times. This technique has such an ancient history that E. B. Huey described it in his famous book on reading in 1908. However, the central problem with this technique is whether improved speed on one story will transfer to another story. If fluency is specific to only one passage or story, the rereading technique is worthless.

The NRP data search on *rereading* was much like the previous one, covering a wide range of programs with fanciful names like "echo reading" and "neurological impress." The same tireless search was carried out, with the result that 98 articles met preliminary screening requirements and were carefully coded. From this analysis, they found that there were a variety of different experimental approaches, which they classified into four categories. Only one category met the requirements for inclusion in a meta-analysis. This was a group of 16 studies (1970–1996) that were properly designed with pretest and posttest measures of reading, plus a control group. The other categories not included were the following: 14 studies on the immediate impact of repeated reading (no tests for transfer); 8 studies comparing different rereading methods and approaches, but lacking a true control group; and single-subject designs only.

Due to the differences in populations (younger/older children; good versus poor readers), only the most basic effect sizes could be computed. The first outcome measure was a global reading score based on whatever type of measure was used. The overall effect size for rereading training was moderately positive (ES = .48). Looking at separate measures of reading, the greatest impact appeared to be for word recognition (ES = .55), followed by fluency (ES = .44), and then by comprehension (ES = .35).

When normal versus poor readers were separated, and the data controlled for sample size, the effect size was larger for normal readers (ES = .50) than for poor readers (ES = .33). But, as the authors pointed out, this was confounded with the amount of time the rereading program lasted. Studies on normal readers tended to last longer.

I want to look in detail at the programs with the greatest success and take a more historical perspective. Little research appeared on the effects of rereading until the 1970s, when S. J. Samuels (the senior member of the NRP fluency panel) began to explore the aptitudes and strategies of efficient fluent readers compared to poor readers. He and his colleagues looked at how or whether using context enhanced reading speed. They investigated the impact of training sight-word recognition speed compared to rereading. Samuels (1979) reported that rereading with a target goal of 100 wpm led to increased speed and accuracy, with savings (transfer) from one story passage to the next, an effect that increased in efficiency with each of five story passages. By contrast, sight-word training (visual memory) was not effective.

Samuels's colleague, Dahl (1979), compared three methods (context, sight word, rereading) in a completely crossed research design, in which second-grade children were trained in one, or none, or any possible combination of these three methods. Dahl found that context-based training and the method of rereading were equally likely to enhance reading accuracy, but that rereading was most likely to increase reading speed. Sight-word practice on the 800 isolated words that constituted the text had *no effect* on either accuracy or speed.

While these studies were ongoing, Chomsky (1976) developed a rereading technique in which children read along with an audiotape. She reported that children improved in reading speed and accuracy, but there was not any hard evidence to back up this claim.

Since this early work, a number of important issues have come to light, and there has been increasing scrutiny of the assumptions about what rereading actually achieves. Because so many factors are critical in optimizing the effects of rereading, I will outline them here before discussing the more recent research.

Here are the questions that need to be addressed in doing research on rereading or in designing an effective rereading program:

1. Does reading get faster with or without a target goal (criterion of words per minute)?
2. Do children do better reading alone or with an audiotape?
3. Is rereading more effective than reading the same number of *different* stories?
4. What is the optimum practice time necessary to produce lasting changes?
5. How should this time be allocated: concentrated into a few days, or spread out over weeks or months?
6. How many different stories should be reread to ensure a lasting effect?
7. Does the difficulty level of the text make a difference?
8. Does overlap in the words from one story to the next make a difference?
9. Does overlap in story content/context make a difference?
10. Does prosody (reading expression) improve along with speed?
11. What kinds of transfer effects are there and how should they be measured?

Five main goals or outcomes need to be measured for rereading to be deemed a success. First and second, reading speed should increase with no loss of accuracy (or an increase in accuracy) as readers read faster. Third, oral rereading should produce increasingly appropriate phrasal boundaries and inflection (prosody). Fourth, comprehension should improve. Finally, there should be transfer effects. Reading speed should increase from one story to the next. If a criterion reading speed is set, this should be achieved more quickly with each new story. Accuracy and comprehension should improve with each new story as well. Getting children to read "fast" achieves nothing if they are inaccurate, fail to comprehend what they read, and do not stay "fast" from one story to the next.

Sorting out these issues turned out to be more difficult than people imagined. It is easy to get slow readers, accurate or inaccurate, to read much faster in a short space of time (within an hour). It is not easy to improve comprehension of that same passage or to show transfer effects. We may not have all the answers to the questions raised above, because individual researchers study different problems, and the children in the studies vary in age and reading skill, but we are getting close.

Setting a target criterion seems, on the face of it, a better approach than using an arbitrary number of repetitions—in other words, letting children reread without a goal. Children report they like rereading and enjoy having a goal. Because the studies vary, there is no direct proof of this assertion. What is important is that if a goal is set, children are capable of meeting it. This raises the question of where to set the goal, because rereading stops when the goal is met.

Training Studies on Improving Children's Reading Speed

Herman (1985) did a training study on slow readers in grades 4 through 6 whose reading speed ranged from 35 to 40 wpm. This is exceedingly slow. The slow readers were selected from children attending a reading lab in the school. These children were not only slow but inaccurate, scoring below the 17th percentile on a reading test.

The children read five different stories suitable for their reading level, about 2 years below their grade. A target speed of 85 wpm was set. The initial speed on story 1 was 47 wpm and the final speed 93 wpm, slightly above the target. At this point, the children chose another story and repeated the process. Students worked on this task for 10 minutes per session, twice a week, for total of about 21 days (210 minutes) spaced out over 3 months. The initial speed on the fifth and final story was 70 wpm, a clear improvement over story 1 (transfer effect). The final speed on story 5 was the same as on story 1 (92 wpm) because rereading stopped when the children met the target goal. (Would they have improved further if the target goal had been shifted higher for each story?) Accuracy showed excellent transfer. The average error score was 11 on the first reading of story 1, and this dropped to 7.6 on the first reading of story 5, a highly significant effect ($p < .01$).

Rashotte and Torgesen (1985) were interested in the impact of word repetition on transfer. The children were 8.5 to 12 years old. No target goal was set. Instead, improvement was measured by how much faster the child read after a fixed number of rereadings. Children's initial reading speed ranged from 31 to 62 wpm, with an average of 50 wpm. Because all the stories were at a second-grade difficulty level, reading accuracy was already good, and there was scarcely any room for improvement.

The children read about 15 minutes each day, for a total of 7 days (105 minutes). They were divided into three groups, and each group read slightly different materials. Two groups read various passages from the same story, rereading the same set of passages four times each session. For group 1, 60 common words repeated many times across all the passages. For group 2, the same story and the same passages were read, but the common words were replaced by synonyms and there was little word overlap. Both groups read passages from the same story on 28 occasions. Group 3 read 28 *different* stories, an important control for the impact of "reading a lot."

The two rereading groups increased their speed by 34 wpm to 84 wpm from the first to the last session. The reading speed for the children who read 28 different stories improved by only 5 wpm, proof that rereading increases speed but that "reading a lot" does not. When they looked at transfer in terms of speed, accuracy, and comprehension, only *speed* was found to transfer from one story to the next, and this effect was stronger for group 1, where passages contained the repeating words.

There were differences between the two studies that make them hard to compare. Superficially it looks like the gains in speed (93 and 84 wpm) were similar. But text difficulty varied. Herman's training was spread over 3 months; Rashotte and Torgesen's was concentrated into 7 days. In both studies, documenting improvements in comprehension was a problem. Rashotte reported no gains, but this may be because the stories were too easy and comprehension was nearly perfect to start with. Herman did find gains and transfer, but her comprehension measure was indirect and vague: "errors in context sensitive word substitutions." This measure sheds no light on whether story content was *understood* or remembered.

Nevertheless, there is agreement on certain facts. Rereading is effective almost immediately and children can reach a target speed when required to do so. Reading speed shows a transfer effect, particularly when there is some overlap in the words. Rereading is considerably more effective than reading the same number of different stories. Reading for speed does not occur at the expense of accuracy but actually enhances it. Improvement in accuracy is much easier to demonstrate when story content is close to reading level or grade level (not too easy). Like speed, improvements in accuracy will transfer from one story to the next. Measures of comprehension were confounded in both studies, and better methods were called for.

In 1987, Dowhower published the most comprehensive study to date. She investigated transfer effects for speed, accuracy, and comprehension, along with measures of prosody. She also investigated two types of rereading experience. One group of children read stories out loud without assistance, and the other group read along with an audiotaped version of the same story. The target goal in both cases was 100 wpm.

Dowhower was interested in beginning readers who were just making a transition from word-by-word decoding to more fluent reading. She screened 89 beginning second-grade students and selected 17 who fit the profile of "accurate but slow" readers. Children read the stories aloud, whether working on their own or with an audiotape. The group working with the audiotape listened to the story first, then rehearsed it out loud, with the goal of being able to read in synchrony with the tape.

The study design was complex. There were five stories (numbered 1–5), all at a second-grade level and 400 words long. There were two additional stories (200 words each) at the same level of difficulty: story A was read only once at the very first session (baseline), and story B was read only once at the very last session (the final transfer test). The rereading part of the study began at session 2. The children read the first 200 words of story 1 over and over until they reached the target of 100 wpm. This initially took many sessions. Dowhower timed each rereading to check how close the children were to achieving the target speed. Reliability checks were made throughout by using a second observer. When the children reached the target speed, they were asked to read the *second half* of the story—the last 200 words (the *first transfer test*). This transfer test preserved story context. Word overlap between the two halves of the story was not controlled.

When the children finished reading the transfer passage (once), they were asked to choose another story, and the process began again. This continued until all five stories were read at the target speed of 100 wpm. At the very last session, the children read the unrelated story (story B— *final transfer*) one time, and the experiment ended. Each child met with Dowhower for 15 minutes most days of the week, and this continued for as long as necessary to achieve the target goal on each story. The study lasted a total of about 7 weeks, approximately 7.5 hours per child. This is twice as long as the longest study above (Herman).

Gains and transfer effects were measured for speed, accuracy, and comprehension. Comprehension was measured by asking different questions about each story on the first and last trials. Statistical comparisons were made between the initial and final reading of the same story, the initial reading and transfer portion of the same story, all five initial readings, all five final readings, and the readings of stories A and B. Also, measures of prosody were coded from the child's tapes, and included things like inappropriate pauses, reading phrase length, and intonation. The results of the study are shown in table 7.1.

All contrasts in the table are significant for both groups of children, and there were no differences between reading alone or with an audiotape on any measures of speed, accuracy, or comprehension. Speed improved on the *transfer passage* (the last 200 words) from story 1 to story 5 by about 10 wpm. Accuracy was already good at the outset (the children were chosen for being accurate) and only got better. The results for comprehension were particularly impressive, improving from 57 percent (story 1) to 72 percent (story 5).

Transfer effects were also high when the children switched to a *new story*, as shown in the comparison of the *first* reading of story 1 to the *first* reading of story 5. Both groups began at 41 wpm and improved to 58–65 wpm, which is close to normal for beginning second graders. Again,

Table 7.1

The impact of rereading on transfer of speed, accuracy, and comprehension. (Data from Dowhower, 1987)

	Story 1	Story 5
First reading of the transfer passage		
Assisted Reading Practice		
Speed	53 wpm	64 wpm
Accuracy	188 words	189 words
Comprehension	58%	66%
Unassisted Reading Practice		
Speed	57 wpm	66 wpm
Accuracy	181 words	185 words
Comprehension	58%	66%
First reading of Story 1 and Story 5		
Assisted Reading Practice		
Speed	41 wpm	58 wpm
Accuracy	184 words	189 words
Comprehension	56%	79%
Unassisted Reading Practice		
Speed	41 wpm	65 wpm
Accuracy	180 words	186 words
Comprehension	58%	66%
	Story A	**Story B**
Assisted Reading Practice		
Speed	35 wpm	62 wpm
Accuracy	178 words	191 words
Comprehension	64%	80%
Unassisted Reading Practice		
Speed	38 wpm	67 wpm
Accuracy	179 words	188 words
Comprehension	68%	82%

Note: All passages were 200 words long.

accuracy was good at the outset and there was not much room for improvement. Comprehension improved markedly even though the story contexts differed, from 57 percent correct (story 1) to 66–79 percent correct (story 5).

The most impressive result was the savings across the five stories in how many trials (rereadings) it took to reach the criterion of 100 wpm. Both groups had great difficulty achieving this target goal on the first story, taking an average of 15 attempts. By story 5, the number of attempts was down to 4.5. What was once difficult had now become easy.

There was a large improvement between story A and story B, the stories read only once at the beginning and end of sessions. Speed increased from about 36 wpm to 65 wpm for both groups. Accuracy increased from 178 words correct to 190 correct out of 200 words. Comprehension on story B was 81 percent correct.

The systematic effect of transfer across all sessions is illustrated in figure 7.1, which shows the progression from the very first story (story A), through each initial reading of stories 1 through 5, to the final story (story B).

Nearly all measures of prosody showed significant improvement as well for both groups. However, the children reading with an audiotape improved more noticeably (and significantly) on several measures, showing that "reading with expression" improves more easily with a model. It is interesting that having a model did not have a differential effect on measures of speed, accuracy, or comprehension. One would imagine that hearing a story read with expression would assist comprehension by enhancing meaning.

Dowhower recommended that teachers use the rereading technique (either method), because it obviously works and children like it. She suggested using the assisted method first (audiotape), especially for children who read extremely slowly, and shifting to unassisted reading when children reach 60 wpm, when they seem to do better on their own. She observed that very slow readers were less frustrated working with the tape than working alone. She also pointed out that this is not a quick fix. The children did not make significant gains at the transition from story 1 to story 2, except marginally for speed. She had several suggestions for further research, such as looking at the relationship between prosody and comprehension, examining the different populations of children who

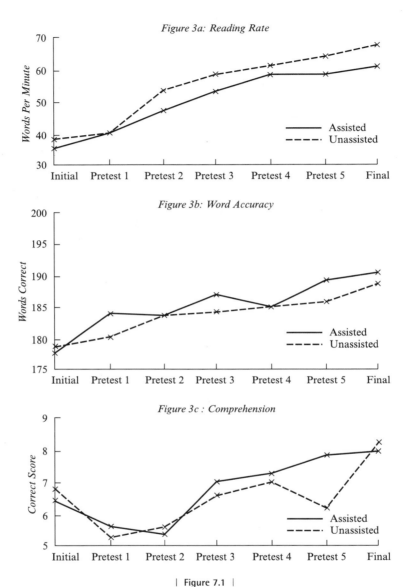

| **Figure 7.1** |

Mean scores for rate (WPM), accuracy, and comprehension for the *first reading* (trial 1) at the initial pretest (Story B). From Dowhower, 1987, p. 400.

benefit best from this technique, and considering whether rereading should be used as a "crash course" in getting children up to speed or as part of normal classroom instruction, interspersed with other lessons.

I want to add another suggestion. All these extremely slow readers dutifully achieved 100 wpm, and this got easier and easier with each story. When target goals are set, the children can never go beyond them. A moving target might produce longer-lasting results. For example, by the third story, the children needed only seven trials to get from a starting speed of 55 wpm to 100 wpm. Achieving 100 wpm, however, did not have much impact on the starting speeds of the next two stories (60 wpm and 61 wpm), despite the fact that the children *could* read at 100 wpm with good comprehension and no loss of accuracy. If the bar is raised a little each time, children might start coming closer to 100 wpm on the first reading.

Reading Faster While Noticing More
There is a speed/accuracy trade-off for any timed task, and people can consciously trade accuracy for speed, as well as vice versa. As a rule, one will suffer to the extent that the other is favored. Levy and her colleagues challenged this notion by asking whether people could read faster while monitoring the accuracy of the text at the same time. This tests the intuitive belief that when people read quickly, they will inevitably miss details.

In a series of studies on college students, Levy and her colleagues (Levy, DiPersio, and Hollingshead 1992) developed a proofreading task to measure the amount of detail picked up by expert readers as they improved in speed with each rereading. This study was designed to prove, one way or the other, a theory originally put forward by Levy and Kirsner (1989) that expert readers process both perceptual and linguistic information simultaneously as they read. The strongest test of this theory would be to find a secondary task that required the students to focus attention on details of the text while they tried to increase their reading speed. In the proofreading task, students had to cross out errors consisting of misspelled words, as well as syntactic or semantic errors that made the sentence meaningless. To measure the level of perceptual awareness, the investigators looked at whether novel (unexpected) changes in typescript or word spacing would disrupt reading and hamper reading speed.

Levy and colleagues got the usual rereading benefits in reading speed and also found that students could do the secondary task equally well as they read faster and faster. Misspelled words were easier to detect (at around 85 percent accuracy) than words that breached rules of syntax or semantics (around 70 percent). An error in word spacing or an abrupt change of font produced some interesting effects. They found that reading speed would slow even though subjects did not consciously notice the change. Apparently when a detail is inessential (does not affect proof-reading or comprehension), it impinges at an unconscious level but does not emerge into consciousness.

Levy and associates demonstrated that readers process perceptual and linguistic/cognitive information in parallel, and they do this so efficiently that much of the lower-level processing takes place below conscious awareness. Good readers are mainly aware of content and meaning, but they can easily become aware of perceptual detail with no loss of under-standing if their attention is directed to it.

Levy wondered whether this effect could be demonstrated with chil-dren, including those with poor reading skills. A similar study was carried out on 144 children in the third through the fifth grades (Levy, Nicholls, and Kohen 1993). Good and poor readers read one story four times and had to locate spelling and word errors. The instructions to the children stressed speed, and they were aware they were being timed with a stop-watch. After the fourth rereading, they transferred to a new story, and transfer effects were measured. The stories varied in difficulty level (easy, medium, hard).

Poor readers read much more slowly, but both reader groups in-creased their reading speed by about the same amount, around 50 seconds faster from the first to the fourth reading. Transfer effects for reading speed were proportionally the same, and were quite large. The children's success rate in spotting errors was similar to the college students', and detection patterns were the same as well. It was easier to spot spelling mistakes than notice errors that violated meaning. Error-detection rates increased modestly for both good and poor readers across rereadings, but improvement was inconsistent. Comprehension transfer did not occur until the fourth and fifth grades, and this varied as a function of story difficulty.

The authors concluded that "the more fluent rereading observed at each grade level, and for both good and poor readers, was achieved without 'guessing' or 'sampling' the printed pages. Word recognition became more efficient, not attenuated, as fluency was acquired" (Levy, Nicholls, and Kohen 1993, 321).

The studies by Levy and her colleagues added a new dimension to the rereading literature by showing that not only do adults and children improve in accuracy as they read faster, but they can also carry out a secondary task (proofreading) with no loss of accuracy. Furthermore, even poor readers can do this, and though they were worse overall, they had slightly higher gains in both speed and accuracy than normal readers did.

Levy and associates attempted to manipulate text difficulty in this study and did not succeed, perhaps because they relied on the publisher's criterion for difficulty ("grade level") instead of objective criteria, such as word frequency, word length, and so forth. In two subsequent studies with Faulkner (Faulkner and Levy 1994, 1999), this problem was remedied. The 1994 study is the most important study on rereading since Dowhower's investigation, because it nails down the final elements that determine what makes rereading successful.

The 1994 study contained four different experiments that manipulated the type of transfer task and text difficulty. The subjects were third, fourth, and sixth graders and college students, divided into good and poor readers. Poor readers were selected on the basis of accuracy (word recognition) and not reading speed. The first two studies involved an in-depth analysis of the impact on transfer of story context and word overlap (repetition of the same words). Each task consisted of two readings: the initial story and a transfer story. There were four kinds of transfer stories: the same story (*rereading*), a story with a high overlap of the same words (*word overlap*), a story with a high overlap in content/context but little overlap in words (*paraphrase*), and a story unrelated in content or words (*unrelated*).

The analysis focused on the reading rates and accuracy for the transfer story only. The results were the same regardless of grade level. *Rereading* the same story produced the fastest times and the fewest errors for everyone compared to the other types of transfer stories. When the remaining transfer stories were compared to each other, good readers improved most on the *paraphrased* version, and got no boost from *word overlap*. Poor readers benefited from both, but most from the overlapping words.

The results showed that when the text is difficult, word repetition is helpful and content overlap is less so. When the text is easy, similar content enhances reading speed and accuracy, and specific words are not as important. In other words, people are more likely to read difficult text at the level of the word (more focus on decoding), and process meaning less well. When people read at an optimum difficulty level, they read for meaning alone, and particular words do not matter as much.

If this is true, then story difficulty "causes" reading speed and determines the amount of meaning extracted from the text. This corresponds to the research on eye-movement control. Rayner (1986) found that text difficulty was the most likely cause of erratic eye-movement patterns. But does this always hold? The children in these studies were reading stories at their grade level. As a result, the stories were easy for the good readers but quite difficult for the poor readers. For this reason, Faulkner and Levy, in a second part of the study, varied text difficulty by tying it to reading skill, comparing good and poor readers across the age span. They used the same four types of transfer stories as before: *rereading, word overlap, paraphrase*, and *unrelated*.

They found that text difficulty level alone could make good readers look exactly like poor readers, reading at the same slow rate and level of accuracy. However, while poor readers did indeed read much faster when stories were easy for them, they never read at rates remotely like those of good readers. In one comparison, second-grade *good* readers and sixth-grade *poor* readers were both given a fourth-grade story to read. The two groups of children read at the same rate (120 and 117 wpm). But when the fourth-grade good readers read a very easy story 2 years below their grade level, reading speed soared to 151 wpm. In another study by Faulkner and Levy (1999), fourth-grade good readers read material at or above grade level at the rate of 159 wpm on the first reading and 182 wpm on the second. Yet poor readers at the college level read easy material at the rate of only 142 wpm.

These were not training studies. Children read stories far fewer times (only twice in the last set of experiments), and results will not be comparable to the true rereading studies. It is clear that a couple of rereadings will not be sufficient to bring poor readers up to speed even on simple stories. And while text difficulty is very important in determining reading speed, it only goes part of the way in accounting for poor readers' extremely slow reading speed. Something else is going on.

Poor readers may get caught in a text-difficulty trap, in which reading slowly becomes a way of life. This would happen if they got off to a bad start and began lagging behind their peers. The reasons would include such things as slow oculomotor development, language delays, lack of early experience with letter shapes and sounds, missing school through illness, poor instruction, and so on. Once behind, children who stay at grade level will always be reading material at a difficulty level beyond their comfort zone. Their reading speed will be slow and will remain slow even if decoding accuracy improves to average or better. This pattern would explain Wimmer's "slow readers," or at least a portion of them.

Summary

The good news is that children do not have to stay slow, and we now have the formula for success. The formula is the same for slow readers (accurate or inaccurate) and beginning readers alike.

Set target reading speeds well above the child's level. So far, no one has reported failing to achieve target levels 50 to 60 wpm higher than the child's baseline speed. I believe targets should be reset each time the child's reading speed improves by a certain amount. The final goal is to have the *first reading of the story* at a normal or superior rate for the child's age. At this point, rereading exercises can cease. Children need to have multiple rereading experiences (many stories), not just a few. Dowhower's time frame of about 7 hours' work over 7 weeks was effective and seems optimal. Time pressure was not excessive, and sessions were not spread so far apart that there were no carryover effects. The ultimate goal is the desired target speed on the first reading, and this goal determines how long the rereading sessions last.

The difficulty level of the text is critically important, because speed is tied to difficulty level. Very slow readers should start off reading passages at or just above their *reading level*, not their grade level. Once reading speed improves, stories should increase in difficulty. Passages with overlapping words are best for struggling readers and very young readers, and are most likely to produce carryover (transfer) effects from one story to the next. Overlapping context helps as well. This creates a situation in which transfer is successful and boosts confidence and motivation to continue.

This is far from the last word on this topic, because more research is needed to sort out the best way to apply these new findings in the classroom and in remedial settings. But the technique of rereading has finally come of age. Nevertheless, fundamental research questions remain. What causes children with good reading instruction to be slow, as found in the Salzburg studies? So far, the evidence is pointing to a low verbal IQ and a weak verbal memory. But other critical variables have not been studied, such as the rate of oculomotor development and the nature of the skills the child acquired prior to going to school.

VOCABULARY AND COMPREHENSION
INSTRUCTION

Printed words are oral language written down. Print is a filter through which people can exchange oral messages across space and time. To make these distant conversations possible, two things are necessary: you must understand the spoken language, and you must know how the code works (decoding accuracy and fluency).

Decoding and fluency are the gateway to reading comprehension, but they do not work in isolation from a child's vocabulary and oral-comprehension skills. This can be observed in a number of ways. A word might be accurately decoded (*vampire*) but have "nowhere to go," because the child does not know what it means. A word that is not in a child's vocabulary (*sympathy*) might lead to a distorted, though "legal," decoding (*sim-pa-thigh?*). A word that is known may fail to be decoded correctly due to anomalies in the spelling code, *glacier* read as "glassier."

Comprehension means more than a good vocabulary. It involves a number of core language skills, such as the ability to use syntax to antici-pate words in a sentence and assign unknown words to the appropriate part of speech. It includes an aptitude for monitoring context, making inferences on the basis of background knowledge, as well as familiarity with oral or literary forms (genres). Children with good oral comprehen-sion who read the phrase "the bunnies huddled in the dense green grass" may not know the meaning of the words *huddle* and *dense*, but they will know that *huddle* is something the bunnies are doing ("verb"), and *dense* is a property of the grass ("adjective"). They know this implicitly because of where these words occur in the phrase.

Other comprehension problems can arise from the nature of the com-munication or the text itself. Young children have particular trouble with a "story grammar"—the special sequential structure of a story and its fictional nature. This is surprising in view of the fact that children hear so many stories. Yet when children are asked to "tell a story," most cannot initiate or order the structural elements until around the age of 8 (Hudson and Shapiro 1991). They routinely omit the "flags" that signal a story beginning and ending ("once upon a time"; "they lived happily ever after"). They fail to provide a setting or any fictional characters. (Young children's stories are invariably autobiographical, with the children themselves in the title role.) They fail to create a problem or obstacle to carry the story forward (story line), which means there is no resolution (story apex). And despite what parents think, young children cannot retell a story they have heard scores of times. They invariably get the story sequence scrambled (Nelson 1998).

Reading comprehension is the end game of learning to read and necessarily involves everything that comes before it: a good vocabulary and good oral-comprehension skills, plus accurate and fluent decoding skills. If children do badly on a reading-comprehension test, any of these four things, alone or in combination, could be the culprit. Children who get low scores on a reading-comprehension test solely because they cannot decode are a very different from children who have low scores due to weak oral-comprehension skills.

In English-speaking countries, reading researchers have focused much more attention on decoding than on reading comprehension. In large part, this is a consequence of the enormous number of children who fail at this level. Nevertheless, the ultimate purpose of being able to read is to *understand* the message conveyed by the print. This is certainly the primary goal of most teachers, even in the earliest grades, as has been seen many times in this book. So far, we have learned that time spent on verbal language skills is time taken away from learning how to decode and spell. But we also know that decoding and basic spelling skills can be learned quickly if they are taught appropriately. And there are excellent techniques to improve reading fluency.

The tests used in the National Assessment of Educational Progress (NAEP) to estimate reading competency in the United States, measure reading comprehension, not decoding accuracy (Mullis, Campbell, and Farstrup 1993; Campbell et al. 1996). When NAEP reported in 1993 and 1996 that 43 percent of fourth graders in America were "functionally illiterate," this did not mean these children could not decode (though that may have been true as well). It meant they could not locate information or use the information conveyed by the text to interpret meaning.

The question here, of course, is whether the failure of these children was due to problems with decoding, to comprehension, or to a combination of the two. This point needs to be stressed, because it is frequently overlooked in the research on reading comprehension, despite the fact that the relative contribution of oral comprehension and decoding to scores on a reading comprehension test has been highlighted in a number of studies.

For beginning readers, decoding accuracy is more strongly correlated with reading comprehension than oral comprehension is (Juel, Griffith, and Gough 1986), but this quickly reverses. Hoover and Gough (1990) studied 254 children who were tracked from grade 1 to grade 4. Decoding was the best predictor of reading comprehension at first grade ($r = .84$), and oral comprehension was not a factor. At second grade a different pattern emerged. Now decoding and oral comprehension were equally important, with oral comprehension gaining ground from second to fourth grade (.71 to .87). However, the product of the two scores (decoding times oral comprehension) was more powerful than either alone ($r = .85$ to .91), accounting for 72 to 83 percent of the variance.

Aaron (1991) tested 180 children in grades 3 through 8 on the Woodcock Reading Mastery tests of word recognition and passage comprehension (Form G was used for reading and Form H for listening). The correlation between oral and reading comprehension grew larger over time, from $r = .65$ at third grade to $r = .75$ at eighth grade. The impact of decoding skill was not nearly as great; it decreased over time, ranging from $r = .36$ to $r = .21$. As in the previous study, the combined score (oral comprehension plus decoding) was a much stronger predictor than either alone, with fairly consistent values across the age range (mean = .85).

Aaron also discovered a large increase in reading speed over this age range. When words were read in context, children averaged 7.5 letters per second at third grade and 12.5 letters at eighth grade. Reading speed for isolated words was slower and less variable (6.0 to 7.6 letters per second). This shows that older children have learned to make good use of context in anticipating words.

Joshi, Williams, and Wood (1998) confirmed the listening-reading relationship on 273 bilingual children in grades 3 through 6. They used the same Woodcock tests, but modified the listening version of the test to a "cloze" format ("supply the missing word"). The correlation r between oral and reading comprehension ranged from .68 (grade 3) to .75 (grade 6), with a mean of .67, values almost identical to Aaron's. They also found that correlations fluctuated depending on the tests. They gave third and fifth graders three different standardized oral-comprehension tests and correlated these scores with a composite measure of reading comprehension. Correlations for the Wechsler were modest (around $r = .45$), but were stronger for the Woodcock ($r = .60$ for third grade and .65 for fifth grade), and stronger still for the Peabody comprehension test ($r = .69$ and .90).[1]

Nation and Snowling (1997) confirmed these findings in a factor analysis. Children were given a variety of decoding and oral-comprehension tests. A factor analysis is a mathematical tool for determining which test scores cluster or group together (known as "loading"), and is essentially a measure of the redundancy of the tests. The four decoding tests loaded on one factor at very high values (all above .86). Oral comprehension loaded on a second (different) factor at .95. Reading comprehension loaded on both factors equally (.62 and .67). Once more, we see that skill in reading comprehension is due to a combination of oral comprehension and decoding.

This is unassailable evidence that good oral-comprehension and decoding skills are not only critical to being able to understand what you read, but they are the only two skills that matter, accounting for nearly all the variance on tests of reading comprehension. There is no support here for the notion that reading comprehension is a special or isolated skill. We will come back to this issue later in the chapter.

These are critical findings with important ramifications for research. Studies of instructional methods for improving reading comprehension

---

1. As a general rule, *if correlations are real*, the better the test, the higher the values will be. This is a function of the items on the test, their difficulty level, and the number of items at each level. A good test increases the likelihood of a normal distribution, which will increase correlational values. The Peabody is considered one of the best tests available for oral and reading comprehension.

must control decoding skill. In view of the enormous overlap between oral and reading comprehension, methods of enhancing "reading comprehension" need to specify what is unique to *reading* comprehension—if anything.

In the remainder of the chapter I will look at the research on two types of instruction: vocabulary training and methods for improving reading comprehension. I will be departing somewhat from the format of the previous chapters, because the National Reading Panel's analysis of the vocabulary and comprehension studies was not handled in the same way as the previous topics. No meta-analysis was carried out in either case, and few effect sizes were reported. For these reasons, I have singled out certain studies for special attention and have computed effect sizes myself in all cases where this was appropriate.

Vocabulary Instruction

There is a popular theory that listening to stories and "reading a lot" causes vocabulary and comprehension skills to improve. This is assumed to be true because written text contains more complex and rare words than appear in everyday conversations. Haynes and Ahrens (1988) found that children's literature contains 50 percent more rare words than prime-time television or college students' conversations. When adult readers encounter unknown words, they try to work out meaning from syntax, context, and word derivation. This is a lifelong process that is never completed.

Thus there are two propositions one could hold about the relationship between vocabulary and reading. One is that "vocabulary causes reading," because the more words are stored in memory, the easier it is to decode them. The second is that "reading causes vocabulary," because if you "read a lot," you learn more new words. Both lines of reasoning could be correct (and probably are), and this has important consequences for reading instruction in the classroom. (We have already seen that "reading a lot" does not cause fluency or decoding accuracy.) But there are more fundamental issues.

Vocabulary Development

Research on vocabulary instruction has to build on basic knowledge of how vocabulary skills develop. So far, there has been a disconnect between the scientific knowledge of language development and the methods promoted by the educators and researchers. A prime example of this problem is Chall's descriptions of the 1960s basal-reader lessons, which showed that teachers took up most of the reading lesson explaining the meaning of words in the lesson that children already understood. We see it today in whole-language classrooms, where children are supposed to acquire new vocabulary (among other things) from listening to stories, and to guess word meaning from context cues as they read. We saw it in Sumbler's observational study on 20 kindergarten classrooms, where teachers spent the bulk of the language-arts period reading stories and doing vocabulary work, time that was *negatively* correlated with every reading test score, *including reading comprehension*. Evans and Carr's data showed that this negative correlation to reading comprehension increases across grades 1 through 3 ($r = -.70$ to $-.80$), the opposite of what teachers believe. This is strong evidence that not only do language activities take time away from learning the code, they do not even contribute to comprehension skills.

Given the fact that educators hold such strong views about the merits of vocabulary training, we need to establish a baseline, or starting point, for what children bring to the table. The average 5-year-old has a vocabulary of approximately 10,000 words and a 6-year-old, about 13,000 words. Throughout childhood, the average child learns about 3,000 words each year, though this number varies enormously from one child to another (Nagy and Herman 1987; White, Graves, and Slater 1990). This is about 10 new words per day. Children would have to learn at this rate in order to acquire even a garden-variety adult vocabulary of 55,000 words, the number of words that John and Mary Smith need to participate in everyday conversations. This pattern of rapid, untutored vocabulary acquisition begins in infancy at around 18 months and has been christened *fast mapping* by developmental psychologists. Children's books and other texts (printed school English) go well beyond the 55,000-word level. They contain about 88,500 words, according to Nagy and Herman's estimate.

Children are not taught these words. They pick them up from parents, friends, and other sources like television. If children stay true to the patterns observed in early childhood, they remember words that interest *them*, words that make it possible to discuss important events from *their* point of view (Nelson 1998). The rapid expansion of vocabulary is a central problem for vocabulary instruction and for empirical research. The amount of time it takes to teach new vocabulary directly, compared to what children are able to learn indirectly, must be taken into account. If it takes 6 months of daily drill to teach 40 vocabulary words so that all children know them, is this a productive way to spend class time? This point was also raised by Nagy and Herman.

The Importance of Parents' Input

But there is much more going on than "developmental rate." A remarkable study was carried out by Hart and Risley (1995), who monitored the enormous individual differences in vocabulary growth and the possible causes of these differences. Having studied children in Head Start programs, they became frustrated by the fact that it was hard to make a noticeable difference in the children's language skills. They believed the problem started much earlier and decided to study parent-child interactions in the home. These interactions were videotaped for 1 hour every month from the time the children were 9 months old until they were 3. Ultimately, 42 children and their families made it to the end of the study. Thirteen families were from the highest socioeconomic group and designated "professional." Twenty-three families were middle class, and six families were on welfare.

The focus was on the child's spoken vocabulary, and on how parents (usually the mother) spoke to the child. The mother's communications were scored for the number of words per hour, and for simple number counts of nouns, adjectives, past-tense verbs, and *wh*-questions used in each session, as well as her style of verbal interaction with her infant. The investigators tallied the number of imperatives, statements of approval and disapproval, examples of positive and negative feedback, and so forth. In the final analysis, these measures were grouped into five categories: *language diversity* (number of different nouns and modifiers), *positive feedback tone* (repetitions, extensions, expansions, confirmations, praise, approval), *negative feedback tone* (imperatives, prohibitions, disconfirmations, criticisms, disparagements), *symbolic emphasis* (the degree to which parents made connections between things and events, as indicated by richness of nouns, modifiers, and number of past-tense verbs), *guidance style* (the number of invitations—"Shall we?"—divided by the number of imperatives—"Stop it!"), and *responsiveness* (the number of responses to the child—"Oh, you want Mommy to take the ball"—divided by the number of initiations to the child—"Let's play with the blocks").

There were enormous differences between the high-, middle-, and low-socioeconomic groups on a simple measure of the mothers' verbal output to their children. The average number of words per hour addressed to the child between the ages of 13 and 36 months was over 2,000 for the professional mothers, 1,250 for the middle-class group, and 616 for the welfare mothers. This was despite the fact that welfare mothers spent, overall, more time in the same room with the child than the other groups did.

There were differences, as well, as a function of the child's age. Professional mothers not only talked much more to their babies (1,500 words per hour at 9–12 months) than the other mothers did, but this verbal barrage increased systematically with the child's age, leveling off by 30 months at around 2,500 words per hour. The middle-class parents spoke less overall, and their initial rate was lower and increased more modestly (1,000 to 1,500 words). The range for the welfare mothers was virtually nonexistent (600–750 words). Based on these numbers, it was estimated that by age 3, a child from a professional family would have heard 33 million words, a middle-class child, 20 million, and a child of a welfare mother, 9 million.

But this did not tell the whole story. The three groups were noticeably different in the way mothers interacted with their children. Professional mothers used a much richer vocabulary. Interactions with their children were consistently positive, at twice the rate of middle-class mothers and five times the rate of welfare mothers. Professional women rarely used negative feedback of any type. They were highly responsive and far less inclined to be directive. Middle-class parents were "similar but less so" in terms of the positive measures. Welfare mothers had a very different style of verbal interaction with their children. Almost 80 percent of the feedback to the child was negative and prohibitive ("Stop it." "What did I tell you?" "Put that back or else." "I said no!"). They frequently discouraged or disparaged their youngsters, calling them "stupid" or "dumb." Encouragement was rare, and sometimes absent altogether. This did not mean that mothers on welfare were cruel and did not love their children. They were affectionate and met their baby's needs.

The children's vocabulary development was strongly related to the sheer *quantity* of the words they heard. At age 3, children in professional families had an average spoken vocabulary of 1,115 words (true count), middle-class children, 750 words, and children of welfare mothers, 525. IQ differences between the groups were large as well (117, 107, and 79 respectively), which raises the question of how much of this effect was genetic. Verbal intelligence is highly heritable, genes accounting for over 50 percent of the variance, with shared environment accounting for the remainder (Plomin et al. 1999). Professional parents with high verbal IQs would be more verbal (talk a lot), use a more complex vocabulary, and handle the interaction with their child more sensitively (more "intelligently"). There is certainly evidence for this interpretation. Mothers' vocabulary scores were strongly correlated with their children's actual (recorded) vocabulary and with their children's IQ—possible support for the effect of heredity.

But heredity is not destiny. When they looked at the quality and character of the mothers' interactions with their children, these interactions turned out to be more important than the parents' vocabulary. All five categories of parenting style were highly predictive of the child's vocabulary, IQ score, and performance on general language tests at age 3. Not only this, but the parents' communicative style predicted their children's language skills almost as well when the children were followed up at age 9.

Although the mother's communicative style cannot be completely disentangled from her verbal IQ, we *can* see the impact of style on the child's language development. And there is certainly no reason why any parent *or any teacher* cannot copy what works best. Here are the key implications:

• The sheer *quantity* of parents' verbal input (total number of words per hour) predicts a child's spoken vocabulary later in time. (Other research has shown that speech must be child directed and not adult directed.)
• The *quality* of the communicative style (its richness, as well as the type of feedback the child receives) was a stronger predictor of the child's verbal development than socioeconomic status was. This was seen in the data for individual children, where socioeconomic status mattered much less than how the mother interacted with her infant.
• Five key communicative styles were identified. These are, in order of importance:

Guidance style. Provide gentle invitations to play and engage in positive interactions. Avoid prohibitions.

Symbolic emphasis. Make connections between words and things and other words.

Feedback tone. Positive feedback is good. Negative feedback is bad.

Language diversity. Use different nouns and adjectives as much as possible.

Responsiveness. Tune in. Follow the child's lead. Avoid telling the child what to do.

These guidelines are just as important in the classroom as in the home if the goal is to teach vocabulary and oral comprehension. Vocabulary training requires lots of repetition. It should include attempts to link new words to the child's vocabulary and knowledge via symbolic emphasis and use of analogy. New vocabulary needs to be embedded in a context-rich mélange of nouns and adjectives. Other items on the list are simply good pedagogy: the importance of offering positive and not negative feedback, as well as of finding ways to engage interest without demanding or ordering it.

Another basic issue is the question of the orderly progression of learning to read as it relates to vocabulary lessons. This question has become obscured by whole-word teaching methods, especially whole language. In the early twentieth century, children's readers were composed of words with "regular" (decodable) spellings that children understood. Story line, topic, content, and syntax were also geared to the age of the child. As children acquired decoding skills, books gradually increased in complexity and difficulty until children were encountering words they did not understand. Whole language has muddied the waters by substituting children's literature for simple readers and making this the only resource for teaching reading. Not only do the children in whole-language classrooms lack decoding skills (because they are not taught any), but they are faced with comprehension difficulties as well.

If reading is taught properly, there is a means-end reversal in the relationship between reading skill and vocabulary acquisition. As seen above, children's oral vocabulary is in advance of what they are able to read. After this, print vocabulary begins to outpace oral vocabulary. When this happens, books become an additional resource for children's vocabulary development. Do children pick up new vocabulary from reading books in the same way they pick up new words from listening to people? The short answer is that we do not know, because this is hard to demonstrate empirically. However, there are clues from studies investigating whether children learn new vocabulary from being read to by an adult.

At this point we encounter the Achilles heel of vocabulary research: how to measure vocabulary acquisition. The typical study involves exposing children to a set of new words, with or without special training, and measuring whether they learned them. Standardized tests are not good measures of vocabulary acquisition, because the training is specific to particular words. For this reason, researchers design in-house tests using a multiple-choice format. Children are asked to point to one of four pictures, or to circle the correct word among four words after hearing a word or definition spoken by the teacher.

Multiple-choice tests are *forced-choice* tests and susceptible to guessing. To control for this possibility, the binomial test must be carried out, as noted in chapter 6. Recall that this test computes the minimum score that is significantly greater than chance at a specific probability (i.e., $p = .05$). The formula takes into account the number of *choices* for each item and the number of *items* on the test. As a basic principle, tests with few items and few choices are very bad tests. To score significantly above chance at $p < .05$ on a two-choice test (true-false) containing ten items, a person must get eight or more correct (not five, as many people believe).

Despite the fact that multiple-choice tests are the most common measure used in vocabulary research, I have not come across any studies where the researchers knew how to address this problem, and most were unaware it was a problem. We can see the consequences of this oversight in the following group of studies.

Do Children Learn New Vocabulary from Listening to Stories?

Do children, in fact, do what teachers and parents assume and learn new words from listening to stories? Robbins and Ehri (1994) found (inadvertently) that much more is required to imprint new words on memory than listening to stories. They read a story to 38 kindergarten children (individually) in which 11 target words (new words) appeared either one or two times. A day or so later, the same story was read again. The story was read with no expansion or explanation about the target words.

After the second reading, the children were asked to listen to a series of sentences that contained either the target word or a novel word that was not in the story ("foils"). They had to point to one of four pictures that best fit the meaning of the sentence (25 percent correct by chance). The success rate for the foil words (words not in the story) was just over 3 words. The success rate for the target words was 4.4 words, not much better. Neither score was significantly above chance (5.6 correct is significant at $p = .05$). Only the high-vocabulary group scored this well, and just barely.

There is no evidence from this study that the majority of children learned *any* words, despite the authors' conclusions to the contrary. Even the high-vocabulary group learned only two or three words.

Senechal and Cornell (1993) reasoned that if parents or teachers used a more interactive style, this would enhance memory for new words. There were 80 four-year-olds and 80 five-year-olds in the study. All were middle or upper middle class. The design of the study was similar to the one above, with target words embedded in a story. The story-reading session (only one) took about 30 minutes. The target words were odd and unfamiliar (as they were in Robbins and Ehri's study): *angling, corridor, elderly, gazing, infant, lineman, reposing, sash, satchel, snapshot.* All had a familiar synonym: *fishing, hall, old, looking, baby, repairman, resting, window, purse/bag, picture.*

The children were tested initially on their knowledge of the target words and their synonyms. All children knew the familiar synonyms, but none knew the target words. The next day, they met with an experimenter (individually) and listened to the story. The story was read in one of four ways, which varied in how much repetition or questioning was involved. Immediately after this, the child took recall and recognition tests, and one week later, the recognition test was given again.

We can dispense with the four treatments, because they made no difference whatsoever to either age group. Children remembered just as well (or badly) when they heard the story read with no help or with explanations of the target words. We can also dispense with the data for the recall-memory test, because children did not do what they were supposed to do. When they were shown a picture representing a target word, instead of saying the word from the story, they gave the common word (the synonym) almost exclusively. Only 18 of the 160 children provided any target words throughout testing.

The recognition-memory test suffered from the same problem as in the Robbins and Ehri study: the fact that children would get 25 percent correct by chance. To their credit, Senechal and Cornell did address this problem, but their solution (subtracting pretest scores) does not take into account the number of items on the test. A child needed to score 5.0 or higher to do statistically better than chance in this study. As seen in the accompanying table, none of the scores met this criterion. (Scores are averaged across treatments.)

	Pretest	First posttest	Second posttest
4 years	1.6	2.9	3.5
5 years	1.8	3.5	4.3

These results show that a handful of children learned one to two words from initial testing to follow-up, but most children were just guessing. Even viewed in the most generous way, it takes 30 minutes per individual child to add one word to their vocabulary, and even then children will not use the word spontaneously, making it hardly worth the effort.

The target words in this and the previous study were decidedly odd. Children add words to their vocabulary so they can say something they could not say otherwise. There is no reason they would prefer the archaic/technical/literary target words in these stories as replacements for common synonyms they already know. This may be one explanation why these experiments did not work.

If experimenters reading to a child have no impact on vocabulary acquisition, would preschool teachers do any better? And if so, what type of teacher-child interaction works best? These were the questions addressed by Dickinson and Smith 1994. This study only serves to illustrate just how difficult an assignment this was. This was a naturalistic study in which the teacher's style of interaction during story time was uncontrolled. It was coded after the fact from videotapes in 25 different Head Start classrooms. At the end of the year, 25 children (5 years old) were randomly selected from these classrooms and tested on vocabulary and story comprehension.

The videos were coded for the amount of talk during story time for teachers and the children in each class, plus styles or types of interaction. The investigators coded 21 different measures, which were combined to represent three types of classroom interactions. The first was labeled *co-constructive* (5 classrooms), in which a high number of analytic conversations took place between the teacher and the children, prior to, during, and after reading the story. The second type was called *didactic-interactional* (10 classrooms). Talk was limited generally, and what talk did occur consisted of repetition (saying a sentence again) or answering a question. The final type was *performance-oriented* (10 classrooms). Here, talk largely occurred prior to and following reading the story, and the story was read with little interruption. The preamble to reading the story was often extended, analytic, and evaluative. When the story was finished, questions were asked about story recall and understanding. Sometimes this involved reconstructing the entire story piece by piece.

This was Dickinson and Smith's interpretation of what the data showed. But a table of probability values indicated that only five measures discriminated among the classrooms at a conservative $p < .01$. Most of these measures had to do with how much talk was going in the classroom by both teachers and children prior to, during, and after story reading. The only other discriminating measure was the proportion of teacher and child clarifications about the story. Using these more conservative measures, classroom "style" boiled down to two things: the total amount of talk by teachers and children, and how this talk was distributed between the prestory and poststory phases and during the story.

Vocabulary and story-comprehension measures were compared for the three types of classrooms. Children in the performance-oriented classrooms had significantly higher vocabulary scores than children in the didactic-interactional classrooms ($p < .01$). (One assumes no other comparisons were significant because no other values were provided.) No differences were found for story-comprehension scores.

There was a fatal design flaw in this study. *Vocabulary was not measured before the children entered the study.* Without this baseline, there is no way to know whether the children's vocabulary levels "caused" (animated and extended) the type of interaction that went on in the classroom, which seems highly likely, or whether what went on in the classroom "caused" the vocabulary. The authors opted for the second interpretation and did not consider the first.[2]

These are examples of some of the studies carried out on younger children, looking at the impact of simple story telling and story time on vocabulary acquisition. Basically, nothing was found. Children perform at chance on tests of story vocabulary, and while the classification of classroom "style" may have some validity, its impact on vocabulary acquisition cannot be determined without knowledge of the baseline measures of vocabulary.

Some insight about why children do not learn more from listening to children's books was provided by a study by Brett, Rothlein, and Hurley (1996). Earlier, Elley (1989) had reported that when difficult words were defined and explained, receptive vocabulary improved noticeably. Brett and colleagues set out to explore this systematically. Teachers were provided with two storybooks along with scripted definitions for 10 target words from each story, plus synonyms to help clarify meaning. The teacher would read "As the boy went back to the village, he felt despondent," followed by "As the boy went back to the village, he felt helpless." Target words were abstract, and included words like *indulgent, reverie, imminent, disdain, sauntered, obscure, emanated, immerse, exemplary*. There were 175 fourth graders in the study, divided into three groups. The first group heard the two books read over a 10-day period (5 days each), and the 10 target words were defined as described above. The second group heard the same books but had no explanation about the meaning of these words. The third group did not hear either book.

A multiple-choice vocabulary test was constructed for each set of target words. Children took this test prior to hearing the stories, immediately

---

2. A series of regression analyses were carried out in which the children's language scores were "correlated" with the various measures of classroom behaviors. I am unaware of any statistical tests in which *individual* scores from one set of tests can be correlated with *group* scores on a different set of tests. The investigators' claim that the "joint proportion of prompted or responsive analysis, prediction and vocabulary utterances by teachers and children" accounted for 50 percent of the variance in the children's vocabulary is unsupportable.

after the 5-day book-reading period, and also 6 weeks later. Only the children who were taught the meanings of the target words scored significantly above chance. They did well on both books immediately after training and also 6 weeks later, scoring around 50 percent correct. The control group that heard the books read for the same amount of time with no explanation, did no better than the control group that had never heard the books, both groups scoring at chance.

These results showed that simply listening to a story does not impact vocabulary acquisition. If new words are explained and synonyms provided in context, there is some success. Nevertheless, even a 5-day training period was not long enough for the children to remember more than half of 10 new words. Meanwhile, they would have acquired 50 words on their own without any training.

Direct Vocabulary Instruction in the Classroom
The volume of studies on vocabulary instruction peaks at around fourth grade, according to a tally provided by the National Reading Panel. This is the age where direct instruction in vocabulary becomes an issue, no doubt as a consequence of the format of basal-reader programs. Very little is understood about what methods work best and why.

Stahl and Fairbanks The first attempt at a meta-analysis of the classroom studies on vocabulary instruction was carried out by Stahl and Fairbanks (1986), who deserve a good deal of credit for their efforts. However, it must be noted that neither Stahl and Fairbanks nor the NRP vocabulary group discuss the ubiquitous problem of controlling for guessing on multiple-choice tests. This means that effect sizes will be based on bogus values and will be unreliable. This is a far greater problem than the variations in training methods, which was a major complaint in the NRP report.

Stahl and Fairbanks's review targeted the extreme variability in instructional methods as a key issue in coming to grips with this research. They established five categories for sorting the studies based on the degree to which the instruction was largely definitional, largely context based, or mixture of the two. They also identified another feature of the instruction in terms of the richness or depth at which new vocabulary words were processed. They isolated three characteristics of methods:

purely associational, comprehension oriented (using words in sentences, finding synonyms), and oriented toward generation (using words in novel utterances). The third category was the number of exposures of the words: one, two, or many. The fourth category dealt with the "setting," which included factors like whether the target audience was a group (classroom) or an individual, and, finally, how much time was spent teaching the words. Total time varied enormously from one study to the next, ranging from several weeks to less than an hour.

A study had to meet two criteria to be included in the database: it had to include a control group, and there had to be sufficient statistics to compute effect sizes. The researchers located 52 studies that met these criteria, including a total of 94 comparisons or "cases." The studies were further divided into group versus individual studies, by the number of minutes allocated to each new word, and by the method of instruction. The studies split about evenly among two types of control groups, one where the control children had no exposure to the words, and one where students had exposure (saw them in print or on worksheets) but got no special training. Test scores for both vocabulary and passage comprehension were reported.

The results of the meta-analysis were described as "trends" rather than anything definitive due to the high variability and the lax screening criteria. The total effect size for vocabulary training compared to a no-exposure control group was ES = .97, a substantial effect. Mixed methods of instruction worked better in all conditions than merely providing definitions or having students deduce meaning from context. However, as expected, effect sizes were substantially reduced when standardized tests were used to measure vocabulary and passage comprehension (ES = .30 and .29). Methods using multiple repetitions of the words had double the effect sizes, and this was true for all measures including passage comprehension. Effect sizes did not vary as a function of individual versus group instruction.

Stahl and Fairbanks discussed a variety of limitations with the studies, not the least of which was the vagueness with which the training program was described. However, this is not nearly as serious as computing effect sizes from unreliable test scores, and we have no knowledge of which test scores were reliable.

The NRP Report The NRP subgroup's analysis of the training studies, 14 years on, was disappointing. It would have been helpful to have an update, perhaps adopting Stahl and Fairbanks's classification scheme and comparing this to more recent research. Instead, the NRP declared all research null and void for purposes of a meta-analysis. The initial screening criteria were publication in a scientific journal, inclusion of a control group that was either matched or randomly assigned, and a proper statistical analysis. The initial search turned up 197 papers on "vocabulary" plus "instruction," and after screening, 50 studies remained in the pool. On further analysis of these 50 studies, the panel decided that no research met the NRP criteria that explicitly addressed measurement issues. In the executive summary of this report, the reason for ruling out a meta-analysis was a "heterogeneous set of methodologies, implementations, and conceptions of vocabulary instruction" (p. 4-3).

Instead, the panel provided brief descriptions of 40 studies, set out in various categories. Ten studies overlapped categories and appeared in more than one place. Included among them were the studies I presented above on storybook reading, where the data were invalid due to the failure to control for guessing. The panel was unaware of this problem and their report on these studies is inaccurate (see p. 4-21).

The NRP stated that Senechal and Cornell showed that "a single book reading significantly improved children's expressive vocabulary." However, there was no significant effect for *receptive* vocabulary in this study, and even Senechal and Cornell reported that there was no impact on *expressive* vocabulary, because they found that children used few target words to label the illustrations ... and there was not enough variability in the data to conduct statistical tests.

The NRP stated that Robbins and Ehri's method "helped teach children meanings of unfamiliar words." Yet the data were invalid in this study as well. They claimed that Dickinson and Smith showed that "the amount of child-initiated analytic talk was important for vocabulary gains" when it did nothing of the sort. Gains were never measured in this study (no baseline). The panel's final summary of these 40 studies was even more troubling, because these and other inaccurate conclusions were generalized further.

Direct Vocabulary Instruction Does Work

At this point, I want to provide more detailed information on a few of the better studies in the NRP report, studies that *do* demonstrate that vocabulary training works. I will be focusing on studies that were directed to an analysis of teaching methods and on the amount of exposure to the words (repetition and duration).

The most in-depth series of studies was carried out by Beck and her colleagues. Beck, Perfetti, and McKeown (1982) studied 56 fourth graders, mainly African-American students (70 percent) from lower-income families. They were taught 104 new words taken from the Ginn 720 series for fourth grade. These words were quite difficult and covered 12 semantic categories. Included were words like *philanthropist, filch, famished, scrutinize, diligent, meander, banter, gregarious, audible, introvert, compromise,* and *exotic.*

One classroom received the training and a control classroom did not. The training group was taught 104 words at the rate of 8 to 10 words in daily 30-minute sessions, over a period of 12 weeks (30 hours total). This averages to 17 minutes per word. After this, they continued learning 43 of these words for an additional 18 days, spread out over 6 weeks (45 hours total). This averages to 27 minutes per word. At testing, knowledge of the target words was contrasted with similar words that were not taught (control words) and also contrasted with the control group, which participated in their usual language-arts program. Training involved a mix of approaches, including learning definitions, word associations (synonyms), and creating sentences and contexts for the target words.

Posttest scores on a multiple-choice (in-house) receptive vocabulary test showed that the 43 words (longer exposure) were remembered with 86 percent accuracy, and the 61 words seen less often, with 78 percent accuracy (values significantly above chance). There was a modest transfer effect to the words in the stories not specifically taught, because the trained group scored 10 percent higher than the control group (41 versus 30 percent) and 10 percent higher than their own pretest score. The training also transferred to a standardized test (Iowa Test of Basic Skills). The experimental group gained 10 percentile points on the vocabulary and reading subtests from pretest to posttest, a gain not shown by the control group. These transfer effects were significant.

These are interesting results for several reasons. First, it took 30 hours (over 18 weeks) to bring the class up to an 85 percent accuracy rate on a measure of receptive vocabulary for the 43 overlearned words (27 minutes per word). Children also did well on the less trained words (close to 80 percent correct), but even this took 17 minutes per word. Meanwhile, with no instruction, these children will have picked up over 1,000 words during this period. As for whether the 104 words would enter productive vocabulary (be used), we have no idea, because this was not monitored.

Second, the transfer effect is important, because it suggests that the methods and strategies used in training to help children comprehend new words transferred to nontarget words in the stories, and to words on a standardized test the children had not seen before. This is valuable information.

The children also participated in a semantic-decision task ("Which word is a person?") and in a sentence-verification task (true-false) in which children could score 50 percent correct by chance. Unfortunately, failure to correct for guessing invalidates these data, and none of the statistical comparisons (experimental versus control groups) will be valid.

The impact of training on story recall was also measured. Three stories were created. One used the most exposed target words, one used the less exposed words, and one used control words (not taught). Nobody did well. The group that got the training performed exactly like the controls on the stories with the less exposed or untaught words, and did only slightly better on the story with the most practiced words (33 percent versus 21 percent correct). Peppering stories with 61 or 43 overlearned words did not make them any more memorable than the stories with novel, unfamiliar words. This suggests that the new vocabulary had not been integrated into productive vocabulary (vocabulary use), and/or that the stories themselves were hard to recall for the reasons discussed earlier in the chapter.

Beck's group (McKeown et al. 1985) continued to refine their teaching approach by examining timing and forms of instruction, again studying fourth graders. They contrasted two types of training. One type was described as "rich," involving elaborative and varied techniques. The second was described as "extended" because it involved activities and homework outside the classroom. One classroom was designated "rich only," one classroom "rich + extended," a third classroom used a traditional approach consisting of dictionary definitions and generating synonyms, and a fourth classroom had no training.

There were 24 target words taken from the previous list. They used two exposure levels: 12 repetitions for one set of words and 4 for another. One group learned the 24 words in twelve 30-minute lessons (6 hours), about 15 minutes per word. The other group learned the 24 words in four 30-minute lessons (2 hours), about 5 minutes per word. The training took 3 weeks, in contrast to the previous study, which lasted from October to March.

The measures were those used previously. Test scores for high-exposure words for all training groups (including the traditional classroom) were close to ceiling (95 percent correct) on the vocabulary-knowledge test. The absence of any effect of the different types of training was also found for the less exposed words, though scores were lower (84 percent correct). Obviously, scores are well above chance here, and they were also above chance on a test of semantics.

Group differences were mainly found on tests of productive vocabulary where children had to interpret and describe contexts related to the target words. The two "rich" groups did not differ, both scoring 75 percent correct on questions related to the most exposed words, and 50 percent correct on the less exposed words. The "traditional" group had significantly lower scores (60 percent and 40 percent).

Finally, the children were asked to recall stories written with the target words. Again, performance was poor. The two "rich" groups had higher scores on stories with the high-exposure words, but not much higher—averaging only 26 percent correct. Again, this result is curious. It appears that story memory poses a distinct problem in and of itself, and this may be relatively independent of vocabulary. It should also be noted that there was no advantage for the "extended" learning experience on any test.

There are some interesting comparisons between the two studies. In the second study, children scored higher on the vocabulary test after *fewer* learning sessions (fewer minutes per word). There are two possible explanations for this effect. One was a better teaching method. The other reason relates to Lloyd's (1992) discovery that fast and intense training is more effective for young children. Because McKeown et al. changed three variables that relate to timing—the number of words taught (24 versus 104), the exposure time for each word (shorter), and the length of the training (shorter)—there is more than one explanation for why all three methods (even the traditional method) produced almost perfect receptive-vocabulary scores (95 percent correct) for high-exposure words, and nearly as high (85 percent correct) for the low-exposure words. Was this due to learning fewer words, the compressed learning time, or both? The impact of the "rich" teaching approach versus the traditional approach appeared only on measures of productive vocabulary, which suggests that the teaching method matters most in enhancing recall memory.

These studies suggest that any method that calls attention to meaning *and* engages the student cognitively, produces gains in receptive vocabulary. Exposure duration and intensity of learning impact how well and how much is remembered. This general hypothesis may or may not be accurate, but it is certainly worth further study.

Jenkins, Matlock, and Slocum (1989) also found a "frequency" and "method" effect in a short-term study on vocabulary instruction. There were 135 fifth-grade children in the study, primarily middle class, with exceptionally high vocabulary and reading-comprehension scores on standardized tests. The goal was to teach 45 target words. The children were taught with either of two methods. In one, word meanings were taught directly, and in the other, meaning was derived from context. In addition, words were seen once, three times, or six times. Training took place over 9, 11, and 20 days depending on the amount of exposure. Children spent 15 minutes per day learning these words, about 5 hours for the long-exposure group (6.5 minutes per word).

"Training for meaning" included memorizing definitions, using the target words in a sentence, and substituting synonyms for the target words. "Context training" involved applying a sequence of strategies: (1) substitute a word or expression for an unknown word, (2) check other context clues to support this choice, (3) determine whether the substitution fits all context clues and if not, (4) revise the word and start again.

Knowledge of the target words was tested for both productive and receptive vocabulary. The context-learning group did not do well on any of the tests at any exposure condition (low, medium, or high). They scored about 1 correct for finding synonyms for isolated words, and were only marginally better for finding synonyms for words in context (3.25 words across all conditions). The context group did not score significantly above chance on receptive-vocabulary tests, so the authors' statistical analyses of these data will be invalid.

The group taught the meaning-based method did much better, and their performance was strongly affected by the number of exposures to the word. In the synonym test, they scored three times higher after six exposures than after one, whether words appeared in isolation or in context. And they scored twice as high after six exposures on easy and difficult receptive-vocabulary tests (85 percent and 75 percent correct). The high-exposure group scored well above chance throughout.

Summing Up

The results from these well-executed studies are very consistent. Frequency of exposure to new words makes a big difference *only* if students have some guidance (instruction) and gain a deeper understanding of what these words mean. Deriving meaning from context analysis is not effective. It appears to be too abstract, even for bright fourth graders. This finding contradicts the major tenet of whole language, that children can easily derive meaning from the pictures and context clues *and* do this while they teach themselves to read.

Vocabulary can be taught, and there is solid evidence on which teaching methods have value. We also see that repetition is critical, and that short-term (intense) teaching works better than lessons spread out over a long period of time. As to whether teaching new vocabulary is "worth it," the fact that these abstract words would be unlikely to be acquired spontaneously suggests that this is a good idea. Using the right method and approach, the cost is only around 5 minutes per word. Stahl and Fairbanks pointed out that learning just 300 words a year will increase vocabulary size about 10 percent. This is around two new words per day of *classroom* days (175 days). However, there is considerable debate about the effectiveness of teaching isolated words rather than learning new vocabulary in the context of general comprehension training. As we will see in the next section, a good comprehension program dramatically enhances vocabulary, even when this is not a specific feature of the lessons.

Teaching Reading Comprehension

There is an implicit assumption behind much of the research on reading comprehension that it is different in kind from oral comprehension. This can be seen in the absence of any consideration of the connection between them in almost every study on this topic. It is evident in the NRP comprehension panel's opening remarks. They cite Markman (1978) as a primary catalyst for interest in doing research on reading comprehension. The tenor of Markman's remarks is that certain comprehension skills are specific to reading, noting, for example, that readers often fail to detect logical or semantic inconsistencies in text. The NRP panel paraphrased some of her ideas:

Reading comprehension was seen not as a passive receptive process, but as an active one that engaged the reader. Reading came to be seen as intentional thinking during which meaning is constructed through interactions between text and reader....

Reading comprehension was seen as the construction of the meaning of a written text through a reciprocal interchange of ideas between the reader and the message in a particular text. (p. 4-39)

It is not clear whether this is intended to mean that before Markman had these insights, people believed that reading comprehension was "passive" and that readers "failed to contruct meaning," or that Markman believes that reading comprehension is unique. But it is obviously the case that *listeners* are equally likely to fail to "detect logical or semantic inconsistencies" in speakers' utterances, as well as the fact that *listeners* always engage in active interpretation and reciprocal exchanges of ideas during a conversation.

What then is special about reading comprehension? *Why does it need to be taught?* We never get an answer to this question.

The numerous attempts to discover ways to teach reading comprehension have spawned a variety of methods, but there is little substantive work in this field. The NRP classified 16 different approaches, and even this was difficult. Various strategies have been proposed that involve a wide range of different techniques for targeting certain modes of thought, such as predicting what will happen, noticing contradictions, making inferences, asking specific types of questions, and so forth.

Because these methods are for the purpose of impacting *reading* comprehension, another key variable comes into play that gets short shrift in this research. Poor comprehenders are the subject population in many of these studies. As noted earlier, children are poor comprehenders for different reasons. Poor decoding skills influence reading comprehension. Slow but accurate readers also have reading-comprehension problems. There is a striking relationship between reading fluency and measures of oral syntax (Willows and Ryan 1986). Rayner (1998) cites 40 studies on the connection between eye-movement patterns, reading speed, and syntax. Children with low verbal skills are also poor comprehenders. Without proper control over these variables, a research study has no validity. After reviewing much of the literature, I found that this is often the case.

Furthermore, when you teach "reading-comprehension" skills to children with good or excellent *listening* comprehension but who score badly on *reading*-comprehension tests, what exactly are you teaching? How is the teacher supposed to know where the child is in the reading process if listening comprehension, decoding accuracy, and reading speed are never measured?

A Meta-analysis

Apart from these concerns, there are problems with how reading comprehension is measured in these studies. Unlike the research on vocabulary instruction where specific words are taught and tested, training in reading comprehension *must generalize* to other text to prove the validity of the method. The results of a large review show that it does not. Rosenshine, Meister, and Chapman (1996) did a meta-analysis on 26 studies that dealt with "questioning" types of instruction. As they put it, "Teaching students to ask questions may help them become sensitive to important points in a text and thus monitor the state of their reading comprehension" (p. 183).

The method had to include a large proportion of time spent generating questions to help students understand a passage for the method to be included in their analysis. Also included were studies using "reciprocal teaching," in which both teacher and students collaborate to interpret a passage. Rosenshine and colleagues excluded all studies where the children were tested on the same passage they had been trained on. The overall result was an effect size of .86 for experimenter-generated tests—test passages that had a *similar structure* to the passage on which the children were trained. However, this training did not generalize, and there was little transfer to standardized measures of comprehension (ES = .36).

The studies were broken down further into five different types. One was "signal words" in which the student is prompted by words like *who*, *what*, *where*, *when*, *why*, and *how*. The second type involved "generic questions." Here the student is trained to ask a variety of questions, such as how two things are alike or different, what the main idea is, or how events or actions are related to one another. The third type was "main idea only," in which children find the main idea and then ask questions about it. "Question types" comprised the fourth category. Here students are first directed to find specific information, then to relate two or more pieces of information, and finally to answer questions where information must be inferred or deduced by logic and background knowledge. (The NAEP tests are based on this approach.) The fifth type encompassed questions about story grammar like those reviewed earlier: "Who is the main character in this story?"

On the experimenter-designed tests, the "generic-questions" approach generated the largest effect sizes, followed by the "signal-words" technique. Finding the "main idea" did not fare well. Other types included too few studies to make effect sizes meaningful. As for performance on standardized tests, the "signal-words" group produced an effect size of .36, and the "question-type" group an effect size of zero. Even more interesting, Rosenshine, Meister, and Chapman found no evidence for the impact of length of training. Paradoxically, studies with positive results had fewer sessions overall (4 to 25) than those with nonsignificant results (8 to 50). This fact alone calls most of this research into question. With a good method, learning time ought to translate into better learning, not worse.

The authors commented on the contrast between experimenter-designed tests and standardized tests. Experimenter-designed tests were more highly structured, with a clear "main idea" and obvious supporting detail. Standardized test passages were more typical of normal text, without such a clear and obvious structure. It should also be noted that standardized tests are normed and control for age, whereas experimenter-designed tests are not. Experimenter-designed tests usually employ multiple-choice questions and are subject to guessing. As we have seen, researchers in this field generally do not correct for guessing. In view of these facts, much of this research is likely to be meaningless.

The NRP Report

The NRP group located 203 studies that survived their final screening protocol. However, because these 203 studies included over 16 different methods, with few, if any, studies carried out in the same way (same training, same duration, same tests), the panel felt that a meta-analysis would be out of the question. Instead, they categorized the methods and made some observations. This was not a productive exercise, and their analysis was contradictory and uncritical to the point of being biased.

Of the 16 types, the panel reported that only 7 had a "firm scientific basis for concluding that they improve comprehension in normal readers" (National Reading Panel, 2000, 4-42). (The report did not reveal what this basis was.) Six of the types included *comprehension monitoring, cooperative learning, graphic organizers, question answering, question generation*, and *story structure*. Several of these approaches can also combine to form a seventh, a *multiple strategy* approach.

It should be noted that the NRP screening protocol did not include important methodological considerations that would bias the outcome of a study, such as situations where (1) the subject pool consisted of poor readers whose decoding skills were ignored while they were taught to "comprehend" what they could not read, (2) the tests measuring gains used the same passages on which the children were trained, (3) experimenter-designed multiple-choice tests were utilized and the data were not corrected for guessing, and (4) no measure existed to ensure the method was implemented as described. Comprehension training programs are very complex, often taking pages to describe. Documentation is needed (in the form of classroom observations or video) to show that the teacher actually taught the method as intended.

Aside from these concerns, the NRP authors provided no evidence on the generality of the studies they believed were valid. There were 96 studies in the 7 categories, yet only 20 percent of these studies were cited as using standardized tests. The NRP did not provide the data from these tests. Comprehension instruction must impact reading comprehension for a variety of texts, not just for one unique text.

Instead, the panel accepted the evidence from the experimenter-designed tests as valid. In their summary of the methods under review, they came out strongly in favor of the *multiple strategy* approach, particularly one that included a *reciprocal teaching* method. The main support for this conclusion came from a meta-analysis carried out by Rosenshine and Meister (1994) on 16 reciprocal-teaching studies. They reported an effect size of .88 on experimenter-designed tests, but only .32 for when standardized tests were used (9 of the 16 studies). In other words, this method did not generalize to other texts.

It is disconcerting for the NRP authors to claim that the 203 studies remaining in their data pool could not be submitted to a meta-analysis, and then to cite a meta-analysis carried out by someone else on a fraction of these studies as the sole support for their evaluations of the methods. This is especially problematic in view of the fact that a subsequent meta-analysis by the same group (Rosenshine, Meister, and Chapman 1996)—which the NRP did not cite—compared reciprocal teaching to other instructional methods, and found it had *no advantage*, either on standardized tests (ES = .23 versus ES = .27) or on experimenter-designed tests (ES = .88 versus ES = .70). Effect sizes were not significantly different in either case.[3]

It is of some interest to provide evidence on one of the better (methodologically sound) studies using reciprocal-teaching techniques. Johnson-Glenberg (2000) compared two types of reading-comprehension training with each other and with an untutored control group. Children in the third through fifth grades were trained in small groups for 10 weeks with either a reciprocal-teaching (RT) approach or a visualizing/verbalizing (V/V) program developed by Bell (1986). They received an average of 28 half-hour sessions (14 hours total). The children had good to high decoding skills but poor comprehension skills.

The reciprocal-teaching approach was adapted from Palincsar and Brown (1984) and consisted of four strategies: summarization, clarification, prediction, and question generation. The lessons began with exer-

---

3. I did not include cases where there was one study only per method in these effect sizes.

cises in summarizing very short passages, and then gradually expanded so all strategies were engaged using longer text passages. In reciprocal teaching, the teacher and the children have equal input in the process. The visualizing method trains imagery by having students describe verbally in great detail how they "see" certain characters, settings, objects, and events, in their mind's eye.

The children were tested on 12 different measures prior to and after training, including four standardized tests. Interrater reliability was computed for all in-house tests and was consistently high. The investigators also computed effect sizes for pretraining and posttraining scores. Children improved over time on most tests, with the exception of the control group on the WRAT word recognition (standard scores), a measure of reading speed, explicit questions on story recall, and open-story recall.

WISC vocabulary scores were controlled (covaried) in the group comparisons, and this significantly dampened the differences between groups. Nevertheless, the RT groups outscored controls on six measures: WRAT word recognition, question generation, explicit-questions story recall, implicit-questions story recall, listening story recall, and visual questions. I computed effect sizes for these specific comparisons, and these were, respectively, ES = .34, 1.0, .78, .65, .35, and 1.55. The V/V groups outscored the controls on three measures: question generation, implicit-questions story recall, and visual questions (ES = .54, .76, and .37). Interestingly, the V/V groups did not score higher than the other two groups on the remaining *visual* measures: the paper-folding test and a test of visual imagery. The RT groups also outscored the V/V groups on question generation, explicit story recall, and listening story recall (ES = .51, .66, .53). However, despite the strong effects of training on the mainly in-house tests reported above, no group differences were found on the only standardized measure of reading comprehension (Gates-MacGinitie) or on the Detroit Test of Learning Aptitude.

This was a fairly rigorous test of the RT approach, and while it had an advantage over the V/V training, differences were not that great. It is important to note that Johnson-Glenberg reported highly significant gain scores for the trained groups on all 12 measures before vocabulary was statistically controlled. These differences were seriously curtailed after these controls were introduced. Here is another wild card that is certain to influence outcomes in these studies. Vocabulary is rarely controlled in most studies on reading comprehension.

There is some evidence here to support the NRP comprehension panel's recommendation in favor of RT, but the evidence does not support their general conclusions, which they furnished in a summary to this section. They provided a hearty endorsement of teaching comprehension strategies in general: "The past 2 decades of research appear to support the enthusiastic advocacy of instruction of reading strategies" (p. 4-46).

This positive outcome was attributed to methods in which teachers

demonstrate, explain, model, and implement interaction with students in teaching them how to comprehend a text. In studies involving even a few hours of preparation, instructors taught students who were poor readers but adequate decoders to apply various strategies to expository texts in reading groups, with a teacher demonstrating, guiding or modeling the strategies, and with teacher scaffolding. (p. 4-47)

The effectiveness of this reciprocal interaction between teacher and students was alleged to be consistent with "socially mediated learning theory." No specific study or evidence was referenced in support of these conclusions. The only source cited was Rosenshine, Meister, and Chapman 1996, which found nothing of the sort.

Following this endorsement, the next and final section of the panel's report was highly critical of the research on reading comprehension, and largely contradicted everything that came before. Lysynchuk et al. 1989 was the main source for this critique. This publication screened 37 studies on comprehension instruction and coded 24 variables of methodological relevance. There was a substantial fail rate on 9 of them. These were, in order from the very worst to the least: used the correct unit of analysis for statistics (83 percent fail); monitored the strategies the students actually used, as opposed to the ones they were supposed to use (73 percent fail); provided information on training time (70 percent fail); and checked whether students were doing what they were supposed to do (63 percent fail). There were several variables with a 35 percent fail rate: random assignment of children to groups, exposing the controls to the same materials as the experimental subjects, ceiling and floor effects on the tests, and lack of interrater reliability checks on in-house tests.

Overall, this is a very gloomy analysis from all points of view. I do not regard this research, taken as a whole, as providing any proof whatsoever of the validity of comprehension instruction. Instead, I want to examine the only two studies I could locate that are both methodologically rigorous and that illustrate the true power of good comprehension training. Both methods involved extensive efforts over long periods of time and produced solid gains on standardized tests.

Reading-Comprehension Programs That Work

Brown et al. (1996) employed a method known as *transactional strategies instruction* (TSI), a form of reciprocal teaching in which everyone cooperates to ask and answer questions. This process is teacher directed. As they put it, "The short-term goal of TSI is the joint construction of reasonable interpretations by group members as they apply strategies to texts" (p. 19).

Students are trained to "predict upcoming events, alter expectations as text unfolds, generate questions and interpretations while reading, visualize ideas, summarize periodically, and attend selectively to the most important information" (p. 20). Students think aloud while they are learning to do all this.

The authors report that it takes several years of training and experience before teachers can implement this method effectively.

Five reading groups using TSI were compared to five groups taught with an eclectic approach (specific to teacher) over the course of one school year. Students were second graders, reading below grade level. They were matched on Stanford Achievement Test scores and randomly assigned to ten groups of six children each ($N = 60$). I was unable to locate information on the number and duration of lessons per week.

A number of in-house tests were designed to measure outcomes. However, I will focus only on the standardized tests. After training, the TSI children were significantly advanced on the SAT comprehension subtest and the "word-skills" test (word recognition). I computed effect sizes and found the ES value was .67 for word-study skills and .89 for comprehension, compared to controls. These are substantial effects and show that this program generalizes beyond the texts used in training. However, it cannot be known how much is due to method and how much to exposure, because Brown and colleagues did not report how much time was devoted to teaching this program. Also, in the case of children with poor reading skills, there is a strong possibility that a fair proportion of these children had lower-than-average verbal IQ scores, and verbal IQ was not controlled.

The last study (Block 1993) was the only study I was able to locate in which the method of instruction had great generality for improving critical-thinking skills beyond the immediate task. It was also the only study that solved nearly all the methodological problems, and the only study where there was a clear understanding that reading comprehension is a consequence of oral comprehension. The paramount goal of transfer and generalization was set out in the introduction. I paraphrase:

1. If instruction helps students use strategic processes consistently and reflectively as they read, they should comprehend and use more information in their daily lives.
2. Students who have trouble comprehending may need a new type of instruction, involving new strategies and thinking/reading competencies.
3. Students who are confused about important concepts, inferences, and relationships in a text may never have encountered the inductive or deductive reasoning patterns the author used to create the text. If these thinking strategies are explained prior to reading, thinking repertoires should expand.
4. Students may be more able to generalize this new knowledge to solve decoding and comprehension problems on their own.

Block uncovered eight strategies that are important and need to be taught. These reflect such things as basic cognitive operations, analytic thinking, decision strategies, problem solving, metacognitive analysis (awareness of one's current state of knowledge), creative thinking, plus skills for working in groups, and skills for working effectively alone. Sixteen lessons were designed to teach these strategic skills, and these lessons were carefully field tested across all grade levels on a large number of children prior to this study.

The lessons were structured so that one critical-thinking technique was introduced per lesson, plus strategies for improving comprehension. This constituted part 1 of the lesson. In part 2, children selected reading material to apply this new knowledge. They could choose from a large selection of books among a variety of genres: fiction, nonfiction, poetry, autobiographies, folk literature, periodicals, and science fiction. Children were given simple and useful handouts for how to attack an unknown word, and to increase their understanding of what they read. They were encouraged to ask questions and to learn to recognize what a good (productive) question is. There is no space here to review this program in depth. The description of the method was detailed and precise.

There were 16 classrooms in the study ranging from grades 2 through 6 (352 children). Half the classrooms received the special lessons, and half acted as controls. A trained research assistant was present in every classroom during the language-arts period and worked together with the teacher. In the experimental classrooms, these assistants helped with the prescribed lessons, and in the control classrooms they helped the teacher present lessons that did not include the strategy instructions. The lessons continued throughout one school year, 3 hours per week for 32 weeks, for a total of 96 hours.

Treatment fidelity was measured by videotaping the last lesson in each classroom. Tapes were coded "blind" by raters who did not know which classroom got the training. There were ten significant and important differences in the children's verbal and physical behavior between the two types of classrooms. The trained children had more highly skilled interactions (verbal exchanges) and far less nonproductive behavior (near absence of interruptions, random remarks, noise, use of jargon or slang, and off-task behaviors/boredom), which is remarkable in and of itself!

On the reading-comprehension subtest of the Iowa Test of Basic Skills, the trained group scored significantly higher than the control group ($p < .001$), and they improved in vocabulary as well ($p < .001$), although this was not a focus of the training. There was little impact on grammar. This was expected, because grammar was not taught. I computed effect sizes for these results. The effect sizes were 2.24 for comprehension, 2.62 for vocabulary, .32 for grammar, and 1.34 for Total Reading. These figures are very impressive, one could even say extraordinary, in view of the typical results in this field.

Block used a number of additional tests to measure generalization effects. Children from the trained group were much more likely than control children to represent analytic thought in their writing ($p < .0001$), and to report that what they had learned at school was useful outside school (92 percent reporting "useful," versus zero for the controls). The trained children had significantly higher self-esteem, though the groups had not differed at the outset of the study. On tests of problem solving, the trained groups used a greater number of critical-thinking strategies, were more precise in their statements about these strategies, and offered a larger number of alternative solutions to the various problems. The results in these comparisons were highly significant ($p < .0001$ in all cases).

Block's outstanding work was published in 1993 and, so far, seems to have had little impact on the research community. No other method comes close to achieving the goals of what a good comprehension program is supposed to do. Not only does it generalize to standardized tests (with huge effect sizes), but to all forms of analytic thought, academic performance, and classroom behavior, and it works across a broad age range, requiring little teacher training. Furthermore, it produces a huge impact on vocabulary, even when measured by standardized tests. This is quite beyond anything achieved in the vocabulary-training studies cited in the previous section.

Overall, the research is this field is extremely problematic. There are certainly good instructional methods, but for the most part, they have been ignored by the research community. Instead, educators and reseachers seem more interested in designing their own unique approach than in building on one another's work. As a result, instructional methods are highly idiosyncratic and difficult to classify.

General Conclusions

The past few chapters have shown that there are some remarkable instructional methods for almost every type of reading skill, methods that produce close to 100 percent success for every child. This is the good news. Wouldn't it be exciting if everyone knew about these methods, especially teachers? Unfortunately, due to the enormous volume of published and unpublished research, these excellent methods are very hard to locate.

It is difficult to be neutral about the fact that there is such a vast quantity of poor research ("junk science") clogging the reading-research databases. In the real world of science, the most rigorous and most important studies tend to find their way to the top journals. Here, quite the opposite is true. The flagship journals, of which there are only two, are just as likely to publish research that is methodologically flawed as not.

(Among a very large pile of papers on comprehension I had to set aside because of fundamental problems with methodology, 80 percent were published in the top two journals.) This creates the impression that either the editors and reviewers know next to nothing about research methodology, or that they are overly influenced by who is "important" in the field and who is not. As a result, talented unknowns must seek publication in journals near the bottom of the food chain. This makes the problem doubly difficult, because readers are just as likely to find high-quality work hidden amidst the dross almost anywhere they look. Readers should not need a Ph.D. in statistics and research methodology because they are forced to analyze the research design, redo the statistics, and critically assess authors' conclusions from the data. That is the reviewers' job and the responsibility of journal editors.

The combination of quantity (too many articles without any peer review on the databases, and too many journals) plus the lack of any mechanism for determining quality (no way to rely on journals; no way to rely on databases), means that the scientific study of reading is basically going nowhere and has been going nowhere for over 30 years. One might even argue that it is going backward, in view of the fact that the majority of researchers in the field still seem to believe that children need an extensive phoneme-awareness training program in addition to an effective phonics program. That belief is so powerful that the NRP ignored the evidence in its *own* database and in its analysis of what children need to be taught.

When we come to spelling, a topic not even considered by the NRP, the situation is far worse, as we will see in the following chapter.

HOW DOES ANYONE LEARN TO SPELL?

In a deeply opaque writing system like the English alphabet code, most phonemes have multiple spellings. Only eight are reliable, and another six, relatively so. But even here, half of the "predictable" phonemes have single- and double-letter spellings: /b/, /d/, /l/, /p/, /t/, /g/, /m/, and /n/, as in *cab/ebb*, *lad/ladder*, *curl/hill*, *tap/tapped*, *bat/batter*, *fog/egg*, *ham/ hammer*, *win/winning*). Some phonemes can be spelled nine or ten different ways. Because spelling requires recall memory and reading requires only recognition memory, spelling is much more difficult than reading. It is easy to read a word like *hill*, but quite another matter to remember whether to double the *l* when you spell it (*boil, ball, deal, will, pal, pull, bail, doll*).

As we saw in chapter 3, there have been four attempts, historically, to systematize the English spelling code, and I was only able to locate three studies where these systems were tested empirically. Typically, spelling instruction consists of lists of random words that go up on the board on Monday for the spelling test on Friday. The yardstick of spelling difficulty is syllable length, as well as "regular" versus "rare" spellings, but seldom emphasizes the *structural* elements of the code—such as the spelling patterns linked to phoneme position within words.

Research on classroom spelling programs is so rare that there was no section on spelling in the NRP report. Graham (2000) managed to locate only 60 studies on spelling by scouring the journals back to the 1920s. These studies compared the two dominant approaches: "natural" learning (self-taught spelling) versus "traditional" instruction, consisting mainly of random word lists. Most of these studies were methodologically flawed, but the general message was that children cannot teach themselves to spell simply by reading or through creative writing, and that "traditional" programs were superior. As for what these programs contained, little was said. Graham noted that, apart from rote memorization, spelling lessons were made more enjoyable by "including student choice in the selection of spelling words and methods of study, guided discovery in learning the patterns underlying the spelling of words, opportunities to work with peers, and use of games" (p. 245).

How "student choice" and "guided discovery" are supposed to work in the absence of any knowledge on this subject was not explained.

The fact that many children do learn to spell is, therefore, a bit of a mystery, and how children succeed at this task has been the central question in research on spelling. This question occupies us for the next two chapters, and there are some surprising answers.

The "how" question is approached differently depending on the researcher's background knowledge. For the most part, researchers who study spelling have little or no understanding of how writing systems work and no knowledge of the structure of the English spelling code. Because of this, spelling research is based on a set of implicit assumptions. It is assumed that it is "natural" for children to teach themselves to spell, and that spelling skill proceeds in stages. It is assumed that children learn to spell by reinventing the spelling code (invented spelling). Using this logic, a poor speller is someone with a developmental delay or a deficit. Yet if children are not taught something as complex as the English spelling code in a structured and meaningful fashion, how can anyone learn it? To someone with greater knowledge, *the good speller seems unnatural and the poor speller seems normal*.

There a deeper issue here, which I call the *many-word problem*. Even if the world's best spelling program could be devised, it would never be possible to teach the spelling of every word. Because the English spelling system is so opaque, and only a handful of phoneme-to-grapheme correspondences are consistently reliable, the only way it can be mastered is through its probability structure, the reoccurring regularities in spelling patterns as outlined in chapter 3. For the brain to set up this structure, it needs exposure to thousands of examples of correctly spelled words. A good spelling program can jump-start this process by grouping words with these redundant patterns, but it will never succeed in teaching every word. There will always be words that a fluent English reader is unable to spell, words that have to be looked up in a dictionary.

Nevertheless, some people can master most of this structure unaided, while others cannot. Do good spellers have special visual or linguistic skills that make this possible? These kinds of questions have given rise to three major lines of inquiry: the study of "spelling stages"; an exploration of how linguistic knowledge might affect spelling skill; and the study of structural redundancies in the spelling code, which is intimately tied to computer models of reading. But before we turn to these issues, we need to look at more fundamental skills that might underpin an aptitude for spelling.

Spelling Predictors

There are three important factors that will impact spelling scores regardless of method.

IQ IQ is a consistent contributor to spelling skill. IQ has an impact on spelling ability from the outset, and this connection increases with age. Kindergartners' aptitude for producing modestly accurate "phonetic spellings" is correlated with the WISC Full Scale IQ at $r = .51$ (Mann 1993). Bond and Dykstra (1967) found the identical value in their monumental study on over 9,000 first-graders, Full Scale IQ correlating with spelling at $r = .51$. Muter and Snowling (1997) found this connection was a long-lasting one. Full Scale IQ measured at age 4 and 5 predicted scores on a standardized spelling test at age 9 ($r = .42$). In a large-scale study by Shanahan (1984), scores on the Stanford IQ Vocabulary subtest (receptive vocabulary) correlated with spelling at second grade (.45), and at fifth grade (.62). These are remarkably consistent findings, and show that IQ predicts spelling skill across the age range, accounting for about 25 percent of the variance.

Sex Girls outnumber boys in high-reader groups and are relatively scarce in low-reader groups (see my book *Language Development and Learning to Read*). Girls have an even greater advantage in spelling. First-grade girls were superior spellers in Bond and Dykstra's study in every methods comparison. Allred (1990) tested over 3,000 children in grades 1 through 6 from various regions across the United States. Girls did better on both spelling-dictation and spelling-recognition tests, and this was highly significant ($p < .001$) *at every grade*. And while spelling skill varied significantly by region, the sex difference did not. (No region × sex inter-actions were found.)

The Spelling-Reading Connection   Even with a transparent writing system, the correlation between reading and spelling will not be perfect, because skill in reading and spelling depends on different types of memory. This connection will be weaker with an opaque writing system, since spelling is much more difficult than reading. Bond and Dykstra reported a strong correlation between spelling and word recognition ($r = .63$) and reading comprehension ($r = .66$). Shanahan (1984) tested over 250 second graders and 250 fifth graders on the Stanford Diagnostic Reading Tests and the Gates-MacGinitie reading-comprehension test. Spelling was measured by a well-designed in-house spelling test (reliabilities around .90). Spelling was correlated with basic decoding skills at $r = .66$ (second grade) and $r = .60$ (fifth grade), and with reading comprehension at $r = .58$ (second grade) and $r = .56$ (fifth grade). Again, the correlational values in these studies are in remarkable agreement. However, had IQ and sex been con-trolled, these values would be lower.

Taking these uncontrolled factors into account, reading and spelling are unlikely to share more than about 25 percent common variance. This is too low to support the notion that reading and spelling skill are tightly linked, but high enough to show a consistent connection. Nevertheless, this leaves 75 percent of the variance in spelling scores unaccounted for. There are a number of options for how and why reading and spelling part company. People may have different aptitudes in recognition and recall memory. Or they may exhibit different facilities for reading and spelling as a consequence of instruction (or noninstruction), causing them to focus on the wrong perceptual units of the writing system. This would lead to two separate strategies, one for reading and one for spelling.

Bearing these important facts in mind, we turn next to the research on spelling.

Stage Models under the Microscope
The dominant model in spelling research is the "stage model"—the theory that spelling skills progress in developmental stages. The fact that the majority of children learn to spell is taken as evidence that people have a special aptitude for spelling. (There are stage models for reading as well,

but they do not dominate the field of reading research to nearly the same degree.) Unfortunately, much of this work is as weak methodologically as it is logically. Researchers consistently fail to control factors known to affect spelling skill, such as age, IQ and sex. And they tend to ignore reading and spelling *instruction* altogether, a point also emphasized by Ehri (1992, 330): "One important issue that has been neglected in studies of spelling stages is the relationship between stages and instruction. The concept of developmental stages implies that the growth patterns are relatively impervious to specific instructional experience. However, in the case of spelling development, the nature and extent of instruction very likely makes a big difference to development." This oversight is puzzling, because inappropriate or absent classroom instruction causes the spelling errors that researchers *use as data* to construct their stages. The basic instructional failings are these:

• Teaching letter names rather than correspondences between letters and sounds
• Teaching the alphabet code backward: letter to sound only (visual orientation) rather than sound to letter
• Excessive reliance on sight-word memory (random-word lists)
• Teaching practice that actively divorces reading and spelling instruction from one another (taught on different days, different words, different modes of learning)
• Teaching a hodgepodge of spelling "rules" that get broken most of the time
• Failure to let the structure of the spelling code dictate the sequence of instruction, because nobody knows what the structure of the spelling code is.

To put this in context, let's begin in the real world. Molly's mother began teaching her the alphabet at age 3. Molly learned to chant letter names in alphabetical order. She learned to match letter names to letter shapes. She was cycled through a "letter-of-the-week" regime in which a new magnetic letter appeared on the refrigerator door each Monday. By the time Molly entered school at age 5, she and most of the children in her middle-class neighborhood had a fair-to-good knowledge of letter shapes and letter names. The children could name the letters they were shown, point to letters that were named, and some children (mostly girls) could write their name and a fair number of letters from memory.

Molly believed that letter names were extremely important in learning to read, otherwise why had she spent so much time learning them? When she arrived in kindergarten, this belief was reinforced. Her teacher spent more time reviewing letter names and letter shapes and taught some sight words. In first grade, Molly was "immersed in print," told to use all her "cueing systems," taught some "sight words," and encouraged to guess words by context clues, as well as to "sound out" words using "phonics clues." For Molly, as well as for most of the other children, the only sound-out clues at their disposal were letter names. In the time set aside for creative writing, she was encouraged to write stories using her own "invented spelling" system. Molly had two available strategies for spelling words in her stories: visual memory (sight words) and letter names. By an amazing coincidence, she used these two strategies to spell words.

In 1971, these strategies were documented for the first time when Read published an analysis of preschool children's invented-spelling errors. He later discovered that the most common spelling mistakes consisted of using letter names instead of phoneme-grapheme correspondences (Read 1986). This type of error was more likely to be observed with vowels (*KAM* for *came*). Read viewed this as a "psycholinguistic process" in which children bring their awareness of the language to bear on the task. Read's article is the most frequently cited work in the research literature on spelling stages, where his findings are taken to mean that children spell with letter names *because they are in the letter-name spelling stage*.

Note that for a period of four years, Molly received training in activities supposedly related to learning the English writing system. Yet in all that time, she had never been taught anything she needed to know, nor was she exposed to any useful exercises that could instill this knowledge: (1) A writing system is a code. *Reading* means decoding letters into speech sounds (sounds in *your* speech). *Spelling* means encoding speech sounds into letters. (2) Reading and spelling are reversible processes. (3) There is a one-to-one correspondence between many sounds and their spellings, and a one-to-many correspondence for others. (4) There are patterns (recurring regularities) in the spelling code to help us remember how words are spelled.

Molly was never taught these things because neither her mother nor her teacher knew them.

This is the backdrop against which researchers frame their theories and carry out their studies. They seem to believe that Molly's situation is *reasonable*, because if it was not reasonable, there would be little purpose in studying it. I can show that it is anything but reasonable by shifting the focus a little. Molly's mother also taught her ten number symbols and ten number names. She taught Molly that numbers "stand for" quantities. She bought workbooks with pictures of pies, pieces of string, and rows of hippopotamuses, and as well as floating balloons for Molly to count in order to connect quantity with a number code. Molly learned there was a direct correspondence between the *quantity 5* (five balloons, five hippopotamuses, five pieces of pie or string) and the *number 5*. This is all very good, because a number system divorced from an understanding of quantity is not much use.

Then Molly went to school. It was during the era of "invented arithmetic." Children were supposed to discover the principles of addition, subtraction, multiplication, and division by being immersed in numbers. They were encouraged to invent formulas or systems for solving numerical word problems. Researchers descended on classrooms to annotate and classify the errors that children made while they invented arithmetic, or rather, tried to rediscover the invention of arithmetic unaided. "Arithmetic stages" were carefully documented. Researchers were intrigued by the discovery of a universal initial stage of "protoarithmetic," in which numbers were ordered in rows or columns in the same increasing order as the quantities they represented. One person called it the "protoarithmetic" stage, another the "serial-order" stage, and another the "initial combinatorial equity" stage.

I may joke about reading and spelling stages (and I do not intend to spend much time on them), but there are genuine issues here that have been muddled together with the issue of stages. I will address these issues as I review this work.

Stage Models of Spelling Acquisition

A Little History of Stages

Stage models in psychology came into prominence at the beginning of the twentieth century largely through the work of Freud and Piaget. Both were trained in biology, Freud as a neurologist and Piaget as a zoologist. During their training, they learned about biological stages of development, such as the larval stage of an insect. Later, in searching for a framework for their discoveries, they borrowed the concept of stages from biology, just as Hans Selye borrowed the concept of psychological and physiological stress from physics. In his psychoanalytic model, Freud claimed to document stages of psychoemotional/sexual development that, if not negotiated appropriately, could lead to subsequent neuroses.

Piaget studied the development of logical reasoning. He discovered that when children acquired a certain level of intellectual capacity, they were able to think about more than one spatial dimension at a time (length, breadth, height), or to realize that quantity is "conserved" through transformations in form, and that this process is *reversible*. The classic experiment is on the conservation of volume—water being poured from a short, fat container into a tall, thin one, and back again. Piaget viewed these new capacities as cognitive developmental stages and as specific to logical reasoning about objects and object properties. He believed that language development was more continuous than stage-like (Piaget [1964] 1993).

Stage models have special properties (Flavell 1963). Stages follow in a fixed sequence. They tend to come into being rather abruptly, then stabilize, resembling a staircase when plotted over time. Skills acquired at earlier stages are integrated with later ones, but children in a higher stage abandon naive solutions used at earlier stages (stages do not go backward). According to Piaget, if a child solves the problem of conservation of quantity and reversibility, this will generalize to similar problems (a block of clay smashed into a long thin tube), if not immediately, then certainly with brief instruction. Nor does the child revert to being unable to solve these problems merely through lack of opportunity.

Both Freud and Piaget viewed stages in a biological sense as intrinsic to the organism, and brought about through interactions with the world. These models have to do with problem solving, psychosocial in the first case, and logical/mathematical in the second. This is a far cry from the ability to master human inventions, especially because one of the hallmarks of a true stage of development is that it cannot be taught!

Stage models contrast with two other models in developmental psychology. One is a continuous developmental model in which a biological program unfolds in tandem with exposure to a minimally suitable environment. A cumulative sequence of subskills emerges that combine and continue to work together. Infant language development is a prime example, where children acquire more and more aptitudes and sensitivities as time goes by (see *Language Development and Learning to Read*). The difference between this model and a stage model is that skills gradually improve over time as each skill is added to the one before. Multiple subskills work simultaneously in a reciprocal fashion to increase the accuracy and fluency of speech perception and production.

The second model is learning, which is not specific to childhood (reading and spelling can be taught at any age). New skills and insights are acquired through discovery, demonstration, training, and repetition. Learning is cumulative in the same way as continuous development; one thing builds on another. But learning is not a biological program. It is prone to setbacks and failure that arise for various reasons, such as being exposed to misleading instruction, adopting inappropriate strategies, and, in some cases, the lack of a critical level of certain subskills. Children or adults *learn* to read and spell. They do not go through spelling stages or developmental spelling levels.

To gain a fuller understanding of how a stage model has been abused by researchers studying "spelling development," we turn next to some of these studies.

Research on Spelling Stages

Stage models for spelling (and reading) began to pop up in the early 1980s, spurred on by Read's report on children's invented spelling. These models were based on an analysis of children's spelling errors in their creative writing, or errors produced by specially designed spelling tests. The most influential models were those developed by Henderson and his colleagues (Henderson and Beers 1980; Henderson 1982, 1992), by Frith (1980, 1985) in the United Kingdom, and by Ehri (1986, 1989b, 1995).

Although the basic assumption behind these models is similar (children teach themselves to spell), the way the stages are derived is quite different. Henderson's model is based on the surface structure of the error patterns, what Ehri (1992) described as *orthographic features*. In Henderson's model there are five stages: Prephonetic, Letter Name, Within Word Pattern, Syllable Juncture, and Derivational Constancy. They reflect the child's growing awareness of spelling detail, as well as the characteristics of the English language. Common words are short, less common words have more than one syllable, and the least common words have lots of syllables. Multisyllable words tend to be "morphological" in structure (combining units of meaning: *un-happi-ness*), and this structure is reflected in the spelling code.

Frith's stages are more akin to global strategies than stages, and are less specific. The child begins as a "logographic" (whole-word) reader and speller, graduates to an "alphabetic" stage (phonetic), then to an "ortho-graphic" stage, when spelling "rules" and conventions are mastered. In this model, reading and spelling stages do not necessarily develop in parallel. Dissociations appear, leading to three types of children: good readers/good spellers, good readers/poor spellers, and poor readers/poor spellers. The existence of the middle group led Frith to propose that some children read by eye (visually) and spell by ear (phonetically).

Ehri (1992, 326) contrasts her model with the others as being more oriented toward "the nature of the correspondence between written (or-thographic) units and spoken (phonological and morphemic) units that spellers exhibit in their invented spellings." In other words, she views "spelling development" as a search for predictable mappings between a growing awareness of sounds in words and the symbols that map to these sounds. As such, Ehri's model ties directly to the phoneme-awareness re-search. The model also links spelling to reading, because reading experi-ence is believed to have a direct impact on spelling. There are four stages in her model: Precommunicative (preliterate), Semiphonetic (only por-tions of sounds are represented, and letter names are used), Phonetic (represents all sounds, some spellings accurate, some letter names), and Morphemic (uses functional multiphoneme patterns).

A stage-model approach has a number of pitfalls. Framing a research problem in terms of a stage model leads to a dangerous (unscientific) mode of investigation in which the data are constrained at the outset by the classification system. This is especially problematic when there is so much latitude in the classification process. Not only this, but because the spelling errors must fit the categories and the categories must be stages, the description and interpretation of these error patterns are adapted to comply with the stage model, rather than simply reflecting what the data show. To illustrate this, I provide evidence from research by C. S.

Beers and J. W. Beers (Beers and Beers 1992), former colleagues of Henderson.

The first thing one notices in their report is that their stages are different from Henderson's, and are based more on phonological and linguistic knowledge: Prephonetic, Early Phonetic, Phonetic, Structural, and Correct. Yet, in summarizing the earlier work in the field (i.e., Henderson's), Beers and Beers wrote: "There are indeed identifiable stages of orthographic awareness through which children pass as they become more proficient in their writing, [and] children proceed through these stages at varying rates" (p. 231). Apparently, these stages are not sufficiently "identifiable" to be constant from one decade to the next, or from one group of collaborative researchers to another.

Beers and Beers tested first through sixth graders on a nonsense-word spelling test in which the words had to be altered to represent the plural, regular past tense, or progressive verbs. Test items took the form: "John saw a blinch in the woods. Then he saw two _____." Errors were tallied and assigned to "spelling stages" for each age group.

For purposes of this illustration, I will focus on the top stage (Correct), which would reflect a high degree of accuracy for most children who were at the Structural stage (Beers and Beers), or the Derivational Constancy stage (Henderson)—the stage of morphologically based spelling "rules." Specific ages are never claimed for any stage model (including Piaget's). Nevertheless some age constraints must apply, otherwise stages cannot be "developmental." In view of the 6-year age spread, "mastery" scores (percent correct) should appear for most children at a particular age, and for the remainder shortly thereafter. Furthermore, because all the test items reflect knowledge of "orthographic rules" for adding common suffixes, *they belong in the same stage.*

Neither of these things happened. There were huge age differences for "stages" depending on the particular transformation required. Mastery appeared at first grade for adding -s for the plural, at second grade for adding -es, but the transformation *sky → skies* did not materialize until sixth grade. Which one is the correct measure of the "spelling stage" for plurals, or do we need a stage for each kind of plural?

Similar anomalies appeared for past-tense spellings. First graders did poorly. There was a big jump at second grade, no change whatsoever for 3 years, then sudden mastery in sixth grade. Is this a stage with a 4-year plateau, or did the teacher *teach* past-tense spellings in sixth grade? There seem to be two stages for mastering the "add -*ing* rules" (drop *e*, double the consonant). For some reason it is easier to master the "drop *e*, add -*ing* rule," though certainly not for everyone. Only 70 percent succeeded by second grade. Following this, there was *no change for the next 4 years*. The letter-doubling trick appears to be much later "developmentally."

These peculiar results are just as likely to reflect what was going on the classroom. Because no information was provided about this, these results are uninterpretable. In any case, they do not support a stage model that places "structural" or "derivational" spelling errors at a single stage. In fact, no stage model can explain these data, not even one that proposed a different stage for every type of plural and every type of verb transformation.

A classification process must follow standard scientific principles; otherwise this work does not count as science. Evidence for a stage model requires that at least these criteria be met:

- An objective (not subjective) classification scheme must exist.
- Interrater agreement (reliabilities) should be provided.
- All errors must be classified, not just some of them.
- A numerical tally (frequency count) of each type of spelling error should be provided in a published report.
- Shifts in patterns of spelling errors across age must be documented in either cross-sectional or longitudinal studies.

And for a classification scheme to count as "science,"

- It must be sufficiently robust that it can be replicated by others in the field.
- It should be adopted unanimously by everyone in the field (this does not mean it cannot be modified).

Imagine what the field of chemistry would be like if every investigator developed his or her own unique table of chemical elements.

As I reviewed the numerous studies on spelling stages, other concerns arose about the validity of stages as a proper interpretation of the data. Here are some of the problems:

- Error scores are the basis for the coding scheme, but errors provide no information on how children spell words correctly.
- Because stages are defined by the error-classification process itself, the logic is circular: larger to fewer spelling errors = lower to higher "spelling stages."
- The data are often represented inappropriately, as tallies (head counts) of children "at each stage." Stages can only be demonstrated by shifts for individual children to prove that spelling stages are not mixed. That is, children could not be in a "visual" stage once they were in a "phonetic" stage.

I provide examples of four well-known studies to illustrate these problems. Two claim support for stages and two found no support.

Morris and Perney (1984) were interested in the relationship between spelling skill (stages of development) at the beginning of first grade, and reading scores at the end of the year. They designed a spelling test that had words containing consonant and vowel digraphs, consonant blends, and a variety of e-controlled and vowel + r spellings. All spellings were "regular." First graders took this spelling test (the same test) in September, January, and May. Reading tests were also given in May.

A scoring system was devised for spelling errors that fit their four-stage (six levels) model: The Prephonetic stage was a simple letter tally, with three levels corresponding to zero, one, or two letters in the correct sequence. The Phonetic stage consisted of getting a single vowel letter in the right location plus any minor error (BAC for *back*). The Transitional stage consisted of "legal" orthographic patterns (*CK*), but with a minor error. The Transitional stage was combined with the Correct stage in all analyses, reasons unstated, probably due to too few correct spellings. Each word was scored as being in one of these stages and awarded points. The circular logic is obvious. Spelling errors are coded in accordance with the number of correctly spelled phonemes in the correct sequence. The spelling-error coding scheme = the "stages."[1]

---

1. Morris and Perney's scheme is different from Henderson's and from that of Beers and Beers, yet Morris formerly worked with Henderson.

A tally was made of how many children were in a particular stage in January as a function of where they were in September. These numbers reveal that children can get stuck at a stage or skip one or two stages entirely. Given the fact that these children had the same exposure, and everyone started school knowing all the letters to spell these words, this weakens the argument for stages. Stages mean a similar *developmental sequence* given the same environment. Nothing in Morris and Perney's data suggests this.

Nunes, Bryant, and Bindman (1997) in the United Kingdom studied "developmental stages" by focusing on one spelling issue: adding *-ed* to indicate past tense. They set out guidelines for what a stage model meant to them:

Any stage model should pass at least three tests. One is that all, or very nearly all, the children should clearly belong to one of the stages in each session.... Second, the developmental stages should be related to external criteria: The children at more advanced stages should be the older or educationally more successful children in the sample. The third test is the most stringent and unfortunately the least often applied.... Children should move in one direction but not in the other. (p. 642)

Despite this clear statement, the descriptive language in the report is quite at odds with the notion of stages. The language reflects children's slowly emerging awareness of spelling conventions. The researchers wrote that at first children "ignore" spelling conventions, then "they begin to realize" there is an *-ed* spelling convention but cannot apply it, later they "grasp [its] grammatical significance" but misapply it to irregular verbs, and finally they "learn about exceptions."

This gradual process of becoming aware of spelling patterns is not a description of anything "stagelike." It is a description of *learning*.

This was a longitudinal study with 363 children tracked from second through fourth grade. They were given a spelling-dictation test in which ten words were regular past-tense verbs ending in /d/ or /t/ that take the *-ed* spelling (*load*, *loaded*; *wilt*, *wilted*), ten were irregular past-tense verbs ending in /d/ or /t/ (*found*, *felt*), and ten were common nouns ending in /d/ or /t/ (*bird*, *belt*).

The spelling test was given three times: at the start of the study, 7 months later, and 13 months after that. Spelling errors were classified as *unsystematic* errors (no connection to the word stem), *phonetic* errors in which the letter *d* or *t* was simply added to the root word, and *generalizations* of the *-ed* spelling to the foil words (irregular past-tense verbs, and nouns).

The results were surprising. Generalization errors of the *-ed* spelling to irregular past-tense verbs were common (*felted*), and the number of children making these errors actually increased over time, from 34 percent at the first testing to 38 percent at the second and 42 percent at the third. More remarkable, this effect also appeared for nouns (*birded*). Roughly 30 percent of the children made noun-generalization errors at all three testings. Overall, 71 percent of the children made at least one generalization error for irregular verbs, and 56 percent did so for nouns. A stable or increasing error rate over a 20-month period is strong evidence against stages. (It is also strong evidence against learning!) It seems that the nature of the task, and the experience of taking the identical test three times, led children to believe that the correct response was to add *-ed* wherever possible.

Faced with these unexpected results, the authors ignored this simple explanation and created new "stages" on the basis of the overgeneralization errors. A five-stage model was superimposed on the pattern of error scores, very much in the style of Morris and Perney. Children were classified according to their predominant type of spellings error (a.k.a. "stages") and assigned to stages (a.k.a "spelling errors"). These categories were even less convincing than those used by Morris and Perney. As an example, the stage 2 classification was "Spell *half or more* of the endings of irregular verbs and nonverbs correctly.... Make *at least five* phonetic transcriptions of regular past verbs but should produce very few (*less than three*) ed spellings for any of the words" (pp. 641–642; my emphasis). Some "stages" even permitted a 50-50 split between one stage and another.

Nunes, Bryant, and Bindman tracked the fate of children from the first to the second testing 7 months later, which provides some sense of the movement of individual children through stages. Of the children who started out in stage 1, 28 were still there 7 months later, 11 moved up one stage, 8 moved up two, and 2 were in stages 4 and 5 respectively. Children who were initially at stage 2 behaved even less stagelike, 43 got stuck there, 5 went backward to stage 1, none went up one stage, 5 went up two, and 6 went up three. Children's movement from one stage to the next is scarcely progressive or orderly. The follow-up testing produced similar results. Of the 58 children initially assigned to stage 1, 15 children (25 percent) were still there 20 months later.

A second hypothesis in this study was that knowledge of grammar (past tense) would directly impact children's ability to spell past-tense verbs. However, their in-house grammar test was far too advanced for 7- to 9-year-olds. Test scores were near zero and changed little over 20 months. This did not prevent the authors from doing statistics on the data. The authors interpreted their findings as follows:

These generalizations are at the heart of our new model of the development of spelling. This proposes that a child's first step in spelling is to adopt a phonetic spelling strategy; the next step is to notice and to try to incorporate exceptions to these rules, but without a complete understanding of their grammatical basis; the next step is to understand fully this grammatical basis for some of the spelling patterns that do not fit well with the letter-sound rules; and the final step is to learn about the exceptions to the grammatically based rules. (p. 647)

There is no evidence that children are progressing in "steps." There is no evidence that these children "understand fully [the] grammatical basis" of the past-tense -ed rule, because "awareness" of this knowledge was never measured. The data actually run counter to this argument, since error scores increased over time. It is equally likely that children learn to spell these words through exposure and practice, not because they are in an "orthographic spelling stage."

Morris and Perney's work as well as that of Nunes and colleagues is typical of the research in this area. The logic is circular, and "stages" are often rerigged to suit the experimental hypothesis. There is a strong bias toward stage models and few studies in the literature where this model is challenged. We turn next to two such studies.

Canadian psychologists (Varnhagen, McCallum, and Burstown 1997) decided to take a long, hard look at the validity of "spelling stages." They adopted Gentry's (1981) classification system, and used Morris and Perney's (1984) error-scoring method. This was a cross-sectional study on 272 children in first through sixth grade. The children were asked to write a composition about "A Special Day." They were told not to worry about spelling errors and not to correct them.

The analysis of spelling errors was limited to words with *e*-controlled vowel spellings (*lake*), and with the three phonetic forms of regular past-tense verbs: *helped* (help't), *grabbed* (grab'd), *listed* (listed). The stages were as follows: Precommunicative (random), Semiphonetic (minimally phonetic), Phonetic (consonants correct but letter name for vowel, or all phonemes correct but ends with *-d* for past tense), Transitional (correct phonetically but incorrect orthographically), and Correct spelling. Three raters independently scored a portion of the errors, and interrater reliability was high, above .90 in all cases. (This critical step is missing in most of the research on stages.)

The first finding was that the classification system did not hold up. There were no Prephonetic errors. Semiphonetic errors were in evidence at first grade but not after that. Stage 4 (Transitional errors) were virtually nonexistent, and nearly all the children jumped from stage 3 to 5. The only two categories that reliably classified the spelling errors and that *varied systematically as a function of age* were the Phonetic and Correct categories.

When spelling scores were plotted by age, there was zero evidence for stages. Instead, there was a simple trade-off between Phonetic and Correct spellings. Phonetic errors gradually declined (sloped gently down) and Correct spellings gradually increased (sloped gently up) as mirror images of each other. The same pattern appeared for every type of spelling error, *e*-controlled vowel spellings and past-tense suffixes alike. These patterns are typical of *learning curves* and are not remotely stagelike. Furthermore, these are the only age-related functions I have seen in the research on spelling stages.

When the investigators looked at the individual data for vowel + *e* spelling errors, they classified 27 children as being in three stages at the same time. They arrived at similar results with past-tense spelling errors.

They concluded that there was no evidence for stages, only evidence for a transition from a purely "surface" phonetic approach to an increasing knowledge of spelling patterns. Children are *learning* to spell, and this is influenced by classroom instruction. As they noted: "Different rates in this progression appeared to be related to the spelling curriculum" (p. 160).

In the second study from this group (Steffler et al. 1998), the notion of stages was abandoned and replaced by "strategies," which were solicited from the children. Children took a spelling-dictation test and responded to the question "How did you spell that word?" after every word. This was a cross-sectional study on children in grades 2 through 5.

Four strategies appeared with sufficient frequency to tabulate them. The most common responses were "I just knew it" (*Retrieval*) and "I sounded it out" (*Phonetic*). Some children reported using analogies to similarly spelled words—"*Clip* is *lip* with a *C* in front of it" (*Analogy*)—as well as orthographic rules: "*e* makes the *A* say its name" (*Rule*). Idiosyncratic responses were scored as *Other*. Analogy, Rule, and Other strategies were rare at all ages and diminished with age. By grade 5, the proportion of analogy strategies had dropped to 2 percent (opposite the prediction of stage models).

Rule-based strategies were reported only for CVCe words (18 percent at grade 2, 13 percent at grade 3, zero at grade 5), and were very helpful indeed. Again, this is opposite to the prediction of many stage models, which are supposed to end up at the "rule-based" stage. Second graders who reported they knew the *e* worked with the preceding vowel scored 95 percent correct on CVCe words (*home*, *late*), as opposed to children who used Analogy (37 percent correct), a Phonetic approach (48 percent correct), or Retrieval (73 percent correct). The two most common strategies, Phonetic and Retrieval, traded off with age. A Phonetic strategy dominated at second grade, and a Retrieval strategy dominated at fifth grade.

The term *retrieval* is difficult to interpret. The process is too instantaneous to be a "strategy." The authors' treatment of this was somewhat vague and contradictory. They used definitional terms like *automatic* as well as *choose* and *adaptive approach*, suggesting that a retrieval strategy is under voluntary control. This led them to infer that "retrieval" replaces a phonetic strategy, marking the end of "phonetic spelling" for a particular group of words. But it is just as likely that *rapid phonetic analysis* continues and combines with visual memory to equal "retrieval," a sense of instant awareness. As noted often in this book, what seems instantaneous in subjective time is not instantaneous in neural time. People are not aware of their eye movements when they read, yet their eyes move nonetheless.

Taken as a whole, these studies provide no support for a stage model, even assuming there were no methodological problems. I will leave the final word to Ehri (1992), taken from her commentary on the "feature"-oriented stage models. I believe these comments apply to all stage models:

We might also consider whether a focus upon spelling features necessitates a conception of stages to organize the features, or whether it might be sufficient to describe the emergence of the features themselves and leave it at that. This would resolve the controversy over which features are hallmarks of particular stages. Also, it would eliminate expectations that certain features emerge at the same time, which data show are false. (p. 328)

Ehri called for longitudinal studies to look at

individual children's spellings, how consistent their appearance is at first and later on, what effect one feature has on other features when it appears (i.e. overgeneralization errors), and how the emergence of features corresponds to or is influenced by explicit instructional experiences.... Presently our basis for believing that there are stages of spelling development is primarily conceptual and quite limited empirically. (pp. 328–329)

There are more longitudinal studies in the literature today than there were in 1992, but the data continue to show that stage models are false. Stage models of spelling will continue to be limited empirically because they are circular and logically untenable.

What Do Good Spellers Know That Poor Spellers Do Not?

Another popular approach to the study of spelling is based on the theory that good spellers have certain knowledge that poor spellers lack, such as knowledge of the linguistic structure of English words and of how this structure relates to the spelling code. Knowing that the past tense is usually represented by *-ed* is one example.

This type of study attempts to pinpoint specific skills peculiar to good spellers that are absent in poor spellers, using word lists that feature particular types of spellings. Poor spellers will, by definition, be worse on every type of test (they are selected to be worse). The goal is to show *differential* performance on the tests, a worse performance on some tests than on others. For instance, one might anticipate that differences would be small to nonexistent on one-syllable "regularly" spelled words, but greater on words where spellings obey a convention or "rule" (past-tense endings) or are determined in some way by morphology (language structure).

The validity of this research is entirely dependent on whether the word lists actually measure what they purport to measure. Knowledge of the structure of the spelling code is imperative for in-house spelling tests to be valid. Otherwise, there is no way to know whether performance is due to a visual or phonetic strategy, to ignorance of the orthographic or morphological spelling "rules," or to insufficient exposure to print. Unfortunately, few researchers have any knowledge of this structure.

As an example of this problem, it is assumed that morphological spelling clues like those bequeathed to us by Samuel Johnson in 1755 are of great benefit to readers and spellers alike (Johnson [1755] 1773). Linguists, echoed by reading researchers, often point to "linguistic" connections between word forms and the spelling code. But they are highly selective. The word *sign* is said to contain the *gn* spelling because it is morphologically related to *signal* and *signature*. This may be true, but it does not matter a fig unless this morphological clue is consistent and predicts these transformations: *deign, deignal, deignature; reign, reignal, reignature; design, designal, designature; impugn, impugnal, impugnature; benign, benignal, benignature*. As you can see, it does not. In order to use this "morphological clue," a person would have to remember that the *gn* in *sign* occurs because of *signal* or *signature*, "BUT NOT" (a blocking rule— or exception to a rule you have to remember) for other words with the *gn* spelling. It is far simpler to remember that *gn* is a spelling alternative for the sound /n/ (except for *signal* and *signature*), and be done with it. There are 15 common words with this spelling.

Research on College Students
Fischer, Shankweiler, and Liberman (1985) were the first to try this approach using good and poor spellers at the college level. They designed

a spelling test consisting of various types of words like those described above. They predicted that poor spellers would be differentially worse on words where spellings were most influenced by linguistic features, and differ least on words with the most transparent ("regular") *and* most opaque spellings (rare sight words). They designed a spelling test with three levels of "transparency of orthographic representation." They consulted Hanna et al. 1966 (see chapter 3), a book on spelling rules by Witherspoon (1973), and two dictionaries. These sources provided spelling "rules" of this dubious variety: "Words of more than one syllable, ending in a single consonant preceded by a single vowel, if accented on the last syllable usually double the final consonant before a suffix beginning with a vowel" (Fischer, Shankweiler, and Liberman 1985, 439). Clymer (1983), who showed that spelling "rules" or "generalizations" are meaningless, would be amused by the word *usually*.

Fischer and colleagues set up the spelling tests correctly using *spelling* alternatives (possible spellings for 40+ phonemes), not *decoding* alternatives (possible readings of a letter). The various levels were described as follows:

Level 1. Words where the phonetic realization is close to the orthographic representation and has a high frequency in written English.

Level 2A. Words that contain an ambiguous segment departing from straightforward phonetic mapping and that require an application of orthographic conventions or a sensitivity to regularities at the surface phonetic level. (This refers to such things as knowing when to double final consonants when adding a suffix.)

Level 2B. Also has an ambiguous segment, reflecting "abstract morphophonemic knowledge." For the most part, these transformations were assumed to call on an awareness of how root words and affixes combine. That is, a good speller was supposed to *know* that the final *r* is doubled in *confer/conferring* but not in *confer/conference* as a consequence of syllable stress.

Level 3. Words were "demon" spelling words that contained segments not normally found in English spelling and often of foreign derivation.

Words on the lists were mainly multisyllable words and were balanced across levels for syllable length and frequency in print.

The distinction between Levels 1 and 3 is clear. There is no question that words like *blunder*, *alternate*, and *unemployment* are more transparent and easier to spell than words like *diphtheria*, *sergeant*, *annihilate*, and *pygmy*. And these words were noticeably different from Level 2 words. The problem arose in the contrast between Level 2A and 2B words. For example, letter doubling was supposed to work by an "orthographic rule" at Level 2A in words like *sobbing*, *clannish*, and *thinned*. Yet these words were not qualitatively different from words of "morphophonemic" origin, such as *omitted*, *regrettable*, and *equipped* (Level 2B). Thus the distinction between Levels 2A and 2B was based on bogus phonics-type rules.

The results showed that Level 1 was easiest, Level 2 next easiest, and Level 3 hardest, for good and poor spellers alike. Both groups had the same error patterns, and in the same proportions, phonetic substitutions being the most common errors (around 88 percent), confirming the findings of Varnhagen and colleagues. The two groups parted company on Levels 2A and 2B. Poor spellers were equally bad on both word lists, but good spellers spelled the morphophonemic (2B) words more accurately than the orthographic (2A) words (contrary to expectation).

Fischer and associates also tested good and poor spellers on a nonsense-word spelling-recognition test. The students had to choose which of two words was most likely to be spelled correctly. Poor spellers had the most difficulty when an added prefix or suffix required a modification to the root word.

When they looked at other possible contributors to these results, the poor spellers were found to score well below good spellers on the WRAT reading test and on the Stanford reading-comprehension test. The groups did not differ in vocabulary (WAIS vocabulary), showing that these students' spelling problems were not related to verbal IQ. And equally important, poor spellers did not do worse on a visual-memory test for abstract visual patterns, evidence that visual memory is not the source of the poor spellers' difficulties.

Fischer and colleagues surmised that because the greatest discrepancy between good and poor spellers appeared on the "morphological" spelling test (Level 2B), "linguistic sensitivity" was at the root of their reading and spelling difficulties. However, it is just as likely that these students are poor spellers because they are poor readers and do not read (or write) frequently enough to observe the more difficult spelling patterns very often.

Australian psychologists, Holmes and Ng (1993) were unable to replicate Fischer, Shankweiler, and Liberman's findings for Level 2A and 2B type words, and attributed this to an artifact in the word lists used by Fischer and colleagues. Holmes and Ng found the least difference on regular words, and the greatest difference between the spelling groups on the idiosyncratic words (contrary to Fischer, Shankweiler, and Liberman's prediction). Othographic and morphophonemic word lists were intermediate in difficulty. Overall, Holmes and Ng's results showed that good and poor spellers were most alike when words are easy to spell, and least alike when words are hard to spell, suggesting that poor speller's problems are due to insufficient exposure to words with unusual spellings.

They reasoned that poor spellers' relatively weaker performance on idiosyncratic words might be because there are more ways to spell them incorrectly. They did a second experiment to control for this possibility. Groups of poor and good spellers were given a reading task in which the students had to decide (yes/no) whether a word was a real or nonsense word (*blurge*), using "regular" and "idiosyncratic" spellings. The time to initiate a response (voice-onset latency) and errors were recorded. Poor spellers needed more time to decode longer, more complex words than good spellers did, and another experiment was carried out to pinpoint the problem.

Nonsense words were created from real words by systematically changing one letter in the initial, middle, or final position. Good and poor spellers differed only when the change appeared in the *middle* of the word. It took poor spellers 100 milliseconds longer to read these words. It appears that poor spellers focus mainly on the outer segments of words as they read, rather than decoding phonetically from left to right. If this is the case, it means that exposure is confounded with decoding strategy —the failure to pay close attention to internal spelling patterns in multi-syllable words.

Visual-processing skill was also measured. The students had to decide whether pairs of words, nonwords, random-consonant sequences, and random-symbol sequences were the "same" or "different." Poor spellers were significantly slower on judgments involving words and nonwords, though both groups were very accurate on this part of the experiment. Matching pairs of random letters or symbol sequences was incredibly slow, twice as slow (4,000 ms versus 2,200 ms) in some cases. But there were no differences between good and poor spellers on either visual task for speed or for errors. Once more, the evidence shows that poor spellers do not have visual-processing problems.

These are important results. First, they show that it takes only half the time to judge whether a pair of words is the same as it does to decide whether a random string of the same letters is the same. This means that processing speed improves as a function of exposure, and the redundant syllable patterns in speech, and how these are represented by spelling code, make this possible.

Holmes and Ng also found that poor spellers were far more likely to have low vocabulary scores, but did not differ in nonverbal IQ. The students took the Author Recognition Test (Stanovich and West 1989) to estimate exposure to print. The task is to check off famous authors' names, which are mixed with names of unknown persons. The differences were enormous. Good spellers correctly identified an average of 18 authors out of 40, poor spellers only 7.5 (pure guessing), proof that poor spellers do not read nearly as much as good spellers.

These studies provide a excellent profile of the poor speller at the college level. They score well below good spellers on standardized reading tests; they also read far less and have a weaker vocabulary. They have no visual-perception problems, but they do have an unusual visual-scanning patterns for reading multisyllable words, focusing most attention on the outer segments of the word. None of this, of course, sheds much light on cause. For example, a weak vocabulary or poor decoding skills might depress interest in "reading a lot," so that print exposure is a result of reading skill, and any "causal" link to spelling is indirect.

Ressearch on Children

Waters, Bruck, and Malus-Abramovitz (1988) adapted this research design to study children. They set up five types of spelling lists suitable for children age 8 to 12 years (see pp. 172–173). Precise descriptions of each type were provided. Here they are in slightly reduced form:

Regular words. "*Must* contain spellings that directly reflect the surface phonology of the word, and which can be derived through the application of sound-spelling correspondences. Sounds have few spelling alternatives" (original emphasis). Later in the article, they referred to regular words as words where "spellings can be derived on the basis of invariant sound-spelling correspondences."

Regular words*. These are similar to regular words but contain a phoneme represented by several legal spelling alternatives. (Example: *street, streat, strete*.)

Orthographic words. Contain a phoneme or segment that is spelled according to orthographic conventions. (Example: when to use *ch* or *tch* for final /ch/.)

Morphologic words. Knowledge of word structure and conventions for attaching affixes to words, and of spellings based on relationships to other words. (Examples: *sign, grammar*.)

Strange words. Contain at least one orthographic segment that rarely appears in English spelling. (Examples: *yacht, ocean*.)

This is a well-designed scheme, so it was surprising how little the words on the spelling lists reflected these descriptions. Regular words were not "regular." "Surface phonology" means that connections between *individual* phonemes and their *individual* spellings are unaffected by surrounding phonemes (context free). Five words (*program, unit, finding, push, album*) are not spelled with the most probable (regular) spelling *and* they can be spelled phonetically a number of ways (*proagram, ewnit, fineding*, and so on). Nor are they context free, as these hyphenated examples show: *prog-ram, un-it, fin-ding*.

Regular words* were defined as "regular" (most probable spellings) but containing a phoneme with more than one spelling. But six of these words did not have high-probability spellings: *money* (*munny*), *true* (*trew*), *duty* (*dooty*), *absolute* (*absoloot*), *event* (*eavent*), and *fever* (*feever*). Two words lacked any viable spelling alternatives: *foolish* (? *fulish/foulish*) and *woodpile* (? *wouldpile/wudpile*). I defy the reader to spell them differently.

Similar anomalies appeared on the Orthographic and Morphologic word lists. Morphologic words were more like "spelling demons." They contained uncommon spelling patterns (*bomb, sign, obey*), schwa vowels (*German, destructible*), and words spelled with double letters (*really, hopefully, dissolve*). It is highly unlikely that children (or adults) spell these words by reflecting on morphological "rules" having to do with analogies to *bombadier* or *signature*, or because they are aware of a final *-l* doubling rule for adverbs.

Waters and colleagues remarked that there were flaws in Fischer, Shankweiler, and Liberman's word lists, but there were also flaws in the word lists used by Waters and associates, making it difficult to interpret the data. The most straightforward description of the word lists is that they increase in difficulty with each level as they depart from a surface phoneme-grapheme relationship.

This study involved 158 children at four grade levels (3 through 6), consisting of the top and bottom thirds in spelling performance. Poor spellers were also very poor readers. Results for all groups combined (main effects) showed that high-frequency words were easier to spell than low-frequency words (frequency in print), Regular words were spelled more accurately, Regular* and Orthographic levels did not differ from each other, and the remaining levels differed significantly from each other in the expected direction. Grade level was also significant.

However, while poor spellers did worse overall, there was no differential impact as a function of the types of spelling words. This result is particularly interesting, not only for purposes of this study, but because a stage model would predict that these spelling "levels" would be acquired by good and poor spellers at different times or rates. This was one of three requirements of a stage model as specified by Nunes, Bryant, and Bindman 1997.

The patterns across age were very revealing. First, good spellers made systematic gains across all spelling levels between grades 3 and 4, while gains for poor spellers during this time period were virtually nil. Second, the size of the gains was comparable for all categories of spelling words with the exception of "Strange words." Third, not only did poor spellers score far below good spellers on every test, but they made proportionately fewer gains at every grade level. They are late out of the starting gate and run more slowly as the race progresses.

This is more evidence against developmental stages (not that Waters and colleagues were interested in stages). A stage model would predict variations in acceleration as a function of age and the category of words the child was asked to spell, assuming these categories were meaningful. Instead, there were similar rates of improvement across all levels.

Waters and associates also compared the performance of the same children on a spelling-recognition task. The children had to choose the correct spelling from three foils (*trane, train, trayn*). Poor spellers had a disproportionate boost in accuracy compared to good spellers. They improved at five times the rate of good spellers on Regular* words, double the rate on the Morphologic words, and by 25–50 percent for Strange words. Of course poor spellers had more room for improvement, but results were the same after the top spellers were removed from the data analysis. Poor spellers clearly have more accurate spellings in mind (available in recognition memory) than they are able to retrieve (recall memory). There is also a hint in these results that poor spellers may be learning the code in only one direction, from print to sound, because they were so much more accurate in judging spellings (visual-recognition memory) than in producing them (recall memory).

As a rule, children tend to score similarly on reading and spelling tests. It is uncommon for a child to be very good at one and very poor at the other. Bruck and Waters (1990) managed to locate 13 children among 175 sixth graders who scored normally on a reading-comprehension test, and extremely poorly on a spelling test. They were matched to two control groups that were either good at both or poor at both. We will call them the *good, poor,* and *mixed* groups. The mixed group was characterized by very weak reading and spelling scores but normal reading-comprehension scores. They also had above-average verbal ability vocabulary standard scores: good, 107; mixed, 105; poor, 86.

In a series of carefully designed tests, Bruck and Waters showed that both the mixed and poor groups read difficult or "incongruous" words equally slowly and inaccurately. Both groups relied heavily on context to read words, but the mixed group was far more successful, no doubt because of having superior vocabulary skills. However, one should not get carried away with theorizing about this unusual population of children. The mixed group in this study represented only 3 percent of the 175 children originally tested, and the children in this group were not good but *poor* decoders/poor spellers (their only advantage being in comprehension).

Summary

Poor spellers are more likely to have a limited vocabulary and weak decoding skills, and do not read as much as good spellers do. However, as a group they are not differentially worse than good spellers on tests designed to tap knowledge of specific orthographic "rules" or morphological patterns. Their spelling ability falls short across the board, no matter how the tests are constructed. There is indirect evidence that reading and spelling skill are linked (supporting the correlational research), because it appears difficult to find children who perform normally on a reading test and abnormally on a spelling test. However, this research suffers from the problem of not knowing how these children and young adults came to be poor readers and spellers in the first place. In other words, we have no idea how they were *taught*.

Some Instructional Tips

Finally, we do know something about certain aspects of spelling instruction that do or do not work. Some of this research was described briefly in chapter 4.

Writing Words Helps You Learn How to Spell Them

Cunningham and Stanovich (1990b) taught first graders to spell a list of words, learning a third on the computer, a third with letter tiles, and a third by writing them out. On half the trials the children said the letter names as they typed, arranged letter tiles, or wrote the letters, and half the time they said nothing. The children practiced these three tasks for four days, 30 minutes each day. Writing the words was superior to the other two conditions, though spelling was hardly exemplary. Out of 10 words in each condition, the average score was 1.5 (tiles), 1.6 (computer), and 3.1 (writing). Saying letter names had no effect. These results support Hulme and Bradley (1984), who also found that children learn to spell faster and more accurately by writing words than by arranging letter tiles.

Research has shown that it is easier to remember something in the same environment in which you learned it (a phenomenon known as *context-dependent learning*). To test for this effect, Cunningham and Stanovich taught children a set of words in three modes: tiles, computer, and writing. The children were tested with tiles or by computer, stacking the deck against the writing group. Despite this manipulation, the writing group still excelled. It is the *learning* phase that matters most, not how learning is tested. Visually guided movement, like copying, boosts memory in a way that purely visual learning does not.

The authors commended Montessori for her wisdom in insisting that children write as a major method for learning to spell. Montessori also believed that spelling should precede reading for this and other reasons.[2]

Cunningham and Stanovich did not point out Montessori's other insight (and that of Dale 1898)—that children should say the *sound* each letter stands for as it is being written (not the letter name). So far, there are few empirical studies on Montessori's important ideas.

Learning Letter Names Can be Hazardous to Your Spelling

Much of the research on spelling is based on spelling errors, errors that are often a consequence of ineffective instruction. After Read documented the numerous letter-name spelling errors in children's creative writing, a "letter-name stage" appeared in stage models, as if these errors were part of the inevitable scheme of things (Gentry 1981; Henderson 1982).

The stage-model research showed that letter-name substitutions produced numerous spelling errors. A thorough documentation of letter-name substitution errors has been carried out on a large sample of children's writing by Treiman (1994). She replicated Read's findings entirely: the ubiquitous use of vowel letter names in CVCe words (CAK), the use of the letter name *ar* (R) as a vowel: *car* = CR, and the use of consonant letter names for final open syllables in words like *baby* = BAB.

In their study on spelling "stages," Varnhagen, McCallum, and Burstown (1997) commented that their "Phonetic" category was swamped with letter-name errors, particularly in CVCe words: *lake* spelled LAK, *hide* spelled HID, and *home* spelled HOM. The proportion of first graders making errors on these particular words was 79 percent, 44 percent, and 50 percent, respectively, and this persisted into second grade: 22 percent, 15 percent, and 0 percent. Recall that only two spelling categories held up: Phonetic errors and Correct spelling. Because the Phonetic category contains a large number of letter-name spelling errors, if these errors could be eliminated by not teaching letter names in the first place, the Phonetic

---

2. As noted earlier, Montessori believed that if spelling is taught first, children can automatically decode (read) what they have just written and will "discover" how to read. This is an excellent way to ensure the code is reversible.

category ought to disappear. And if it did, the only category left would be *Correct spelling*!

Treiman discovered that letter-name knowledge can have a negative impact on children's spelling accuracy. A study was designed to find out whether children knew the letter names in their own name, and whether this would generalize to knowing letter-sound correspondences (Treiman and Broderick 1998). Kindergarten and first-grade children were asked to identify letters in the alphabet by name and by sound. Children knew far more letter names than sounds. Only the letter name for the initial letter in the child's first name was consistently (and significantly) likely to be known, and this was true for both age groups. However, knowing this letter name did not ensure that these children knew the first *sound* in their names.

The second experiment was a replication of the first, with a writing component added. Preschoolers (4:3 to 5:9 years old) were tested for letter-printing accuracy, plus letter-name recognition. Scores were significantly higher for the letter that began the child's first name, but, again, this did not lead to knowledge of the sound the letter stood for. Despite the fact that young children are very familiar with the shape and "name" of the first letter of their name, knowing this provides no clue to the sound it represents even by first grade. The supposed "generalizability" effect has been the *only argument* for the importance of teaching letter names.

Treiman and Tincoff (1997) designed a special spelling test to pin down letter-name spelling errors in multisyllable words. Kindergartners and first graders were asked to spell nonsense words like *tuzzy*, *tuggy*, and *tuzzigh*. The first word ends in a letter name—*zee*—and the others do not (*ghee* and *zigh*). They found children commonly spelled open syllables (CV-CV) with single consonant letters (*b*, *z*, *d*, *g*). These "letter-name" errors were three times more likely to appear in the kindergartners' spellings than in first graders' spellings. This shows that letter names are something a child has to *unlearn* to be able to spell. Treiman and Tincoff observed that the error patterns showed that children were processing words at the level of the syllable, not the phoneme, and they were matching letters and sounds at the level of the syllable as well. They emphasized the significance of this fact: "These letter-name spellings reveal that the alphabetic principle is fragile for beginning spellers. Children find it difficult to represent speech as a sequence of individual phonemes. They sometimes take an easier path—the path of symbolizing groups of phonemes as units" (p. 447). In other words, letter names mislead children in two ways, by directing attention to the wrong phonological unit for the writing system, and by causing them to misrepresent the sound-to-print correspondences.

Yet despite the obvious negative effect of letter-name knowledge on spelling, Treiman and Tincoff did not believe this was cause for alarm or a reason to change what we are doing: "Knowledge of letter names thus has both positive and negative effects on early spelling. It can help children to spell alphabetically by helping them learn the links between phonemes and letters and by setting up expectations about how words are spelled. However, knowledge of letter names sometimes leads children to deviate from the alphabetic principle" (p. 449). This is a surprising statement in view of the finding by Treiman and Broderick (1998) that letter-name knowledge does not spontaneously generalize to letter-sound knowledge!

There is a vast literature on letter-name knowledge and letter-naming speed that proves conclusively that knowledge of letter names per se has nothing to do with reading or spelling skill (see *Language Development and Learning to Read*). Digit-naming speed and accuracy are just as highly correlated with reading skill (decoding accuracy and speed) as letter-naming speed. Because naming digits has nothing to do with reading, this means the apparent connection between letter-name knowledge and reading is artifactual. Something else is causing the relationship. What this something might be is unknown. It could be an aptitude for paired-associate learning, or it could be the fact that when mothers and teachers teach letter names, they also teach digit names.

We have more direct and practical evidence as well. Wimmer (1993) pointed out that Austrian teachers actively discourage the use of letter names when teaching children to read and spell, and focus exclusively on the phoneme-grapheme relationship instead. Every child learns to read and spell with a high degree of accuracy. Of course, the fact that the German spelling code is transparent matters a lot. But we know from these studies that letter names do not matter.

Jeffrey and Samuels (1967) and Samuels (1972) showed long ago that learning letter-sound relationships cut the learning time to decode words spelled with those letters by approximately 50 percent as compared to learning letter names. Furthermore, letter-name knowledge never generalized to the sounds inside the names. Learning letter names was no more beneficial than memorizing names of geometric shapes or cartoon characters! In fact, it was no more beneficial than being taught nothing at all.

The message is clear: *Discourage and eliminate the use of letter names and encourage the teaching of phoneme-grapheme correspondences.*

THE MANY-WORD PROBLEM:
MORE TO SPELLING THAN MEETS THE I

The studies reviewed in the previous chapter failed to show either how children learn to spell, or why some children fail and others do not. The concept of stages of spelling development is untenable on both logical and scientific grounds. The notion that poor spellers lack some linguistic knowledge or insights that would allow them to access "orthographic rules" or "morphological levels" of the spelling codes has not been substantiated. Poor spellers do worse across the board and have the most difficulty with rare, irregularly spelled words that appear infrequently in print—words whose spelling patterns do not reflect "orthographic rules" or "morphological structure." The most parsimonious explanation of the poor spellers' problem is lack of exposure to print. I address the reasons this might be the case later.

One of the major problems with these research efforts is that they reflect two main sources of confusion. The first relates to these fundamental questions: What processing skills are involved in mastering our spelling system? Is it phoneme awareness, knowledge of phoneme-grapheme correspondences, rote visual memory, memory for redundant visual patterns, or all the above? The second source of confusion is ignorance of the structure of the English spelling code. Unless we can get beyond these basic holes in knowledge, we are unlikely to make much headway toward the ultimate goal, which ought to be figuring out how we teach children to spell. The question "What's wrong with people who can't spell?" is, after all, a rather foolish question when researchers do not know the structure of the spelling code or how to teach it.

An analysis of the English spelling code was provided in chapter 3. This showed that the spelling code contains multiple components or aspects. It is a phonemically based system, but a strict one-to-one relationship holds over a very limited portion of phonemes. It is strongly linked to the phonotactic structure of the syllable, and scores of common spelling patterns reflect this structure. There are transformations for adding suffixes that come very close to "rules," and when they do, they are well worth teaching, not as rules, but through suitable examples and repetition. However, the bulk of the code is made up of hundreds and hundreds of *patterns*, systematic (redundant) grapheme sequences that are highly context dependent, *context* meaning the order of sounds and letters and the relative position of those letters: *batch* and *botch*, but *watch*, not *wotch*; *teach*, not *teech*; *church*, not *churtch* or *cherch*; *fault* and *fall*, not *falt* and *faul*.

Apart from the more obvious structural elements in the spelling code as outlined in chapter 3, the central concern for researchers is the *many-word problem*. How do people learn these patterns, and what sort of processing is going on in the brain to allow them to do this? The many-word problem encompasses the fact that it would be impossible to teach children to spell every word in the English language that deviated from a common set of phoneme-grapheme correspondences. This is a problem that does not exist in countries with a transparent alphabet. If the brain did not spontaneously record and update the thousands of redundant patterns in our spelling code, no one could learn to read or spell unless they had a photographic memory. For a brain to solve the many-word problem, it must see a lot of print. The problem certainly cannot be solved by taking scores of spelling tests consisting of random word lists, or by writing compositions riddled with misspelled words.

Measuring Print Exposure

If a large part of spelling skill is dependent on the brain's ability to code the structural redundancies of our complex spelling code, then how can we know if this is true? One way is to measure print exposure and study its impact on spelling. Stanovich and his colleagues explored the interactive or "knock-on" effects of reading a lot on spelling skill. In particular, they were concerned that the one-sided view that phoneme awareness explains everything misses a critical aspect of reading and spelling skill—the fact that unless phoneme analysis is connected to the spelling patterns of the written code, it is of little use.

The initial research (Stanovich and West 1989) was designed to look at the contribution of both phonological decoding and orthographic knowledge to spelling skill. The general view had been that phonological analysis was mainly responsible for the integration of phoneme sequences and spelling patterns. However, Stanovich and West felt that while this may be true, the ability to store orthographic patterns in memory might be an independent skill. If this is the case, then a measure of *exposure* to orthographic patterns would be most likely to tease the two apart.

They hit on a novel solution to measure exposure to print by designing a test to estimate how much people read. Questionnaires on reading behavior are fatally prone to "halo effects," people reporting they read far more than they actually do. To avoid this problem, Stanovich and West designed the Author Recognition Test (ART) and the Magazine Recognition Test (MRT). We met the ART in the previous chapter.

The tests are straightforward, simple to administer, and easy to take. The Author test consists of a list of 50 authors (well known by virtue of book sales and critical reviews), mixed with 50 foils of names of unknown persons. The Magazine test lists 50 names of real magazines and 50 of made-up magazines. The task involves a simple yes-no choice.

In one study, college students took the two tests described above plus a Reading Habits questionnaire, asking for a list of favorite authors and magazine subscriptions. Students took two spelling tests, a standardized test (WRAT spelling) and Fischer's test described in the previous chapter.

Of the self-report measures, the ART was far and away the best predictor of spelling skill, with the following correlations: composite spelling, $r = .46$; segment errors on the WRAT, $r = .38$; and Fisher's test, $r = .43$. Correlations between the spelling measures and self-reported reading habits and scores on the MRT were essentially zero.

In a second study, involving a much larger number of students, Stanovich and West used a battery of tests to tease apart phonological decoding from "orthographic" analysis. Reading was measured by the Word ID (word recognition) and Passage Comprehension subtests of the Woodcock. Other tests were Phonological Choice (select the word from a pair of misspelled words that "sounds like" a real word: *trane, clane*), Nonsense Word decoding test, Orthographic Choice (choose the correctly spelled word: *trane, train*), and Homophone Choice (which of these two words is a fruit? *pair, pear*).

The students were divided into skilled and less skilled readers on the basis of their reading test scores and compared statistically on 25 tests. Three tests failed to distinguish the two reader groups: the MRT, Orthographic Choice, and Homophone Choice. Clearly, the MRT is not a discriminating test, nor were the tests designed to measure "orthographic" visual memory. Because good readers read a lot and poor readers read very little, the absence of any difference on these tests is evidence against their theory that exposure to print enhances memory for orthographic patterns.

The most discriminating spelling measure was a count of word-segment errors on the WRAT spelling test, followed by "exception words." Poor readers differed most from good readers on words with unusual spellings that appear infrequently in print, supporting the results of Holmes and Ng, as well as of Waters, Bruck, and Malus-Abramovitz (see the previous chapter). Spelling test scores were strongly correlated with Word ID ($r = .50$ to $.63$) and somewhat less with Passage Comprehension ($r = .26$ to $.44$). These values are similar to those reported on children (Bond and Dykstra 1967; Shanahan 1984). Taken together, these results confirm the consistent connection between reading and spelling skills, with around 25–30 percent of shared variance.

The main purpose of the study was to look at the separate contribution of print exposure to spelling, with phonological decoding skill controlled. Phonological Choice and Nonword decoding were entered first in a regression analysis, followed by the ART (the measure of print exposure). The two decoding measures accounted for 25 percent of the variance on WRAT spelling, and the ART contributed a small (3 percent) but significant amount of variance beyond this. This cannot constitute *cause*. Verbal IQ is consistently correlated with spelling and was not controlled. The ART scores could be partially attributable to "reading a lot" because you have good verbal skills. If verbal ability and decoding skill "cause" print exposure, the connection between print exposure and spelling will be spurious. The authors were well aware of this problem and of the fact that correlational research cannot sort this out.

The failure to control for verbal IQ, and the problem of determining the direction of causality in a correlational study did not get solved in subsequent research from this group. In later studies on print exposure, the focus shifted to children. Cunningham and Stanovich (1990a) developed a new test called the Title Recognition Tests (TRT). The children had to identify real titles of children's books from a list of foils. But this only made the causality issue murkier, because, as the authors acknowledged, children's awareness of book titles could reflect a literary environment, or print exposure, or both—something heard as well as something seen (e.g., bedtime stories).

Because the TRT is not a clean measure of print exposure, and because of the methodological problems in these studies (small sample size, unstable results from one study to the next), the research on children (Cunningham and Stanovich 1990a; Cunningham, Stanovich, and West 1994) sheds no light on whether "reading a lot" improves one's knowledge of the spelling code.

The idea that print exposure plays an important role in learning the redundant patterns in the spelling code seems so intuitively plausible that most people want to believe it. Yet, so far, the evidence is too weak to show that print exposure plays a causal role in enhancing this skill.

Spelling without Phonology: A Study of Deaf Children

The goal of Stanovich and West (1989) was to tease apart phonological decoding from knowledge of orthographic structure to study the impact of print exposure on orthographic knowledge alone. They did not succeed. But there is another way.

Aaron et al. (1998) devised an ingenious way of tackling this problem by comparing the spelling of profoundly deaf children to that of normally hearing children on a variety of spelling tests. Profoundly deaf children have little or no phonological awareness so it is not clear how they learn to spell, which many do with some success. Because they are obliged to rely solely on visual memory, what kind of visual memory is it?

Aaron et al. pointed to a number of anomalies in the research literature on this topic, largely due to the lack of control over the degree and type of hearing impairments (some children had spoken language). There were disagreements in the literature about how to account for the fact that some deaf children and adults spell rather well. One theory was that they relied on pure rote visual memory, making them logographic spellers. Others believed that they acquire "phonological sensitivity" through speech training or lip reading, while still others suggested that they learn by mastering morphological spelling clues or "rules." Aaron et al. proposed a fourth theory—that deaf readers rely on the statistical probabilities of spelling sequences in words. They referred to this as a "frequency" model, meaning *frequency in print*.

They located 35 profoundly and congenitally deaf children in grades 5 through 12 who passed a rigorous screening. The children had no speech, or completely unintelligible speech, and could not communicate vocally. They were matched in reading age on the SAT and Woodcock reading tests with normally hearing children. The hearing children were evenly distributed by reading age across grades 2 through 5. This established a baseline. If spelling varied systematically between the deaf and hearing children on different types of spelling tests, this would be independent of reading and specific to spelling.

A variety of spelling tests was used to test the various theories described above. The first was the critical test of phonological encoding. Aaron and colleagues used a homophone-production task, in which the children were asked to write in the missing word in a sentence (correct spelling) and then add a "homophone" (same sounds, different spelling): "Clouds are white, but the sky is b _ _ _." (Answer: *blue, blew*.) In another homophone test, children had to write all the pairs of words they could think of that "sounded" alike (or were "spoken" alike) but were spelled differently. Deaf children had great difficulty understanding this concept and needed extra instruction. (Instruction was done in sign and was provided by a highly qualified teacher.)

The deaf children scored 90 percent correct on spelling words in context, equivalent to the grade 5 children. However, their success rate dropped to 10 percent when they were asked to supply a homophone, far below the grade 2 readers, who scored 47 percent correct. In the second homophone task, deaf children scored 20 percent correct and grade 2 readers 60 percent correct. Inspection of the individual data indicated that two deaf children did rather well on the last task. Their data were excluded from the remaining analyses, leaving a group of 33 children whose phonological sensitivity was essentially zero.

Next, the visual theories were put to the test. The children read sentences with a missing word that was spelled with a digraph with an inessential letter. Thus *sno* still sounds "snow" without the *w*. Deaf children spelled these words about as well as grade 5 readers (average 12/13 correct). When they looked at the proportion of spelling errors due to missing letters, hearing children made 80 percent of their errors in this category and deaf children only 38 percent. This shows that hearing children rely more on phoneme-grapheme patterns, and deaf children rely on visual memory, which is not supported by phonological processing.

But what kind of visual memory is it? Visual memory was tested by showing a series of word sets flashed on a screen for 30 seconds. Following each set, the children wrote down as many of the words as they could remember and tried to spell them correctly. The deaf children succeeding in writing down 90 percent of the words, the hearing children around 80 percent. The deaf students were much older, so this was expected. However, despite their superior memory for the words, the deaf students made far more spelling errors, 48 percent correct compared to 70 percent, 76 percent, and 89 percent for the hearing children at reading grades 3, 4, and 5. Deaf children made more transposition errors, visual errors, and unclassified errors, and virtually no phonetic errors (2 percent). This shows that visual memory alone is inadequate to spell common English words, even though deaf students remembered more words.

The final and critical task manipulated the statistical properties of spelling patterns in the words. The investigators used short nonwords spelled legally or illegally based on bigram and trigram frequencies (the number of times two- and three-letter sequences appear in words). The question was whether deaf students learned to spell by remembering redundant (probable) spelling patterns rather than by pure rote memory (random-letter sequences). If so, they would not do any better than hearing children on spelling words that are phonotactically illegal (unpronounceable), like *prta*, *hrda*, and *tneh*. The task took the same form (word sets) as the previous experiment. Children had to remember the words in each set, write them down, and try to spell them correctly.

Again, deaf students succeeding in recording (recalling) more words than even the fifth-grade children. The totals across all word sets combined were 391 (deaf) versus 259 (normal) for pronounceable words, and 309 versus 162 for the unpronounceable words. Apart from this, the deaf and normal children were remarkably alike. Both remembered significantly more legally spelled nonwords and spelled them more accurately. Deaf children performed much like the grade 3 and 4 reading groups, scoring 67 percent correct on *legal* nonwords. However, both deaf and hearing children did much worse (48 percent correct) in spelling *illegal* nonwords.

Deaf and hearing children find legal spelling patterns much easier to remember and spell. Not only this, but deaf children do not have superior visual rote-memory skills to hearing children. It appears that deaf and hearing children alike rely on both types of visual memory—pure rote memory and memory for redundant orthographic patterns—and they do so to the same extent.

A qualitative analysis of spelling errors on this task revealed that hearing children made mainly phonological errors, and deaf children hardly any. Their errors were visual and included letter reversals, and missing or substituted vowels and consonants. Deaf children made vowel and consonant errors in the same proportion, whereas the hearing children's errors mostly involved vowel spellings.

This is strong evidence that profoundly deaf children learn to spell by relying on the statistical properties of *visual* spelling patterns. These children had no phonological skills and no special advantage in rote visual memory. Yet they were able to spell nearly as well as grade 5 readers on some tasks. The other important result was that the hearing children were using a combination of three different skills: phonological processing for phoneme-grapheme relationships, pure rote visual memory, and memory for the statistical probabilities of "orthographic" patterns in words. It is this combination of skills that allows us to remember words and spell them accurately, and that accounts for why spelling improves with age. As Aaron pointed out, deaf children are at a distinct disadvantage: "A lack of acoustic phonological skills sets an upper limit at about the fourth grade level, beyond which spelling skills may not progress. This may be so because beyond a certain level, children encounter many cognate verbs, adverbs, and multi-syllable words whose spelling is influenced by morphophonemic conventions" (p. 18).

A related finding on a very different population of children was reported by Siegel, Share and Geva (1995) in Canada. They tested 257 poor readers who scored below the 25th percentile on the WRAT reading test, and 342 normal readers who scored above the 35th percentile.

The task was a spelling-recognition exercise: look at pairs of nonwords and select the one that looked "most like a word." The children were also tested on the Word Attack subtest of the Woodcock. The normal and poor readers differed on the Word Attack test in the expected direction. But the poor readers were superior (statistically) on the spelling-recognition task, supporting the findings of Waters, Bruck, and Malus-Abramovitz (1988). The poor readers behaved more like the deaf children, overly relying on visual memory for the common patterns of letter sequences, and were less aware of phonemes and phoneme-grapheme correspondences.

How Does the Brain Solve the Many-Word Problem?

Now we are at the heart of the matter. Aaron et al. proved that deaf and hearing children alike learn the statistical probabilities of orthographic patterns. But what exactly are those statistical patterns? Their study contrasted illegal letter strings with pronounceable letter strings based on bigram and trigram frequencies. But our spelling code cannot be mapped accurately by bigrams and trigrams. Readers have to be on the lookout for single letters (*t*), digraphs (*th*), and multiletter phonograms (*ough* in *though*), and constantly shift among them as they scan each word. If people rely on the statistical probabilities of orthographic sequences in addition to phoneme-grapheme correspondences, what are those sequences, and how does this work? If we had precise answers to these questions, if we knew what the brain did automatically, perhaps we could optimize instruction to work with the brain and not against it, as we are doing at the moment.

Twenty years ago, cognitive psychologists began a quest to discover how reading skill (speed and accuracy) is impacted by redundant orthographic patterns. This was the beginning of the discovery of the "third way" to decode and spell, as revealed by Aaron's elegant study on deaf and hearing children. In this research, however, the expression "orthographic patterns" refers to the *reading code* and not the spelling code (keeping in mind that writing systems are spelling codes, not reading codes). The research was intended to discover how spelling patterns map to pronunciations, and not how sounds in the language map to the spelling patterns. This is a nontrivial distinction, because the spelling code has a logic and a true probability structure, and the reading code does not. This will become more apparent in the analysis of the orthographic patterns that researchers assume impact decoding speed and accuracy.

Much of this research has been intimately connected with the development of computer models of reading. An early and influential model was the *dual-route* model. According to this theory, there are two independent pathways in the brain that process a printed word to its final destination (Coltheart 1978; Coltheart et al. 1993). One path (*lexical entry*) is "logographic" (purely visual) and maps directly to semantic memory and the stored phonological representation of the word. The other path involves translating from letters to individual phonemes and assembling them into a word. The translation is said to proceed via *grapheme-phoneme correspondence rules* (GPC rules). This route bypasses semantic memory and links to the output phase just prior to "saying" the word. GPC rules are the *decoding* counterpart of phonics-type spelling rules.

The concept of GPC rules had its roots in the work of Chomsky and Halle (1968), who proposed that phonology and morphology were linked by a set of correspondence rules. If a rule failed in a particular instance, this violation would be marked (presumably by the brain) with a "blocking rule" ("BUT NOT"). Venezky's (1970, 1999) attempt to discover "rules" of the spelling-to-sound code (chapter 3) fits this line of thinking. The dual-route model holds that GPC rules can be revealed by a complete analysis of printed words of the type Venezky embarked on. These rules are presumed to be deduced by the learner (or taught) and will explicitly guide the learning process. The dual-route model also includes the dictum that once a GPC analysis of a word is sufficiently fast, the word is transferred to the lexical path and becomes a sight word, recognized instantly (which, as chapter 2 showed, is impossible).

A similar idea was developed to explain the behavioral data on adult readers and children learning to read. It was believed that people have two (equally efficient) reading styles, reading whole words by sight (logographically), or reading phonetically. Baron and Strawson (1976) christened them "Chinese" and "Phoenician" readers. This reflects a mistaken belief that the Chinese (or anyone else) have a logographic writing system, and that people can learn to read by memorizing whole words as if they were telephone numbers.

The dual-route, Chinese/Phoenician models had their detractors, but none as important as Robert Glushko. His pioneering work is directly linked to the latest computer models of reading based on "parallel distributed processing" (Seidenberg and McClelland 1989; Plaut et al. 1996). These models mimic what is thought to occur in the brain when someone learns to read. These are statistical models. They "learn" by virtue of processing the structural redundancies in the input, along with the feedback from the environment about success rates.

On the Trail of Structural Redundancies in the Spelling Code
Glushko became disenchanted with the dual-route model as a graduate
student and set off in a different direction. The result was a new way to
think about how reading (decoding) occurs (Glushko 1979). It was
Glushko's work that led to the realization that there was a third process at
work during decoding, distinct from rote visual memory and grapheme-
to-phoneme correspondences.

A New Logic Glushko's insights stemmed from a logical analysis of the
problem. A dual-route model is illogical whether routes are considered
separately or in combination. Glushko proposed that all the information
about a word—visual, phonological, orthographic, semantic—is processed
at the same time *in parallel*. This means that no matter how many elements contribute to successful decoding, processing is not carried out in
separate (disconnected) pathways.

Furthermore, the proposal that "orthographic rules" could be distinguished separately from an analysis of the whole word was patently false.
For one thing, how does one identify the particular size of the unit that
qualifies it as an "orthographic rule"? Glushko did not give an example,
but there are many to choose from. Consider the "orthographic rule" that
a consonant should be doubled when adding -*ing*. Where does one draw
the line between this rule and the remaining letters in the word? Should
this rule contain a drop -*e* clause, or an antidoubling clause, or are these to
be separate rules? And because this rule must also specify where a reader
has to look to find out whether to double, it needs two additional sub-
clauses and a blocking rule to make it work: (1) if the word ends in *e*, drop
the *e* before adding -*ing* (*dine, dining; bridge, bridging*); (2) double the consonant when the preceding vowel is a "simple" checked vowel (*bat, batting*) BUT NOT when it isn't (*beat, beating*).

And these were not the only problems. Dual-route theorists use the
term *orthographic rules* to mean three different things. One meaning has to
do with linguistic descriptions, the second, knowledge of language structure, and the third, procedures or mechanisms of pronunciation. A *linguistic description* of the spelling code was supposed to be a reflection of a
reader's implicit or explicit knowledge of it. But as Glushko pointed out,
"There is no necessary relationship between linguistic descriptions of the

orthographic and phonological regularity in the language and a reader's knowledge of such language structure" (p. 675).

This is like my argument against the notion that people are aware of the "morphological rules" that govern spelling patterns. There is no reason to expect that spelling patterns are perceived by the speller (or reader) in a linguistic framework rather than simply as probable spellings of those words. This is not to say that some morphological rules or patterns cannot be taught or might be useful to know, but, rather, that they are not automatically deduced from spoken language or from text. Fischer, Shankweiler, and Liberman (1985) found that when they interviewed the college students about their strategies on the spelling test, they were completely unaware of any orthographic or morphological rules.

Glushko also pointed to difficulties with Venezky's 1970 analysis, and with his notion that readers generate GPC rules: "Since each word in the language is weighted equally in deciding whether a correspondence is regular or not, descriptive rules like these would be extremely difficult for readers to induce" (Glushko 1979, 675).

There are two issues here. First, Venezky's analysis was not probabilistic. He did not specify which print-to-sound "decodings" are most to least likely and to what degree. Second, the fact that only linguists with extensive training are able to generate these "orthographic rules" makes it highly unlikely that the average reader would do so spontaneously, something even Venezky (1967; 1999) acknowledged.

Glushko made several new proposals concerning how decoding could occur. First, the decoding process must take into account the contextual dependencies of the entire word. No purely surface decoding via GPC rules will work, just as no attempt at whole-word decoding, independent of the sequential redundancies in the orthography, will work.

Second, decoding proceeds by a variety of means, operating in parallel and integrating orthographic and phonological information. "Orthographic information" consists of all relevant featural components and their sequential patterns. Glushko used the analogy of natural language, in which the speaker and listener use all linguistic elements at the same time (semantic, syntactic, phonological, prosodic) as well as the context in which the conversation is taking place.

Third, he adopted the term *activation* to refer to a hypothetical "state" in which the brain automatically processes this information:

I suggest that it is more appropriate to focus on the functional properties of the lexical and orthographic knowledge bases, and to replace the unnecessarily specified mechanisms with a more neutral term such as "activation."

In this simpler framework, I propose that words and pseudowords are pronounced through the integration of orthographic and phonological information from a number of sources that are activated in parallel, much as readers comprehend sentences by integrating lexical, syntactic, and contextual information. As letter strings are identified, there is parallel activation of orthographic and phonological knowledge from a number of sources in memory. This knowledge may include the stored pronunciation of the letter string, pronunciations of words that share features with the letter string, and information about the spelling-to-sound correspondence of various subparts of the letter strings. (p. 678)

The central problem, then, became one of determining which of these sources or features of the word's spelling were more or less relevant.

The goal in this research has been to find an objective or quasi-objective way to quantify the "orthographic patterns" that lead to success in decoding English words. Many approaches have been attempted, but all have failed. One reason is a lack of understanding of the structure of English words (phonotactics) and the way the spelling code maps to this structure. A second reason follows from the first. Because the analysis is exclusively in the direction of decoding and never in the direction of encoding, the "structural patterns" do not reflect the way the code was written and how it developed. The fact is that spellings are assigned to words. Words are not assigned to spellings. A third reason is one Glushko pointed out. Orthographic structure consists of "the contextual dependencies of the entire word" and "all relevant featural components and their sequential patterns" (p. 678). It has proven extremely difficult to meet the goal of defining "all relevant features."

There have been two main approaches to this problem, one quantitative and the other subjective. The quantitative approach makes no prior assumptions about "patterns," but relies on frequency counts of letter sequences (bigrams and trigrams). The subjective approach is based on the observation that many final VC or VCC units in one-syllable words are spelled consistently, providing orthographic clues for how to read the word. In cognitive models, this component is known as the *word body*.

Teachers have known it for at least two centuries as a *word family*, and more recently it was rechristened the *rime*. I will refer to the visual representation of the VC or VCC letter sequences in one-syllable words as the *orthographic rime* and the phonological "decoding" of that rime as the *phonological rhyme*. It is very important to keep this distinction straight, or this research will seem even more complex than it already is.

Orthographic Rimes Have Consistent and Inconsistent Neighbors Glushko's interest in orthographic structure led him to the orthographic rime. He set up lists of words based on whether the rime was consistent or inconsistent in terms of how it was decoded—its *pronunciation*. This was the logic: the orthographic rime (*ile* in *mile*) will automatically activate words stored in memory that have the same rimes both visually and phonologically. In Glushko's theory the orthographic rime maps directly onto the phonological rhyme. The theory does not take into consideration the fact that a phonological rhyme would also map to an orthographic rime (/s/ /t/ /ie/ /l/—*style*), if, indeed, rimes are even relevant in the first place.

The word lists consisted of regular words (those with many consistent neighbors) and exception words (those with inconsistent neighbors). Words were matched for word frequency. For example, *dean* is regular (there is only one way to read words ending <u>ean</u>); *deaf* is an exception word because it inconsistent due to the word *leaf*. Two sets of nonsense words were also created by changing the initial consonant of word pairs: *hean* and *heaf*. The hypothesis was that regular words/nonwords would be decoded faster and more accurately than exception words/nonwords.

It was as at this point that Glushko's otherwise impeccable logic began to fail. Already, one can see the problem. Because the initial consonant was not part of this scheme, other readings besides the ones he expected were not acknowledged. What if <u>heaf</u> was read as *hef* by analogy to *head*, producing the same outcome as *deaf*, but for a different reason? What if *hean* was read as *hen* as an analogy to *head* instead of to *dean*?

More problematic was Glushko's use of the term *error*. The "errors" were not really errors in any objective sense. Instead, errors occurred when the subjects did not read a nonword as Glushko expected them to (with a consistent pronunciation), even though the rendering was perfectly legal. For instance, the mathematical likelihood of reading <u>heaf</u> as *hef* or *heef* is identical, because there are only three real words spelled with this rime, *deaf, leaf,* and *sheaf.* This selective scoring biases the error rate in the direction of the hypothesis, which appears to be what happened.

And there were problems with the word lists, the data, and the inferences from the data. I will run through the studies briefly to illustrate these effects. College students in the first experiment saw 172 words and nonwords plus 100 filler words presented randomly (one at a time) by computer. Their task was to read each word as accurately and as quickly as possible into a microphone, and the time to start speaking was recorded (voice-onset latency).

Glushko provided an item analysis for the response-time data, one of the few people in this field to do so. These values are extremely illuminating. For one thing, contrary to Glushko's prediction, the students read 14 exception words faster than the regular words, and there were 4 ties. This is 42 percent of the words on the lists. And even though the results were "significant" in the predicted direction, regular words were read, on average, only 29 ms faster than exception words ($p < .05$). Yet the difference between the word pairs that went opposite to prediction was much larger, 51.4 ms.

What could explain this? Certainly not regularity and exceptionality or consistent and inconsistent "rimes." Perhaps this was a word-frequency effect. High-frequency words like *both, done, most, none, some,* and *were* might be read faster because they are "activated" more quickly, to use Glushko's terminology. Some of these words fit little "families" phonologically: *done, none, some (one, come), most, post (ghost, host).* But there are no easy answers for why *foot* was read faster than *feet, hood* was read faster than *heed,* or *comb* was read faster than *cold.* The fact that *spook*—the only inconsistent "rime" in the <u>ook</u> family—was read 90 ms faster than *spool* is a mystery, and this goes directly against the idea of consistency as being the determining factor in decoding these words.

Experiment 2 was designed to counter the objection that there were too many overlapping words on the lists (words with the same rimes), which may have biased the way people responded. This problem was remedied by using nonwords only. Some pairs were taken directly from the old list, some had the same rime but different initial consonant, and some were new. I prepared a table with the following information: (1) the pairs used in experiment 2; (2) whether the same or a similar pair was used in experiment 1; (3) response-time differences between experiments 1 and

2; and (4) whether or not the response times followed prediction. The table illustrated some disconcerting facts about these kinds of word lists. In the first place, it is tempting for experimenters to drop out words that go against the prediction and retain those that do. I am not saying that this is a conscious act or that Glushko did this; otherwise all word pairs would have gone in the prediction direction. But he did have a better hit rate for the reused word pairs than for the new word pairs he created: 16 out of 26 old pairs going with the prediction (62 percent), versus only 3 out of 7 new pairs (43 percent). The response-time data represents an additional concern, because the values for the same word pairs fluctuate wildly from experiment 1 to experiment 2.

Glushko himself appeared to have considerable doubts about his classification scheme. In the third experiment, he reclassified words into three categories. He used the word *have* to explain how this worked. *Have* is both an exception word and inconsistent, in that the spelling <u>ave</u> is only decoded /av/ in this word, whereas it is usually decoded /aev/ (*cave*, *gave*). Thus, *have* is the only word with this pronunciation. The word *gave*, on the other hand, is no longer regular by the old scheme, but inconsistent by virtue of the existence of *have*. Another group of words were both regular and consistent, having lots of neighbors and no competitors. Two sets of consistent words were derived from the exception and inconsistent words by changing a single consonant (*haze* and *wade*), and these became the control words.

In general, Glushko's predictions for this complex set of contrasts was borne out statistically, but it is doubtful that the categorization process fits his activation theory, or that the findings are even supported by the data. First of all, the pairs of regular/consistent control words (*haze*, *wade*) were supposed to be read at more or less the same speed, having been derived from the same word (*gave*), both having lots of neighbors. But only 66 percent of these word pairs were processed at comparable speeds, when all should have been.

Furthermore, because the activation theory predicts that neighbors will automatically be activated together and boost the likelihood of a particular reading of a word, regular/inconsistent words like *wave* (lots of consistent neighbors) ought to be read more quickly than an exception word like *have* (all neighbors inconsistent). This, after all, is the basis for the consistency effect. Yet reaction time was 492 ms for *have* and 528 ms for *wave*. Similarly, the exception word *love* took 472 ms to read, and the regular word *grove* took 642 ms. Altogether, 12 regular/inconsistent words took longer to read than exception words, and 4 were tied—39 percent going against prediction.

Some Conclusions   Comparing the reaction times of some "exception" words that were used in both experiments 1 and 3 revealed some startlingly erratic values. Often the differences between the reaction times for the *same word* were larger than the comparisons between different words, which seriously compromises this work. Perhaps voice-onset latency relayed through a microphone is an unreliable technology, and/or people are not consistent in naming speed.

There are a host of factors involved in how quickly people can read words, and they take us far beyond the realm of consistent or inconsistent "word bodies." These are the number of times you have seen the word (familiarity), the emotional saliency of the word (*love* has high emotional salience), and idiosyncrasies due to word type.

More important issues have to do with the spelling code, which is very different from the reading code. For example, <u>have</u> is a completely "regular" spelling; there is no other way to spell it, given that final /v/ is always spelled <u>ve</u>. The <u>e</u> in the <u>ve</u> spelling does double duty in some words, also marking the vowel. The fact that the *e* plays two roles in words like *gave* makes the *ve* spelling unusual. A number of "exception" words on Glushko's lists are not exceptional in the least, because this is the only way they can be spelled. These are words like *give, foot, hoof, pint, plow,* and *soot*. (I challenge the reader to spell them differently.) Then there are words where vowel spellings are linked to the *initial* consonant: <u>b</u> and <u>p</u> take the <u>u</u> spelling for /oo/ (*bush, bullet, put, push—book* is the exception). The vowel spelling is controlled by the <u>w</u> in words like *wand* and *work* (rather than *wond* and *werk*).

Glushko confessed in a footnote that things were a lot more complex than simple rime patterns would allow, and perhaps his remarks are the best conclusion to this work: "A more general activation and synthesis model, with a broader experimental base, would allow for the contribution of neighbors in all positions, and would differentially weight them in different tasks" (p. 684).

At this point, I must address the problem created by the notion that orthographic rimes are major sources of brain activation. In Glushko's initial work and in the subsequent research on computer models of reading, the word body or rime means *a letter string* mapping to a *pronunciation*. Whether activation generates a brainstorm of related words with identical rimes is unknown. This is complicated by the fact that we read so fast that we are not aware of how we do it. Nevertheless, it takes the brain 450–700 ms to read a simple word—quite a long time for brains. Simple reaction time (see a light, press key) ranges from 150 to 200 ms, so a brain can do quite a lot in that much spare time.

Something undoubtedly gets activated, but what? If both orthographic *rimes* and phonological *rhymes* light up, chaos would ensue. A number of Glushko's words illustrate this quite nicely. A person reads great and the visual system activates words with the same *visual rime*: eat, beat, cheat, defeat, heat, meat, neat, peat, pleat, seat, treat, wheat. A few milliseconds later, the phonological system gets a match (/eet/). Meanwhile, memory traces have linked great to the *phonological rhyme* (/aet/), activating phonological rhymes for the words: *bait, crate, date, inflate, freight, gate, hate, mate, plate, slate, state, spate, straight, trait, wait*. Because the systems work in parallel, I assume the spellings above (visual rimes) are supplied rather quickly as well. What is the brain to do with this? A systems collapse seems inevitable! Yet Glushko found that the reaction time for *great* (an exception word) was 41 ms faster than for *greet*, a highly regular spelling with no "enemies."

It is unlikely that the system works this way. Decoding may occur largely through generating the most likely connection between a visual image and its phonological image, and where both images are much more highly specified than by word fragments like rimes or rhymes, which on the face of it is an extremely quaint notion. How does anyone learn to read or spell words that do not rhyme?

I have taken time to survey the problems in constructing these word lists to illustrate the danger of making inferences from these results about how the brain processes spelling patterns. I did this, as well, because Glushko's word lists march inexorably on and are still being used today to confirm or disconfirm the validity of influential computer models of reading.

More Attempts to Pin Down Orthographic Structure
Glushko's work led to an explosion of research on this topic, and there is no space to cover this here. Here, I want to deal briefly with the fate of the orthographic rime and then review more recent discoveries that show what is really going on.

Juel and Solso Glusho's article was followed by a more quantitative attempt using bigram (letter-pair) frequencies in a series of studies by Juel and Solso (Solso and Juel 1980; Juel and Solso 1981; Juel 1983). They provided an informative and thoughtful analysis of the problem, though this was largely a failed attempt because bigram frequencies are a very bad fit to the spelling code. In 60 percent of the words in their lists, at least one bigram unit was discordant with the word's phonology.

Juel and Solso's analysis did go some way toward identifying important structural elements of the spelling code. They identified two types of information contained in the spelling patterns. Their language has been changed to some extent to be consistent with the use of terms in this book.

1. The probability (or number of occurrences) with which a specific letter pair (bigram) appears in *specific* word positions in a syllable, estimated on a large corpus of words. They called this *orthographic redundancy*.
2. The probability with which a letter pair appears in *any* position in a large number of different words. They called this *orthographic versatility*.

These categories tie letter sequences to positions within words, but do not specify what the reader does with them. This led to a third orthographic category:

3. The probability with which a particular letter pair represents a particular phoneme or phonemes. Using their terminology, this would reflect "orthographic consistency," but they called this *coding* or *decoding*.

As can be seen, this is essentially a visual logic, and does not include the probability structure of the spelling code from the phoneme out. Thus, there are two missing variables on the list. One is the *frequency* of occurrence in print of a particular spelling for a particular phoneme. The other is the *probability* or likelihood that spelling alternatives for the same phoneme occur in a large corpus of words. This problem was never solved in future research, and remains unsolved as this book goes to press.

There were several interesting findings in this work. Juel (1983) reported that the probability that a bigram consistently represents a phoneme was much more important for beginning readers (second graders). Orthographic versatility was more important to older children (fifth grade) and adults, and they read "versatile" letter pairs (bigrams that appear in lots of positions in lots of words) much faster. This result seems counterintuitive, because one would expect that positional knowledge of spelling patterns (*chat*, *catch*) would be extremely important and should improve with age, and *not* that positional stability is less beneficial. However, this may be an artifact of the bigram technique and of their word lists.

After investigating the instructional implications of these findings, she reported that first graders taught by a letter-to-sound method learned the letter-sound relationships faster for "versatile" letter pairs (those that appear in many slots in words) than for nonversatile letter pairs. Juel (1983, 325) had this to say:

There is a possible instructional implication that emerges from the current study. A real advantage that adult readers have over children is their sensitivity to versatile letter combinations. Versatile letter combinations appear to be more quickly processed both visually and phonologically. Presenting children with large numbers of words that contain similar letter combinations would seem facilitative to developing a set for versatility.

Versatility represents a simple frequency measure, the fact, for example, that the letters *ad* appear in a lot of words in lots of different positions. However, children should never be taught letter pairs unless they are legitimate digraphs. Tailoring reading instruction to words representing certain classes of bigrams would be extremely counterproductive because they so strongly misrepresent the phonetic nature and structure of our spelling code.

Zinna, Liberman, and Shankweiler Zinna, Liberman, and Shankweiler (1986) were the first to study children using Glushko's approach. The children were asked to read real and nonsense words, and were scored for accuracy, not speed. Zinna and colleagues provided a thorough analysis of how the children decoded the vowel digraphs on each word on their test, which tells us more than average scores and significance levels do. As in the Glushko study, words were assigned to "consistent" and "inconsistent" neighborhoods on the basis of the VC rime: *beach* was consistent because the spelling each is likely to be decoded "eech"; *head* was inconsistent because ead can be decoded "heed" or "head."

The results showed that children are just as idiosyncratic as adults in how they respond to "rime consistency" and "neighborhoods," indicating that orthographic rimes have little connection to what the brain is doing. I report here on the nonsense words, because there were ceiling effects on real words.

Some neighborhoods were more consistent than others. The consistent oo group *mooth*, *looth*, *troom*, *poom*, *shoon*, *smoon*, *woon* behaved in an orderly way, with nearly everyone opting for the /oo/ vowel sound. The nonwords ending each, ean, eam were consistently read as /ee/. But none of the remaining rimes in the "consistent" group were read consistently. The children decoded the rimes oup, oung, oud with five different vowel sounds. Children read the three oup words (the *soup* neighborhood) as "oop" 30 percent, 50 percent, and 73 percent of the time, depending on the word—not remotely consistent. Decoding was unstable for words with the rimes ield, ief, and iece as well.

On the other hand, many rimes in the "inconsistent" group produced highly consistent responses, most children opting for /o͞ol/ in *bool* and *smool* (not /o͝ol/ as in *wool*). Preferences were strong (around 90 percent) for reading eak words as /ee/ and not as /ae/ (*steak*). Children were split, as expected, on the ow words, reading them as /ou/ (*cow*) or /oe/ (*low*) equally often.

In reviewing these words, I can confirm that the orthographic patterns fit the authors' intentions. The variability in responding was due to the children and not to the word lists. Some children seemed to be decoding by analogy to a word family, others by analogy to CV initial letters (chead was read as an analogy to *cheap* and not *head* 77 percent of the time). Some nonwords contained whole real words, which may have encouraged the children to seek out little words inside bigger words: *zoo* in *zook* and *moo* in *mook* won the battle with the powerful ook, family whose only enemy is *spook*. The *cow* in *cown* and *how* in *hown* may be responsible for the children's preference for /ou/ versus /oe/ readings, which garnered nearly 100 percent of responses.

In analyzing these responses, Zinna and colleagues concluded that "the influence of the initial segment appears to account for most of the variability" (p. 474). They suggested that because people read from left to right, the first sequence activates a word: *prou_ = proud* instead of *proup = soup*. But this explanation does not hold up consistently, not even for *proup*, which was read *proop* 50 percent of the time. In short, children's decoding did not obey either the CV onset or the VC "rime," and seemed to involve the whole word.

Treiman and Colleagues   The first attempt to provide a quantitative account of the consistency with which all orthographic units represent language did not appear until 1995. This was the work of Treiman and her colleagues (Treiman et al. 1995). The authors stated that while the English writing system is alphabetic, there are structural redundancies in its orthography. It was their belief that the most important structural element was the VC unit or "rime":

We argue here that a consideration of orthographic and phonological units that are larger than single graphemes and single phonemes can shed new light on the nature, use, and acquisition of the English writing system. Specifically, we claim that letter groups that correspond to the *rimes* of spoken syllables, or units that include the vowel and any following consonant, play an important role in adults' and children's pronunciation of printed words. (p. 107; original emphasis)

And they were quite clear about this direction of the relationship: "The consonant that follows the vowel helps to specify its pronunciation" (p. 108). They referred to this as a "special dependency."

These statements are troubling, because the goal is so circumscribed, suggesting a lack of objectivity in the quest to classify orthographic structure.

The article was in three parts. The first was a tabulation of the frequency count of the "neighbors" of the orthographic units: C, V, C, CV, VC in 1,329 CVC words. These units were analyzed correctly, in that each phoneme could be represented by one to four letters: s<u>i</u>t, s<u>oa</u>p, s<u>igh</u>t, s<u>ough</u>t.

The tabulation proceeded as follows. Each letter, digraph, or phonogram in each position in the 1,329 CVC words was given a value according to whether that letter—in the same position in all comparison words—was pronounced alike or differently in a much larger corpus of multisyllable words. A "neighborhood" (the same letter or letter sequence) was quantified according to its *consistency*, the frequency with which this occurred.

Pronunciations that matched were "friends," and those that mismatched were "enemies." Each of the orthographic units was scored for the number of friends relative to the number of friends plus enemies by the formula $F/F + E$. This provides a single value for "*neighborhood consistency*" for all letter units in each set: C, V, C, CV, VC.[1]

The tabulated data showed that the most consistent reading of any letter in a CVC word is the initial consonant (95 percent consistent), followed by the final consonant (92 percent consistent). The VC unit was more consistent than the CV unit (80 versus 55 percent), and more consistent than the vowel alone (62 percent). These values are for the probability of the spelling in all words in the corpus. The values for frequency of occurrence in print were somewhat lower for all units involving vowels, but single consonants maintained the same high values. When the number of different pronunciations and their probabilities across all monosyllabic words in the corpus were calculated, the most regular (predictable) were the final consonant and the VC unit. Next came the initial consonant and the CV unit. The vowel pronunciation was least predictable.

Treiman and colleagues drew the following conclusions from this effort:

---

1. This was a formidable undertaking, because orthographic units had to be "decoded" to be compared. The pronunciation determined how each item was scored, and this cannot be done by computer. However, there was no explanation about how this critical process was carried out, nor any reliability checks on the coding process. On the one hand, this effort appears highly objective (frequency counts), and on the other hand, there is an unknown degree of subjectivity that was not controlled.

The results for individual graphemes paint a rather bleak picture of the English writing system.... English is not very regular. For vowels especially, a single grapheme often maps onto several phonemes.... If we incorporate large orthographic and phonological units into our description of the English writing system, however, the picture becomes more encouraging. The pronunciation of orthographic units that contain *a vowel grapheme and a final consonant grapheme* are more consistent than the pronunciations of single vowel graphemes. (p. 112; emphasis added)

There are two problems with this and the statement above. First, it is no more likely that the VC consistency is due to the consonant controlling the vowel pronunciation, as the authors claim, than for the vowel to control the consonant spelling (co-occurrence is not cause). Second, these 1,329 common CVC words, constitute only .07 percent of all words in a college dictionary of 200,000 words, scarcely a sufficient number of words to advocate incorporating larger orthographic and phonological units in descriptions of our writing system. Finally, there is no evidence for, and considerable evidence against, the assumption that people's *behavior* will follow this particular statistical pattern in these particular words, as earlier results have shown. The obvious next step was to find out if it did. Students from two universities (27 from Wayne State and 30 from McGill) were asked to read the 1,329 CVC words as quickly and accurately as possible.[2]

I will present the results that were consistent between the two student groups. Unless results can be generalized across similar populations, they have no validity. Of the 42 variables entered into a regression analysis, only those shown in the accompanying table accounted for significant

---

2. Reaction time (voice-onset time) and error scores were averaged across subjects for each word, for the two groups of students separately. Thus, there were a total of 1,329 reaction-time scores, one for each word. These were used in a multiple-regression analysis to look at the relationship between the speed involved in saying a word and the various properties of that word. In effect, "words" were substituted for subjects in the statistical analysis, and all the "variance" (variability) came from the words and not from the students. This is a very unusual procedure.

amounts of variance for *both* the Wayne State and McGill students. These values represent unique variance for each variable, with shared variance controlled.

	Wayne State	McGill
Word familiarity	3.8%	1.3%
Word frequency	2.2	.3
No. of letters in C, V, C (summed values)	2.7	1.4
Consistency: initial consonants	2.2	.9
Consistency: VC	.8	1.3
Variance due to producing the initial phoneme	5.2	22.8

The table illustrates two things. First, the figures in the bottom row reflect a serious problem with the technology used to measure voice-onset latency. Variation in the physical act of producing the initial phoneme in a word accounted for the largest amount of variance in voice-onset time and was quite different for the two groups. In essence, this is a huge source of noise in the data. As such it should have been subtracted or set aside, yet the authors *added it* in their analysis.

Second, whatever it is that accounts for the speed it takes to read a word, this study has not found it. Word frequency or familiarity will not play a big role in college students' ability to read high-frequency, simple CVC words, and we see that it does not here. But even so, it accounted for more variance than anything else that was measured. The number of letters per phoneme and the consistency rating for the initial consonant both accounted for more variance than the VC rime, which accounted for less than 1 percent in the Wayne State data and 1.3 percent for the McGill students. Although these tiny values were "significant" due to the fact that the 1,329 words acted as "subjects" in the study, they have no practical significance.

Treiman and colleagues reached the following conclusion:

Readers appear to have picked up the statistical regularity documented in Part 1, that VC units are fairly reliable guides to pronunciation. Given a word whose VC had a single pronunciation, people pronounced the word relatively quickly and accurately. When the VC had multiple pronunciations, performance was comparatively poor. This was a robust finding, emerging in all of the regression analyses for both the Wayne State and McGill participants....

Together with the effect of VC consistency, this finding suggest that, at least in the speeded naming task, printed words are processed to a large extent in terms of orthographic units that correspond to onsets (C units) and orthographic units that correspond to rimes (VC units). (pp. 121, 122)

The data do not support this extreme position.

The final section included a study of children in first, second, third, and fifth grades. Word lists were set up on the basis of high or low CV and VC consistency scores (proportions of friends and enemies). There were four kinds of lists: (1) words with high-CV/high-VC consistency scores; (2) words low on both; (3) high-CV/low-VC; (4) low-CV/high-VC.

Treiman and associates predicted that children would make fewer errors on words with highly consistent VC rimes, because, according to the theory, the final consonant is the primary cue to how the vowel is pronounced in these words. The data appeared to confirm this, because words in the "high-VC" lists were read significantly more accurately by first, second, and third graders. Fifth graders were equally accurate on all four lists.

My analysis of the word lists showed that something quite different was going on. In many words, the *vowel* controlled how the consonant was spelled in VC units (watch, beach), or the *initial consonant* controlled how the vowel was spelled (/b/ and /p/ take the u spelling for /oo/, as in *bush*, *push*). Words like these were scattered throughout the lists and did not fit the designations used by Treiman and colleagues. In a large number of words, there was no relationship between any of the phonemes or graphemes in the word, which is typical of the "simple-vowel" CVC words on their lists: *bob, mob, thin, gum, gun, wet, met*. In perfectly "regular" CVC words like these, any letter can be swapped out, and this does not affect how the other letters are decoded.

I carried out a thorough analysis of all the words on these lists (see appendix 2) and found only 2 words out of 60 where the final consonant in a VC rime definitely influenced how the vowel is decoded: *ball* and *tall*.

In all other cases there was little or no connection. This means that the "significant" advantage in reading accuracy for "consistent" VC rimes is an artifact of the words on the word lists. What might this factor be?

It turns out that the main reason children made more mistakes reading low-consistency VC words was because these words were considerably harder to read. They were longer (had more letters), and they were spelled with less common spelling alternatives: *bear, shall, none, ton, won, cough,* and *rough.* Four words on one list used the Old French spelling se for the phonemes /s/ and /z/, and the vowel could be decoded in two ways: *chose, dose, pose, lose.* It is not surprising that children had more trouble reading these kinds of words. If these anomalous spellings cause a decrease in reading accuracy, is this really because the "rime" is inconsistent? Can the absence of something be a cause?

So far, there are no satisfactory measures for studying which "orthographic" patterns are processed by the brain to help retrieve information in order to decode words. These measures are not only unsatisfactory, but misleading, especially when the interpretation of the data tends to be biased.

Computer Models of Reading

For reasons unknown, Glushko left off his study of the statistical properties of orthographic patterns and went on to other things. As things have progressed, perhaps this was a wise decision. Nevertheless, Glushko's fundamental questions are still important since computer models of reading have started to come of age. The current problem is not so much whether a computer program can learn to read, but which of the various models fits the way humans read. Unless the model behaves like people do, one cannot infer that the computer is doing anything remotely "brain-like." After all, a computer can play chess by running through every possible move, ten moves in advance, in the time it takes to say *nanosecond,* but this is not what chess masters do.

For historical reasons (one assumes), the major players in *parallel-distributed* or *neural-network* models of reading (Seidenburg and McClelland 1989; Plaut et al. 1996) have relied on Glushko's original logic and have attempted to validate their models on tasks identical to or similar to Glushko's, even to the point of using Glushko's original lists of words. We have already seen that those lists are problematic. After a decade or so, one would imagine that everything had been nailed down, and that all the head scratching that Glushko suffered through was over and done with. Not so.

A Can of Worms Gets Some More Worms

In 1990, Jared, McRae, and Seidenberg published what was intended to be the definitive study to get this sorted out, especially in view of the fact that so many people were finding it difficult to replicate Glushko's results. At the same time, they were interested in finding reliable behavioral support that a model based on strict grapheme-phoneme correspondence rules was untenable. Orthographic patterns were important, but what were they?

One of the central problems was that the computer models of "behavior" (referring to Seidenberg and McClelland 1989) did not mimic human behavior and the tests designed to measure it, such as Glushko's. The computer is given 3,000 words to learn to read, along with some initial "training" on basic letter-to-sound correspondences. The computer gradually organizes "patterns of activation" encoded by a set of weights (interneuron substitutes). These eventually link a spelling to its most probable decoding based on common patterns (statistical redundancies) that appear in the entire corpus of 3,000 words. As the computer learns, it gets feedback on each trial for whether it did or did not print out the correct phonetic rendering of the word. The outcome is fed back into the system, and the weightings are modified. Various mathematical models have been tested, the most recent outlined by Plaut et al. (1996).

The difference between these models and behavioral measures is that all relevant words contribute to an outcome, plus the data are continuous, precisely weighted values and constantly updated. By contrast, behavioral research relies on discrete categories of words in which there is competition between inconsistent and consistent neighbors, or on other variables. In the computer models, "neighbors" (friendly or unfriendly) cooperate to a supply pool of information. Thus, "The weights come to encode facts about the consistency of spelling-sound correspondences in the training corpus. The models' performance is evaluated in terms of a phonological error score that indicates the discrepancy between the computed phonological code and the correct code" (Jared, McRae, and Seidenberg 1990, 689). The two most important points about this statement include the computation of consistency (how often a match occurs or does not occur), and the fact that phonology is wrapped into the process—a process that serves the function of integrating letter patterns and speech sounds. There is no need nor reason, therefore, for "dual routes" or different "pathways."

The work of Brown (1987) had seemed to show that the largest impact on decoding speed was not consistency of the "rime" but the frequency with which orthographic rimes appeared in print. Jared and associates suggested that perhaps the notion of consistency is correct, but that this will only appear in certain kinds of words, having something to do with the "neighborhood size" of enemies *relative to* the neighborhood size of friends. For instance, if an orthographic rime has few enemies that are low frequency in print, there will be little interference in decoding the word. On the other hand, if the rime has a lot of enemies all of high frequency in print, decoding will take longer. It must be stressed that by neighborhood "consistency," Jared and colleagues meant the *orthographic rime* only.

In a series of four experiments, Jared, McRae, and Seidenberg more or less "proved" the theory outlined above, or at least thought they did. But this theory held for a limited corpus of words, with far too many constraints.[3]

The results showed that the "consistency effect" was isolated to words with orthographic rimes that had lots of enemies, but it failed to appear when enemies were few. The investigators believed they had settled the dilemma that had plagued this research for so long: the fact that the

---

3. In the definitive experiment, the following constraints had to apply for the "orthographic rime theory" to work. Words were selected that fit two main categories: words with high-frequency friends (rime segments that appear often in a lot of words) and words with low-frequency friends. They were divided further into words with consistent and inconsistent rimes (one possible decoding versus more than one). The inconsistent words were split further into words with high-frequency enemies (rimes with different pronunciations that appeared often in print), and those with low-frequency enemies (infrequent in print). Each word was then matched to a control word on everything except consistency. Also controlled were a variety of other measures such as word frequency and word length.

frequency in print of the orthographic rimes had not been controlled. They argued that these results provided a strong refutation of a dual-route model and GPC rules, because a rule-based system cannot explain the impact of the "rime" consistency and frequency effects on word-recognition speed.

Further experiments added some nuances. Jared and colleagues attempted to tease apart the impact of the *visual* orthographic rime and the *phonological* rhyme on the "consistency effect." Results showed that the consistency effect was found only when the students responded verbally (not manually), leading the researchers to conclude that the consistency effect was due to phonological factors. It is not clear what this means. Structural redundancies are certainly visual as well; otherwise deaf children could not use them to read and spell.

More Worms

We need to put Jared, McRae, and Seidenberg's results in perspective, especially because they underpin the rationale for the latest computer models on reading from this group (Plaut et al. 1996). It is insufficient to argue merely that these studies did or did not prove a consistency theory about word-recognition speed and accuracy, because all the constraints that made this statement possible should be part of the equation. An accurate statement of what happened in this study follows.

Given words of equal frequency in print, all one syllable long and containing the same number of letters, the same bigram-frequency count, and the same orthographic-error score, consistent words (rimes pronounced only one way) are read faster and more accurately than inconsistent words (rimes pronounced more than one way) *only if* the inconsistent words have enemies seen frequently in print. This effect is most marked if the frequency of friends is low as well. This result is not affected by the simple tally of friends or enemies.

There are two ways to look at this outcome. Here is the authors' version, presented in light of the fact that they controlled all the relevant variables listed above: "It is very likely that the observed effects are due to the one stimulus property that systematically differed between groups: consistency of spelling-sound correspondences" (p. 707).

I was more struck by the fact that as the controls kept mounting, the corpus of words became so small that the investigators had to repeat word lists twice to have enough words to do the study. Thus, even if these effects are robust and replicable, are they relevant when they pertain to a very special group of words constituting a minute fraction of all words?

Jared and colleagues attempted to link these results to computer models of word recognition, especially that of Seidenberg and McClelland 1989. This model has no representations for individual words. Instead, properties of the model give rise to consistency effects:

> Words that are similarly spelled and similarly pronounced (e.g., rhyming neighbors such as FEAT and TREAT) have similar effects on the weights: therefore exposure to one word improves performance on the other.... Words that are orthographically similar but phonologically dissimilar have mutually inhibitory effects: training on TREAT has a negative impact on the weights relative to GREAT and vice versa. The net effect of the entire ensemble of learning experiences is poorer performance on inconsistent items compared to entirely consistent ones. (Jared, McRae, and Seidenberg 1990, 709)

Is reading really about patterns of reciprocal activation between orthographic rimes and phonological rhymes? There is no convincing evidence so far that it is. And Jared and associates introduced this little conundrum near the end of their article:

> Throughout this paper we have assumed, as others have before us, that pronunciation is largely determined by properties of neighborhoods defined in terms of word bodies.... However, there are some words in English that have word bodies found in no other words (e.g. SOAP is the only OAP word).... Performance on SOAP, for example, may be affected by exposure to words such as SOAK and SOAR. Therefore, our studies should not be taken as indicating that only neighborhoods defined in terms of word-bodies are relevant to naming. (p. 711)

But what if there is a simpler explanation? What if the word *soap* is read

$$/s/ \quad /oe/ \quad /p/$$

For some reason the alphabet code has gone astray in this research!

There is a far simpler explanation of Jared, McRae, and Seidenberg's results than the one they provided. This has to do with the fact that the words in their consistent and inconsistent lists contained different vowels and unequal ratios of the same vowels. When words on these two lists are balanced for counts of the same vowel sounds, and their spellings are examined, rime-based explanations fall apart, a problem similar to the one with Treiman et al.'s word lists.

My analysis was extensive, and I provide one small example here, using the words from experiment 3 (Jared, McRae, and Seidenberg 1990, 698). The words on the consistent and inconsistent lists had only 6 vowels in common out of a total of 19 vowels. The vowels on the consistent lists were more likely to be "simple" (short) vowels: /a/, /e/, and /i/. That is, they tended to be the vowels that had the fewest spelling alternatives and that were the easiest to decode. As to what this has to do with rimes or rhymes, the answer is nothing. But we can probe deeper. The alleged function of the orthographic rime is that the final consonant provides a clue to the pronunciation of the vowel sound. Did the final consonant help in these word lists?

We can take as an example the /oe/ sound, which was used the most on any list, for a total of nine words. Here is a list of the /oe/ words from the "consistent" list on the left, with the total number of words that are read consistently (*friends*) in brackets. They are paired with words on the "inconsistent" list—that is, words with different pronunciations of the same orthographic rime (*enemies*), with the number of enemies in brackets. Counts are based on a corpus of 3,000 words.

Consistent words	Inconsistent words
dome (4)	*some* (2)
foes (11)	*shoes* (1)
prone (9)	*gone, one* (5)
wove (8)	*move, shove* (7)
comb (1)	*tomb, bomb* (3)
dough (2)	*tough, cough, through* (5)
dose (3)	*nose* (6)

If the orthographic rime (VC, VCC) is relevant to decoding, the final consonant(s) must affect the pronunciation of the vowel, and must do so by a *statistically* meaningful value. Only one rime on the list has odds in its favor sufficient to cause it to be read faster. Reading <u>foes</u> as *foze* has an 11:1 probability over *fooz*. But remember Glushko? He found that the word *shoes* was read nearly 100 ms faster than the high-frequency word *goes*. If *goes* cannot conquer *shoes*, certainly *foes* cannot either. (There is no way to know what happened in this study, because response times were not reported.) When I carried out this type of analysis on all words in the lists where vowel sounds overlapped, *final consonants had no effect on how a vowel was read*. Jared, McRae, and Seidenberg's results are therefore an artifact of the particular vowel sounds in the words and their particular spellings.

There is not the slightest evidence from any of these studies that the orthographic rime is an important structural pattern, so it comes as no surprise that it vanishes without a trace in a new computer model.

The Orthographic Rime Gets Lost in Attractor Space

In 1996, Plaut et al. (Seidenberg and McClelland are coauthors) provided a major update on their original model (Seidenberg and McClelland 1989). In particular, I want to discuss the results for the third model in a series of four, a model described as an "attractor network." (The first and second models are most like their original model, and the fourth model included a semantic component.) An attractor model is an advance on the other models because it allows for feedback within the network, which Plaut et al. called "recurrent connections," a feature of real neural systems.

They described it this way:

Processing in a network is interactive when units can mutually constrain each other in settling on the most consistent interpretation of the input.... A common way in which interactivity has been used in networks is in making particular patterns of activity into stable *attractors*. In an attractor network, units interact and update their states repeatedly in such a way that the initial pattern of activity generated by an input gradually settles to the nearest attractor pattern. (p. 82)

An "attractor" essentially represents a point in a "multidimensional state space" in which, at any given time, the pattern of activity across all units engaged in processing corresponds to this single point. This is similar to a "node" in a network that contains all the information about particular input-output relationship. Furthermore, "A set of initial patterns that settle to this same final pattern corresponds to a region around the attractor, called its basin of attraction. To solve a task, the network must learn connection weights that cause units to interact in such a way that the appropriate interpretation of each input is an attractor whose basin contains the initial pattern of activity for that input" (p. 82). Whether neural networks behave like attractors or work by superposition and Fourier analysis/synthesis (Pribram 1991), or both, is a problem for the future. What is interesting now is how well the attractor model mimics human performance. For one thing, it can "decode" nonwords never seen before just as well as humans do. This had been a failing of the earlier models. Another bonus of this model is that it can be directly compared to the reaction-time data. Previous models could only be compared to error scores.

Two properties of the model are of greatest interest here. The first is that the mutual redundancies of orthographic "rimes" and phonological "rhymes" are mapped together in an attractor basin. The authors explain it this way: "The reason is that, in learning to map orthography to phonology, the network develops attractors that are *componential*—they have substructure that reflects common sublexical correspondence between orthography and phonology. This substructure applies not only to most words but also to nonwords, enabling them to be pronounced correctly" (p. 83; original emphasis).

The second property of interest is that an attractor model can be systematically and continuously degraded until its "boundary state" for mapping a particular feature(s) of the input begins to collapse. This allows for a direct measure of each feature's robustness, as well as of which features work together to produce a correct outcome (the correct pronunciation of a word).

The model (a computer program) was set the task of learning how to read 3,000 words. These words varied in things like neighborhood consistency (friends/friends + enemies), word length, number of phonemes in the word, and a measure of word frequency. The results for the time it took to learn to read a word showed that all four factors accounted for unique variance: 10 percent for word consistency, 5.6 percent for log frequency, .8 percent for orthographic length, and .1 percent for phonological length. But this analysis did not reveal what orthographic features created the consistency effect.

To look at the orthographic features, the investigators reduced the activity in the "network" of each feature separately and in combination until the system started to misread words. This was precisely quantified as a "boundary value," which ranges from 0 to 1. Zero means that a letter or letter combination (digraph or consonant cluster) is relevant to the pronunciation of the word, but not relevant to the pronunciation of adjacent letters; 1 means it is absolutely essential to decoding other letters. This provides a pure measure of orthographic probability. The system was tested on the four types of words (see figure 10.1).

For regular consistent words (words that are consistently decoded one way), the units corresponding to initial consonant(s), vowel, and final consonant(s) were largely independent, which, as Plaut et al. (1996, 88) put it, "indicates that the attractor basins for regular words consist of three separate, orthogonal sub-basins (one for each cluster)." As already noted, letters in CVC words with "simple" vowels are "context free." Any letter can be swapped without affecting how the other letters are pronounced (*pot, top, dot, pod, pit, tip,* and so on). Thus, the model confirms what is known about the spelling code at this level.

As words became less "regular" (regular/inconsistent words), the units still remain independent, except the vowel needs some minimal support from both initial and final consonants. In the two remaining types of words, the vowel must have mutual support from both consonants to be recognized. This shows that the initial and final consonants have two values in "attractor space," one for their independent contributions and another for their contributions to a correct decoding of the vowel. For ambiguous words, the vowel had a higher boundary value than the supporting consonants, showing the vowel was a stronger cue to how it was decoded. But for the exception words, the supporting consonants had higher boundary values than the vowel, showing they are *critical* to decoding it.

There are two important points here. First, this analysis supports my observation that Jared, McRae, and Seidenberg's results were largely due to the different kinds of vowels on the lists, which would grossly alter

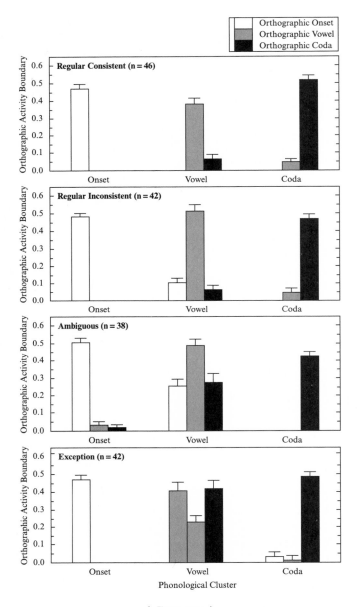

| Figure 10.1 |

The amount of activity in the attractor network (boundary state) for initial consonants (onset), vowel, and final consonants (coda) necessary for the computer to read words correctly. In words with regular spellings (*trip*) all phonemes are context free (decoding is not influenced by surrounding spellings). In words with irregular spellings (*dead/read, break/beach*) the vowel cannot be decoded independently of the surrounding consonants. From Plaut et al. 1996. Copyright APA. Reprinted with permission.

these sequential dependencies. Second, even though these words were chosen for the presence or absence of consistent VC rimes, the VC unit played no more important role than the CV unit. Both the initial and final consonant(s) were necessary to the same degree in helping decode the vowel in words where it was ambiguous. There is no basis in fact to the notion that the VC rime unit makes some special contribution to decoding. It contributed far less than the independent contributions of isolated initial and final consonants.

These results confirm my analysis of the word lists presented in this chapter, which led to the same conclusion. This analysis was based on the orthographic structure of the spelling code, not on the orthographic structure of the "reading code." This investigation clarifies key theoretical problems and raises fundamental questions for future research:

1. Glushko's original insight that all the letters in a word contribute to a statistical template of orthographic redundancy was mainly correct except for a certain class of CVC-type words.
2. If the attractor network was taught the structure of the spelling code directly (sound to print), would it learn to read more quickly? Would it learn to read at all? (Humans would.)
3. Can a network trained entirely on the "reading code" also spell? This would be an interesting test of the model, because humans are inconsistent here.

These studies provide strong support for a third way to decode print in addition to knowledge of phoneme-grapheme correspondences and rote visual memory. This third way is a gift of the brain's capacity to automatically encode the statistical redundancies of *any kind of pattern*. The third way was first proposed by Glushko, and has been operationalized mathematically in research by Plaut et al. Aaron and colleagues provided further proof in their discovery that deaf children rely on visual statistical redundancies to read and spell.

We have come full circle. Chapters 1 and 2 showed that knowledge of the English spelling code is the key to understanding how English-speaking peoples learn to spell and how they decode (read) orthographic patterns. This knowledge is as important for designing spelling and reading programs for the classroom and clinic as it is for behavioral research and for designing computer models of the decoding process. In view of the fact that the classroom research shows we now know how to design effective reading and spelling programs, we need a new road map for where to go next. The research questions for the twenty-first century are entirely different questions from those addressed so far, and it is time to move on.

NEW DIRECTIONS FOR THE
TWENTY-FIRST CENTURY

It is our good fortune that the National Reading Panel's fishing expedition led to such a harvest of treasures. We now have precise knowledge about how to teach every child to decode, read fluently, and comprehend what they read. No child needs to be left behind. This is exciting news indeed. It has been long in coming. We have been held up by two major road-blocks: the difficulty of unearthing properly controlled research on successful programs amidst the vast wasteland of publications on this topic, and the difficulty of identifying the basic elements of reading instruction that consistently lead to success. The NRP has gone some distance toward solving the first problem. And I hope this book will help in solving the second.

The NRP's analysis showed that research on reading instruction is still being cast in the phonics versus whole-word ("reading wars") framework. In virtually all 66 "cases" in the NRP database, the control group was taught with a whole-word method. These methods were identified in the NRP tables as "whole word," "basal," "whole language," or "unspecified"—meaning "regular classroom program" (i.e., whole word). Few studies contrasted two types of phonics program.

It is time to move on. The goal of this chapter is help us do that. First, I want to summarize the important discoveries presented in this book, and second, I would like to make some suggestions for how to move reading research into the twenty-first century. I will begin with the prototype. This is the first set of objective guidelines for reading instruction based on the historical and scientific evidence. They establish the ground rules, though they are still incomplete. Much more research is needed to pin down specific details, like the order (if any) in which phonemes should be taught, how fast they should be taught, what type of lessons work best, and which materials, special exercises, and activities matter, and which do not.

The Prototype: Putting It All Together

Several chapters have addressed the historical and empirical evidence for how a writing system should be taught, and how an *alphabetic* writing system, in particular, should be taught. The evidence is overwhelming that whole-word writing systems cannot work, never did work, and never will work. The evidence is equally clear that all writing systems are based on one (and *only one*) phonological unit below the level of the word.

Two principles determine which phonological unit is chosen for a particular writing system. First, the unit must fit the phonotactic structure of the language. Second, the choice follows the principle of least effort, and represents a trade-off between perception and memory. The unit chosen should be the easiest to hear (segment from the speech stream) but not impose an excessive memory load. This obeys the following simple rule: too many units = too many symbols = unmemorable. English has over 55,000 phonotactically legal syllables. Chinese has 1,270. This is the reason the Chinese use a syllabary writing system, and we use an alphabet.

These facts rule out all reading programs based on the whole word, and all reading programs that teach phonetic units *not* represented by the code. For an alphabetic writing system, this means syllables, consonant blends taught as single units, and word families (rhyming endings).

The lessons from the 5,000 years of the history of writing systems are fully supported by the evidence from the National Reading Panel report. Whole-word programs are consistently inferior to phonics programs, and multisound phonics has no advantage over the whole-word programs. Not only this, but phoneme-awareness training that also includes multiple phonological units is consistently inferior as a predictor of reading skill to teaching phoneme awareness alone.

Thus we have two lines of support for the first set of guidelines that constitute the general prototype. These are reiterated here:

1. Make sure the complete structure of the writing system has been worked out (or thoroughly understood) before a method of instruction is developed.

2. Teach the specific sound units that are the basis for the code. (Do not teach other sound units that have nothing to do with the code.)

3. Teach the arbitrary, abstract symbols that represent these sounds. These symbols constitute the code.

4. Teach the elements of the system in order from simple to complex.

5. Ensure that the student learns that a writing system is a code and that codes are reversible.

6. Make sure that encoding (spelling) and decoding (reading) are connected at every level of instruction via looking (visual memory), listening (auditory memory), and writing (kinesthetic memory).

On the basis of this knowledge, phonics versus whole-word research is a nonissue and has been a nonissue for 5,000 years. The real and important research question is *which phonics methods* work best? Research in the twenty-first century should be directed toward the study of the effectiveness of the various types of phonics programs outlined in chapter 5. First, we need to compare general types of phonics where it is reasonable to do so. Second, we need to compare methods within types, such as the different forms of linguistic-phonics programs.

Types of Phonics Programs: Which Work Best?

The NRP came up with one list of phonics types under the general rubric of "explicit, sequential" phonics. I came up with another. Here is my list once more:

JUNK PHONICS   The practice of teaching aspects or elements of the alphabet code in a chaotic, nonsensical, and unstructured fashion. Most basal phonics falls in this category.

VISUAL PHONICS   The *short version* (a) teaches the 26 "sounds" of the 26 letters of the alphabet. The *long version* (b) teaches the 27 to 200+ "sounds" of the letters, digraphs, and phonograms.

WHOLE-TO-PART PHONICS   (also known as *embedded, analytic, intrinsic*). The practice of easing children into phonemes by starting with whole words, then syllables and word parts (word families, blends), then individual phonemes taught overtly or covertly (embedded).

MULTISOUND PHONICS   Same as above, but the different-size sound units are mixed up and taught together.

LINGUISTIC PHONICS   *Incomplete* (a) (called *synthetic*) teaches from the sound to the letter. Teaches the 40+ phonemes of English and their main spellings, plus some spelling alternatives. *Complete* (b) includes (a) above plus 136 spelling alternatives.

We can rule out "junk phonics" at the outset based on the evidence from the NRP report. Children taught with basal-reader phonics generally did poorly compared to children taught with other types of phonics programs. We can eliminate whole-to-part and multisound phonics programs as well, based on the historical evidence and on their dismal showing in the NRP report.

This leaves visual phonics and linguistic phonics. There is considerable confusion about the nature of these two types of programs, especially the distinction between teaching from the letter versus teaching from the phoneme, and the issue of which one is "synthetic" phonics. The NRP reading committee, along with most U.S. phonics advocates, either do not recognize this distinction or do not know it exists.

Let's clarify the distinction once more. Linguistic phonics anchors the code in the sounds of the language, and bases initial reading instruction on a basic code. This avoids several pitfalls created by our highly opaque spelling system. The code is temporarily set up with a manageable number of units (40+ phonemes), and this number does not change as the lessons progress. Children see that an alphabet code works from a finite number of speech sounds to their individual spellings. They observe that the code can reverse (all codes are reversible mapping systems by definition). Later, spelling alternatives can easily be pegged onto the system without changing the logic: "There's another way to spell this sound. I'll show you some patterns to help you remember when to use this spelling."

Visual phonics does the opposite. Because letters and letter sequences (digraphs, phonograms) drive the code and phonemes do not, this deprives the code of any anchor or endpoint. As the number of "sounds" begins to expand (there are over 250 "sounds" that letters "can make"), there is no way to get back to the 40 phonemes that are the basis for the code. The child is soon awash in letter patterns and there is no discernible structure, no limit, no logic, and no pivot point around which the code can reverse.

Thus, the code loses one of its essential properties—its reversibility—and cannot function as a code. There is no way to teach spelling alternatives, except as *letter-sound* alternatives, flipping the logic of the code on its head: "There's another way to *say* this letter." "This letter *makes* another sound here." As these letter sounds proliferate, there is a high risk of confusion and failure.

We have seen many examples of the confusion created by visual phonics in this book. When Griffith, Klesius, and Kromrey (1992) stated that children were taught "90 different individual sounds" in the basal-reading program used in their study, there is no doubt that they were referring to 90 different, individual phonemes in the English language.

Berninger et al. (1998) attempted to teach children to spell using Venezky's recommended sequence (see chapter 3), which relies solely on visual logic. This sequence has 47 spellings representing an unknown number of "sounds," and *no spellings* to represent 7 missing phonemes. Using this sequence, children were taught with several different methods. Children learning Venezky's "visual phonics" did no better on a spelling test than children taught purely by rote (sight words). And none of the training groups (regardless of method) did any better on a standardized spelling test than a control group that was taught nothing!

For these reasons, visual phonics leads to the unanswerable questions posed by the NRP, such as: How many letter sounds should be taught? If this was a legitimate question, the proper answer should be all of them. We know from the analysis of the spelling code in chapter 3 that there are 40 basic-code spellings, 136 remaining common spellings, and 80 high-frequency sight words with unusual spellings. But in visual-phonics logic, this would mean there are 256 common sounds in the English language represented by 256 spellings. And if one was a purist and wanted to include Venezky's tallies on the outer reaches of the code, we could add 100+ more rare letter sounds.

Framed in visual-phonics logic, the NRPs question would be a genuinely formidable one: Which of the 356 decodings should be taught? Framed in linguistic-phonics logic (the logic of an alphabet code), this question is meaningless.

The NRP attempted to answer its question as follows: "It is clear that the major letter-sound correspondences, including short and long vowels and digraphs, need to be taught" (National Reading Panel, 2000, 2-135).

But *what* is "clear"—and clear to whom? And what is "major"? In the first place, English vowels do not vary systematically by length (or by height). In the second place, which digraphs are they referring to? More to the point, what sounds of these digraphs are they referring to, given that (in visual phonics) digraphs have so many sounds? (The digraph *ou* can stand for /o͞o/, /ow/, /oe/, /o͝o/, /u/, /o/, and /er/, as in *soup, proud, soul, could, young, cough,* and *journey*.)

The visual versus linguistic-phonics issue has another face. There is an influential and vocal minority that does recognize the "letter-first" versus "phoneme-first" distinction. Nevertheless, this group believes that children *should be taught* from letters to phonemes. They argue that phonemes are abstract and transient, whereas letters are concrete (visible and tangible). From their perspective, it is okay to tell children that letters "have sounds" during early reading instruction, because this will not matter in the long run. It is not clear why letter shapes would be more tangible and less abstract to children than the sounds of their own speech.

The danger of vision-first phonics can be seen in any remedial-reading setting. Many children actually believe that letters "make sounds" and do not have the slightest idea where these "sounds" come from. I have met many functionally illiterate adults (including some of my college students) who are amazed to learn that a writing system is a code, and that this code represents sounds in their speech. There is no need or reason to take this risk.

In practice, a phoneme-first versus letter-first approach requires a simple shift in orientation to achieve maximum effect as learning progresses. The instructional implications are so minor initially that this is probably why people think they do not matter. In linguistic phonics, the teacher begins the lesson by introducing a phoneme. The teacher can produce this or can ask the children to listen for a phoneme featured in a story or poem. Once the children are familiar with the phoneme and can produce it, they are shown the letter that represents its most common spelling. In visual phonics, the teacher points to a letter shape and/or draws it on the board, and the children are told the sound it "makes." This is referred to thereafter as a "letter sound." This shift in logic blocks understanding of *where this sound comes from* (that it is part of natural speech and is one of forty sounds that are the basis for the code), leading children to believe that the sound comes from the letter.

The differences between visual phonics and linguistic phonics need to get sorted out, semantically, logically, and empirically. An important first step would be to compare a visual-phonics method like those advanced by Venezky or Beck to a linguistic-phonics method like Lippincott or Jolly Phonics.

Linguistic Phonics: What Works Best?

More fundamental research questions have to do with the linguistic-phonics programs themselves. We need to pin down the elements that make a difference. Given their complexity and variety, this is not a straightforward task. We can begin by establishing what we know for sure and move forward from there. To do this, here is the final version of the prototype, which takes into account the classroom observations, spelling research, and studies in the NRP database. The first two activities in the list are italicized, because they produced negative or zero correlations between time on task and reading/spelling test scores in several large-scale studies.

The Prototype for Teaching the English Alphabet Code

1. *No sight words* (except high-frequency words with rare spellings).
2. *No letter names.*
3. Sound-to-print orientation. Phonemes, not letters, are the basis for the code.
4. Teach phonemes only and no other sound units.
5. Begin with an artificial transparent alphabet or basic code: a one-to-one correspondence between 40 phonemes and their most common spelling.
6. Teach children to identify and sequence sounds in real words by segmenting and blending, *using letters.*
7. Teach children how to write each letter. Integrate writing into every lesson.
8. Link writing, spelling, and reading to ensure that children learn that the alphabet is a code, and that the code works in both directions: encoding/decoding.
9. Spelling should be accurate or, at a minimum, phonetically accurate (all things within reason).
10. Lessons should move on to include the advanced spelling code (the 136 remaining common spellings and 80 sight words).

Given that at least five programs reviewed by the NRP follow all or nearly all of these guidelines (minus the complete spelling code), the differences in the effectiveness of these programs have to do with specific features such as pacing and depth, special activities, and curriculum materials. Research varying these details, element by element, would be extremely time consuming and tedious, but not all elements are in question.

Let's begin with the definitive proof about what children can learn, at what age, and in what time period, to provide a baseline or set of criteria for what can be accomplished.

One important "rule" needs to be stressed. If your goal is to teach the alphabet code, all components of the prototype must be taught *at the same time*, because each component bolsters the remainder. It is counterproductive to ease children into reading by teaching these elements slowly in disconnected and unrelated bits.

The youngest children in these studies were in the Jolly Phonics/Fast Phonics First classrooms in the United Kingdom. They were between 4:8 and 5:0 years old at the start of training. The training period lasted from 10 to 16 weeks depending on the study, and the total number of hours in whole-class lessons varied from 26 to 60 h. In these training sessions, children learned the 40+ phonemes, their basic-code spellings, and how to write every letter and digraph for the 40 phonemes. Children learned to identify phonemes in all positions in a word, segment and blend phonemes in words, and read, write, and spell common words. Immediately after training, these children were 8 months above U.K. age norms on standardized reading and spelling tests. The control groups scored exactly at age norms. These gains increased at the second and third testings to 1 year above norms, and by the fourth and fifth grades children were 2 years above norms on tests of decoding. Effect sizes were consistently around 1.0 or higher compared to the children learning via analytic phonics.

Now we have a useful baseline. If children this young can learn to read and spell 40 phonemes and their common spellings in 10 to 16 weeks, certainly any older child can do the same. We also know from Lloyd's account of the development of Jolly Phonics that children are eager learners and willing to work hard. Because these programs involve only the elements in the prototype and the learning period is so compressed, children see gains almost immediately. They begin reading words after the first six sounds are introduced. This is highly motivating, especially because children start school with the strong expectation that the "main event" is learning to read.[1]

Jolly Phonics Actions   The interesting difference among the U.K. studies is the shorter training time in the Scottish study (26 hours versus 50 to 60) while achieving similar gains that held up well over time. A large part of the savings came from omitting the Jolly Phonics (JP) actions. On the other hand, Sumbler in Canada reported that of all the phonics activities they assessed, the time spent learning and using JP actions produced the highest correlation to reading test scores. The problem here is that JP actions are confounded with lessons on phoneme-identification as well as segmenting and blending activities, as they are taught and used simultaneously. Nevertheless, Sumbler's data suggest that JP actions matter, while Johnston and Watson's data suggest they do not.

Nellie Dale, who developed the first successful linguistic-phonics program, warned teachers to "never teach anything you have to discard later." Does this warning apply to the JP actions, or might learning them be helpful *even though* they will be discarded? This is an interesting research question from a number of perspectives. Lloyd believes that the action patterns supply a "motor" component in a multisensory type of learning, and this helps automate learning sound-symbol correspondences. One could argue, as well, that the action patterns help focus attention on the differences between the phonemes, increasing auditory discrimination. (Children must listen carefully to know which action pattern to use.) I pointed out in chapter 5 that the actions may help the teacher during whole-class instruction by providing visual signals for who is participating and who is not, or who is "getting it" and who is not.

Lessons on Speech-Motor Features   A similar question applies to the speech-motor patterns used extensively in the Lindamood program, an idea that

---

1. At the end of his first week in kindergarten, my son had this tearful complaint: "I've been in school a *whole* week. It seemed like a hundred years, and I haven't even learned to read!"

originated with Dale. Dale had the onerous task of engaging 70 children from the front of the room. She reported that focusing attention on the parts of the mouth, tongue, and vocal cords that produce each phoneme makes the phoneme easier to hear and identify, and therefore faster to learn. It also makes it easier to tell phonemes apart (auditory discrimination improves).

Unlike the JP action patterns, speech-motor patterns are executed spontaneously. Because there is no need to learn them, only to be made aware of them, this will take up little extra time. Dale used these patterns strictly for auditory support as each phoneme was taught. In the Lindamood program, however, the motor patterns form a major part of training and are taught in depth. Each motor pattern for 44 phonemes is given a special name, which children have to memorize. For example, a bilabial plosive (/b/, /p/) is called a *lip popper*. The voiced plosive (/b/) is called a *noisy lip popper*.[2]

We now have the ingredients for an interesting and important study on whether these "add-ons" assist learning. A study could be designed in which there are three groups of beginning readers all taught with the same linguistic-phonics program. One group learns the basic program only, a second group learns this plus Jolly Phonics actions, and the third group, the basic program plus speech-motor patterns (à la Dale). Any benefit from these additional components would be expected to impact *learning rate*—the time it takes to master 40+ phoneme-grapheme associations) and *automaticity*—the speed to match a letter to a phoneme and vice versa. Other important measures, of course, would include reading, spelling, and phoneme awareness (segmenting, blending).

The automaticity issue is extremely important. Lloyd (1992) observed that the most persistent differences between children was the time it took to "automate" the phoneme-grapheme associations. Without automaticity, children have difficulty blending sounds into words (auditorally or from

---

2. Memorizing these names and which phonemes they apply to is not easy, as anyone who has used the Lindamood program can attest. Using them during lessons is even harder: "In this word the 'quiet lip popper' comes after the 'little skinny,' not after a 'scraper.'"

print), because they lose track of phoneme sequence and which phoneme came first. She found it was helpful for children to accent the first phoneme in the word, causing it to stick in memory and act as an anchor for the sequence.

Lloyd's observations on the extensive timeline to achieve automaticity are borne out in a study on letter-name knowledge and letter-naming speed. Mann and Ditunno (1990) found it took to the end of first grade for all children to achieve a error-free performance on naming letters. However, naming *speed* (automaticity) still showed high individual variability and continued to improve. These are surprising results, because children begin learning letter names from a very young age. This is usually the first "reading activity" taught both at home and at school. This study showed that children can take up to 2 years or more to memorize the 26 "names" of the letters of the alphabet, and it takes much longer to automate this knowledge. (Since knowing letter names serves no purpose in learning to read, this is another powerful argument for not teaching them.)

In view of the individual differences in learning rate, and the long timeline to achieve automaticity, the children in our hypothetical study need to be followed for several years. This is the only true test of whether these extra components matter in the long run. For example, Johnston and Watson (1997) reported that at 7.5 years, 9 percent of the Jolly Phonics children scored more than one standard deviation *below* national norms. Although this compared favorably with the control group (30 percent of them below 1 s.d.), one wonders why any child scored this low. Unfortunately, we know nothing about these children. Did they miss lessons due to illness, or did they transfer in from another school? Did they fall behind because they did not automate sound-letter correspondences at the same rate as the other children? Did they become confused because this program does not teach the complete spelling code?

Do Beginning Readers Need Special Phoneme-Awareness Training?
The evidence showed that a separate phoneme-awareness training program for beginning reading instruction is largely a waste of time. No phoneme-awareness program reviewed in chapter 6 had any advantage over a linguistic-phonics program, either for reading and spelling, *or even for improving phoneme awareness.*

There is, however, a good argument for special training in phoneme awareness in the clinic. Poor readers have extremely maladaptive decoding strategies, guessing whole words from the first letter only, assembling little word parts into something like a word, or refusing to read altogether (McGuinness 1997b). An ineffective decoding strategy leads to habits that can be hard to break. It is almost a given that these children (or adults) have few or no phoneme-analysis skills. Because print can be aversive, causing anxiety and even panic, initial phoneme-awareness training is more effective in an auditory mode using blank tiles. A three-step process is necessary: developing phoneme awareness with blank markers, learning phoneme-grapheme correspondences, and reading simple (easily decodable) text.

Reading Fluency
The research on reading fluency is a curious mix of nonsense and brilliance. The vast majority of publications uncovered by the NRP were devoted to the premise that "reading a lot" increases accuracy, reading speed, and comprehension. Research (or quasi-research) on this topic turned out to be so methodologically flawed that only 14 studies out of the 1,000 or so screened by the panel had any merit. These studies showed essentially nothing. There is a central problem with this premise, because, without a highly sophisticated research design, there is no way to account for reading habits, and no way to tell whether children read more *because* they are fluent readers, or whether they turn into fluent readers *because* they read a lot. The best research on this topic has been provided by Stanovich and West (1989), and even this study could not solve all the research-design problems. This study and similar studies are reviewed in *Language Development and Learning to Read*.

Fortunately, the "reading a lot" issue is a red herring, because there is a much better way to ensure that children read fluently, accurately, and with understanding. This is through the technique of rereading. I want to provide a brief summary of this work along with suggestions for future research.

Due to the large individual variation in the rate at which the phoneme-grapheme associations become automated, a small portion of children have difficulty decoding at sufficient speed to comprehend what they read. Advances in research on rereading techniques as a means of alleviating this difficulty have been enormous, and we know exactly how to cure this problem. The basic format for this training has largely been worked out by Dowhower (1987), with the final missing pieces added by Faulkner and Levy (1994, 1999).

The research just cited is notable for its methodological rigor, something sadly lacking in the field as a whole. Among other things, good methodology means asking the right questions. In view of the fact that good research on reading instruction has barely begun, it is informative to look closely at the questions all the researchers in the field had to identify to prove that rereading has a real and long-lasting effect.

Research Questions on the Technique of Rereading

1. Does reading get faster with or without a target goal—that is, a criterion of words per minute?
2. Do children make greater gains reading alone or with an audiotape?
3. Is rereading more effective than reading the same number of *different* stories?
4. What is the optimum practice time necessary to produce lasting changes?
5. How should this time be allocated: concentrated into a few days, or spread out over weeks or months?
6. How many different stories should be reread to ensure a lasting effect?
7. Does the difficulty level of the text make a difference?
8. Does overlap in the words from one story to the next make a difference?
9. Does overlap in story content/context make a difference?
10. Does prosody (reading expression) improve along with speed?
11. What kinds of transfer effects are there and how should they be measured?

Five main goals or outcomes had to be measured for rereading to be deemed a success. Reading speed should increase with no loss of accuracy (or an increase in accuracy). Oral rereading should cause an improvement in prosody (melody, inflection). Comprehension should improve. Most importantly, there should be transfer effects. Reading speed should increase from one story to the next. If a criterion reading speed is set, this should be achieved more quickly with each new story. Accuracy and comprehension should improve with each new story as well.

I have provided a list of suggestions, based on the data, to help ensure that rereading is a success. Here they are again. Target reading speeds should be set well above the child's initial reading speed. So far, no one failed to achieve targets 50 to 60 wpm higher than the child's baseline. It is my personal view that targets should be reset each time the child's reading speed improves by some critical amount. The final goal should be to have the *first reading of a story* at a normal or superior rate for the child's age. At this point, rereading exercises can cease.

Children need multiple rereading experiences (across many stories), not just a few. Dowhower's time frame of about 7 hours of work over 7 weeks was effective and seems optimal. Time pressure was not excessive, and sessions were not spread so far apart that there were no carryover effects. The ultimate goal is the desired target speed on the first reading, and this goal determines how long the rereading sessions last.

The difficulty level of the text is critically important, because *speed is tied to difficulty level*. Very slow readers should start off reading passages at or just above their reading level, not their grade level. Once reading speed improves, stories should increase in difficulty. Passages with overlapping words are best for struggling readers and very young readers, and are most likely to produce carryover (transfer) effects from one story to the next. Overlapping context helps as well. This creates a situation in which transfer is successful and boosts confidence and motivation to continue.

Vocabulary and Comprehension Instruction

The last categories covered in the NRP report are vocabulary and comprehension. The contrast between the studies on basic reading instruction and studies on comprehension, in particular, is interesting. New phonics programs are created all the time by making minor changes in curriculum detail and emphasis (and given colorful new names by their authors), yet the basic platforms change very little. As we saw above, phonics programs reduce to very few common types. Comprehension programs, on the other hand, are designed from the ground up by individuals who seem to have never heard of one another's work. The NRP was so overwhelmed by the variety of these programs that it was unable to categorize them. Instead it set them up loosely in 16 types, largely characterized by semantics and not by anything objective.

Fortunately, none of this matters, because one program is so extraordinary that all other programs (for vocabulary or comprehension) pale in comparison. I will be summarizing the elements of this program below. First, I would like to say something about the efforts to improve children's vocabularies, especially because teachers spend so much time working on this, as the classroom observational studies showed.

We know that children rapidly and automatically acquire new vocabulary on the order of around 8 to 10 new words per day. We also know that children from impoverished environments do not have the same vocabulary skills as children from more affluent homes. It makes sense for teachers to want to help the children who need special assistance. This was one of the major goals of Hart and Risley's study, presented earlier. The impetus for that study was the failure of Head Start to have any impact on vocabulary and verbal skills generally. The main question is what is the best way to approach this problem. Let's look once more at the bottom line for vocabulary training.

It is possible to teach vocabulary in the short term, though it took a lot of research to prove it. McKeown et al. (1985) found that by keeping the word list short (24 or so words at a time), compressing the learning time, and providing a rich or in-depth explanation of the words, children needed about 5 minutes per word to ensure nearly perfect performance on a vocabulary test for those words. Using a similar format, Jenkins, Matlock, and Slocum (1989) confirmed these results, based on 6.5 minutes per word. We do not know, however, whether these words ever become part of productive vocabulary—the vocabulary children actually *use*. Nor does this represent a major shift in vocabulary size, because children learn about 8 words a day just by minding their own business.

It turns out that these vocabulary gains are minor compared to what children can achieve with proper training in oral and reading comprehension, as seen by the brilliant work of Block (1993). Block's program had an enormous spin-off for vocabulary skills, even though this was not a focus of the training. The effect size was unlike anything seen in the vocabulary-instruction research: 2.62 on a standardized test. In the NRP studies overall, the effect size for vocabulary gains (all types of tests) was

ES = .97. But this fell substantially when standardized tests only were used (ES = .30).

Block's program is the gold standard for the field as a whole. Most important, it shows that short-term interventions are not the way to improve vocabulary and comprehension skills. To make a difference, the training needs to fit into the scheme of ordinary school lessons, and continue for months and possibly years. Block's program took up 3 hours a week over an entire school year (about 96 hours of classroom time). Ninety-six hours sounds like a lot of hours, until you consider that this is a mere fraction of the total time children spend at school. On average, lessons take up about 5 hours per day, 5 days a week (25 hours), for a school year of 32 weeks (800 hours). Block's program took up about 12 percent of total classroom time, yet it literally transformed these children. One wonders what schoolchildren could achieve if the remaining 22 hours of the week (700 hours of the school year) were spent in such rewarding and enlightening activities. This is a stunning indictment of our educational system.

The other notable feature of Block's study was the outstanding methodology. The program is also unique for setting up a purpose or set of goals. These were not parochial or limited academic goals, but life-changing goals, and I list them once more:

1. If instruction helps students use strategic processes consistently and reflectively as they read, they should comprehend and use more information in their daily lives.
2. Students who have trouble comprehending may need a new type of instruction, involving new strategies and thinking/reading competencies.
3. Students who are confused about important concepts, inferences, and relationships in a text may never have encountered the inductive or deductive reasoning patterns the author used to create the text. If these thinking strategies are explained prior to reading, thinking repertoires should expand.
4. Students may be more able to generalize this new knowledge to solve decoding and comprehension problems on their own.

The eight strategies that Block believed were crucial for improving children's comprehension skills and increasing progress toward these goals included strengthening basic cognitive operations like analytic thinking, decision strategies, problem solving, metacognitive analysis (awareness of one's current state of knowledge), and creative thinking. Children also needed social skills for working in groups and skills for independent learning.

What made the lessons effective was their structure, a structure that evolved over months and years of pilot work. Lessons worked best if one strategy was taught at a time, and then followed up by group or independent activity. Materials were carefully chosen that were relevant to the lesson and added insight for problem solving.

Not only did children have dramatic increases in vocabulary, but reading-comprehension skills soared as well. The training generalized to oral comprehension, so that students became more articulate, asked better and more penetrating questions, wrote more coherent papers and stories, and improved dramatically in behavior and confidence.

Scores on the reading-comprehension subtest of the Iowa Test of Basic Skills showed astonishing gains over a control group. The effect size for reading comprehension was 2.24, and it was 1.34 for the Total Reading score (though reading was not taught directly). These are extraordinary results in view of the typical findings in this field.

There were other improvements as well. Children in the program were much more likely to represent analytic thought in their writing to an astonishing degree ($p < .0001$). They reported that what they had learned at school was useful outside school (92 percent reporting "useful"), whereas *none* of the control group found that what they learned was useful (which makes quite a statement about the school system). The trained children had significantly higher self-esteem, though the groups did not differ initially. The trained group used a greater number of critical-thinking strategies, were more precise in their statements about these strategies, and offered a larger number of alternative solutions to the various problems. These comparisons were highly significant ($p < .0001$ in all cases).

I would urge readers interested in this program to read the books by Block and her colleagues, because these books outline the program, the ideas behind it, and the effort that went into designing it (Block, Gambrell, and Pressley 1997; Block and Mangieri 1997; Block and Pressley 2001; Block 2002).

New Frontiers

Linking Linguistic Phonics to the Advanced Spelling Code

Even the most successful reading programs are missing a major component of reading and spelling instruction. This is the advanced spelling code, comprising the remaining spelling alternatives that need to be taught once children have mastered the basic code. The advanced code consists of an additional 136 common spellings alternatives.

There are few programs that teach the advanced spelling code (Jolly Phonics teaches 22 additional spellings for vowels only, and Lindamood, 16). I am aware of three programs, and only two of these programs are published at this time. The study by Smith (1999), reported in chapter 3, used a spelling program I designed (McGuinness 1997a, 1998a). Adolescents, who were extremely poor readers and spellers, had 12 hours of individual instruction on the advanced code, up to and including all Latin suffixes. These children not only made large gains in spelling (9 standard-score points), but even larger gains in reading and reading comprehension (10 to 14 standard-score points). Total Reading scores were at the 50th percentile (normal) on standardized tests by the end of the sessions.

Another published program—by C. McGuinness and G. McGuinness (1998)—was originally designed for the clinic for one-on-one sessions with poor readers. It has been adapted for parents to teach poor and beginning readers, and for beginning readers in the classroom. In a study on 87 consecutive clients to the clinic (C. McGuinness, D. McGuinness, and G. McGuinness 1996), gains were comparable to those reported above, except spelling and comprehension were not measured. Nearly all poor readers read at grade level in about 12 hours or less based on standardized tests of word recognition and word attack.

Because this program was designed initially for poor readers (age 6 or older), it was possible to speed up the introduction of the advanced spelling code by overlapping it with the basic code about halfway through. This works well for older children, but it is not clear whether a sudden shift in logic (one sound–to–one spelling versus one sound–to–many spellings) is as successful with younger children. Young children may become confused by this.

So far, there are no methodologically valid studies on the classroom version of this program. Research carried out by local school districts shows strong gains, but, so far, these studies do not meet NRP standards.

Finally, there is a comprehensive new reading/spelling program for parents and teachers designed for children age 4–6 years (McGuinness, forthcoming). This program integrates a linguistic-phonics program with the advanced spelling code. Lessons are sequenced by spelling complexity. For example, children begin learning the phonemes that can appear in any position in a word without changing their spelling. This makes it possible to teach "transitivity" from the outset, the fact that the same sound can appear in all positions in a word—something young children have trouble with. The first three phonemes in the lessons (/p/, /o/, and /t/) make four CVC words, so children can begin reading almost immediately. After six phonemes (and one sight word), children can read little phrases, such as "a tan man on a mat."

Lessons follow the same format and are self-explanatory (foolproof), so no training is necessary. Each lesson begins with a story read by the parent (or teacher) that introduces the phoneme for the lesson. An excerpt from "Poppy Pig" was provided earlier. This is followed by a structured listening exercise to teach phoneme identity and transitivity (all positions in a word). Next, the child sees the letter for that phoneme and learns to trace, copy, and write it from memory. As phonemes accumulate, words appear. These are visually segmented and read in a segmented fashion, then blended into the word. Spelling dictation follows. As more words are added, phrases and stories appear as "little readers." The recommended speed for parents is one phoneme every other day, or a minimum of three phonemes per week. Teachers can move faster. Lessons are cumulative, and include only the sounds and the spellings taught to that point (no surprises). At the end of the lessons (after approximately 5 to 7 months), the child can read all the parent stories, and should have reading and spelling skills at the second- to third-grade level.

As far as I am aware, this is only program that weaves the structure of the spelling code (from easy to hard) into the lessons from day one. It includes the advanced code up to the Latin level, in both single-syllable and multisyllable words.

These three programs, all of which feature the advanced spelling code in one format or another, need extensive research to demonstrate their merit. In terms of the gains reported so far, it is predicted that at least in the long term they will outdistance the basic linguistic-phonics programs, which provide minimal or no instruction in the advanced spelling code.

———

Computer Models of Reading and the Real Spelling Code

What is the connection, if any, between the structure of the advanced spelling code set out in chapter 3, and the computer models discussed in the previous chapter? The stated goal of computer simulations of reading is that if the computer mimics human behavior, one can infer that it reflects something about how the brain processes information and "learns." The major problem with this assumption is that while computer models may seem objective and scientific, the computer can only do what it is programmed to do, and it is rated on its performance by what humans deem to be correct. There is no guarantee that the researchers will have an accurate knowledge of the structure of our spelling code, any more than there is any guarantee that they understand how the brain works.

This is an important issue because the "parallel-distributed model," which is part and parcel of this work, is purported to work like the human brain. If any mathematical model succeeds in mimicking human behavior, *even though the model is wrong, or the scoring of the model's performance is wrong*, this may have dangerous consequences. The attempt of these researchers to link the computer's performance to "types of dyslexia" is a prime example of this danger. (See Coltheart 1978; Coltheart et al. 1993; Plaut et al. 1996; Seidenberg 1992.)

In the last chapter, I noted two central problems with these computer simulations. One has to do with the types of words the computer is given to read, and the other is that the models are based on visual phonics, in which the probabilities of spelling patterns are derived from letters. The true structure of the English spelling code is based on phonemes. Spellings are assigned to phonemes in words; words are not assigned to spellings.

If you map the structure of the spelling code the way it was written (see chapter 3), this brings a huge array of patterns (statistical redundancies) into focus that would otherwise not be noticed by human observers, even though they are certainly "noticed" by the brain. In the Plaut et al. 1996 studies, several patterns *not* discernible to the research team appear to have been discerned by the computer program that was optimized to record probabilities.

Nothing illustrates this better than the computer's nonword decoding "errors." The computer was trained on 3,000 real words (CVC, CCVC,

CVCC only) for 2,000 repetitions. The number of times each word appeared was controlled by its frequency in print. The "attractor model" was then tested for transfer of training on 86 *nonwords* from Glushko's (1979) lists.

According to the team, the computer "failed" on 19 of these nonwords. But these "failures" were more in the eye of the beholder than being anything objective. If the computer substituted a different *legal decoding* for the one the researchers wanted, this was scored as an error. Based on the real spelling code, the computer misread only 3 of the 19 words. Here are some examples. The responses are phonetic renderings of the actual output.

Computer Errors?

Computer sees	*Computer says*	*Researchers say*
BLEAD, WEAD	bled, wed	bleed, weed
BOST, SOST	boast	bossed

Here are the actual probabilities (options) for making analogies to real words:

BLEAD, WEAD:
Analogy to onset/vowel (CV)

as /e/	(none)
as /ee/	bleach, bleak

Analogy to rime (VC)

as /e/	bread, dead, dread, head, lead, read, spread, thread, tread
as /ee/	bead, lead, plead, read

BOST, SOST:
Analogy to onset/vowel

as /oe/	bold, both
as /o/	Bob, bog, bond, box

Analogy to rime

as /oe/	ghost, host, most, post
as /o/	cost, frost, lost

In these examples, the computer selected an equally probable or more probable decoding than the researchers, one based on actual probabilities.

In another corpus of words, the vowel spelling was the issue. The phoneme /u/ can be spelled *o-e* in a number of high-frequency words (*come*). The *o-e* spelling is also the most probable spelling for the sound /oe/ in a large number of common words (*home*). The former represents "frequency in print," the latter, "probability" across all words in a corpus (total vocabulary). For whatever reason, the computer preferred the frequency solution. It decoded LOME, MONE, PLOVE, WONE as *lum*, *mun*, *pluv*, *wun*, a match with common words like *above*, *come*, *done*, *dove*, *glove*, *love*, *none*, *one*, *shove*, *some*. Nevertheless, these renderings were scored as errors. If the computer was a child, she would say this "wasn't fair!"[3]

The point here is profound. It goes back to the first premise in the general prototype, which states that you must have a complete understanding of the structure of a writing system before you teach it. Ergo, you must have a complete understanding of the structure of a writing system before you model it. At the very least one needs to be aware that our spelling system is a *spelling* system, not a *decoding* system. Until this occurs, computer models of reading will not be reliable. And if they are not reliable on these very simple words, how can they cope with words like *artificial*, *parallel*, and *intelligence*, or with the hundreds of thousands of words that do not have "word bodies" and do not share "rimes."

Before we leave this topic, I want to try to clear up a serious misconception about neuroanatomy that permeates the cognitive and computer models of reading. This is the notion that "processing" goes on in "pathways." The use of the term *pathway* to refer to types of neural processing during reading originated in the "dual-route" model of Coltheart (1978). Since then, this term has become ubiquitous, even in the computer models that disprove Coltheart's theory (Plaut et al. 1996). Ehri speaks of "estab-

---

3. The authors did state that if they scored the errors on the basis of whether *any word* in the original corpus of 3,000 had the "same body" (rime) as the nonword, the computer's errors reduced to 9. But the network model is based on statistical redundancy (probability), not isolated cases, so this does not solve the problem.

———

lishing access routes" as if learning is about co-opting or carving out "channels" in the brain, rather like digging a trench to lay a pipeline or stringing a telephone cable.

Here are the facts. Neurons come in two main flavors. There are cells with dendrites and axons, and cells with only dendrites. Dendrites are short, branching fibers. Axons are long (nonbranching) fibers. Neural processing goes on in networks of dendrites. This processing is recursive, with feedback from every neuron to every other neuron in the network via the dendrites. The final output of this computational effort arrives at the layer of neurons with axons. Axons relay this output to other regions of the central nervous system. *Axons are the neural pathways.* Axons are like telephone lines, and like telephone lines, *they do not process anything.* They merely transmit. Learning does not occur in "pathways," but via anatomical and neurochemical changes in dendrites and adjacent cell membranes. (This information is available in any good undergraduate textbook on neurobiology; e.g., see Pinel 1997.)

How Does the Brain Read?

Early in the book, I described a new type of sight-word recognition that some researchers believe occurs late in reading acquisition. This is essentially another armchair theory about how the brain "reads." It is contradicted not only by brain science, but also by studies that reveal the complex processing that goes on at an unconscious level *before* we produce a conscious, behavioral response. This is yet another misleading theory that can lead to dangerous consequences, as we will see.

Trying to infer how the brain works from behavior involves reasoning backward from the behavior to what might be occurring in the brain. This can lead to a fallacy in which brain processing is thought to be analogous to how we experience or characterize the behavior. The mistake is that brains do not work like humans think, nor do they work like *products* of human thought (machines, telephones, digital computers). The complexity of brain processing is far beyond anything our conscious mind can fathom.

Beware Old Messages in New Bottles   The comparative analysis of writing systems proves that a whole-word (logographic) writing system is impossible. Research on children learning to read continues to show that whole-word (sight-word) methods of instruction are ineffective. Time spent memorizing sight words was found to be negatively correlated with reading skill (Evans and Carr 1985; Sumbler 1999). Meanwhile, some reading researchers, including those who know that whole-word methods do not work, have adopted a new kind of sight-word model. I will call this *late-stage* sight-word reading, to distinguish it from basic (logographic) sight-word reading.

These two types of sight-word reading are exemplified by Frith's (1980, 1985) stage model. At stage 1, the *logographic stage*, children memorize words by sight as random letter sequences. As reading vocabulary grows, the *alphabetic stage* begins, and children figure out how to match phonemes to graphemes. As this becomes efficient, a final sight-word stage emerges, the *orthographic stage*. Words that are decoded by "orthographic rules" are ultimately processed instantly (by sight) via a visual pathway. This model is directly tied to Coltheart's dual-route computer model of reading.

Adams and Huggins (1985) proposed a similar idea. They studied the effect of word frequency and context on decoding accuracy in elementary school children, and measured what they called *functional sight vocabularies*. They found that reading accuracy was strongly affected by word frequency and improves more when words are read in context than in isolation. Based on these results, they proposed a *stage theory* of sight-word acquisition. A word becomes a sight word in three stages. At the third or highest stage, "The word [is] securely represented in the reader's visual lexicon. It is this third stage of mastery that permits the level of word recognition automaticity that is so characteristic of skilled readers and so central to theories of their behavior" (p. 275). Adams and Huggins proposed this third stage of "automatic direct access" despite the fact that they measured accuracy and not speed.

Ehri (1991) added a new twist to the "late-stage" level. Sight-word reading is the final product of internalizing the "reading code" (grapheme-to-phoneme correspondences): "Sight-word reading involves establishing visual-phonological access routes rather than strictly visual logographic routes into lexical memory" (p. 402).

Ehri's (1998) version of sight-word reading apparently created considerable confusion, which she felt obliged to resolve. Instead, the hole only got deeper:

Misconceptions about sight word reading persist. One is that only irregularly spelled words are read by sight. This is not true; *all words*, once they have been read a few times, *become sight words....* The term "sight" indicates that the sight of the word triggers that word in memory, including information about its spelling, pronunciation, and meaning." (p. 91; emphasis added).

Ehri provided no operational definitions for what constitutes a "sight word," retreating to semantics with words like *quickly* and *automatically*. A sight word is defined by what *it is not*. If a reader must consciously decode a word, this means it has not yet achieved sight-word status: "Words not known by sight may be read in other ways, although these ways require attention and consume more processing time. Readers might apply their knowledge of grapheme-phoneme relations to convert the spelling into a pronunciation" (p. 90).

The notion that all words are ultimately read by sight because *it seems that way* is rapidly gaining acceptance in the field despite the absence of any proof. Aaron et al.'s (1999) remarks illustrate this quite clearly: "Even though the importance of sight-word reading is recognized *almost universally*, how it is accomplished remains an unsolved issue" (p. 91; emphasis added). They are referring here to "late-stage" sight-word reading, not to "logographic" reading.

The danger that this idea will find its way into the classroom is real. Aaron et al. (1999) had several suggestions for how teachers could enhance this kind of sight-word reading through vocabulary training.

A Century-Old Fallacy of Inferring Brain Processing Time from Response Time The idea that reading speed mirrors brain-processing speed has a long history, and has already had a profound effect on reading instruction. The story begins in 1886 when Cattell published a little paper in the journal *Mind* on comparing the time it took to name letters and to read simple, common words. He found that adults can read common words as fast as they can name letters, and they can read words in context twice as fast as they can read them in isolation.

This paper was cited as the ultimate "scientific proof" for the importance of teaching sight words as the major method of reading instruction by the advocates of the look-say movement in the early twentieth century. Later, Cattell's paper came to the attention of reading researchers and his basic findings were replicated and extended. Biemiller (1977/1978) reported that second and third graders took longer to name words than to name letters, but that the speeds were identical by fourth grade and remained so through college, while overall naming speed increased at each grade. Reading words in context was much faster than reading words in isolation, and this effect appears by second grade.

Samuels and colleagues speculated that if a word is read as a single unit (holistically), then word length would not matter (see Samuels, Laberge, and Bremer 1978; Samuels, Miller, and Eisenberg 1979). They found that word length (three to six letters) did have a strong effect on naming speed at second grade, and continued to do so at higher grades when words were over five or six letters long, but there was no word-length effect for college students. They concluded that younger readers process words letter by letter, whereas college students read "holistically." This was interpreted as some kind of "activation" process: "What is apparently being changed as one progresses through the grade levels is a reduction of the contribution of activation of each letter code to the word code" (Samuels, Laberge, and Bremer 1978, 719).

However, as Samuels, Laberge, and Bremer noted, "activation units" cannot explain how college students process all words at the same speed regardless of length. Instead, they proposed that "there must be a tradeoff in the activation threshold with word length, such that the letter codes of three-letter words produce *more activation* than the letter codes of the six-letter words" (p. 719; emphasis added).

To such complexities do our theories lead us!

I have surveyed a mere sprinkling of the many studies over the past 120 years in which researchers concluded that if you can read a word as fast as you can name a letter, this is proof that the word has become a "sight word," processed holistically, instantly, and automatically.

No one stopped to consider that the same results could reflect the limits of *motor* processing (speech-output rate) across the developmental span, not visual-processing speed. In other words, the similarity in speeds to name letters and words may be caused by limits on the time it takes to program an output and produce it, not how long it takes to perceive or recognize it.

The idea that you can infer something about perception, cognition, and brain processing from a single measure of simple response time is extremely naive. This problem was recognized early in the twentieth century by psychologists studying reaction time, and scientists who measure eye-movement patterns during reading have made this point many times. No single measure can reliably predict a reader's efficiency in decoding text. Rayner (1998, p. 377) summed up this work as follows: "Any single measure of processing time per word is a pale reflection of the reality of cognitive processing."

Eye-movement research shows that extremely precise measures of fixation time per word (225 ms is average), recorded by the most sophisticated eye-movement camera, are too imprecise to make inferences about how processing occurs. Imagine how much this imprecision multiples when it includes the entire reading/speaking act: focus, scan, transform visual image to word, program output of word, execute output program. Nor would this include the fact that individuals have such highly inconsistent response times for reading the same words, as shown by Glushko's data.

There can never be a metric to pin this process down. There is no way to estimate how the brain reads from response times as sluggish as 450–800 ms, the time it takes to read a single word aloud. Nor is there any evidence (or reason) that phonological decoding stops because motor (vocal) responses speed up. The speed and complexity of the brain's neural systems are at a rate and quantity far outside the limits of what a simple measure of behavior can show.

The late-stage sight-word theory is based on the assumption that because a word *seems to be* recognized instantly, it is processed instantly as well. The sense of "seems to be" is beautifully captured by the children's spontaneous remarks in Varnagen et al.'s study on spelling strategies: "I just knew it."

Well, the mind plays tricks on us, as Freud observed long ago in *Project for a Scientific Psychology* (Freud 1966; Pribram and Gill 1976). Freud, who was trained as a neurologist, was apparently the first to realize that the brain cortex makes conscious reflection possible, and then only portions of it depending on what you are conscious of. Span of consciousness, or "attention span," is restricted to one domain or event at any point in time. We cannot be aware of everything at once (McGuinness and Pribram 1980). Most of what goes on in the brain cortex, and all of what goes on in subcortical regions, operate outside our conscious awareness or our conscious control.

A century later, we know that the brain processes all incoming sensory signals but only alerts us to what is relevant *after processing it*. We can ask our brain to hold something "in mind" if we choose to focus on it, but usually at a metabolic cost (Pribram and McGuinness 1975). Furthermore, conscious awareness of external events can be incredibly slow, especially when they are novel and unexpected. When President Reagan was shot, a film recorded nearly a minute of silence before any reaction was seen or heard (brains were churning while bodies were frozen in inaction).

There is another brain principle at work. With experience and learning, neural processing increases in efficiency (in terms of precision, speed, and neural organization) to the point where multiple or "parallel" processing goes on automatic pilot, outside our awareness. There are in-built properties of neural systems that allow for such rapid processing that we can never become aware of it, no matter how hard we try. People do not hear or feel phoneme coarticulation in speech. Yet we know it is there all the same. We do not hear the microsecond differences between the arrival time of sounds to each ear that allows us to localize objects in space.

Our sense that we read whole words instantly by sight via some direct pipeline from the eye to meaning is an *illusion*. No matter how much something "seems like" it happens instantly, it does not. Conscious awareness and brain processing run on different clocks. The brain can map grapheme-phoneme correspondences, analyze patterns of orthographic redundancies, register degrees of word familiarity, perceive context cues, and work out possible decodings of odd or unpredictable spellings, in parallel. Everything else the brain does works this way. In ordinary conversations, we map phoneme sequences into words, process syntax and semantics, perceive quality and tone of voice, note vocal inflection, and watch mouth movements, facial expressions, body posture, and mannerisms *all at the same time*. The brain has an amazing capacity for "multiplexing" or "multitasking" hundreds or thousands of operations simultaneously. Brains are redundant parallel processors even when they do not need to be.

Your Brain Can Read Before You Know What It Has Read   We have barely begun to scratch the surface of how the brain processes the printed page. Recent breakthroughs have shown that readers' expectations based on syntax and semantics govern how the text is read, and what they look for or ignore. This is contrary to the view presented above, in which reading is essentially passive and linear: see word … automatically decode word … move to next word, and so on. The crucial tests for this new insight are based on function words, those ubiquitous little words that one would expect to be read most automatically of all: *a, the, on, in, for, and.*

Healy (1976) developed a useful technique for measuring what people are conscious of as they process text, called the *missing-letter effect.* People were asked to locate a target letter as they read continuous text at a normal rate. Letters in function words were more likely to be missed. The error rates for detecting *t* in words like *the* were much higher than for detecting *t* in *think.*

At that time, it was discovered that readers focus less often and for shorter periods on function words than on other words (Rayner 1977). Various explanations were proposed for this effect. One was that function words are redundant and can be skipped. Another was that because readers focus on meaning, function words are missed because they are semantically empty.

Greenberg and Koriat (1991) thought differently. They discovered that Hebrew readers detect function words largely on the basis of their syntactic and semantic role in the sentence. They followed up this research with U.S. college students and adapted it to the English language by varying the linguistic roles of prepositions.

In one experiment, the word *for* appeared in sentences either in its simple prepositional role, or in one of two common phrases. In "for better or worse" it acts as a preposition, while in "for or against" it acts as a modifier (adjective/adverb). The expectation was that the error rate (detecting the target letter *f* in *for*) would be the same when *for* was in its usual prepositional role, but that error rates would drop when *for* acted as a modifier. This is exactly what was found. The error rate for *for* as a preposition was 23 percent in a sentence and 25 percent in a common phrase, but only 6 percent when it acted as a modifier.

Greenberg and Koriat replicated this effect using the preposition *on* in sentences where *on* functioned like a preposition or as an adjective in compound terms such as *on switch, on call, onlooker, on side.* The error rate for finding the target letter *n* was 42 percent when *on* was a preposition, but only 17 percent when it was an adjective.

The investigators looked for the source of this effect by experimenting with the location of information in a sentence. Sentences were constructed where the context of the initial phrase was the same, but the word *for* was used differently. In one case ("for or against") it was a modifier; in the other ("for abortion") it was a preposition. They predicted that detecting function words would vary as a function of context, even when its function was in the future (in the second phrase), evidence of a "late-stage" analysis of sentence structure. In other words, people either anticipate the second phrase before they read it, or they actually read it *before they are conscious of reading it.*

The students missed 35 percent of the targets when *for* was a simple preposition and 27 percent of the targets in the phrase "for abortion," but only 3 percent of the targets in "for or against." Because prior context could not have influenced these results, and the word *for* was detected quite easily in one phrase but not in the other, this ruled out the theory that function words are part of some "unitized word frame" (sequential dependencies).

To pin this down more precisely, Greenberg and Koriat constructed sentences with controls both on content and on functional phrases. Meaning, for example, was held constant across all critical phrases, while content varied. They created sentences in which the word *for* could be linked to something that either preceded or followed it, as in the following questions: "Are you for abortion or against it?" and "With regard to this issue of abortion, are you for or against it?" In the first sentence, *for* is the preposition of the object word *abortion*, and the statement is *explicit*. In the second sentence, the word *abortion* comes early and *for* comes late, serving as a modifier ("for or against"). In this case the meaning is *implicit* (it refers back to something earlier).

Greenberg and Koriat predicted that the explicit phrase, where *for* plays its usual prepositional role, would produce more errors than the implicit phrase. This would show that the missing-letter effect is tied to a function word's specific syntactic role, and also clarifies how sentences are processed. The error rate was 22 percent for detecting the letter *f* in *for* in the explicit phrase, but only 14 percent in the implicit phrase.

Taken together, these results support an active, structural approach to reading sentences, which psychologists call *top-down processing* or *analysis by synthesis:*

We propose that although the coding of structure and the coding of meaning go hand in hand during reading, the coding of structure generally leads the way. Readers try to establish a tentative structural frame for the phrase and then use it to guide the interpretation and integration of the constituent units into a meaningful representation. The establishment of these frames appears to occur at a relatively early stage in text processing on the basis of a cursory and shallow visual analysis.... Letter detection is more difficult in function words which normally serve to anchor and support phrase structure than in the semantically informative content words. However, when function words are forced into a content role, their constituent letters remain available. (p. 1058)

The author viewed the "structural frame" as local in the sense of the immediate context. The location of a particular word that disambiguates meaning changes the depth of the perceptual analysis in surrounding words, even when it "appears in mind" before it is read and/or is expected in the future.

This research shows that reading is far more complex and more amazing than anyone could possibly imagine. It highlights the fact that this complexity, which, in these studies, required visual search, decoding, the processing of meaning, and syntactic analysis, is also accompanied by an attempt to carry out a global structural analysis of every sentence and anticipate which words need to be briefly scanned or receive full attention. *And this goes on completely outside conscious awareness.* A good reader is only conscious of meaning. The print on the page is all but invisible.

We are not the conductors of this symphony. Our brain is. This is why it is foolish to imagine that anyone can decree how a particular word is read by the brain, simply because reading seems automatic, and then presume to know what this process entails.

Appendix 1: How Nations Cheat on
International Literacy Studies

In 2001, the media in the United Kingdom reported that English students outscored Sweden in a recent international reading survey, citing PISA 2000 (Programme for International Student Assessment, OECD 2001). Yet a mere four years earlier, in another OECD study on twelve countries, Sweden came first in the 16-to-25 age group while the United Kingdom, Australia, New Zealand, Ireland, and the United States barely outdid Poland. Contradictory results also appeared in a recent study on nine-year-olds from thirty-two countries—PIRLS 2001 (Progress in International Reading, April, 2003). England was third in this study after Sweden and the Netherlands. The United States was ninth. The apparent spurt in literacy rates for England and the United States is not mirrored by well-conducted domestic studies, such as the National Assessment of Education Progress (NAEP).

In the most recent NAEP report on fourth-grade children (NAEP 2002, U.S. Department Education 2003. See USDE Web site), 38 percent of the children were "below basic" (functionally illiterate), 32 percent were at "basic level," 23 percent were "proficient," and 6 percent were "advanced." These values are similar to earlier results of 43 percent, 33 percent, 20 percent, and 4 percent, respectively. Certainly, a 38 percent functional illiteracy rate is unlikely to catapult the United States into ninth place internationally. NAEP studies are extremely rigorous. In NAEP 1992 (Mullis et al. 1993), 140,000 children were tested on an individual basis. Test items were secured, and outside testers monitored protocols and compliance rates.

Earlier international reading studies sponsored by the OECD were also well conducted. Yet a senior official on this project told me that some countries put pressure on them to obscure or disguise the data. One country withdrew from the study because they did not like their results.

Today, the situation has deteriorated to the point where results are meaningless. PISA 2000 is the most recent of the OECD studies, involving thousands of 15-year-olds from thirty-two countries. Pages 232 to 236 of the report provide information on population sampling along with tables on exclusion and compliance rates (tables A3.1, p. 232, and A3.2, p. 235). Compliance was monitored in the following ways: (1) Target schools representing a demographic sample were provided to local school districts. (2) If a school would not or could not participate, a replacement school from a second list had to be chosen. To avoid selection bias, the compliance rate at step 1 was set at 85 percent minimum. (3) A fixed number of students per class had to participate based on classroom size (usually about 35 children), with a minimum compliance of 80 percent student participation.

Exclusion rates refer to children in the population who cannot be tested because of mental retardation, being blind or deaf, and so forth. The guidelines were: "The percentage of 15-year-olds excluded within schools had to be less than 2.5 percent of the nationally desired target population." The last part was in boldface type. This section of the report also expressly stated that "special education" was not a criterion for exclusion.

The PISA consortium, a body of various government officials and statistics experts, were apparently unable to enforce even these lenient guidelines. Failure to comply with exclusion rates was ignored completely. Poor compliance rates were explained away with the statement (p. 236) that countries with poor compliance rates supplied documentation that adequately explained why rates were low! The Netherlands, with a 27 percent compliance rate, was the only country dropped from the study. The compliance rates for the remaining worst offenders are provided below. The score in column 1 must be 85 percent to meet the requirements of the study. If not, reading scores will be unreliable, especially when the percentage of missing schools is added to the percentage of missing students. Even with replacement schools, the United States tested only 55 percent of students they should have tested.

Countries with poor compliance rates:

	Target schools	With replace-ment	Students
United States	56%	70%	85%
United Kingdom	61%	82%	81%
Belgium	69%	86%	93%
New Zealand	78%	86%	88%
Poland	79%	83%	88%
Australia	81%	94%	84%
Japan	82%	90%	96%

However, as shown by the following countries, there is no excuse for low compliance rates.

Countries with excellent compliance rates:

Korea	100%	100%	99%
Sweden	100%	100%	88%
Austria	99%	100%	92%
Italy	98%	100%	93%
Finland	97%	100%	93%
Spain	95%	100%	92%
Mexico	93%	100%	94%

I compiled lists representing the true facts about exclusion and compliance rates for all countries. Composite reading test scores are included, taken from table 2.3a, p. 253 in the report.

Countries failing to meet requirements for both exclusion and compliance:

	Exclusion rate	Reading score
Ireland	4.6%	527
Luxembourg	9.1%	441
Netherlands	4.4%	NA
New Zealand	5.1%	529
Poland	9.7%	470
United Kingdom	4.9%	523
United States	4.1%	504

Countries failing to meet the exclusion cut-off only, scoring above 3 percent:

Canada	4.9%	534
Denmark	3.1%	497
France	3.5%	505
Sweden	4.7%	516

Countries failing to meet the 85 percent compliance rate only:

Australia	528
Belgium	507
Japan	522

The following countries played by the rules.

Countries meeting all requirements ranked by reading test scores:

Finland	546	Germany	484
Korea	525	Liechtenstein	483
Austria	507	Hungary	480
Iceland	507	Greece	474
Norway	505	Portugal	470
Switzerland	494	Russia	462
Spain	493	Mexico	422
Czech Republic	492	Brazil	396
Italy	487		

In this last list, what is most significant is the absence of English-speaking countries. From the tables overall one notices the highly inflated scores for the "cheaters" as compared to the countries that did not cheat. It is evident that the top-scoring countries in the final list are there for a reason. Finland and Korea have the most transparent writing systems in the world. Nearly as good are the Scandinavian, German, Italian, and Spanish writing systems. It's a pity Sweden violated the exclusion criterion, because there was no need to. They would have scored near the top in any case.

Think about how misleading this report is. If one merely looked at the tables of reading test scores, being unaware of, or skipping over, the complex tables on exclusion and compliance rates, it would appear that the United States had scored in the mid range, and the United Kingdom ranked with Korea.

Control over sampling and compliance rates was also a problem in the PIRLS 2001 study on 150,000 students from thirty-five countries. This study was sponsored by Boston College, with support from the International Association for the Evaluation of Educational Achievement. One example of the problem is the fact that Singapore tested 7,000 children while the United States tested only 3,763. Although Sweden came out on top in this study, not much else fit expectations. The Netherlands and England (major culprits in the PISA 2000 study) came in second and third, followed by Bulgaria and Latvia. Iceland and Norway scored a dismal twenty-first and twenty-fifth, the penalty for playing by the rules.

As project directors obviously have lost control over these studies, international testing has become an exercise in futility. It is an enormous waste of time and resources, and proves nothing.

Appendix 2: Misuse of Statistics

Statistical Problems in Bond and

Dykstra 1967

Use of Means Instead of Individual Data in ANOVA Statistics

The use of simple means to represent the data from a small population (20 to 30 children per classroom) is liable to serious distortion. This would occur if one or two children in a class had extreme scores, a common situation in reading research. The mathematics that underpins analysis-of-variance (ANOVA) statistics, and the probability tables formulated to work with these statistics, are based on variances and not on means.

The ANOVA computes a ratio of the between-groups variance to within-groups variance. In this study, each classroom should contribute a range of scores. These scores are used to compute the ratio of the variance due to treatments (between-groups variance) to the variance due to the children across all treatments and all classrooms (within-subjects variance). Between-groups variance is the numerator, and within-subjects variance is the denominator or error term. These terms should reflect a normal distribution (normal variance of the all the children's reading ability). Replacing individual scores with classroom mean scores means that scores are unlikely to be normally distributed.

The probability of obtaining a significant result (large F ratio) is determined by the size of the difference between the groups, and by the power in the study. "Power" translates to the number of subjects. Thousands of subjects is very high power, and tens of subjects is low power. By using the means instead of individual scores, all the variance (the variability) from the children was eliminated and replaced by the variability between classroom means. This not only changed the focus of the Bond and Dykstra 1967 study from one comparing children to one comparing classrooms, but dramatically reduced statistical power so that the probability of obtaining a significant result was far too low.

Appendix 2

About Units of Measurement It is currently fashionable to use classroom means as the unit of measurement in cases where the "treatment" (the teaching method) is delivered to the whole class rather than to individuals (or groups). From a logical standpoint it is unclear why this is necessary, and from a mathematical standpoint it makes no sense. ANOVA statistics were invented for field trials in agricultural research. If plants are substituted for children, the analogy is nearly perfect, except that the dependent variables are height and weight. In field trials, plants are set out in plots and each plot gets the same treatment (specific proportions of nutrients). Plots are counterbalanced or randomized across the terrain to control for such things as sunlight, drainage, wind, mineral content of the soil, and so forth. After treatment, each plant contributes one score to the analysis. This is essential to compute the variance within plots as a function of treatment unless the number of plots is vast. Using mean height per plot would eliminate this variance, and statistical analysis would be invalid.

Analysis of Covariance

The analysis of covariance (ANCOVA) is justified when subjects differ widely in a particular skill at the beginning of a study where the *same skill* is being trained, or when subjects differ widely on something likely to contribute to this skill, such as IQ or vocabulary. In other words, covariance would be used where it would be logical to pair or match subjects between groups, or when a difference between groups occurs that does not seem due to chance. Even if one assumes that Bond and Dyskstra's study met these requirements, one must be able to answer the following question: Did the groups consistently differ on the baseline measures? Unfortunately, this question cannot be answered, because the incorrect data (means again) were used for the statistical analyses. Furthermore, when comparing the statistics for all projects combined, versus individual project analyses, the results from the baseline tests suffered from a "now you see it now you don't" effect. In the basal-reader versus i.t.a. comparisons, letter-name knowledge was significantly better for i.t.a. Yet when the five projects were analyzed separately, the letter-name effect disappeared *for every group*. However, a group difference in phoneme discrimination appeared that had not been there before. These results are typical of what happens when means instead of individual scores (variances) are used in a statistical analysis.

ANCOVA is based on correlational statistics with the twist that it allows you to make all groups comparable on the baseline measures, and then adjust the outcome measure accordingly. The mathematics requires the data to be linear and normally distributed, with similar variances on each test. By reducing the data to means, none of these requirements can be met. In addition, the computations in an ANCOVA analysis must include values for sampling error and residual variance (the square of the standard-deviation estimate), neither of which can be computed with means.

Degrees of Freedom

Degrees of freedom translates to the number of subjects in a study, minus the levels or conditions under each treatment or factor, minus 1. In computing ANOVA statistics, the total variance for treatments is divided by the number of levels for that treatment (for i.t.a. versus basals, df = 1), and the total variance for subjects across treatments (within-subjects error) is $N - 1 - 1$. If the degrees of freedom for the error term is very large (lots of subjects), then the final value for within-subjects error (the denominator in the F ratio) is very small. This, in turn, would make the final F value too large and more likely to be significant. In this study, individual projects were analyzed one at a time, and the degrees of freedom should have represented only the classrooms in that project. Instead, the value for the degrees of freedom represented all the projects in a method group. In the i.t.a. comparison, the degrees of freedom for the error term was five times larger than it should have been for every comparison. And the same problem continued throughout.

As an illustration, by analyzing each project separately, this reduces to a two-factor random-group design (gender × treatment). Project 1 had 32 classrooms (64 means), so degrees of freedom would be 1 (treatment) 1 (sex) and 61 subjects. The table values given, however, were 1 and 292, which is clearly incorrect. This was not a typographical error, because the same mistake appeared on all other tables where individual projects were analyzed separately (see tables 27, 38, 49, 60, and 71). The same mistake appeared in the analyses for the individual tests as well. This means one cannot rely on the results for any of the outcome measures.

Appendix 3: An Analysis of Word
Lists from Treiman et al. 1995

CVC Spelling Word Lists are Sorted by High and Low Consistency of Initial (CV) and Final (VC) Segments

Words are listed by spelling type, starting with vowel + *r*.

Low CV/High VC
bar, jar, beer, dear, rear, turn, ball, tall, lock, cook, loss, bob, mob, heap, thin

High CV/High VC
deck, pick, suck, Dutch, mess, gum, gun, met, wet, file, game, hope, rode, role, sung

Low CV/Low VC
bear, pull, push, wash, watch, none, ton, won, cough, rough, lose, dog, fog, death, bade

High CV/Low VC
word, worm, chose, dose, lease, pose, gas, yes, doll, shall, hood, mood, wood, limb, mead

Problems with High-Consistency VC Units

1. One list contains six vowel + *r* words: *bar, jar, beer, dear, rear,* and *turn.* The /r/ is a vowel in its own right (/r/ in *her*). When it is combined with another vowel (VV) as in *for*, this creates a diphthong: /oe/-/er/. A diphthong is taught as one unit (a digraph or phonogram) and not as two separate phonemes (/oe/ and /r/), which would make no sense. The words listed above are actually CV words, not CVC words, and so have no VC

unit. The letter *r* cannot "control" the pronunciation of the vowel because it is part of the vowel.

2. That this is the case is revealed by the word *turn*, which is treated as a CVC word in which the /r/ (spelled *ur*) counts as one vowel.

3. The word *bear* is on one of the low-VC lists, yet has the identical rime to *dear* and *rear* on the high-VC list. It is not clear how *ear* can be consistent and inconsistent at the same time. And, of course, these are CV words in the first place and have no VC unit.

4. There were eight words on the high-VC lists where the vowel controls the final-consonant spelling, exactly the opposite of the claim. These words are *lock, cook, deck, Dutch, pick, suck, loss,* and *mess.* Vowel phonology determines the spelling of final /k/, /ch/, /f/, /j/, /l/, and /s/. "Simple vowels" usually take the spellings *ck, tch, dge, ff, ll,* and *ss.* All other vowels or consonants take *k, ch, ge,* and *l* as well as *ce, se,* or *s.* The final consonant does not control how the vowel is pronounced in these words. The pronunciation would be unchanged if the other legal spellings were used: *lok, dek, duch, pik, suk, los,* and *mes.* It is the *spellings* that are controlled, not the pronunciation.

5. There were nine CVC words of the "simple" ("short") vowel type: *bob, bog, thin, gun, gum, met, wet, sun,* and *sung.* In these words, all phoneme spellings are "context free." No phoneme (or its spelling) has the least effect on how the others are decoded or spelled. They are pronounced consistently, not because the VC unit makes them consistent, but because nothing is affected by what it sits next to.

6. The words with V + *e* vowels are also stable: *file, game, hope, rode,* and *role.* The vowel is unaffected by changing the final consonant: *file, fine, five / gage, gale, game, gape, gate, gave / hope, hole, hone, home, hose / rode, role, robe, rose, rote, rove.*

7. There are only two words where a final consonant controls vowel pronunciation. These are the "*l*-controlled" vowels. When the letter *l* follows *a,* this causes it to be read as /o/, as shown: *ball, tall* (though not always: *shall, fallow, gallows, tallow, pal, pallid*). This would meet their criteria for "high consistency," but they are the only two words on any of the lists that do.

8. One of the high-VC words is *heap.* The *p* is supposed to signal that *ea* is read /ee/ and not /e/ (*head*). The orthographic *eap* family consists of four words—*heap, cheap, reap,* and *leap*—but this does not hold up in multisyl-

lable words (*weapon*). The VC unit is not productive here in view of the fact that the *phonological eep* family has two spellings, those above plus *beep*, *cheep*, *creep*, *deep*, *keep*, *peep*, *seep*, *sheep*, *sleep*, *steep*, *sweep*, *weep*.

Problems with Low-Consistency VC Units

When we turn to the words with low-VC units—orthographic rimes where the consonant is *unlikely* to help decode the vowel—we encounter entirely different kinds of words. In the first place they are considerably harder to read. The words are longer and have more irregular spellings. It is not surprising that children had more trouble reading these words. But was this a function of the low-VC consistency? Can the absence of something be a cause?

1. There are far more irregularly spelled words on the low-VC lists. I have mentioned *bear*, which is "irregular" compared to *dear* and *rear*. There is *shall* (one of the renegades in the *all* family), as well as *none*, *ton*, and *won*, with uncommon spellings of the vowel /u/. *Cough* and *rough* both appear on the same list, causing confusion because *ou* stands for different vowel sounds, and *gh* is a low-probability spelling for /f/. Did children have trouble reading these words because of their irregular spellings, because of the fickleness of *ough* (*bough*, *bought*, *though*, *through*), or because the VC "rime was too inconsistent" to provide a clue to how to pronounce the vowel, as they claim?

2. These lists contained many words in which the initial consonant controls the vowel spelling: *pull*, *push*, *wash*, *watch*, *word*, *worm*. As noted above, /p/ (and /b/) take the *u* spelling for the vowel /ŏŏ/, as in *pull*, *push*, *pudding*, *pulley*, *pullet*, *put* (and in *bull*, *bullet*, *bully*, *bush*, *butcher*). The sound /w/ takes the *a* spelling for the vowel sound /o/: *wad*, *waffle*, *wan*, *wand*, *wander*, *want*, *wash*, *wasp*, *watch*, *water*, also true for /sw/ blends (*swab*, *swamp*, *swap*, *swat*) and even for /skw/ blends (*squab*, *squabble*, *squall*, *squander*, *squash*, *squat*). The sound /w/ takes the *or* spelling for the vowel sound /er/, as in *word*, *work*, *world*, *worm*, *worry*, *worse*, *worst*, *worth*, *worthy*. It is noteworthy that four of these strongly CV-controlled spellings were not on the high-CV consistency list, showing that these lists reflect little understanding of the spelling code.

3. Four words use the Old French spelling *se* for /s/ and /z/: *chose*, *dose*, *pose*, and *lose* (*choze*, *doass*, *poze*, and *looze*), and are unstable for both

consonant and vowel, thus being highly likely to cause decoding errors. To add to the confusion, uncommon final /s/ words were also on the list: *gas*, *yes*. They are part of a tiny group of words ending in /s/ (not plural) that use the *s* and not *ss* spelling (*bus*, *gas*, *us*, *this*, *yes*).

4. The words *hood*, *mood*, and *wood* were on the same list. This creates confusion because this is the main spelling (basic-code spelling) for two vowels (nothing to do with "control" by a final consonant), as in *food*, *mood*, *noodle*, *poodle* / *good*, *hood*, *stood*, *wood*.

5. Two other words seemed designed to cause reading errors—*limb* and *mead*—because few children will have heard of these words.

6. Finally, the words *dog* and *fog* are on these lists. These are part of the "context-free" CVC group, and it is not clear why the *og* spelling is "inconsistent" with any other pronunciation.

Glossary

alphabet A writing system based on phonemes (individual consonants and vowels).

analogy decoding An instructional approach in which children are encouraged to decode an unknown word by searching in memory for a word with the same ending sounds, and then swapping the initial sound(s). ("*Hand* looks like *land*, except it starts with an aitch.")

artificial transparent alphabet Used during initial reading instruction. Each phoneme in the language is represented by a letter, digraph, or artificial symbol.

basal reader A reading program that includes all elements of a curriculum. Designed by education publishing houses for use in the classroom.

basic code Used during initial reading instruction. Each phoneme in the language is represented by its most common or least ambiguous spelling.

binomial test A statistical test that computes a numerical score that will exceed chance (guessing) at a specified level of probability. The computation takes into account the number of items on a test and the number of alternatives for each response.

categorical perception The inability to hear the acoustic transitions between two similar consonant contrasts (*ba/pa*) and the tendency to hear only one or the other.

ceiling effects A situation in which a test or task is so easy that most people get perfect scores.

character   In Chinese writing, a symbol standing for a syllable (or word).

classifier   In Chinese writing, a symbol acting as a marker for a semantic category.

coarticulation   Phonemes overlap one another in speech. The phonemes coming later in the word modify the production of phonemes coming earlier in the word, creating a complex acoustic envelope of sounds.

code   Any system in which arbitrary symbols are assigned to units within a category. The number symbols 1–10 represent units of quantity. Letters represent units of speech sounds (phonemes).

consonant   A phoneme that involves contact and movement between one or more speech articulators. **Voiced consonant** engages the vocal folds. **Unvoiced consonant** does not engage the vocal folds.

consonantal alphabet   A writing system in which symbols are assigned only to consonants. Suitable for languages where consonant sequences stand for meaning, and vowels signal grammar and are inferred from context.

consonant blend or **consonant cluster**   Two or more consonants in sequence in a word: *str* in *street*.

construct validity   The aspect of test design in which items faithfully reflect the construct being measured and not some other construct.

covariance analysis   A statistical tool to adjust posttest scores to reflect individual differences in these scores at initial testing (e.g., intelligence is covaried in order to look at the correlation between phoneme awareness and reading, independent of intelligence).

decoding   The act of translating symbols that represent units of something back into those units (translating from letters to phonemes).

degrees of freedom   In statistics, the number of scores in a study that are free to vary given one known value.

determiner   A symbol standing for a semantic category (plant, man, water).

diacritic   A special mark or extra letter written above, below, or beside a letter to indicate pronunciation.

digraph   Two letters standing for one phoneme: *ch* in *church*.

diphone system   A system of writing in which one symbol represents each consonant-vowel (CV) unit in a language.

diphthong   A vowel sound that elides two vowels in rapid succession and counts as one vowel (/e/ + /ee/ = /ae/ in *late*).

dyslexia   Greek for "poor reading." Taken to mean a genetic predisposition to difficulties in learning to read in some countries (U.S.). Means poor reading, whatever the cause, in other countries.

eclectic reading method   A method of teaching that includes a variety of approaches not necessarily relevant to what needs to be taught.

effect size   A conversion of the difference in scores between two groups to standard-deviation units. This provides a standard metric for comparing two or more studies with similar research designs and measures.

encoding   The act of transcribing units within a category into arbitrary symbols assigned to each unit (phonemes to their spellings).

expressive vocabulary   A spoken vocabulary. The number of words someone is able to say and have understood.

factor analysis   A complex type of correlational statistics in which the relations between scores on a variety of tests are explored in geometric space. Tests are sorted according to their similarity to one another (proximity in this space), and factor scores or "factor loadings" are computed for each test in relation to every other test. Tests that "load" together (are highly correlated) constitute a factor. A factor is an abstraction, and the researcher must determine what the tests have in common. In general, a factor loading is not meaningful unless it is .80 or higher.

factor loading   A final value assigned to a test after a factor analysis has been carried out. This represents the power of that test to represent a factor in correlational values.

floor effects   When a test or task is so difficult that most of the scores are at zero.

frequency   Used here as a measure of the frequency of occurrence of a particular spelling in printed text. Frequency is the number of times it would occur in a specified number of words in text.

functional illiteracy   A designation of reading difficulty used in national testing in which the reader is unable to find, use, and interpret the meaning of printed text.

hieroglyphic   A writing system used on religious or public monuments for sacred or political purposes.

hiragana   One of two systems for marking diphones used in the Japanese writing system.

homophones   Words that sound exactly alike but have a different meaning.

invented spelling   An instructional method in which children are encouraged to recreate the spelling system based on whatever knowledge they might possess.

isomorphic   Same form.

item analysis   In test construction, an analytic technique to determine the power and reliability of individual items to measure a construct, such as which items produce consistent or inconsistent responses, and which are too easy or too difficult.

kanji   Symbols standing for whole words used in the Japanese writing system.

katakana   One of two systems for marking diphones used in the Japanese writing system.

logograph   An abstract symbol standing for a whole word.

look-say   A reading method in the early twentieth century in which children memorized isolated printed words as random letter sequences by visual memory alone.

mapping   A process by which units of one type are assigned to units of another type.

meta-analysis   The weighted mean of series of effect-sizes. This provides a global overview in standard deviation units of many studies using similar research designs and measurements.

morpheme   The smallest unit of a word that conveys meaning (*boat* contains one morpheme; *boats* and *boating* contain two morphemes).

morphology   A division of grammar in which morphemes determine grammatical form.

normal distribution   A mathematical distribution of a series of measurements in which the form of the distribution can be entirely determined by the mean and the standard deviation. This distribution takes the form of a bell.

onset   A technical term that refers to the initial consonant or consonants that precede a "rime." *str* in *street* is an onset.

ontogeny   The biological development of an individual.

opaque alphabet   An alphabetic writing system in which there are multiple spellings for the same phoneme.

orthography   "Standard spelling." The patterns of permissible spellings for sounds in words in a writing system.

paired-associate learning   A type of learning that requires memorization of arbitrary pairs of something (letter symbols for phonemes).

paleography   The study of ancient writing systems.

percentile rank   A conversion of a test score from a standardized test to reflect the level at which this score exceeds a percentage of the population. A percentile score of 90 means this person exceeded 90 percent of the population.

perceptual span   In eye-movement research, this is the distance in the periphery from central visual focus that people can see and/or use information. In reading research this is measured by the number of letters to the left or right that influence speed of decoding.

phoneme   The smallest unit of speech that people can hear; corresponds to consonants and vowels.

phoneme awareness   The ability to hear and remember the order of phonemes in words.

phonetic   Speech sounds in words.

phonics   A generic term for any reading method that teaches a relation-ship between letters and phonemes.

phonological awareness   The ability to hear and remember a variety of units of sound within words: syllable, syllable fragment (onsets/rimes), phoneme.

phonology   A system of speech sounds that make up a language.

phonotactics   The permissible or legal phoneme sequences in words in a particular language.

phylogeny   The evolutionary patterns or lines of descent of an organism.

pictogram   A stylized picture standing for a whole word. Used in ancient times for business purposes (invoices, inventory lists) or as part of an early writing system.

probability   The likelihood of a particular event or occurrence as a func-tion of a total range of possibilities (_a_ is the most probable spelling for the sound /a/ (_cat_)).

prosody   The general term for variations in the acoustic properties of speech for a given language that do not carry meaning directly, such as fluency, melody, stress patterns, and inflection.

radical   The part of a Chinese character that represents a semantic cate-gory. Identical to a determiner.

recall memory   Memory retrieved from a long-term memory store with-out the benefit of prompts or clues. (An essay test involves recall memory.)

receptive vocabulary   The number of words that someone can understand when spoken by others.

recognition memory   Memory retrieved from a long-term memory store that is assisted by prompts and clues. (A multiple-choice test involves recognition memory.)

reliability   In test construction, a reliable test is one where people score similarly on different occasions.

rime   A technical term for the final portion of a word that "sounds like" other words (rhymes). *and* in *band, bland, brand, hand*.

schwa vowel   A swallowed "uh" sound in a nonstressed syllable (*hesitate, abundance*).

semantic or **semantics**   The content or sequence of words in phrases that conveys meaning. In linguistics—the study of how language represents meaning.

sight words   Printed words that children are asked to memorize visually as random string of letters. A true sight word contains rare spelling patterns ("yot" = *yacht*).

spelling alternatives   All possible spellings of a single phoneme.

standard deviation   A measure of the variance (variability) in a set of scores that represents the square root of the sum of the squared differences of each score from the mean.

standardized test   A test administered to a very large number of people (normed) over a wide age range, in which test scores are "standardized" to fit a normal distribution. This is often converted to a standard metric, with a mean of 100 and s.d. of 10. Individual test scores take into account age (in months) and the distance from the mean in standard-deviation units.

statistical power   The number of scores on a particular test or task. The greater the number, the more likely there will be a normal distribution. This translates to the number of subjects in a study: large number = high power = more reliable result.

syllabary A writing system based on the syllable.

syllable A speech unit contained within a word, or constituting a whole word, which consists of one vowel plus any consonants. *I* and *straight* are one-syllable words; *Basket* and *triumph* are two-syllable words; and so on.

tonal language A language in which changes in pitch signify meaning.

transparent alphabet An alphabetic writing system in which there is rarely more than one spelling for the same phoneme.

vowel A phoneme in which the articulators do not stop or curtail the flow of breath. All vowels are voiced.

vowel + *r* A category of vowels in English in which the sound /r/ is either a vowel on its own (*her* contains the sounds /h/ /r/), or it forms a diphthong with another vowel (*for* contains the diphthong /oe/ + /r/). The are nine such vowels in English.

whole language A philosophy which holds that learning to read is similar to the acquisition of natural language. Children learn to by read by exposure, reading along with the teacher, and by guessing words using the context, pictures, and other cues.

word attack A type of reading test that consists entirely of nonsense words.

word family A group of words that share the same ending sounds, that are spelled the same, and that rhyme (bright, night, fight, sight).

word identification Same as word recognition.

word recognition A type of reading test in which a child decodes unrelated words one at a time.

writing system A systematic mapping of the elements of a unit of speech into a set of arbitrary symbols, such that every word in the language can be represented. No writing system marks whole words. Writing systems mark one of four sound units (and only one): syllable, CV diphone, consonants only, consonants and vowels (phonemes).

References

Aaron, P. G. 1991. Can reading disabilities be diagnosed without using intelligence tests? *Journal of Learning Disabilities*, *24*, 178–186, 191.

Aaron, P. G., Joshi, R. M., Ayotollah, M., Ellsberry, A., Henderson, J., and Lindsey, K. 1999. Decoding and sight-word naming: Are they independent components of word recognition skill? *Reading and Writing: An Interdisciplinary Journal*, *11*, 89–127.

Aaron, P. G., Keetay, V., Boyd, M., Palmatier, S., and Wacks, J. 1998. Spelling without phonology: A study of deaf and hearing children. *Reading and Writing: An Interdisciplinary Journal*, *10*, 1–22.

Adams, G. L., and Engelmann, S. 1996. *Research on Direct Instruction: 25 Years Beyond DISTAR*. Seattle: Educational Achievement Systems.

Adams, M. 1990. *Beginning to Read*. Cambridge, MA: MIT Press.

Adams, M. J., and Huggins, A. W. F. 1985. The growth of children's sight vocabulary: A quick test with educational and theoretical implications. *Reading Research Quarterly*, *20*, 262–281.

Allred, R. A. 1990. Gender differences in spelling achievement in grades 1 through 6. *Journal of Educational Research*, *83*, 187–193.

Aslin, R. N., Saffran, J. R., and Newport, E. L. 1998. Computation of conditional probability statistics by 8-month-old infants. *Psychological Science*, *9*, 321–324.

Ball, E. W., and Blachman, B. A. 1988. Phoneme segmentation training: Effect on reading readiness. *Annals of Dyslexia*, *38*, 208–225.

Ball, E. W., and Blachman, B. A. 1991. Does phoneme awareness training in kindergarten make a difference in early word recognition and developmental spelling? *Reading Research Quarterly*, *26*, 49–66.

———

Balmuth, M. 1992. *The Roots of Phonics*. Baltimore: York Press.

Baron, J., and Strawson, C. 1976. Use of orthographic and word-specific knowledge in reading words aloud. *Journal of Experimental Psychology: Human Perception and Performance*, 2, 386–393.

Barr, R. C. 1972. The influence of instructional conditions on word recognition errors. *Reading Research Quarterly*, 7, 509–529.

Barr, R. C. 1974/1975. The effect of instruction on pupil reading strategies. *Reading Research Quarterly*, 4, 556–582.

Beck, I. L., Perfetti, C. A., and McKeown, M. G. 1982. Effects of long-term vocabulary instruction on lexical access and reading comprehension. *Journal of Educational Psychology*, 74, 506–521.

Becker, W. C., and Gersten, R. 1982. A follow-up of follow through: The later effects of the Direct Instruction model on children in fifth and sixth grades. *American Educational Research Journal*, 19, 75–92.

Beers, C. S., and Beers, J. W. 1992. Children's spelling of English inflectional morphology. In S. Templeton and D. R. Bear, eds., *Development of Orthographic Knowledge and the Foundations of Literacy*, 231–252. Hillsdale, NJ: Erlbaum.

Bell, N. 1986. *Visualizing and Verbalizing for Language Comprehension and Thinking*. Paso Robles, CA: Academy of Reading Publications.

Berninger, V. W., Vaughan, K., Abbott, R. D., Brooks, A., Abbott, S. P., Rogan, L., Reed, E., and Graham, S. 1998. Early intervention for spelling problems: Teaching functional spelling units of varying size with a multiple-connections framework. *Journal of Educational Psychology*, 90, 587–605.

Biemiller, A. [1977]1998. Relationship between oral reading rates for letters, words, and simple text in the development of reading achievement. *Reading Research Quarterly*, 13, 223–253.

Blachman, B. A., Tangel, D. M., Ball, E. W., Black, R., and McGraw, C. K. 1999. Developing phonological awareness and word recognition skills: A two-year intervention with low-income, inner-city children. *Reading and Writing: An Interdisciplinary Journal*, 11, 239–273.

Block, C. C. 1993. Strategy instruction in a literature-based reading program. *Elementary School Journal*, 94, 139–151.

Block, C. C. 2002. *Improving Comprehension Instruction: Rethinking Research, Theory, and Classroom Practice.* Jossey-Bass Education Series, no. 20. San Francisco: Jossey-Bass.

Block, C. C., and Mangieri, J. N. 1997. *Reason to Read: Thinking Strategies for Life through learning.* Pearson Learning report, no. 20.

Block, C. C., and Pressley, M., eds. 2001. *Comprehension Instruction.* New York: Guilford Press.

Block, C. C., Gambrell, L., and Pressley, M. 1997. *Training the Language Arts: Expanding Thinking through Student-Centered Instruction.* Boston: Allyn and Bacon.

Bond, C. L., Ross, S. M., Smith, L. J., and Nunnery, J. A. 1995–1996. The effects of the Sing, Spell, Reading and Write program on reading achievement of beginning readers. *Reading Research and Instruction, 35,* 122–141.

Bond, G. L., and Dykstra, R. 1967. The cooperative research program in first-grade reading instruction. *Reading Research Quarterly, 2,* 1–142.

Bond, G. L., and Dykstra, R. 1997. The cooperative research program in first-grade reading instruction. (Reprint of the 1967 paper.) *Reading Research Quarterly, 32,* 342–344.

Boronat, C. B., and Logan, G. D. 1997. The role of attention in automatization: Does attention operate at encoding, or retrieval, or both: *Memory and Cognition, 25,* 36–46.

Bradley, L., and Bryant, P. E. 1983. Categorizing sounds and learning to read—a causal connection. *Nature, 301,* 419–421.

Bradley, L., and Bryant, P. E. 1985. *Rhyme and Reason in Reading and Spelling.* Ann Arbor: University of Michigan Press.

Brady, S., Fowler, A., Stone, B., and Winbury, N. 1994. Training phonological awareness: A study with inner-city kindergarten children. *Annals of Dyslexia, 44,* 26–59.

Brennan, F., and Ireson, J. 1997. Training phonological awareness: A study to evaluate the effects of a program of metalinguistic games in kindergarten. *Reading and Writing: An Interdisciplinary Journal, 9,* 241–263.

Brett, A., Rothlein, L., and Hurley, M. 1996. Vocabulary acquisition from listening to stories and explanations of target words. *Elementary School Journal, 96,* 415–422.

Brown, A. S. 1988. Encountering misspellings and spelling performance: Why wrong isn't right. *Journal of Educational Psychology, 80*, 488–494.

Brown, G. D. A. 1987. Resolving inconsistency: A computational model of word naming. *Journal of Memory and Language, 26*, 1–23.

Brown, I. S., and Felton, R. H. 1990. Effects of instruction on beginning reading skills in children at risk for reading disability. *Reading and Writing: An Interdisciplinary Journal, 2*, 223–241.

Brown, R., Pressley, M., Van Meter, P., and Schuder, T. 1996. A quasi-experimental validation of transactional strategies instruction with low-achieving second-grade readers. *Journal of Educational Psychology, 88*, 18–37.

Bruck, M., and Waters, G. S. 1990. An analysis of the component spelling and reading skills of good readers–good spellers, good readers–poor spellers, and poor readers–poor spellers. In T. H. Carr and B. A. Levy, *Reading and Its Development: Component Skills Approaches*, 161–206. New York: Academic Press.

Bus, A. G., and van IJzendoorn, M. H. 1999. Phonological awareness and early reading: A meta-analysis of experimental training studies. *Journal of Educational Psychology, 91*, 403–414.

Byrne, B., and Fielding-Barnsley, R. 1989. Phonemic awareness and letter knowledge in the child's acquisition of the alphabetic principle. *Journal of Educational Psychology, 81*, 313–321.

Byrne, B., and Fielding-Barnsley, R. 1990. Acquiring the alphabetic principle: A case for teaching recognition of phoneme identity. *Journal of Educational Psychology, 82*, 805–812.

Byrne, B., and Fielding-Barnsley, R. 1991. *Sound Foundations*. Sydney: Peter Leyden Educational.

Byrne, B., and Fielding-Barnsley, R. 1993. Evaluation of a program to teach phonemic awareness to young children: A 1 year follow-up. *Journal of Educational Psychology, 85*, 104–111.

Byrne, B., and Fielding-Barnsley, R. 1995. Evaluation of a program to teach phonemic awareness to young children: A 2 and 3 year follow-up and a new preschool trial. *Journal of Educational Psychology, 87*, 488–503.

Byrne, B., and Fielding-Barnsley, R. 2000. Effects of preschool phoneme identity training after six years: Outcome level distinguished from rate of response. *Journal of Educational Psychology, 92*, 659–667.

Calfee, R. C., and Henry, M. K. 1985. Project READ: An inservice model for training classroom teachers in effective reading instruction. In J. V. Hoffman, ed., *Effective Teaching of Reading: Research and Practice*, 199–229. Newark, DE: International Reading Association.

Campbell, J. R., Donahue, P. L., Reese, C. M., and Phillips, G. W. 1996. *National Assessment of Educational Progress 1994: Reading Report Card for the Nation and States*. Washington, DC: Office of Educational Research and Improvement, U.S. Department of Education.

Cattell, J. M. 1886. The time taken up by cerebral operations. *Mind, 11,* 220–242, 377–392, 524–538.

Chall, J. 1967. *Learning to Read: The Great Debate*. New York: McGraw-Hill.

Chall, J., and Feldman, S. 1966. First grade reading: An analysis of the interactions of professed methods, teacher implementation and child background. *The Reading Teacher, 19,* 569–575.

Chaney, C. 1992. Language development, metalinguistic skills, and print awareness in 3-year-old children. *Applied Psycholinguistics, 13,* 485–514.

Chang, Kwang-chih. 1963. *The Archeology of Ancient China*. New Haven, CT: Yale University Press.

Chomsky, C. 1976. When you still can't read in the third grade: After decoding, what? *Language Arts, 53,* 288–296.

Chomsky, N., and Halle, M. 1968. *The Sound Patterns of English*. New York: Harper and Row.

Civil, M. 1973. The Sumerian writing system: Some problems. *Orientalis, 42,* 21–34.

Clanchy, M. T. 1994. *From Memory to Written Record: England 1066–1307*. Oxford: Blackwell.

Clay, M. 1985. *The Early Detection of Reading Difficulties*. Tadworth, Surrey: Heinemann.

Clymer, T. 1983. The utility of phonic generalizations in the primary grades. In L. M. Gentile, M. L. Kamil, and J. S. Blanchard, eds., *Reading Research Revisited*, 113–119. Columbus, OH: Merrill.

Coltheart, M. 1978. Lexical access in simple reading tasks. In G. Underwood, ed., *Strategies of Information Processing*, 151–216. San Diego, CA: Academic Press.

Coltheart, M., Curtis, B., Atkins, P., and Haller, M. 1993. Models of reading aloud: Dual-route and parallel-distributed processing approaches. *Psychological Review, 100*, 585–608.

Cooper, J. S. 1996. Sumerian and Akkadian. In P. T. Daniels and W. Bright, *The World's Writing Systems*. New York: Oxford University Press.

Cossu, G., Rossini, F., and Marshall, J. C. 1993. When reading is acquired but phonemic awareness is not: A study of literacy in Down's syndrome. *Cognition, 46*, 129–138.

Coulmas, F. 1989. *The Writing Systems of the World*. Oxford: Blackwell.

Cunningham, A. E. 1990. Explicit versus implicit instruction in phoneme awareness. *Journal of Experimental Child Psychology, 50*, 429–444.

Cunningham, A. E., and Stanovich, K. E. 1990a. Assessing print exposure and orthographic processing skill in children: A quick measure of reading experience. *Journal of Educational Psychology, 82*, 733–740.

Cunningham, A. E., and Stanovich, K. E. 1990b. Early spelling acquisition: Writing beats the computer. *Journal of Educational Psychology, 82*, 159–162.

Cunningham, A. E., Stanovich, K. E., and West, R. F. 1994. Literacy environment and the development of children's cognitive skills. In E. M. H. Assink, ed., *Literacy Acquisition and Social Context*, 70–90. New York: Harvester Wheatsheaf.

Dahl, P. R. 1979. An experimental program for teaching high-speed word recognition and comprehension skills. In J. E. Button, T. Lovitt, and T. Rowland, eds., *Communications Research in Learning Disabilities and Mental Retardation*, 33–65. Baltimore, MD: University Park Press.

Dale, N. 1898. *On the Teaching of English Reading*. London: Dent.

Dale, N. 1902. *Further Notes on the Teaching of English Reading*. London: G. Philips and Son.

Daniels, P. T., and Bright, W. 1996. *The World's Writing Systems*. New York: Oxford University Press.

Dickinson, D. K., and Smith, M. W. 1994. Long-term effects of preschool teachers' book reading on low-income children's vocabulary and story comprehension. *Reading Research Quarterly, 29*, 105–122.

Dixon, M., and Kaminska, Z. 1997. Is it misspelled or is it mispelled? The influence of fresh orthographic information on spelling. *Reading and Writing: An Interdisciplinary Journal, 9*, 483–498.

Dowhower, S. L. 1987. Effects of repeated reading on second-grade transitional readers' fluency and comprehension. *Reading Research Quarterly, 22*, 389–406.

Dykstra, R. 1967. *Continuation of the Coordinated Center for First-Grade Reading Instruction Programs.* Report of Project No. 6-1651. Minneapolis: University of Minnesota.

Dykstra, R. 1968a. The effectiveness of code and meaning-emphasis beginning reading programs. *The Reading Teacher, 22*, 17–24.

Dykstra, R. 1968b. Summary of the second-grade phase of the Cooperative Research Program in primary reading instruction. *Reading Research Quarterly, 4*, 49–70.

Ehri, L. C. 1980. The development of orthographic images. In U. Frith, ed., *Cognitive Processes in Spelling*, 311–338. London: Academic Press.

Ehri, L. C. 1986. Sources of difficulty in learning to spell and read. In M. L. Wolraich and D. Routh, eds., *Advances in Developmental and Behavioral Pediatrics*, 121–195. Greenwich, CT: JAI Press.

Ehri, L. C. 1989a. Knowledge and its role in reading acquisition and reading disability. *Journal of Learning Disabilities, 22*, 356–365.

Ehri, L. C. 1989b. Movement into word reading and spelling: How spelling contributes to reading. In J. Mason, ed., *Reading and Writing Connections*, 65–81. Boston: Allyn and Bacon.

Ehri, L. C. 1991. Development of the ability to read words. In R. Barr, M. L. Kamil, P. B. Mosenthal, and P. D. Pearson, eds., *Handbook of Research in Reading*, vol. 2, 383–417. New York: Longman.

Ehri, L. C. 1992. Review and commentary: Stages of spelling development. In S. Templeton and D. R. Bear, eds., *Development of Orthographic Knowledge and the Foundations of Literacy*. Hillsdale, NJ: Erlbaum.

Ehri, L. C. 1995. Phases of development in learning to read words by sight. *Journal of Research in Reading, 18*, 115–125.

Ehri, L. C. 1998. Word reading by sight and by analogy in beginning readers. In C. Hulme and R. M. Joshi, eds., *Reading and Spelling: Development and Disorders*. Hillsdale, NJ: Erlbaum.

Ehri, L. C., and Wilce, L. S. 1987. Does learning to spell help beginners learn to read words? *Reading Research Quarterly, 22*, 47–65.

Eldredge, L. 1991. An experiment with a modified whole language approach in first-grade classrooms. *Reading Research and Instruction, 30*, 21–38.

Elley, W. B. 1989. Vocabulary acquisition from listening to stories. *Reading Research Quarterly, 24*, 174–187.

Ellis, A. J. 1870. *Transactions of the Philological Society*, 89–118. London.

Engelmann, S., and Bruner, E. 1969. *Distar reading program*. Chicago: Science Research Associates.

Evans, M. A., and Carr, T. H. 1985. Cognitive abilities, conditions of learning, and early development of reading skill. *Reading Research Quarterly, 20*, 327–350.

Falkenstein, A. 1964. Das Sumerische. Reprint from *Handbuch der Orientalistik*. Leiden: Brill.

Faulkner, H. J., and Levy, B. A. 1994. How text difficulty and reader skill interact to produce differential reliance on word and content overlap in reading transfer. *Journal of Experimental Child Psychology, 58*, 1–24.

Faulkner, H. J., and Levy, B. A. 1999. Fluent and nonfluent forms of transfer in reading: Words and their message. *Psychonomic Bulletin and Review, 6*, 111–116.

Fischer, F. W., Shankweiler, D., and Liberman, I. Y. 1985. Spelling proficiency and sensitivity to word structure. *Journal of Memory and Language, 24*, 423–441.

Fisher, R., and Craik, F. I. M. 1977. The interaction between encoding and retrieval operations in cued recall. *Journal of Experimental Psychology: Human Learning and Memory, 3*, 701–711.

Flavell, J. H. 1963. *The Developmental Psychology of Jean Piaget*. Princeton, NJ: Van Nostrand.

Flesch, R. [1955] 1985. *Why Johnny Can't Read*. 3rd ed. New York: Harper and Row.

Foorman, B. R., Francis, D. J., Beeler, T., Winikates, D., and Fletcher, J. M. 1997. Early interventions for children with reading problems: Study designs and preliminary findings. *Learning Disabilities, 8,* 63–71.

Foorman, B. R., Francis, D. J., Fletcher, J. M., Schatschneider, C., and Mehta, P. 1998. The role of instruction in learning to read: Preventing reading failure in at-risk children. *Journal of Educational Psychology, 90,* 37–55.

Foorman, B. R., and Liberman, D. 1989. Visual and phonological processing of words: A comparison of good and poor readers. *Journal of Learning Disabilities, 22,* 349–355.

Freud, S. 1966. *Project for a Scientific Psychology.* Ed. J. Strachey. Standard Edition of the Complete Psychological Works of Sigmund Freud, vol. 1, 281–397. New York: Norton.

Friederici, A. D., and Wessels, J. M. I. 1993. Phonotactic knowledge and its use in infant speech perception. *Perception and Psychophysics, 54,* 287–295.

Frith, U. 1980. Unexpected spelling problems. In U. Frith, ed., *Cognitive Processes in Spelling.* New York: Academic Press.

Frith, U. 1985. Beneath the surface of developmental dyslexia. In K. E. Patterson, J. C. Marshall, and M. Coltheart, eds., *Surface Dyslexia: Neuropsychological and Cognitive Analyses of Phonological Reading.* London: Erlbaum.

Fulwiler, G., and Groff, P. 1980. The effectiveness of intensive phonics. *Reading Horizons, 21,* 50–54.

Gelb, I. 1963. *A Study of Writing.* Chicago: University of Chicago Press.

Gentry, J. 1981. Learning to spell developmentally. *Reading Teacher, 34,* 378–381.

Gersten, R., Darch, C., and Gleason, M. 1988. Effectiveness of a direct instruction academic kindergarten for low-income students. *Elementary School Journal, 89,* 227–240.

Geva, E., and Siegel, L. S. 2000. Orthographic and cognitive factors in the concurrent development of basic reading skills in two languages. *Reading and Writing: An Interdisciplinary Journal, 12,* 1–30.

Glushko, R. J. 1979. The organization and activation of orthographic knowledge in reading aloud. *Journal of Experimental Psychology: Human Perception and Performance, 5,* 674–691.

Goodman, K. 1967, May. Reading: A psycholinguistic guessing game. *Journal of the Reading Specialist*, 126–135.

Goswami, U. C. 1990. Phonological priming and orthographic analogies in reading. *Journal of Experimental Child Psychology*, *49*, 323–340.

Graham, S. 2000. Should the natural learning approach replace spelling instruction? *Journal of Educational Psychology*, *92*, 235–247.

Graves, M. F., and Dykstra, R. 1997. Contextualizing the first-grade studies: What is the best way to teach children to read? *Reading Research Quarterly*, *32*, 342–344.

Greenberg, S. N., and Koriat, A. 1991. The missing-letter effect for common function words depends on their linguistic function in the phrase. *Journal of Experimental Psychology: Learning, Memory and Cognition*, *17*, 1051–1061.

Griffith, P. L., Klesius, J. P., and Kromrey, J. D. 1992. The effect of phonemic awareness on the literacy development of first grade children in a traditional or a whole language classroom. *Journal of Research in Childhood Education*, *6*, 85–92.

Haddock, M. 1976. Effects of an auditory and an auditory-visual method of blending instruction on the ability of prereaders to decode synthetic words. *Journal of Educational Psychology*, *68*, 825–831.

Hanna, P. R., Hanna, J. S., Hodges, R. E., and Rudorf, E. H. 1966. *Phoneme-Grapheme Correspondences as Cues to Spelling Improvement*. Washington, DC: U.S. Department of Health, Education, and Welfare, Office of Education.

Hart, B., and Risley, T. R. 1995. *Meaningful Differences*. Baltimore: Paul H. Brookes.

Hatcher, P. J., Hulme, C., and Ellis, A. W. 1994. Ameliorating early reading failure by integrating the teaching of reading and phonological skills: The phonological linkage hypothesis. *Child Development*, *65*, 41–57.

Haynes, D. P., and Ahrens, M. 1988. Vocabulary simplification for children: A special case of "motherese"? *Journal of Child Language*, *15*, 395–410.

Healy, A. F. 1976. Detection errors on the word *the*: Evidence for reading units larger than letters. *Journal of Experimental Psychology: Human Perception and Performance*, *2*, 235–242.

Helfgott, J. A. 1976. Phonemic segmentation and blending skills of kindergarten children: Implications for beginning reading acquisition. *Contemporary Educational Psychology*, *1*, 157–169.

Henderson, E. H. 1982. *Orthography and Word Recognition in Reading.* New York: Academic Press.

Henderson, E. H. 1992. The interface of lexical competence and knowledge of written words. In S. Templeton and D. R. Bear, eds., *Development of Orthographic Knowledge and the Foundations of Literacy,* 1–30. Hillsdale, NJ: Erlbaum.

Henderson, E. H., and Beers, J. W., eds. 1980. *Developmental and Cognitive Aspects of Learning to Spell: A Reflection of Word Knowledge.* Newark, DE: International Reading Association.

Henry, M. K. 1989. Children's word structure knowledge: Implications for decoding and spelling instruction. *Reading and Writing: An Interdisciplinary Journal, 2,* 135–152.

Herman, P. A. 1985. The effect of repeated readings on reading rate, speech pauses, and word recognition accuracy. *Reading Research Quarterly, 20,* 553–564.

Ho, Ping-ti. 1976. *The Cradle of the East.* Chicago: University of Chicago Press.

Hodges, R. E. 1981. *Learning to Spell.* Urbana, IL: National Council of Teachers of English.

Hodges, R. E. 1982. *Improving Spelling and Vocabulary in the Secondary School.* Urbana, IL: National Council of Teachers of English.

Hohn, W. E., and Ehri, L. C. 1983. Do alphabet letters help prereaders acquire phonemic segmentation skill? *Journal of Educational Psychology, 78,* 243–255.

Holmes, V. M., and Ng, E. 1993. Word specific knowledge, word-recognition strategies and spelling ability. *Journal of Memory and Language, 32,* 230–257.

Hoover, W. A., and Gough, P. B. 1990. The simple view of reading. *Reading and Writing: An Interdisciplinary Journal, 2,* 127–160.

Howard, M. 1982. Utilizing oral-motor feedback in auditory conceptualization. *Journal of Educational Neuropsychology, 2,* 24–35.

Howard, M. P. 1986. Effects of pre-reading training in auditory conceptualization on subsequent reading achievement. Unpublished doctoral dissertation, Brigham Young University.

Hudson, J. A., and Shapiro, L. R. 1991. From knowing to telling: The development of children's scripts, stories and personal narratives. In A. McCabe and C. Peterson, eds., *Developing Narrative Structure*, 89–137. Hillsdale, NJ: Erlbaum.

Huey, E. B. 1908. *The Psychology and Pedagogy of Reading*. New York: Macmillan.

Hulme, C. 1981. *Reading Retardation and Multi-sensory Teaching*. London: Routledge and Kegan Paul.

Hulme, C., and Bradley, L. 1984. An experimental study of multi-sensory teaching with normal and retarded readers. In R. Malatesha and H. Whitaker, eds., *Dyslexia: A Global Issue*, 431–443. The Hague: Nijhoff.

Hulme, C., Monk, A., and Ives, S. 1987. Some experimental studies of multi-sensory teaching: The effects of manual tracing on children's paired associate learning. *British Journal of Developmental Psychology*, 5, 299–307.

Jacoby, L. L., and Hollingshead, A. 1990. Reading student essays may be hazardous to your spelling: Effects of reading incorrectly and correctly spelled words. *Canadian Journal of Psychology*, 44, 345–358.

Jared, D., McRae, K., and Seidenberg, M. S. 1990. The basis of consistency effects in word naming. *Journal of Memory and Language*, 29, 687–715.

Jeffrey, W. E., and Samuels, S. J. 1967. Effect of method of reading training on initial learning and transfer. *Journal of Verbal Learning and Verbal Behavior*, 6, 354–358.

Jenkins, J. R., Matlock, B. A., and Slocum, T. A. 1989. Two approaches to vocabulary instruction: The teaching of individual word meanings and practice in deriving word meaning from context. *Reading Research Quarterly*, 24, 215–235.

Jensen, H. 1969. *Sign, Symbol, and Script*. New York: Putnam.

Johnson, S. [1755] 1773. *A Dictionary of the English Language*. 4th ed. London: Strahan.

Johnson-Glenberg, M. C. 2000. Training reading comprehension in adequate decoders/poor comprehenders: Verbal versus visual strategies. *Journal of Educational Psychology*, 92, 772–782.

Johnston, R. S., and Watson, J. 1997, July. Developing reading, spelling and phonemic awareness skills in primary school children. *Reading*, 37–40.

Johnston, R. S., and Watson, J. 2003. Accelerating reading and spelling with synthetic phonics: A five year follow up. *Interchange 4*, ISSN 1478-6788, 1–8. Edinburgh: Scottish Executive Education Department.

Johnston, R. S., and Watson, J. Forthcoming. Accelerating the development of reading, spelling, and phonemic awareness skills in initial readers. *Reading and Writing.*

Jordan, T. R. 1986. Testing the BOSS hypothesis: Evidence of position-insensitive orthographic priming in the lexical decision task. *Memory and Cognition, 14,* 523–532.

Joshi, R. M., Williams, K. A., and Wood, J. R. 1998. Predicting reading comprehension from listening comprehension: Is this the answer to the IQ debate? In C. Hulme and R. M. Joshi, eds., *Reading and Spelling: Development and Disorders,* 319–327. Mahwah, NJ: Erlbaum.

Juel, C. 1983. The development and use of mediated word identification. *Reading Research Quarterly, 18,* 306–327.

Juel, C., Griffith, P. L., and Gough, P. 1986. Acquisition of literacy: A longitudinal study of children in first and second grade. *Journal of Educational Psychology, 78,* 243–255.

Juel, C., and Solso, R. L. 1981. The role of orthographic and phonic structure in word identification. In M. L. Kamil and A. J. More, eds., *Perspectives in Reading Research and Instruction: 30th Yearbook.* Washington, DC: National Reading Conference.

Jusczyk, P. W. 1998. *The Discovery of Spoken Language.* Cambridge, MA: MIT Press.

Karlgren, B. 1923. *Analytic Dictionary of Chinese and Sino-Japanese.* Paris: Geuthner.

Katz, L., and Frost, R. 1992. The reading process is different for different orthographies: The orthographic depth hypothesis. In *Orthography, Phonology and Meaning,* 67–83. Amsterdam: North-Holland.

Klesius, J. P., Griffith, P. L., and Zielonka, P. 1991. Whole language and traditional instruction comparison: Overall effectiveness and development of the alphabetic principle. *Reading Research and Instruction, 30,* 47–61.

Kramer, S. N. [1956] 1981. *History Begins at Sumer.* 2nd ed. Philadelphia: University of Pennsylvania Press.

Kramer, S. N. 1963. *The Sumerians*. Chicago: University of Chicago Press.

Krevisky, J., and Linfield, J. L. 1990. *The Awful Speller's Dictionary*. New York: Random House.

Landerl, K., Wimmer, H., and Frith, U. 1997. The impact of orthographic consistency on dyslexia: A German-English comparison. *Cognition, 63,* 315–334.

Larson, S. C., and Hammill, D. D. 1994. *Test of Written Spelling*. Austin, TX: Pro-Ed.

Leinhardt, G., and Engel, M. 1981. An iterative evaluation of NRS. *Evaluation Review, 5,* 579–601.

Leslie, L., and Thimke, B. 1986. The use of orthographic knowledge in beginning reading. *Journal of Reading Behavior, 18,* 229–241.

Levy, B. A., DiPersio, R., and Hollingshead, A. 1992. Fluent rereading: Repetition, automaticity, and discrepancy. *Journal of Experimental Psychology: Learning Memory and Cognition, 18,* 957–971.

Levy, B. A., and Kirsner, K. 1989. Reprocessing text: Indirect measure of word and message level processes. *Journal of Experimental Psychology: Learning, Memory, and Cognition, 15,* 407–417.

Levy, B. A., Nicholls, A., and Kohen, D. 1993. Repeated readings: Process benefits for good and poor readers. *Journal of Experimental Child Psychology, 56,* 303–327.

Liberman, A. M., Cooper, F. S., Shankweiler, D. P., and Studdert-Kennedy, M. 1967. Perception of the speech code. *Psychological Review, 74,* 431–461.

Liberman, I. Y., Shankweiler, D., Liberman, A. M., Fowler, C., and Fisher, F. W. 1974. Explicit syllable and phoneme segmentation in the young child. *Journal of Experimental Child Psychology, 18,* 201–212.

Lie, F. 1991. Effects of a training program for stimulating skill in word analysis in first-grade children. *Reading Research Quarterly, 26,* 234–250.

Lindamood, C. H., and Lindamood, P. C. 1969. *Auditory Discrimination in Depth*. Allen, TX: DLM Teaching Resources.

Lindamood, P. 1991. *Reports of Santa Maria-Bonita Project: 1985–1988. Fort Osage follow on 1991*. San Luis Obispo, CA: Lindamood–Bell Learning Processes.

Lloyd, S. 1992. *The Phonics Handbook*. Essex, England: Jolly Learning Ltd.

Lundberg, I., Frost, J., and Petersen, O. 1988. Effects of an extensive program for stimulating phonological awareness in preschool children. *Reading Research Quarterly, 23*, 263–284.

Lundberg, I., Olofsson, A., and Wall, S. 1980. Reading and spelling skills in the first school years predicted from phonemic awareness skills in kindergarten. *Scandinavian Journal of Psychology, 21*, 159–173.

Lysynchuk, L. M., Pressley, M., D'Ailly, H., Smith, M., and Cake, H. 1989. A methodological analysis of experimental studies of comprehension strategy instruction. *Reading Research Quarterly, 24*, 458–470.

Mair, V. 1996. Modern Chinese writing. In P. T. Daniels and W. Bright, eds., *The World's Writing Systems*, 200–208. Oxford: Oxford University Press.

Mann, V. A. 1993. Phoneme awareness and future reading ability. *Journal of Learning Disabilities, 26*, 259–269.

Mann, V. A., and Ditunno, P. 1990. Phonological deficiencies: Effective predictors of future reading problems. In G. T. Pavlidis, ed., *Perspectives on Dyslexia*, vol. 2 New York: Wiley.

Markman, E. M. 1978. Realizing that you don't understand: A preliminary investigation. *Child Development, 48*, 986–992.

Martinussen, R., and Kirby, J. 1998. Instruction in successive and phonological processing to improve the reading acquisition of at-risk kindergarten children. *Developmental Disabilities Bulletin, 26*, 19–39.

Mattingly, I. G. 1985. Did orthographies evolve? *Remedial and Special Education, 6*, 18–23.

Mattys, S. L., Jusczyk, P. W., Luce, P. A., and Morgan, J. L. 1999. Phonotactic and prosodic effects on word segmentation in infants. *Cognitive Psychology, 38*, 465–494.

McArthur, T., ed. 1992. *The Oxford Companion to the English Language*. Oxford: Oxford University Press.

McCracken, G., and Walcutt, C. C. 1963. *Basic Reading*. Philadelphia: Lippincott.

McGuinness, C., McGuinness, D., and McGuinness, G. 1996. Phono-Graphix: A new method for remediating reading difficulties. *Annals of Dyslexia, 46*, 73–96.

McGuinness, C., and McGuinness, G. 1998. *Reading Reflex*. Simon and Schuster/Free Press.

McGuinness, D. 1992. *Allographs Dictionary*. Unpublished manuscript.

McGuinness, D. 1997a. *Allographs I: A Linguistic Spelling Program*. Sanibel, FL: SeaGate Press.

McGuinness, D. 1997b. Decoding strategies as predictors of reading skill: A follow-on study. *Annals of Dyslexia*, *47*, 117–150.

McGuinness, D. 1997c. *Why Our Children Can't Read*. New York: Simon and Schuster/Free Press.

McGuinness, D. 1998a. *Allographs II: A Linguistic Spelling Program. Multisyllable Word Building*. Sanibel, FL: SeaGate Press.

McGuinness, D. 1998b. *Why Children Can't Read*. London: Penguin Books.

McGuinness, D. 2004. *Language Development and Learning to Read*. Cambridge, MA: MIT Press.

McGuinness, D. Forthcoming. *Sound Steps to Reading*.

McGuinness, D., McGuinness, C., and Donohue, J. 1995. Phonological training and the alphabet principle: Evidence for reciprocal causality. *Reading Research Quarterly*, *30*, 830–852.

McGuinness, D., and Pribram, K. H. 1980. The neuropsychology of attention: Emotional and motivational controls. In M. C. Wittrock, ed., *The Brain and Educational Psychology*. New York: Academic Press.

McKeown, M. G., Beck, I. L., Omanson, R. C., and Pople, M. T. 1985. Some effects of the nature and frequency of vocabulary instruction on the knowledge and use of words. *Reading Research Quarterly*, *20*, 522–535.

McNemar, Q. 1949. *Psychological Statistics*. New York: Wiley.

Meyer, D. E., Schvaneveldt, R. W., and Ruddy, M. G. 1971. Facilitation in recognizing pairs of words: Evidence of a dependence between retrieval operations. *Journal of Experimental Psychology*, *90*, 227–234.

Meyer, L. A., Stahl, S. A., Linn, R. L., and Wardrop, J. L. 1994. Effects of reading storybooks aloud to children. *Journal of Educational Research*, *88*, 69–85.

Michalowski, P. 1996. Mesopotamian cuneiform. In P. T. Daniels and W. Bright, eds., *The World's Writing Systems*, 33–36. Oxford: Oxford University Press.

Morris, D., and Perney, J. 1984. Developmental spelling as a predictor of first-grade reading achievement. *Elementary School Journal, 84*, 441–457.

Morris, J. M. 1984. Phonics: From an unsophisticated past to a linguistics-informed future. In G. Brooks and A. K. Pugh, eds., *Studies in the History of Reading*. Reading, England: University of Reading.

Mullis, I. V. S., Campbell, J. R., and Farstrup, A. E. 1993. *National Assessment of Educational Progress 1992: Reading Report Card for the Nation and States.* Washington, DC: Office of Educational Research and Improvement, U.S. Department of Education.

Muter, V., and Snowling, M. 1997. Grammar and phonology predict spelling in middle childhood. *Reading and Writing: An Interdisciplinary Journal, 9,* 407–425.

Nagy, W. F., and Herman, P. 1987. Breadth and depth of vocabulary knowledge: Implications for acquisition and instruction. In M. McKeown and M. Curtis, eds., *The Nature of Vocabulary Acquisition*, 19–36. Hillsdale, NJ: Erlbaum.

Nation, K., and Snowling, M. 1997. Assessing reading difficulties: The validity and utility of current measures of reading skill. *British Journal of Educational Psychology, 67*, 359–370.

National Reading Panel. 2000. *Report*. Washington, DC: National Institute of Child Health and Human Development.

Nelson, K. 1998. *Language in Cognitive Development*. Cambridge, England: Cambridge University Press.

Nisbet, S. D. 1939. Non-dictated spelling tests. *British Journal of Educational Psychology, 9*, 29–44.

Nunes, T., Bryant, P., and Bindman, M. 1997. Morphological spelling strategies: Developmental stages and processes. *Developmental Psychology, 33*, 637–649.

Olson, R., Forsberg, H., Wise, B., and Rack, J. 1994. Measurement of word recognition, orthographic, and phonological skills. In G. R. Lyon, ed., *Frames of Reference for the Assessment of Learning Disabilities: New Views on Measurement Issues*, 229–277. Baltimore: Brookes.

Organization for Economic Cooperation and Development. 1995. *Literacy, Economy, and Society*. Ottawa: Statistics Canada.

Organization for Economic Cooperation and Development. 1997. *Literacy Skills*. Ottawa: Statistics Canada.

Palincsar, A. S., and Brown, A. L. 1984. Reciprocal teaching of comprehension-fostering and comprehension-monitoring activities. *Cognition and Instruction*, *1*, 117–175.

Pearson, D. 1997. The first grade studies: A personal reflection. *Reading Research Quarterly*, *32*, 428–432.

Perfetti, C. A. 1984. Reading acquisition and beyond: Decoding includes cognition. *American Journal of Education*, 40–57.

Piaget, J. [1964] 1993. Development and learning. In M. Gauvain and M. Cole, eds., *Readings on the Development of Children*, 25–33. New York: Scientific American Books. W. H. Freeman.

Pinel, J. P. J. 1997. *Biopsychology*. Boston: Allyn and Bacon.

Pintner, R., Rinsland, H. D., and Zubin, J. 1929. The evaluation of self-administering spelling tests. *Journal of Educational Psychology*, *20*, 107–111.

Pitman, J., and St. John, J. 1969. *Alphabets and Reading*. London: Pitman.

Plaut, D. C., McClelland, J. L., Seidenberg, M. S., and Patterson, K. 1996. Understanding normal and impaired word reading: Computational principles in quasi-regular domains. *Psychological Review*, *103*, 56–115.

Plomin, R., Fulker, D. W., Corley, R., and DeFries, J. C. 1997. Nature, nurture, and cognitive development from 1 to 16 years: A parent-offspring adoption study. *Psychological Science*, *8*, 442–448.

Postman, L. 1975. Verbal learning and memory. *Annual Review of Psychology*, *26*, 291–335.

Pribram, K. H. 1991. *Brain and Perception: Holonomy and Structure in Figural Processing*. Hillsdale, NJ: Erlbaum.

Pribram, K. H., and Gill, M. 1976. *Freud's Project Re-assessed*. New York: Basic Books.

Pribram, K. H., and McGuinness, D. 1975. Arousal, activation, and effort in the control of attention. *Psychological Review*, *82*, 116–149.

Rashotte, C. A., and Torgesen, J. K. 1985. Repeated reading and reading fluency in learning disabled children. *Reading Research Quarterly*, *20*, 180–188.

Rayner, K. 1977. Visual attention in reading: Eye movements reflect cognitive processes. *Memory and Cognition, 4,* 443–448.

Rayner, K. 1986. Eye movements and the perceptual span in beginning and skilled readers. *Journal of Experimental Child Psychology, 41,* 211–236.

Rayner, K. 1998. Eye movements in reading and information processing: 20 years of research. *Psychological Bulletin, 124,* 372–422.

Read, C. 1971. Pre-school children's knowledge of English phonology. *Harvard Educational Review, 41,* 1–34.

Read, C. 1986. *Children's Creative Spelling.* London: Routledge and Kegan Paul.

Robbins, C., and Ehri, L. C. 1994. Reading storybooks to kindergartners helps them learn new vocabulary words. *Journal of Educational Psychology, 86,* 54–64.

Robinson, A. 1995. *The Story of Writing.* London: Thames and Hudson.

Rosenshine, B., and Meister, C. 1994. Reciprocal teaching: A review of the research. *Review of Educational Research, 64,* 479–530.

Rosenshine, B., Meister, C., and Chapman, S. 1996. Teaching students to generate questions: A review of the intervention studies. *Review of Educational Research, 66,* 181–221.

Samuels, S. J. 1972. The effect of letter-name knowledge on learning to read. *American Educational Research Journal, 9,* 65–74.

Samuels, S. J. 1979. The method of repeated readings. *The Reading Teacher, 4,* 403–408.

Samuels, S. J., Laberge, D., and Bremer, C. D. 1978. Units of word recognition: Evidence for developmental changes. *Journal of Verbal Learning and Verbal Behavior, 17,* 715–720.

Samuels, S. J., Miller, N. L., and Eisenberg, P. 1979. Practice effects on the unit of word recognition. *Journal of Educational Psychology, 71,* 514–520.

Schatschneider, C., Francis, D. J., Foorman, B. R., Fletcher, J. M., and Mehta, P. 1999. The dimensionality of phonological awareness: An application of item response theory. *Journal of Educational Psychology, 91,* 439–449.

Schmandt-Besserat, D. 1978. The earliest precursors of writing. *Scientific American, 238,* 50–59.

Schneider, W., Roth, E., and Ennemoser, M. 2000. Training phonological skills and letter knowledge in children at risk for dyslexia: A comparison of three kindergarten intervention programs. *Journal of Educational Psychology*, *92*, 284–295.

Scragg, D. G. 1974. *A History of English Spelling*. Manchester, England: Manchester University Press.

Seidenberg, M. S. 1992. Dyslexia in a computational model of word recognition in reading. In P. B. Gough, L. C. Ehri, and R. Treiman, eds., *Reading Acquisition*. Hillsdale, NJ: Erlbaum.

Seidenberg, M. S., and McClelland, J. L. 1989. A distributed, developmental model of word recognition and naming. *Psychological Review*, *96*, 523–568.

Senechal, M., and Cornell, E. H. 1993. Vocabulary acquisition through shared reading experiences. *Reading Research Quarterly*, *28*, 361–374.

Shanahan, T. 1984. Nature of the reading-writing relation: An exploratory multivariate analysis. *Journal of Educational Psychology*, *76*, 466–477.

Share, D. L., Jorm, A. F., Maclean, R., and Matthews, R. 1984. Sources of individual difference in reading acquisition. *Journal of Educational Psychology*, *76*, 1309–1324.

Siegel, L. S., Share, D., and Geva, E. 1995. Evidence for superior orthographic skills in dyslexics. *Psychological Science*, *6*, 250–254.

Silberberg, N., Iversen, I., and Goins, J. 1973. Which remedial method works best? *Journal of Learning Disabilities*, *6*, 18–22.

Smith, A. A. 1999. The simple logic of sound-to-letter mapping: A reversible code. Unpublished master's thesis, Massey University, Albany, New Zealand.

Solso, R. L., and Juel, C. 1980. Positional frequency and versatility of bigrams for two- through nine-letter English words. *Behavior Research Methods and Instrumentation*, *12*, 297–343.

Stahl, S. A., and Fairbanks, M. M. 1986. The effects of vocabulary instruction: A model-based meta-analysis. *Review of Educational Research*, *56*, 72–110.

Stahl, S. A., and Miller, P. D. 1989. Whole language and language experience approaches for beginning reading: A quantitative research synthesis. *Review of Educational Research*, *59*, 87–116.

Stanovich, K. E., and West, R. 1989. Exposure to print and orthographic processing. *Reading Research Quarterly*, *24*, 402–433.

Stebbins, L., St. Pierre, R. G., Proper, E. L., Anderson, R. B., and Cerva, T. R. 1977. *Education as Experimentation: A Planned Variation Model*. Vols. IVA–D. Cambridge, MA: Abt Associates.

Steffler, D. J., Varnhagen, C. K., Treiman, R., and Friesen, C. K. 1998. There's more to children's spelling than the errors they make: Strategic and automatic processes for one-syllable words. *Journal of Educational Psychology*, *90*, 492–505.

Stuart, M. 1999. Getting ready for reading: Early phoneme awareness and phonics teaching improves reading and spelling in inner-city second language learners. *British Journal of Educational Psychology*, *69*, 587–605.

Sumbler, K. 1999. Phonological awareness combined with explicit alphabetic coding instruction in kindergarten: Classroom observations and evaluation. Unpublished doctoral dissertation, University of Toronto.

Szeszulski, P. A., and Manis, F. R. 1990. An examination of familiar resemblance among subgroups of dyslexics. *Annals of Dyslexia*, *40*, 180–191.

Torgesen, J. K., Wagner, R. K., Rashotte, C. A., Rose, E., Lindamood, P., Conway, T., and Garvan, C. 1999. Preventing reading failure in young children with phonological processing disabilities: Group and individual responses to instruction. *Journal of Educational Psychology*, *91*, 579–593.

Treiman, R. 1994. Use of consonant letter names in beginning spelling. *Developmental Psychology*, *30*, 567–580.

Treiman, R., and Broderick, V. 1998. What's in a name: Children's knowledge about the letters in their own names. *Journal of Experimental Child Psychology*, *70*, 97–116.

Treiman, R., Mullennix, J., Bijeljac-Babic, R., and Richmond-Welty, E. D. 1995. The special role of rimes in the description, use, and acquisition of English orthography. *Journal of Educational Psychology*, *124*, 107–136.

Treiman, R., and Tincoff, R. 1997. The fragility of the alphabetic principle: Children's knowledge of letter names can cause them to spell syllabically rather than alphabetically. *Journal of Experimental Child Psychology*, *64*, 425–451.

Uhry, J. K., and Shepherd, M. J. 1993. Segmentation/spelling instruction as part of a first-grade reading program: Effects on several measures of reading. *Reading Research Quarterly*, *28*, 219–233.

Varnhagen, C. K., McCallum, M., and Burstown, M. 1997. Is children's spelling naturally stage-like? *Reading and Writing: An Interdisciplinary Journal*, *9*, 451–481.

Vellutino, F. R., and Scanlon, D. M. 1987. Phonological coding, phonological awareness, and reading ability: Evidence from a longitudinal and experimental study. *Merrill-Palmer Quarterly*, *33*, 321–363.

Vellutino, F. R., Scanlon, D. M., and Tanzman, M. S. 1994. Components of reading ability: Issues and problems in operationalizing word identification, phonological coding, and orthographic coding. In G. R. Lyon, ed., *Frames of Reference for the Assessment of Learning Disabilities: New Views on Measurement Issues*, 279–332. Baltimore: Brookes.

Venezky, R. L. 1967. English orthography: Its graphical structure and its relation to sound. *Reading Research Quarterly*, *2*, 75–105.

Venezky, R. L. 1970. *The Structure of English Orthography*. The Hague: Mouton.

Venezky, R. L. 1973. Letter-sound generalizations of first, second, and third-grade Finnish children. *Journal of Educational Psychology*, *64*, 288–292.

Venezky, R. L. 1995. From orthography to psychology to reading. In V. W. Berninger, ed., *The Varieties of Orthographic Knowledge, Vol. 2: Relationships to Phonology, Reading and Writing*. Boston: Kluwer Academic Publishers.

Venezky, R. L. 1999. *The American Way of Spelling*. New York: Guilford Press.

Vihman, M. M. 1993. Variable paths to early word production. *Journal of Phonetics*, *21*, 61–82.

Wagner, R. K., and Barker, T. B. 1994. The development of orthographic processing ability. In V. W. Berninger, ed., *The Varieties of Orthographic Knowledge, Vol. 1: Theoretical and Developmental Issues*. Boston: Kluwer Academic Publishers.

Waters, G. S., Bruck, M., and Malus-Abramovitz, M. 1988. The role of linguistic and visual information in spelling: A developmental study. *Journal of Experimental Child Psychology*, *45*, 400–421.

Webster, N. 1783. *A Grammatical Institute of the English Language*. Part I. Facsimile (1968). Menston, England: Scholar Press.

White, T. G., Graves, M. F., and Slater, W. H. 1990. Growth of reading in diverse elementary schools: Decoding and word meaning. *Journal of Educational Psychology*, *82*, 281–290.

Williams, J. P. 1980. Teaching decoding with an emphasis on phoneme analysis and phoneme blending. *Journal of Educational Psychology*, *72*, 1–15.

Willows, D. M., and Ryan, E. B. 1986. The development of grammatical sensitivity and its relationship to early reading achievement. *Reading Research Quarterly*, *21*, 253–266.

Wimmer, H. 1993. Characteristics of developmental dyslexia in a regular writing system. *Applied Psycholinguistics*, *14*, 1–33.

Wimmer, H., and Goswami, U. 1994. The influence of orthographic consistency on reading development: Word recognition in English and German children. *Cognition*, *51*, 91–103.

Wimmer, H., and Landerl, K. 1997. How learning to spell German differs from learning to spell English. In C. A. Perfetti, L. Rieben, and M. Fayol, *Learning to Spell*, 81–96. Mahwah, NJ: Erlbaum.

Witherspoon, A. 1973. *Common Errors in English*. Totowa, NJ: Littlefield, Adams.

Yopp, H. K. 1988. The validity and reliability of phonemic awareness tests. *Reading Research Quarterly*, *23*, 159–177.

Zinna, D. R., Liberman, I. Y., and Shankweiler, D. 1986. Children's sensitivity to factors influencing vowel reading. *Reading Research Quarterly*, *21*, 465–479.

Author Index

Aaron, P. G., 19, 213, 283–286, 341
Adams, G. L., 127
Adams, M. J., 153, 340
Ahrens, M., 215
Allred, R. A., 249–250
Aslin, R. N., 7, 23

Ball, E. W., 146, 170–171, 179–181
Balmuth, M., xviii
Barker, T. B., 45
Baron, J., 288
Barr, R. C, 115
Beck, I. L., 146, 229–232
Becker, W. C., 104–105
Beers, C. S., 257
Beers, J. W., 255, 257
Bell, N., 238–239
Berninger, V. W., 66–68, 71, 321
Biemiller, A., 342
Bindman, M., 260–262, 272
Blachman, B. A., 146, 170–171, 179–181
Block, C. C., 242–244, 331–333
Bond, C. L., 147
Bond, G. L., 86–102, 107, 123, 131, 249–250, 282
Boronat, C. B., 115, 121
Bradley, L., 114, 164–168, 274
Brady, S., 170

Bremer, C. D., 342
Brennan, F., 184–185
Brett, A., 225–226
Bright, W., 7
Broderick, V., 276–277
Brown, A. L., 238
Brown, A. S., 117–118
Brown, G. D. A., 307
Brown, I. S., 132
Brown, R., 241
Bruck, M., 270–273, 282, 287
Bruner, E., 104
Bryant, P. E., 164–168, 260–262, 272
Burstown, M., 262–264, 275
Bus, A. G., 158–160
Byrne, B., 176–178

Calfee, R. C., 68
Campbell, J. R., 1, 212–213
Carr, T. H., 110–112, 340
Cattell, J. M., 341
Chall, J., 80–86, 100–101, 107–109, 123
Chaney, C., 7, 154, 173
Chang, Kwang-chih, 21
Chapman, S., 235–236, 238, 240
Chomsky, C., 197
Chomsky, N., 288

Civil, M., 20
Clanchy, M. T., 14
Clay, M., 182
Clymer, T., 43–44, 86, 267
Coltheart, M., 287–288, 326, 328
Cooper, J. S., 20
Cornell, E. H., 222–223, 228
Cossu, G., 2, 155
Coulmas, F., 7, 14, 16–18, 20, 22, 24, 27
Craik, F. I. M., 18
Cunningham, A. E., 114, 169–170, 274–275, 282–283

Dahl, P. R., 197
Dale, N., xvii, 4, 76–78, 131, 275, 325–326
Daniels, P. T., 7
Darch, C., 127
Dickinson, D. K., 223–225, 228
DiPersio, R., 205–206
Ditunno, P., 327
Dixon, M., 119–120
Donohue, J., 133, 135, 166
Dowhower, S. L., 200–206, 209, 329–330
Dykstra, R., 80, 86–104, 107, 109, 123, 131, 249–250, 282

Ehri, L. C., 45, 116, 168, 170, 221–223, 228, 251, 255–256, 265, 338, 340–341
Eisenberg, P., 342
Eldredge, L., 149
Elley, W. B., 225
Ellis, A. J., xvii, 56, 76
Ellis, A. W., 182–184
Engel, M., 146–147
Engelmann, S., 104, 127

Ennemoser, M., 171–175
Evans, M. A., 110–112, 340

Fairbanks, M. M., 226–227, 233
Falkenstein, A., 20
Faulkner, H. J., 207–208, 329
Feldman, S., 101, 109
Felton, R. H., 132
Fielding-Barnsley, R., 176–178
Fischer, F. W., 266–269, 272, 281, 290
Fisher, R., 18
Flavell, J. H., 254
Flesch, R., 77–78, 80, 86, 108
Foorman, B. R., 45, 135–137
Freud, S., 253–254, 343
Friederici, A. D., 7, 23
Frith, U., 2, 191, 255–256
Frost, J., 163
Frost, R., 24
Fulwiler, G., 132

Gelb, I., 6–7, 17–18, 23–24
Gentry, J., 263, 275
Gersten, R., 104–105, 127
Geva, E., 40, 55, 286
Gill, M., 343
Gleason, M., 127
Glushko, R. J., 288–297, 299, 305–306, 311, 315, 337, 343
Goins, J., 132
Goodman, K., 108
Goswami, U. C., 2, 45, 191
Gough, P. B., 213
Graham, S., 247–248
Graves, M. F., 80, 216
Greenberg, S. N., 345–347
Griffith, P. L., 128, 147–148, 150, 231, 321
Groff, P., 132

Haddock, M., 166
Halle, M., 288
Hammill, D. D., 70
Hanna, P. R., 53–55, 64–65, 267
Hart, B., 217–222, 331
Hatcher, P. J., 182–184
Hay, J., 77
Haynes, D. P., 215
Healy, A. F., 345
Helfgott, J. A., 345
Henderson, E. H., 255, 257, 275
Henry, M. K., 68–69, 71
Herman, P. A., 198–200, 216–217
Ho, Ping-ti, 21
Hodges, R. E., 65
Hohn, W. E., 170
Hollingshead, A., 118–119, 205–206
Holmes, V. M., 269–270, 282
Hoover, W. A., 213
Howard, M. P., 133
Hudson, J. A., 212
Huey, E. B., 195
Huggins, A. W. F., 340
Hulme, C., 114, 182–184, 274
Hurley, M., 225–226

Ireson, J., 184–185
Iversen, I., 132
Ives, S., 114

Jacoby, L. L., 118–119
Jared, D., 306–311, 313
Jeffrey, W. E., 277–278
Jenkins, J. R., 232–233, 331
Jensen, H., 23
Johnson, S., xvi, 43, 266
Johnson-Glenberg, M. C., 238–239

Johnston, R. S., 139–145, 325–327
Jordan, T. R., 45
Joshi, R. M., 213–214
Juel, C., 213, 297–298
Jusczyk, P. W., 23

Kaminska, Z., 119–120
Karlgren, B., 21
Katz, L., 24
Kirby, J., 150
Kirsner, K., 205
Klesius, J. P., 128, 147–148, 150, 321
Kohen, D., 206–208
Koriat, A., 345–347
Kramer, S. N., 26
Krevisky, J., 119
Kromrey, J. D., 128, 148, 150, 321

Laberge, D., 342
Landerl, K., 2, 40, 55, 191
Larson, S. C., 70
Leinhardt, G., 146–147
Leslie, L., 45
Levy, B. A., 205–208, 329
Liberman, A. M., 6
Liberman, D., 45
Liberman, I. Y., 6, 153, 266–269, 172, 290, 298–300
Lie, F., 178–179
Lindamood, C. H., 77, 131–135, 325–326
Lindamood, P. C., 77, 131–135, 325–326
Linfield, J. L., 119
Lloyd, S., 138–139, 141, 232, 324–327
Logan, G. D., 115, 121

Lundberg, I., 163, 166, 172, 182
Lysynchuk, L. M., 240

Mair, V., 21
Malus-Abramovitz, M., 270–273, 282, 287
Manis, F. R., 45
Mann, V. A., 249, 327
Markman, E. M., 234
Marshall, J. C., 2, 155
Martinussen, R., 150
Matlock, B. A., 232–233, 331
Mattingly, I. G., 24
Mattys, S. L., 7, 23
McArthur, T., 17
McCallum, M., 262–264, 275
McClelland, J. L., 288, 305–306, 309, 311, 315
McCracken, G., 78
McGuinness, C., 56, 133, 135, 150, 166, 184, 334
McGuinness, D., xiv, xviii, 12, 22, 24, 27, 48, 55–65, 69, 74, 78, 114–115, 133–135, 150, 166, 184, 328, 334–335, 343–344
McGuinness, G., 56, 150, 184, 334
McKeown, M. G., 229–232, 331
McNemar, Q., 79, 93
McRae, K., 306–311, 313
Meister, C., 235–236, 238, 240
Meyer, D. E., 18
Meyer, L. A., 113
Michalowski, P., 20, 26
Miller, N. L., 342
Miller, P. D., 123
Monk, A., 114
Morris, D., 259–263
Morris, J. M., xviii, 76

Mullis, I. V. S., 1, 212–213
Muter, V., 249

Nagy, W. F., 216–217
Nation, K., 214
Nelson, K., 212, 216
Newport, E. L., 7, 23
Ng, E., 269–270
Nicholls, A., 206–208
Nisbet, S. D., 117
Nunes, T., 260–262, 272

Olofsson, A., 163, 166
Olson, R., 45

Palincsar, A. S., 238
Pearson, D., 100–101
Perfetti, C. A., 45, 229–230
Perney, J., 250–263
Petersen, O., 163
Piaget, J., 253–254, 257
Pinel, J. P. J., 338
Pintner, R., 117
Pitman, I., xvi, xvii, 76
Pitman, J., 77
Plaut, D. C., 288, 305–306, 311–315, 336–338
Plomin, R., 219
Postman, L., 18
Pressley, M., 333
Pribram, K. H., 312, 343–344

Rashotte, C. A., 199–200
Rayner, K., 191–192, 208, 235, 343, 345
Read, C., 252, 255, 275
Rinsland, H. D., 117
Risley, T. R., 217–222
Robbins, C., 221–223, 228

Robinson, A., 34
Rosenshine, B., 235–236, 238, 240
Rossini, F., 2, 155
Roth, E., 171–175
Rothlein, L., 225–226
Ruddy, M. G., 18
Ryan, E. B., 235

Saffran, J. R., 7, 23
Samuels, S. J., 196–197, 277–278, 342
Scanlon, D. M., 45, 115
Schatschneider, C., 165, 173, 188
Schmandt-Besserat, D., 19
Schneider, W., 171–175, 179
Schvaneveldt, R. W., 18
Scragg, D. G., xviii, 76
Seidenberg, M. S., 288, 305–315, 336
Senechal, M., 222–223
Shanahan, T., 250, 282
Shankweiler, D. P., 266–269, 272, 290, 298–300
Shapiro, L. R., 212
Share, D. L., 166, 286
Shepherd, M. J., 70, 116–117, 168
Siegel, L. S., 40, 55, 286
Silberberg, N., 132
Slater, W. H., 216
Slocum, T. A., 232–233, 331
Smith, A. A., 69–70, 116, 334
Smith, M. W., 223–225, 228
Snowling, M., 214, 249
Solso, R. L., 297–298
St. John, J., 77
Stahl, S. A., 123, 226–227, 233
Stanovich, K. E., 45, 114, 270, 274–275, 280–283, 328
Stebbins, L., 104
Steffler, D. J., 264

Strawson, C., 288
Stuart, M., 139–143
Sumbler, K., 111–113, 141–144, 325, 340
Szeszulski, P. A., 45

Tanzman, M. S., 45
Thimke, B., 45
Tincoff, R., 117, 276–277
Torgesen, J. K., 133–135, 146, 199–200
Treiman, R., 117, 275–277, 300–305, 310

Uhry, J. K., 70, 116–117, 168

van Ijzendoorn, M. H., 158–160
Varnhagen, C. K., 262–264, 268, 275, 343
Vellutino, F. R., 45–46, 115
Venezky, R. L., 39, 41, 48–52, 55, 65–70, 288, 290, 321
Vihman, M. M., 153

Wagner, R. K., 45
Walcutt, C. C., 78
Wall, S., 163, 166
Waters, G. S., 270–273, 282, 287
Watson, J., 139–145, 325–327
Webster, N., 47, 55, 78, 82
Wessels, J. M. I., 7, 23
West, R. F., 45, 270, 281–283, 328
White, T. G., 216
Wilce, L. S., 70, 116, 168
Williams, J. P., 163, 166
Williams, K. A., 213–214
Willows, D. M., 235
Wimmer, H., 1, 2, 40, 55, 174, 175, 189–191, 277

Wingo, C., 77
Witherspoon, A., 267
Wood, J. R., 213–214

Yopp, H. K., 166, 185–186

Zielonka, P., 147–148
Zinna, D. R., 298–300
Zubin, J., 117

Subject Index

Advanced spelling code, 55–65, 70, 323, 334–335

Affix, 267

Allophone, 42

Alphabet charts, 32

Alphabetical order, 28, 29

Alphabet principle, 83, 176–177, 276

Articulation (speech-motor) training, 131, 178, 325–326

Artificial transparent alphabet, xvi, 56, 75–76, 323

Attention
 in the classroom, 138
 and memory, 115, 121
 and phoneme awareness, 155

Attention span (brain), 343

Basic code, 56, 59, 75–77, 82, 111, 321–324
 programs for teaching, 130–145
 spelling chart, ix

Binomial test, 164, 221

Brain
 conscious analysis in reading, 190, 192–193, 248, 343–347
 neuro-anatomy and neural pathways, 338–339
 processing print, 280, 288, 296, 305, 315, 336, 338–347

theories of "brain activation," 290, 292, 294, 296, 306, 309, 342

unconscious analysis in reading, 206

Classroom observations, 83–85, 101, 109–115, 323, 331

Clay tablets, 20

Coarticulation, 155, 190, 344

Code overlaps, 46–47, 63, 83

Codes, 252
 as writing systems, 11–13, 17, 39, 49

Cognitive models of reading/spelling, terms and expressions. *See also* Spelling

consistent/inconsistent neighbors, 292–295, 299, 301, 306–307, 312

consistent/inconsistent rimes, 293–295, 302, 304, 306–308, 310

exception words, 292–295

friends/enemies, 301, 304, 307, 312

orthographic consistency, 297–298, 302, 304, 306

orthographic redundancy, 297

orthographic rime, 292–297, 299–300, 304, 307–309, 311–312, 315, 338

orthographic versatility, 297–298

phonological rhyme, 292, 296, 308–309, 312

Subject Index

Cognitive models of reading/spelling, terms and expressions (cont.)
regular words, 292–295, 338
word body, 291, 295, 338
word family, 292, 299
word frequency effect, 292, 303
Color-coded text, 136
Compounding languages, 62
Computer models of reading, 287–288, 296, 305–316, 336–339
attractor network model, 311–315, 337
dual-route model, 287–289, 307, 338
parallel distributed processing model, 288–289, 305, 336, 344
recurrent connections, 311–312
Computer training studies, 159
Consonants
blends, clusters, 9, 61, 83, 176, 313, 318
voiced, 155
Cooperative Research Program, 86–103
Copying/writing as learning tool, 112, 114, 118, 156, 185, 323, 335

Dale, Nellie, 76–77, 325–326
Deaf children and reading/spelling, 19, 283–286
Decoding, xv, 37–39, 48, 113, 164, 211, 252
Decoding strategy, 57, 114–115, 269, 328
Demographic data, 88, 99
Diacritic mark, 2, 31, 54
Digraphs, 2, 44, 45, 50, 77, 83, 180, 287, 299, 301, 313, 320, 322, 324

DISTAR (direct instruction method), 104–105, 127
Down's syndrome and reading, 2, 155
Dyslexia, 2, 3, 6

Effect size
definition, 124–125
formula, 124
Encoding, 37–39, 252
English language structure, 55–56
English spelling classification systems
Webster, 47–48
Venezky, 48–52
Hanna et al., 53–55
McGuinness, 55–65
English spelling system. See also Spelling
Anglo-Saxon spellings, 55, 59, 62
defined, 41
Greek-based spellings in, 54–55, 62, 64–65, 68
Latin-based spellings in, 54–55, 62–64, 334–335
multisyllable words and, 54, 62
Norman French spellings in, 55, 59, 62, 64
predictable patterns of, 51, 61
problems with, 46–47, 65
spelling alternatives, 57–60, 63, 334
structural features, 59–62
ERIC database, 194–195
Experimenter-designed tests, 161
Eye movements and reading, 191–193, 208, 343
context effects, 192, 196–197
functional span, 192
perceptual span, 192
syntax effects, 192–193

Freud's stage model, 253–254
Functional illiteracy
  countries and, 1, 6, 322
  rate of, 1, 5
Function words in reading, 344–347

Head Start, 103, 217, 223
Homophones, 16

International reading surveys, 1,
  349–353

Jolly Phonics actions, 138–139, 141,
  325–326

Kindergarten, origin of, 171

LAC test of phoneme awareness, 169
Languages, impact on writing system
  Akkadian, 20
  Arabic, 19
  Aramaic, 30
  Chinese, 21, 56
  Egyptian, 19
  German, 3
  Greek, 34
  Hebrew, 19
  Indian, xv, 27–28
  Japanese, xv, 22
  Sumerian, 20
Language development, 153
Language types and writing systems
  Hamito-Semitic, 19, 23, 31
  Indo-European, 27, 30
  Tonal languages, 21
Letter names and learning to read,
  184, 251, 323
Letter-sound correspondences train-
  ing, 166, 170, 175, 178–179, 182
Ligature as diacritic, 27

Longitudinal studies, 103–105, 260,
  265, 327

Many-word problem, xiv, 248, 279–
  316
Mapping systems, 11–12, 15, 320
Memorization
  letters as aid, 170
  limits to, 18–19, 22, 26, 34, 74, 318
Memory
  promoted by, 114
  recall, 37, 70, 116, 232, 247, 273
  recognition, 37, 70, 116, 247, 273
  rote visual in reading, 279, 283,
    284–287, 289
  sight-word reading and, 251
Meta-analysis, 124–125
Missing letter effect, 345
Montessori, Maria, 37, 275
Morphology, 62
Moveable alphabet, 131

Naming speed, 277, 327, 341–342
National Assessment of Educational
  Progress (NAEP), 1, 212–213, 236
National Reading Panel, viii, xiii, xiv,
  xviii, 70, 73–75, 107, 247, 317–
  320, 322–334
  comprehension training, 215, 234,
    237, 331
  fluency training, 193–196, 328
  phoneme awareness training, 153–
    188
  reading instruction, 121–152, 323–
    324
  vocabulary training, 226, 228, 330

OECD (1995, 1997), 1, 349–353
Opaque alphabet, xvi, 3, 13, 39–40,
  46, 75, 159, 247, 250

Subject Index

Paired-associate learning, 18, 19, 74, 277
Paleography, 6, 11–13, 23
Parental involvement, 138
Phoneme awareness
  blending/segmenting, 111, 116, 136, 141, 154, 156, 161–163, 166–167, 170–171, 173, 176–179, 187, 323–324, 326, 335
  computer training in, 160
  decoding and, 279, 280–281, 283
  explicit awareness, 153–155
  skills in, 148
  training of, 112, 134, 153–188, 318, 327–328
  training with and without letters, 160–161
Phonemes
  chart of, ix
  consonants, 51, 54
  definition, xv
  schwa vowel, 52, 54
  tasks
    classification, 161
    discrimination, 161, 166, 169, 186
    identification, 161, 166–168, 173, 178, 185–186, 335
    manipulation/deletion, 161, 169, 170, 173, 186
    sequencing (blending/segmenting), 161, 185–186
  transitivity, 176, 335
  vowel +r, x, 51, 53
  vowels, 53–54
Phonics categories
  junk phonics, 130, 320
  linguistic phonics (see Phonics, teaching approaches)
  multi-sound phonics, 130, 320

visual phonics, 130, 147, 149, 151, 319, 320–323, 336
whole-to-part phonics, 130, 320
Phonics and speech-motor training, 131, 152
Phonics teaching approaches
  analytic or intrinsic phonics, 81, 85, 129, 139, 319, 324
  basal-reader phonics, 129, 146, 148, 320–321
  embedded phonics, 133, 136
  explicit phonics, 129, 147
  linguistic phonics, 129–130, 146, 151–152, 155–156, 173, 178, 187–188, 320, 322–323, 325–326, 334–335
  synthetic phonics, 81–82, 85, 107, 129–130, 151, 320
  systematic phonics, 129, 151
Phonograms, 46, 83, 287, 301, 320
Phonological awareness. See also Phoneme awareness
  alliteration, 164–166, 173
  origin of, 6
  rhyme identity, 154, 164–166, 173, 186
  syllable analysis, 180
  syllable/rhyme segmenting tasks, 159, 163–166, 172
  training of, xviii, 109
Phonological development theory, 6, 109, 153–154, 157, 163–164, 186
Phonological/phoneme training programs
  Lundberg program, 163, 172, 182, 184
  Sound Categorization, 164–166, 169, 173
  Sound Foundations, 176

Phonological units in reading
instruction
onset-rime analogy, 126, 129, 141
syllable analysis, 180
Phonotactics, 7, 23, 34, 55–56, 74,
280, 291, 318
Piaget's stages, 253–254
Prefixes/suffixes and spelling, 62–63,
268
Project Follow Through, 103–105
Prototype for reading instruction, 38,
73, 82, 111, 121, 127, 184, 317–
319, 323–324
programs fitting prototype, 131–
145, 152
Proto-writing, 14
PsychINFO database, 194–195

Reading comprehension
measures of
cloze test, 214
factor analysis, 214
functional illiteracy, 212–213
in-house tests, 235–238
meta-analysis, 235–237
NAEP tests, 212, 236
standardized tests, 212–214, 236–
239, 241, 244
treatment fidelity, 243
skills. *See also* Story comprehension
decoding accuracy and, 211–214,
235
oral (listening) comprehension
and, 211–214, 235
reading fluency and, 211–213, 235
vocabulary and, 211
training methods
Block comprehension program,
242–244

critical thinking strategies, 244
length of training, 236
multiple strategy technique, 238
National Reading Panel review,
215, 234, 237
reciprocal teaching programs, 235,
238–241
summary of, 330–333
visualizing/verbalizing program,
238–240
Reading frequency (print exposure)
impact on accuracy, 282–283
tests of, 281–286
for training fluency, 194–195, 199,
328
word familiarity and, 344
Reading instruction
Austria, 175, 210
California, 5
Canada, 40, 139, 141
England, 40, 138, 191
Finland, 39–40
Germany, 4, 39, 171–173
Italy, 39
Norway, 39, 178
Scotland, 139, 141
Sweden, 39
Texas, 187
Reading methods. *See also* Phonics,
teaching approaches
basal readers, 4–5, 77, 80–83, 86,
92, 94, 97, 102–103, 108, 128,
147, 152, 216, 317
basal + phonics, 87, 90–91, 94,
103
eclectic or balanced, 5, 6, 74, 84,
111–113, 146
language experience, 87, 90–91, 94,
110–111, 123–124

Reading methods (cont.)
linguistics-based, 81–82, 90–91, 94, 103
look-say, 4, 77, 85, 341
phonics, 4, 42, 77–78, 83, 85, 97, 110–113, 128, 319
reading schemes (UK), 4, 128
real books, 4
sight-word, xviii, 4, 9, 19, 34, 74, 112, 114–115, 181
whole language, 4–5, 108, 122–124, 136, 152, 147–149, 152, 216, 220
whole word, xviii, 4, 108, 146, 317–318
Reading programs
DISTAR, 104–105, 127, 180–181
Fast Phonics First, 139–145
Ginn basal reader, 82
Glossic, 76
Harper and Row basal reader, 147
Hay-Wingo, 77
Houghton-Mifflin basal reader, 147, 149
Initial teaching alphabet (i.t.a.), 77, 82, 87, 90, 92–94, 97–99, 103
Jolly Phonics, 111, 113, 138–145, 152, 162, 188, 323–324, 327, 334
Letterland, 185
Lindamood Auditory Discrimination in Depth, 77, 131–135, 152, 170, 325–326
Lippincott, 78, 82–83, 87, 90–91, 94, 97–99, 103, 107, 117, 131–132, 188, 323
New Primary Grade Reading System, 146–147
Open Court, 135–137
Orton-Gillingham, 126, 180
Phonic Exercises, 91
Project Read, 68–69
Reading Recovery, 137, 182, 184
Scott-Foresman basal reader, 82, 90, 147, 181
Sing, Spell, Read, and Write, 147
Speech to Print, 91
Success in Kindergarten, 185
Webster's Blue-Backed Speller, 47–48, 78
Word Power, 91
Reading speed and fluency, 159, 189–211, 159, 328. *See also* Rereading method for fluency training
comprehension and, 189, 191, 193, 198, 200–201, 203
good versus poor readers, 208
National Reading Panel report, 189, 193–196
prosody and, 200–203
reading rate, 191–193, 196
sight word training and, 196–197
slow readers, 2, 189–193, 210
speaking rate and, 190–191
Reading tests, generic
fluency, 159, 172
nonsense word decoding, 131, 148, 164, 178
reading comprehension, 110–111, 172
word attack, 133, 334
word identification, 133, 334
word recognition, 133, 334
Reading wars, 78, 86, 317
Rereading method for fluency training
audiotape and, 200–201, 203

decoding accuracy and, 189–191, 193, 196–201, 203, 205, 207–209
proofreading and, 205–208
target goal, 196–205
text difficulty and, 207–210
training studies, 194–210, 328–330
transfer effects, 196–206
Root words, 54–55, 267–268
Rosner test of phoneme awareness, 186

Sex differences
 in reading, 88, 92, 98, 103
 in spelling, 92, 98, 103
Sight words
 functional sight vocabulary, 340
 late-stage sight-word reading, 339–343
 myth of, 9, 34, 343
 as reading method, 288
 traditional sight word lists, 52
 true sight words, 57–59
Silent letters, 57
Speech perception, 153, 155
Spelling
 alternatives, 46–47, 54, 83, 130–131, 139, 151, 270–271, 298, 310, 320–321
 categories of spelling words
  rare spellings (exception words), 267, 269, 271, 279
  regular spelling, 43, 44–45, 56–57, 247, 266–267, 270–271, 273
 errors, 115–121
 linguistic/visual features of spelling code used in cognitive research
  bigram/trigram frequencies, 285, 287, 291, 297–298, 308
  checked vowel "rule," 289

consonant-doubling "rules," 267–268, 271, 289
 grapheme-phoneme correspondence "rules" (GPCs), 44–45, 288–290, 306, 308, 344
 linguistic structure and, 265–266, 271, 279
 morphological structure and, 266–269, 271, 274, 279, 290
 orthographic "rules," 279–280, 290, 340
 orthographic structure, 279–281, 291, 297, 305–306, 313, 315, 344
 orthography defined, 17, 43, 45–46, 48–49, 55
 phoneme-grapheme correspondences, 279, 285, 288–290, 326, 328
 phonotactic structure and spelling, 280, 291
 spelling generalizations, 43–44
 spelling "rules," 43–44, 50, 119, 251, 266, 268, 274
 methods based on structure of the code, 55–65, 69–70
 methods in schools
  invented spelling, 108, 116–117, 120, 184, 187, 248, 252
  letter-name spelling, 116–117
  miscellaneous, 120–121
  research on traditional programs, 247–248
  rule-based, 43–44, 50, 119
 predictors
  reading skill, 250
  sex, 249–250
  verbal IQ, 249, 268, 282
 probability structure of spelling code

Subject Index

Spelling (cont.)
  context-dependent spellings, 280
  context-free spellings, 271, 313
  frequency in print, 50, 53, 57, 284,
    291, 293, 297–298, 301, 307–308,
    338
  statistical probability, 46–47, 53,
    57, 59, 120, 284–286, 287, 297–
    298, 301, 336, 338
  structural redundancy, 45–47,
    59, 61, 280, 286, 297, 300, 306,
    315
  processing strategies, 264
    letter names, 251, 274, 275–278
    letter-sounds, 251, 276–277
    visual memory, 268, 269–270
  reform, xvi
  research on new teaching methods,
    65–70
  stage models, 250–265, 272
  stages, 55, 109, 116–117, 248–250,
    275
  structural analyses of the spelling
    code
    Hanna et al., 53–55
    McGuinness, 55–65
    Venezky, 48–53
    Webster, 47–48
  systems origin, 40–41
  test types
    spelling dictation, 117–119, 167,
      335
    spelling recognition, 118–121, 268,
      272
Standardized spelling, 43, 46
Standardized tests
  general, 79, 149, 158–159, 160–162,
    171–172, 179, 181, 185, 189, 270,
    334

specific
  British Ability Scales, 183
  California Achievement Test, 120
  California Test of Basic Skills, 147
  Comprehensive Test for Basic
    Skills, 120
  Detroit Test of Learning Aptitude,
    239
  Fry Word List, 88–90, 94, 96–98
  Gates-MacGinitie, 149, 239, 250
  Gates Word List, 89–90, 94, 96–
    97
  Gilmore Tests of Accuracy and
    Rate, 88–89, 94, 96
  Iowa Test of Basic Skills, 229, 243,
    333
  McGraw-Hill Basic Study Skills,
    120
  Metropolitan Achievement Test
    (MAT), 104–105, 120, 169
  Murphy-Durrell Letter-Name, 89
  Peabody Comprehension Test,
    214
  Phoneme Discrimination Test, 89
  Pintner-Cunningham IQ Test, 89
  Schonell Spelling, 185
  Stanford Achievement Test (SAT),
    147, 241, 284
  Test of Written Spelling, 70
  Wechsler Adult Intelligence Scale
    (WAIS), 268
  Wechsler Intelligence Scales for
    Children (WISC), 214, 239
  Wide Range Achievement Tests
    (WRAT), 104–105, 239, 268,
    281–282, 286
  Woodcock Reading Mastery, 69,
    147, 150, 170, 176, 179, 213–214,
    281–282, 284

Statistical analysis
  availability of, 79, 85
  invalid methods of, 91–93, 98
  valid methods of, 94–97
Story
  comprehension, 224
  grammar, 211, 236
  recall, 230–231
Sumerian schools, 38, 115

Test construction, 188
Transparent alphabets, xv, 2–3, 32,
    39–40, 55, 75–76, 159, 175, 178–
    179, 191, 277
Treatment fidelity, 100

Universal education, xviii

Vocabulary
  acquisition, 215–219
    children's literature and, 215
    heritability/verbal IQ, 219
    oral comprehension, 215
    productive vocabulary size, 216, 233
    reading and, 215
    television and, 215
    word derivation, 215
  training
    classroom lessons and, 112–113
    dangers of whole language, 220
    deducing meaning from context,
      232–233
    frequency of exposure and, 229–
      233
    Head Start, 217, 233, 331
    listening to stories as method,
      221–226
    meta-analysis of classroom
      research, 226–227

multiple-choice tests in research,
    221–223, 225, 229
National Reading Panel report,
    226, 228
productive vocabulary and, 222,
    230–232, 331
receptive vocabulary and, 223, 230,
    232
standardized tests and, 221, 227,
    229
successful programs, 229–235
teacher-child interaction, 224
Voice-onset latency/response time,
    293–294, 296, 303, 312

Webster, Noah, 37, 44, 82
Word families, 5, 7, 9, 46, 62, 82–83,
    126, 318
Word play in teaching, 154
Writing systems
  ancient
    Akkadian, 11, 20
    Anglo-Saxon, 39, 40–41, 46
    Aramaic, 11, 30
    Assyrian, 24
    Babylonian, 11, 13, 24, 29–30
    Chinese, 18, 20–21, 25–26
    Crete, 11, 27
    Egyptian, 11, 13–16, 18–19, 23,
      31
    Greek, 28, 31, 32, 34, 39, 41
    Hittite, 6, 11, 24
    Indian, 27–29
    Japanese, 21–22, 33
    Korean, 28–29, 30
    Mayan, 11, 15–16, 27
    Norman French, 40–41
    Old English, 40
    Old Persian, 28–30

Writing systems (cont.)
  Phoenician, 29, 31–32
  Roman (Latin), 41, 46
  Sumerian, 11, 13–14, 18–20, 25–26, 38
  Vietnamese, 24
  assumptions about, 32
  comparative analysis of, 6–8, 11, 14–18, 339
  definitions of, xiv, 11–18, 33
  evolutionary theory of, 6–7, 17, 23–24, 33
  function of, 14
  modern
    Arabic, 31
    Cherokee, 28
    Danish, 159
    English, 40–41, 191
    European, 32
    Finnish, 39–40, 159
    German, xv, 40, 159, 172–175, 189, 191, 277
    Israeli, 40, 159
    Italian, xv, 159
    Norwegian, 159, 178
    Spanish, xv, 159
    Swedish, 159
  myths about, 8, 9
  scripts
    Brahmi script, 28
    cuneiform, 30
    Han'gul, 29–30
    hieroglyphics, 16, 19, 31
    hiragana and katakana, 22, 28
    kanji, 21–22, 33
    Linear A, 11
    Linear B, 11, 27, 34
  semantic classifiers, 19–21, 32

  types (*see also* Opaque alphabet, Transparent alphabets)
    alphabet, xv, 6–7, 13, 31–32, 34–35, 75, 83, 154–155, 318
    consonantal alphabet (consonant cueing), xv, 19, 31–32
    consonant-vowel diphone (CV diphone), xv, 22, 26–32, 34, 74
    logographic, 6, 17–21, 27, 33–34, 339
    meaning-based, 17–18, 20, 74
    pictographic, 6, 17, 19–20, 27
    sound-based, 17, 20
    syllabary, xiv, 6, 20–21, 23–26, 31–32
    whole word, 16, 34, 74